ADVANCE PRAISE FOR *Oregon's Others*:

"Kimberly Jensen's exceptional contribution to American gender history deconstructs the chilling connections between the success of woman suffrage in Oregon in 1912 and the shocking attacks on civil rights, particularly of women, in the state during World War I and the white-supremacist 1920s. The targets were the most vulnerable—sex workers, foreign nationals, wards of the state, gender nonconformists, and other 'undesirables.' Yet through these people's tragic stories, including their resistance, Jensen offers hope for the nation."
PETER BOAG · author of *Pioneering Death: The Violence of Boyhood in Turn-of-the-Century Oregon*

"Makes a significant contribution to scholarship on gendered citizenship and relationships of liberty and policing in the early twentieth century through its thorough examination of these issues from various angles in a state that was at the forefront of surveillance in that era."
CYNTHIA PRESCOTT · author of *Pioneer Mother Monuments: Constructing Cultural Memory*

"How safe are our civil rights today? What can we learn from those whose liberties have been challenged? Kim Jensen's scrutiny of Oregon's past exclusionary policies brings caution for our own roles as citizens. Her deep inquiry into those who challenged policies discriminating against gender, race, ethnicity, and ability highlights our need to be vigilant against continual challenges of 'we' versus 'they.'"
LINDA TAMURA · author of *Nisei Soldiers Break Their Silence: Coming Home to Hood River*

OREGON'S OTHERS

EMIL AND KATHLEEN SICK SERIES
IN WESTERN HISTORY AND BIOGRAPHY

With support from the Center for the Study of the Pacific Northwest at the University of Washington, the Sick Series in Western History and Biography features scholarly books on the peoples and issues that have defined and shaped the American West. Through intellectually challenging and engaging books of general interest, the series seeks to deepen and expand our understanding of the American West as a region and its role in the making of the United States and the modern world.

Oregon's Others

GENDER, CIVIL LIBERTIES, AND THE SURVEILLANCE STATE IN THE EARLY TWENTIETH CENTURY *Kimberly Jensen*

Center for the Study of the Pacific Northwest
in association with University of Washington Press / Seattle

Oregon's Others was made possible in part by a grant
from the Emil and Kathleen Sick Fund of the
University of Washington's Department of History.

Center for the Study of the Pacific Northwest / sites.uw.edu/cspn/
University of Washington Press / uwapress.uw.edu

Copyright © 2024 by the University of Washington Press

Design by Mindy Basinger Hill / Composed in Miller Text

All rights reserved. No part of this publication may be
reproduced or transmitted in any form or by any means, electronic or
mechanical, including photocopy, recording, or any information storage
or retrieval system, without permission in writing from the publisher.

LIBRARY OF CONGRESS CATALOGING-IN-PUBLICATION DATA
Names: Jensen, Kimberly, 1958– author.
Title: Oregon's others : gender, civil liberties, and the surveillance state
in the early twentieth century / Kimberly Jensen.
Description: Seattle : Center for the Study of the Pacific Northwest ; University
of Washington Press, 2024. | Series: Emil and Kathleen Sick book series
in Western history and biography | Includes bibliographical references
and index.
Identifiers: LCCN 2024000358 (print) | LCCN 2024000359 (ebook) |
ISBN 9780295752570 (hardcover) | ISBN 9780295752587 (paperback) |
ISBN 9780295752594 (ebook)
Subjects: LCSH: Civil rights—Oregon—History—20th century. | Women—
Oregon—Social conditions—20th century. | Electronic surveillance—
Oregon—History—20th century. | Oregon—Social life and customs—
20th century.
Classification: LCC JC599.U52 J46 2024 (print) | LCC JC599.U52 (ebook) |
DDC 323.4/90979509041—dc23/eng/20240216
LC record available at https://lccn.loc.gov/2024000358
LC ebook record available at https://lccn.loc.gov/2024000359

♾ This paper meets the requirements of ANSI/NISO Z39.48-1992
(Permanence of Paper).

Contents

Preface / *vii*

Acknowledgments / *xi*

List of Abbreviations / *xvii*

Introduction / 1

Chapters 1 Eugenics and Internal Enemy Others / *23*

2 Patriotic Womanhood and Internal Enemies / *41*

3 Trouble at Work / *65*

4 "Alien" Enemies / *88*

5 Held for Health / *110*

6 "Insane" or "Unfit" / *150*

7 Japanese Oregonian Women's Resistance / *179*

Conclusion / *211*

Notes / *219*

Bibliography / *285*

Index / *305*

Preface

Scott Daniels, reference services manager at the Oregon Historical Society Research Library (OHS), introduced me to the first major primary source collection for this book, the "World War I Alien Forms" housed at OHS, for which I am very grateful. Thousands of detailed forms chronicled complex stories of the forced registration of German citizens and also US-born women who forfeited their US citizenship when they married German-citizen men, all designated as "enemy aliens" by the federal government during the First World War. The forms, which include Bertillon identity data and fingerprints, provide powerful examples of the growth of the surveillance state during the war. This collection helped me think about gender, civil liberties, and surveillance in the early twentieth century in more complicated ways and made me want to expand my research to gather other sources. I was able to access additional collections across many archives that illuminated the lived experiences of people whose civil liberties were challenged in the early twentieth century and vital examples of survival, resistance, and advocacy.

In my previous research for *Mobilizing Minerva: American Women and the First World War* and *Oregon's Doctor to the World: Esther Pohl Lovejoy and a Life in Activism*, I was concerned primarily with the history of women and citizenship rights as votes for women movements and the quest for a more complete female citizenship including service in the First World War came together. *Oregon's Others* intentionally juxtaposes the achievements some women made in gathering more rights of citizenship in the early twentieth century with the loss of civil liberties for other people. The projects for identifying and punishing internal enemy "others" in the wartime and postwar climate of fear and nativism and via the eugenics movement, which took such a strong hold on Oregon and the nation in this period, are key frameworks in this history. My focus on the collisions between citizenship and civil liberties as well as the growth of the surveillance state is not meant to denigrate the achievements of diverse suffragists and other activists who pushed the boundaries of citizenship rights for women and other people in historically marginalized groups in the context of human rights struggles. But the history of social movements is not, of course, a progressive line leading directly to the achievement of full civic power, protections, and liberties for all people. The story is one of fragility, varying victories and losses, and the impact of White supremacy, discrimination by gender, gender identity and presentation, ability, race, ethnicity, immigration status, nationality, and other elements of identity and power that have historically divided people and caused great violence and injustice. A knowledge of that history impels us forward with the understanding that until all rights and liberties are protected, none are safe. Once achieved, rights and liberties can be lost, and we must work to maintain and support them.

Historians of diverse women and gender-nonconforming people rely on methods to lift people's stories from the archives at the same time that we engage in what Nupur Chaudhuri, Sherry J. Katz, and Mary Elizabeth Perry have described as "contesting" those same archives. We can read a single source or set of sources—such as "enemy alien" registration forms, or female patient files, or "mental defect" survey results—all designed by those in power to surveil, categorize, and control dangerous others "against the grain" to reveal agency, resistance, and historical subjectivity. And by engaging in additional methodical research of vital records and historic newspapers, "researching around" our subjects, we can give voice to formerly voiceless historical actors and reveal agency and resistance.[1] This practice is reflected in what Susan Burch and Penny Richards have referred to as the intentional analysis of authoritative sources that can restore the lived experiences of people in disability histories.[2]

I am most grateful for the many people who have provided thoughtful perspectives in conversations with me about the responsibilities we as historians have to our subjects and to our readers present and future. I recognize that in this study of state surveillance I am using the products of that surveillance as vital primary sources. Many of our primary sources

viii / PREFACE

exist because of some kind of scrutiny, often state scrutiny: vital records, court cases, historic newspaper articles, and institutional and organizational registers. This is particularly true for people whose historical subjectivity has been marginalized and silenced, including most of the people whose lives are a part of *Oregon's Others*. As I share this research, students, colleagues, and community members want to learn more about the lives of people studied here for a deeper representation of diverse people in our history and to add to our community understanding of our complicated past. Many also want to see themselves and their communities reflected in our history. And the numerous and varied roles and stories of people who experienced, resisted, and survived the hunt for internal enemy others are a significant part of our collective history and the history of social justice movements and actions. In this book I have tried to maintain this complicated and important balance with respect.

I have chosen to use the names of individual subjects in an effort to restore their voices and place their important stories in our diverse and complex history with the permission of archivists who hold and guard these important records and in consultation with activists, community members, and scholars. This includes people who were surveilled and made a part of criminal justice and registration systems. And for some subjects this includes medical records. Oregon Revised Statute 192.398 requires privacy for medical records of less than seventy-five years for a living person, and federal Health Insurance Portability and Accountability Act (HIPAA) regulations protect medical information for fifty years after a person's death. I have used these standards for all of the people in *Oregon's Others* for whom medical records are part of their files.[3] I have used the names of these individuals in all cases but for Anna Weston's sister, for whom I provide a pseudonym in chapter 3. Her records detail information more than fifty years after her death, but they are not yet available at the Oregon State Archives. I appreciate the redacted copy the Oregon Health Authority provided for my use for this project.

PREFACE / *ix*

Acknowledgments

I have so many debts to the consequential people who have helped make this book. Archivists, librarians, and curators are some of the most significant heroes of our world. Their knowledge of collections and their skilled work to preserve them, physically and digitally, and their vast knowledge that opens research doors make the work of historians possible. My thanks to the incredible staff and volunteers at the Oregon Historical Society Research Library (OHS) in Portland who have supported me during my Donald J. Sterling Jr. Senior Research Fellowship and beyond, always with tremendous support and good humor. In particular I wish to thank Geoff Wexler, Shawna Gandy, Scott Daniels, Hannah Allan, Jennifer Keyser, and Adrianna Elerina Aldamar. Nikki Koehlert and Renato Rodriguez have welcomed me at more recent follow-up visits in the splendid tradition of OHS hospitality and support.

At the Oregon State Archives (OSA) in Salem, current and former staff shaped this project in vital ways. Layne Sawyer shared her extensive knowledge of the collections and processes of the state's holdings. Thanks also to Mary McRobinson, Austin Schulz, Andrew Needham, Todd Shaffer, Theresa Rea, Kristine Deacon, and Kim Gorman. Mary Hansen and Brian Johnson at the City of Portland Archives made researching there a gift. My thanks to Portland city archivist Diana Banning; Karen Peterson and Maija Anderson at the Historical Collections & Archives at the Oregon Health & Science University; Terry Baxter at the Multnomah County Archives; Anne LeVant Prahl at the Oregon Jewish Museum and Center for Holocaust Education in Portland; and Sarah Cantor, director of Heritage Center and archivist, Sisters of the Holy Names of Jesus and

Mary, US-Ontario Province, Lake Oswego. Paige Monlux, Ty Thompson, and Jim Carmen of the Multnomah County Library and Penny Hummel assisted me with M. Louise Hunt materials in Portland, and Darcy Mohr kindly provided Hunt's reports at the Racine Public Library.

Others who helped make this book possible include Doug Erickson, then head of Special Collections, Watzek Library, Lewis and Clark College; Rachel Thomas at the George Fox University Archives in Newberg; Liisa Penner at the Clatsop County Historical Society in Astoria; Jane Tucker with Astoria Public Library; and Kelly Cannon-Miller and the Deschutes County Historical Society staff. Thanks to Kylie Pine, curator and collections manager at the Willamette Heritage Center and the staff at the Oregon State Library in Salem as well as my wonderful colleague Linda Long, curator of manuscripts, special collections, and archive at Knight Library, University of Oregon, and staff. My library colleagues at Western Oregon University's Hamersly Library are at the heart of our campus; for this book project Lori Pagel and LoriAnn Bullis assisted with key interlibrary loan materials and collections, and I am most grateful for their long-standing support. At the National Archives at Seattle, Patty McNamee, Susan Karren, and staff provided thoughtful support. I am grateful for the coalition of people and groups whose work and advocacy reversed the sale of the Seattle National Archives and that this vital repository remains open to researchers. Many thanks to the archivists at the National Archives and Records Administration in College Park, Maryland, who assisted during my research visit there.

This book would not be possible without digitized historic newspapers, including the Historic Oregon Newspapers collection housed at the University of Oregon with support from the Library of Congress Chronicling America Program, the National Endowment for the Humanities, and Oregon Heritage Commission grants. I continue to draw on the enormous resources of the historic newspapers on microfilm at the University of Oregon's Knight Library. In 2017 the Oregon Nikkei Endowment, now the Japanese American Museum of Oregon, received an Oregon Heritage Commission grant to translate ten issues of Portland's Japanese-language newspaper the *Oshu Nippo*, the *Oregon Daily News*. A sustained and collaborative translation effort spanning the Pacific made these translations available, and I have benefitted greatly from the talent and knowledge of everyone who made the translations possible. The digitization of journals and public documents on HathiTrust Digital Library at www.hathitrust. org helped me trace policy and process for institutions and agencies in Oregon and the nation. Online collections of vital records increased my ability to find people who left few other traces.

The COVID-19 pandemic made the already digitized sources of newspapers and documents even more precious, and archivists and librarians pivoted mightily during COVID to increase digital and remote services. Public outreach librarian Allee Monheim of Special Collections at the University of Washington and student worker Betty Benson arranged for an innovative virtual reading room appointment during the pandemic. The Oregon State Archives processed many remote requests for records, and I am so grateful for the work of the OSA staff to connect me with these resources time and again. The Oregon State Library's digital collections supported additional research. Professional researcher and librarian Ginger Frere of Information Diggers contracted to conduct research in the Pullman Company Records at the Newberry Library in Chicago.

I received support for this book project as a recipient of the 2015 Donald J. Sterling Jr. Senior Research Fellowship in Pacific Northwest History from the Oregon Historical Society. This important fellowship provided the time for the foundational research for the project, and the results pulse through the entire book. I received two sabbatical leaves from Western Oregon University at the beginning and conclusion of this project—time that was vital to the research and writing process. With the support of my Faculty Development Committee colleagues at Western Oregon University, I received a Major Project Grant for travel and research, awards for travel to scholarly conferences to share and develop my ideas and writing, and a series of three course reassignments to give me the time needed to write and revise. For this committee, and for our Western Oregon University Federation of Teachers Faculty Union that sustains it through collective bargaining, I am most grateful.

I have been most fortunate to present my work at scholarly conferences and at many community events. Great questions and discussion have helped me hone my ideas and develop key elements of this book. Many thanks to the session participants and audience discussants at the Berkshire Conference for Women Historians, the Western Association of Women Historians, the Pacific Coast Branch of the American Historical Association, the Voting Rights Symposium, the University of Utah, the

Remembering Muted Voices Conference at the National World War I Museum and Memorial, and the Pacific Northwest History Conference. My sincere thanks to the staff at the Oregon Historical Society for sponsoring several presentations based on this research project; to Amy Platt and Tania Hyatt-Evenson of the *Oregon Encyclopedia* project for including my research in the Oregon History 101 series; and to the Oregon Health & Science University History of Medicine Lecture sponsors. Many thanks to the sponsors of a number of History Pubs in Portland and Bend, the Willamette Heritage Center's Zooming Back to History series, the Independence Heritage Museum, and to the members of many local branches of the American Association of University Women, the League of Women Voters, the Humanists of Greater Portland, and local public libraries who hosted presentations. Many thanks to editor Eliza Canty-Jones and managing editor Erin Brasell of the *Oregon Historical Quarterly* (OHQ) for their careful support and advice, and to anonymous readers of article manuscripts from OHQ and *Peace & Change*.

I am most grateful to the many people at the University of Washington Press who worked to make this book possible. Larin McLaughlin, Marcella Landri, Ishita Shahi, Jennifer Comeau, Mindy Basinger Hill, Amy Smith Bell, Molly Woolbright, David Schlangen, and Benny Sisson all brought vision, skill, and thoughtful support to this project. They added vibrance, depth, and breadth to the book. My thanks also to the anonymous reviewers whose suggestions strengthened the analysis. I am honored to have this book be a part of the Emil and Kathleen Sick Book Series in Western History and Biography. I thank the University of Washington Press staff, the Sick Series committee members, and the Sick family for their work and contributions to make this series and my part in the series possible.

I was privileged to study with Linda Kerber at the University of Iowa, whose pathbreaking work on gender and citizenship inspired me and my colleagues to investigate questions of citizenship. Her influence flows throughout my work. Thank you, Linda, for all you have given to us. So many additional colleagues and friends have supported me and this project. I particularly want to thank Erika Kuhlman, Alison S. Fell, Ingrid Sharp, Tammy Proctor, Susan Grayzel, Karen Blair, Jean Ward, Sherri Bartlett Browne, Christin Hancock, Febe Pamonag, Kim Nielsen, Linda Tamura, Peggy Nagae, David Lewis, Marisa Chappell, and Michael Helquist. Eliza Canty-Jones inspires me and countless other historians of

Oregon by advocating for histories of our complex past. Janice Dilg's vision and savvy have enriched my work, and she has placed diverse Oregonians in our landscape. Thanks to the other Century of Action/Oregon Women's History Consortium advocates Linda Long, Donna Maddux, Judy Margles, and Nova Newcomer. My sincere appreciation to the vibrant board and staff at the *Oregon Encyclopedia* project for their collegial support and their work to make a complex and diverse Oregon history available to all, with warmest memories and appreciation for the support the late Roger Hull provided along this research journey.

At Western Oregon University many thanks to Maureen Dolan, Mary Pettenger, Sharyne Ryals, David Doellinger, Patricia Goldsworthy-Bishop, Elizabeth Swedo, Ricardo Pelegrin Taboada, Donna Sinclair, Henry Hughes, Ken Carano, Mark Henkels, and many other WOU colleagues whose support and generosity makes this work possible. My students have inspired many of the questions I asked and tried to answer in this book, for which I am most grateful. Thanks to Cindy Massaro, Janice Hoida, Pat Dixon, and Erin Marr for support and sustenance. Karen Jensen has listened across many conversations in all stages of this work, which means a great deal to me. And for support during these tumultuous times and for understanding why this book matters so much, thank you, Todd Jarvis, once again.

Abbreviations

AAUW	American Association of University Women
AMA	American Medical Association
BIA	Bureau of Indian Affairs
BOLI	Oregon Bureau of Labor and Industry
CND	Council of National Defense
CTCA	Commission on Training Camp Activities
DAR	Daughters of the American Revolution
DOJ	Department of Justice
NWLLC	National Woman's Liberty Loan Committee
OSH	Oregon State Hospital
OSHS	Oregon Social Hygiene Society
STI	sexually transmitted infection
USFA	United States Food Administration
WCTU	Woman's Christian Temperance Union
WES	War Emergency Squad
WSS	War Savings Stamp
YWCA	Young Women's Christian Association

OREGON'S OTHERS

Introduction

IN HIS 1915 STATE OF THE UNION ADDRESS, monitoring an expanding world war and the Mexican Revolution, President Woodrow Wilson observed: "Liberty is often a fierce and intractable thing, to which no bounds can be set, and to which no bounds of a few men's choosing ought ever to be set."[1] That same year, in a speech in Salem, Oregon, titled "Prevention of Insanity," Lewis Frank Griffith, MD, first assistant physician and assistant superintendent of the Oregon State Hospital for the Insane, spoke of the need for "stern restrictions" on the rights and liberties of the "unfit" and "defective classes" of Oregon, including state-mandated sterilization.[2] Three years before these speeches, in November 1912, most Oregon women achieved the right to vote, and by 1915 many were using the ballot to exercise a more complete female citizenship.[3] The movement for women's rights in the state and nation in the early twentieth century was also a part of the historic and multilayered conflicts between increased rights and privileges of citizenship for some people and the denial or reduction of rights and civil liberties for others. In this period both the world war and the eugenics movement amplified and legitimized the call for civic action against internal enemy "others," grafting political urgency and pseudoscientific ways of thinking and acting onto practices and policies of racial and ethnic exclusion and discrimination by gender and ability.

Oregon's Others is a study of the multiple collisions of fierce liberties and stern restrictions in Oregon and the nation with matters of gender, gender identity and presentation, ability, race, ethnicity, and class in mind. It centers these questions in the historical events and processes from after 1912, when most Oregon women had achieved voting rights in an era of "progressive" reform, through World War I and into the war's reactionary aftermath, with racism, ableism, nativism, the growing persecution of gender-nonconforming people, the rise of the state's Ku Klux Klan, and increased restrictions on civil liberties. These restrictions included far-reaching state legislation for eugenic sterilization, exclusionary land

and licensing policies directed at Japanese Americans, and restrictive federal immigration legislation. The war and the period of nativist reaction that followed it into the 1920s sharpened concepts of "loyal supporters" and "enemy opponents," binary categories of who was a citizen and who was an "alien" or a dangerous "other." The war and eugenic policies also expanded and deepened surveillance projects and tools for increased scrutiny in the service of identifying and punishing internal enemies. But some Oregonians, including women and gender-nonconforming and nonbinary people, endured and resisted these stern restrictions. Their persistence and fierce insistence on liberties became part of expanding movements for civil liberties and human rights and a citizenship of dissent that reverberate today. These processes, conflicts, and compelling stories comprise *Oregon's Others*.

Public health physician Chester L. Carlisle used the eugenics-inspired 1920 Oregon State Survey of Mental Defect, Delinquency, and Dependency to define "fit" and "unfit" citizens. A person's "fullest success" in life was to be a "constructive" citizen, he wrote. By contrast, an "inadequate" and "non-constructive" person was a "failed" citizen, a category that included people among Oregon's "insane" and "feebleminded."[4] These binary categories informed the eugenics movement and engendered what Robert A. Wilson calls "eugenic thinking" that influenced law and policy in Oregon and the nation.[5] Carlisle's categories also mirror what Allison Carey refers to as the "narratives of productive citizenship." These narratives have historically favored "intelligence, independence, and the ability to contribute to the national well-being through hard work, political participation, and bravery." The concept of productive citizenship has been "a mechanism by which to confer membership, respect, and participation in valued roles and responsibilities" in society and to deny it to those who are judged lacking and therefore designated to be on citizenship's margins.[6]

In addition to ability, many policymakers and their followers counted other "inadequate" or nonproductive citizens in the early twentieth century in categories related to race, ethnicity, immigration status, and class as well as conformity to prevailing ideas about gender roles, sexuality, and gender identity. Martha Gardner calls our attention to the gendered "qualities of a citizen" that have included Whiteness, heterosexual marriage, "respectability, domesticity, economic viability, and moral character," in addition to one's nation of origin. These "qualities" have been enforced at immigration border stations, at the "second border" of federal courtrooms, and by federal, state, and local enforcers of laws and policies.[7] Margot Canaday identifies the period from 1900 through the post–World War I years as the context for "the development of a federal bureaucracy that was just starting to understand sexual perversion—whether evidenced in sexual acts, gender presentation, or physical anatomy—as inversely related to one's desirability for citizenship."[8]

If the status of citizenship brings certain rights, such as the right to vote, Linda Kerber urges us to consider the corresponding obligations placed upon citizens and residents in the United States. These obligations have included jury service, paying taxes, and for some, military service. And the "state can use its power to constrain" individual freedoms and rights if individuals fail to perform their civic obligations.[9] Sandra VanBurkleo traces the ways that questions about women's ability to fulfill civic obligations such as jury service "fatally compromised" the ideal of women's rights and gendered "co-sovereignty" in early Washington Territory during women's voting interlude there from 1883 to 1887. Washingtonians "remade" gender hierarchies when women achieved voting rights once again after statehood in 1910. The "remodeling" categorized women as dependents and as a separate class to be protected in labor legislation and public power.[10] These gendered civic rights and obligations frameworks connect with Ruth Lister's emphasis on the difference between the legal status of citizenship and the practice of citizenship in specific historical contexts. Lister invites us to consider that citizenship is always more than "a set of legal rules governing the relationship between the individual and the state" defined by those in authority. Citizenship is rather a constantly evolving "set of social relationships," the result of people as active agents working within social and cultural relations of power.[11] Ernest Gellner defined a citizenship of shared experiences, and ideas, based on membership in a community—what other scholars, including T. H. Marshall, have termed "social citizenship."[12]

A key element of the practice of productive citizenship in the United States has been the obligation to engage in civically-sanctioned work—that is, the work of the nation. Policymakers have defined "the work of the nation" in specific historical contexts according to gender, race, ethnicity, ability, and class. A "family wage" presumed a male head of household, and women's quests to achieve equal pay for equal work and professional

INTRODUCTION / 3

status have been a path to what Alice Kessler-Harris calls "economic citizenship" through productive work.[13] Kim Nielsen's research emphasizes the links between ideas about productive citizenship and people's ability to labor and manage that labor as a key factor in mental competency hearings and institutional commitments in this period.[14] Wartime called on many women to engage in industrial war work as a patriotic duty, to become the "second line of defense" for the nation, as Lynn Dumenil demonstrates.[15] During World War I, as Gerald Shenk shows us, the Wilson administration created a "work or fight" civic imperative for men and defined unmanly "slackers" as internal enemies. Tera Hunter notes that Southern policymakers used work-or-fight laws intended to fill the male military to punish Black women and force them into domestic work "under oppressive conditions."[16]

Kerber demonstrates that the historical obligation to work has been "a civic obligation legally framed in negative terms; an obligation not to be *perceived* as idle and vulnerable to punishment for vagrancy." The Anglo-American legal tradition has defined vagrancy broadly as being without a "settled home," not engaging in "regular work" to build the community, or making a living in a "disreputable or dishonest way." Authorities have used vagrancy "capriciously," as Kerber notes, to control what counts as work and who counts as a worker in American history, and to police the boundaries of race and gender. Vagrancy has been a remarkably "malleable" tool, as Gardner observes, for immigration exclusion or inclusion and to "distinguish 'others' who lay outside the social community."[17] Evelyn Nakano Glenn notes that for "most of American history" this obligation "has been embodied in state and municipal vagrancy laws."[18] Oregon's capacious 1911 Vagrancy Act penalized many actions and inactions including punishing people "without visible means of living" who were able to work but did not do so.[19]

"Slacker" as a wartime label of contempt mirrored these definitions of vagrancy precisely. And as scholars of the wartime anti–venereal disease crusades have established, reformers and government officials also labeled sex workers and women with sexually transmitted infections (STIS) as internal enemies who posed treasonous threats to national security and whose civil liberties could therefore be curtailed or removed.[20] Vagrancy laws in Oregon and the nation were often the legal tools used to police and restrict them. *Oregon's Others* demonstrates that the obligation to engage in the work of the nation during and after the war also included the requirement to prove loyalty to the state's aims by active participation in the labor and financing of registration drives and patriotic programs, and also the obligation to identify, restrict, and punish people designated as internal enemies by the state. The nation's wartime and postwar work of civic loyalty encouraged some women to engage in work that denied rights and liberties to others to enhance their own status with the rewards of citizenship and belonging.

Deportation has been and is another means by which states, policy-makers, and residents threaten, exclude, and punish people designated as internal enemies. In *Deportation Machine*, Adam Goodman helps us understand the three types of deportation in US history generally and in the period of this study specifically: formal, voluntary, and self-deportation.[21] We know the most about formal deportation. Congress created the federal Immigration Bureau in the 1891 Immigration Act, giving officials the power to deport "undesirable immigrants." Subsequent legislation expanded the categories of people targeted for formal deportation, including people who might become a "public charge," people considered "insane," political radicals, and sex workers or people perceived as prostitutes.[22] Policymakers, individuals, and groups have used violence and threats of violence to convince people to self-deport, and local immigration officials have worked in tandem with administrators of prisons, hospitals, and other institutions outside of due process to induce people to agree to deportation. These frameworks provide the context for the analysis of the deportation, the near deportation, and public calls for deportation of individuals in this book including Margarita Ojeda Wilcox and Louise Burbank at the Oregon State Hospital who were born in Mexico and Canada, suspected sex workers including Leonor Brunicardi, and citizens claiming the civic right of dissent including Portland librarian M. Louise Hunt. "Voluntary" deportation also frames gender-nonconforming Riedl's repatriation to Germany after internment as an "enemy alien" and "sex pervert." And self-deportation describes the impact of surveillance and anti-Japanese policies on rooming house managers Mitsuyo Uyeto and Matsumi Kojima, who decided to leave Oregon and likely the United States because of these practices.

People in Oregon and the nation did not simply receive these categories of civic definitions, rights, and obligations but were active participants in shaping the status and practice of citizenship and civil liberties. The period of the 1910s through the early 1920s was a watershed in the consequential tug-of-war at federal, state, and local levels about the status and practice of citizenship, and the rights, obligations, and liberties of citizens and residents. Many wage-earning working-class Americans and their supporters advocated for a more complete economic citizenship through maximum-hour and minimum-wage legislation and through laws and policies for healthier workplaces, but these laws also established the right of states to protect women as a separate class of residents. Some activists advocated for radical economic and social revolution, while others emphasized a participatory social citizenship to reform community life and to promote social justice and equality before the law across gender, racial, ethnic, and class lines.[23]

As the United States watched a global conflict and then entered the war in April 1917, the duties and obligations of citizenship, service to the state, and loyalty to the nation's war aims became paramount for national and local leaders. Their prescriptions were gendered as "patriotic womanhood" and motherhood for women residents as Barbara Steinson and Kathleen Kennedy have taught us.[24] State-sponsored and sanctioned surveillance and wartime violations of civil liberties such as the right to due process and freedom of speech, curtailed so soundly by the wartime Espionage Act of 1917 and the Sedition Act of 1918, meant that during the war Americans, as Paul L. Murphy described it in 1979, "saw liberty and justice prostituted in ways more extreme and extensive than at any other time in American history." The war's restrictions energized movements for civil rights and what Christopher Capozzola calls "a new discourse on civil liberties" protections and the making of "modern" citizenship. Civil liberties issues gained currency with some Americans during what Murphy identified as the "winding down of wartime hysteria."[25] And some civil liberties activists worked to include "sexual rights" and "sexual citizenship" as civil liberties in the 1920s, as Leigh Ann Wheeler demonstrates.[26]

Oregon's Others amplifies our understanding of the confrontations between citizenship and civil liberties with gender and intersectional identities at the center by tracing people, events, policies, and resistance before, during, and after the First World War in Oregon, a state that was a leader in both early twentieth-century reform and reactions to those reforms. In their introduction to *Behind the Lines*, the classic study of gen-

6 / INTRODUCTION

der and the two world wars of the twentieth century, Margaret Randolph Higgonet, Jane Jenson, Sonya Michel, and Margaret Collins Weitz used the metaphor of the double helix to frame the "paradoxical progress" for women in wartime and postwar society, a model to measure the steps-forward and steps-backward status of movements for gender equality and human rights. Wartime, they noted, "draws upon preexisting definitions of gender at the same time that it restructures gender relations." And in war's aftermath, "messages of reintegration" come with gendered prescriptions for postwar roles.[27]

Post-9/11 surveillance studies scholars have developed the concept of a "permanent emergency" in the "war on terror" to analyze the impact of ongoing wartime crisis thinking and assaults on civil liberties. This framework mirrors what Murphy identified as the "contrived postwar crisis" after World War I when "it became apparent that ambitious national leaders had no intention of dismantling the mechanisms for wartime repression and planned to extend them into peacetime America."[28] In the war's aftermath nativists, White supremacists, eugenic thinkers, and other policymakers created that contrived crisis in Oregon and the nation to add to the scaffolding of the surveillance state and to build additional policies of exclusion in an attempt to compress and isolate citizenship rights and privileges and to challenge civil liberties. By using a comparative lens across diverse group and community case studies and by forging an alternative periodization from the achievement of woman suffrage in Oregon, the war years, and the war's aftermath, this book provides a comprehensive perspective about the confrontations of civic rights and civil liberties in a period of reform and reaction among diverse Oregonians with implications for regional and national developments and comparisons.

GENDER, EXCLUSION, CITIZENSHIP, AND CIVIL LIBERTIES IN OREGON AND THE NATION

The 1859 Oregon Constitution prohibited Black and multiracial men, Native Hawai'ian men, Chinese men, and all women from voting. The state enacted laws excluding Black people from residence at its founding. In 1862 legislators prohibited marriage between White and Black people, and in 1866 increased these categories to include Native Hawai'ians, Chinese residents, and Indigenous Oregonians with "one half" or more "Indian

INTRODUCTION / 7

blood." Oregon's White male state makers, as Peggy Pascoe observed, targeted Black residents and also "built a longer list of non-White races" into Oregon's systems of exclusions with a "western version of White supremacy."[29] In 1893 Oregon legislators again expanded the prohibited categories of marriage to include "Mongolians," and, as Pascoe demonstrated in the case of Helen Emery and Gunjiro Aoki's attempt to marry in Portland in 1909, local authorities "stretched" the law to cover Aoki, a Japanese immigrant. This was in step with other Western states that passed marriage restrictions with "Mongolian" as a capacious term that included Japanese Americans, "reflecting the growing preference for terms that were expansively racial rather than specifically national."[30]

The Bill of Rights of the Oregon Constitution enshrined Whiteness in state systems in another way with Article I Section 31, declaring: "White foreigners who are, or may hereafter become, residents of this State shall enjoy the same rights in respect to the possession, enjoyment, and descent of property as native born citizens." As Amy Platt and Laura Clay demonstrate, the delegates added the category of "White" to this section after debate and also gave the legislature the power to "restrain and regulate the immigration to this State of persons not qualified to become Citizens of the United States," thereby "helping to create one of the most racially exclusionary states in the country."[31] Many Oregonians engaged in forced removal, military conquest, and genocide of Indigenous people and violence against people considered racial and ethnic others as tools of exclusion.[32]

Women of color, immigrant women, and women committed to institutions in Oregon faced a double burden in their work to exercise citizenship rights such as voting. In 1912 Black and Chinese American women in Portland organized suffrage leagues, and the successful 1912 ballot measure removed the words "male" and "white" from the Oregon Constitution's article on voting rights.[33] But continuing discrimination by race and ethnicity, language barriers, poverty, and lack of access impacted voters in this period as they continue to do today. Women incarcerated in state institutions such as the Oregon State Hospital for the Insane or the Oregon Institution for the Feeble-Minded who would have been eligible to vote after 1912 lost those voting rights by virtue of the Oregon Constitutional provision that "no idiot or insane person shall be entitled to the privileges of an elector." They could only vote again if they were officially discharged, usually after a year's parole.[34] In 1914 voters approved an amendment to the state Constitution requiring voters to be citizens. Before this referendum Oregon had allowed qualified residents with "first papers" declaring their intention to become citizens to vote. Oregon was among forty states and territories that sanctioned noncitizen voting at some point, and as Ronald Hayduk's research demonstrates, the practice "came to a grinding halt in the early twentieth century" as nativism and "wartime hysteria" brought "the elimination of this long-standing practice."[35] Oregonians imposed an English-only literacy test for voting in a 1924 referendum, a tool for voter suppression also used in other states to maintain racial, ethnic, US-born, and class privilege.[36]

Federal policy combined with state and local legislation to exclude people in this period. Federal law prevented first-generation Asian American people from obtaining naturalized citizenship and the right to vote. Before the Indian Citizenship (Snyder) Act of 1924, Indigenous people in Oregon had no guarantee of citizenship and voting privileges. After 1924, continuing discrimination and the impact of settler colonialism continued to create barriers to full civic participation.[37] The Federal Expatriation Act of 1907 directed that married women would take the citizenship of their husbands, which meant that women who were US citizens who married noncitizen men lost their US citizenship status, including voting rights. During World War I women in this group had to register as "alien enemies" with other women who were citizens of Germany, some one quarter of Oregon's female registrants. But the same law protected Margarita Ojeda Wilcox from deportation to Mexico from the Oregon State Hospital in 1920. The Cable Act of 1922 began to address the question of married women's citizenship rights but still barred women who married men who were not eligible for citizenship, such as first-generation Japanese and Chinese men, from US citizenship.[38]

Many Oregonians voiced fears of political and labor radicalism with the growth of the Industrial Workers of the World, socialism, the Russian Revolution abroad and "Red Scare" at home, as well as nativist and antiradical fears mirrored by other Americans. At the federal level the restrictive Immigration Acts of 1917, 1918, 1921, and 1924 accompanied the continued exclusion of Asian Americans. A movement to exclude immigrants from Mexico based on the same principles paralleled these developments. Two US Supreme Court cases—the 1922 case of Takao Ozawa and the 1923

INTRODUCTION / 9

Oregon case of Punjabi immigrant Bhagat Singh Thind—declared that Japanese and South Asian immigrants were not White and therefore ineligible for citizenship.[39] The 1923 Oregon legislature, with significant support from Ku Klux Klan and Klan-supporting voters and legislators, passed an Alien Land Act to prevent residents ineligible for citizenship, such as first-generation Japanese Americans, from owning land and created a statewide business licensing law that same year built on Portland's precedent designed to discriminate by race and ethnicity with Japanese Oregonians in mind.[40] The editors of Portland's *Oshu Nippo* (*Oregon Daily News*) named the year 1923 in Oregon "a year full of hatred."[41]

White exclusionist policies had many destructive consequences. One was to make Oregon an overwhelmingly White, Protestant state that discouraged other people from residence. The 1920 census reported a total resident Oregon population of 783,389 with 85 percent, 666,995 people, US-born and White, and 102,151 Whites born outside of the United States—a category that at this time included first-generation Latinx residents, with 569 born in Mexico. There were 4,590 Indigenous; 4,151 Japanese; 3,000 Chinese; and 2,144 Black Oregonians.[42] The *Official Catholic Directory* for 1924 reported 60,000 Catholic Oregonians in the western part of the state and 6,927 in eastern Oregon, including Indigenous and Latinx Catholics, a total of about 8 percent of the state's population. There were some ten thousand Jewish Portlanders. Several hundred Sikh, Muslim, and Hindu immigrants from India and South Asia lived in Oregon.[43]

WOMEN AS VOTING CITIZENS

After November 1912 women voters took action on both sides of the question of inclusive rights for all versus exclusionary policies. But problems with Oregon's new permanent voter registration system brought an almost immediate potential for voter suppression. From 1913 to 1916 Oregon was the first US state, after several cities had done so, to create permanent voter registration as part of the "Oregon System" of institutional reforms. In Oregon's case this meant implementing a voter registration card rather than maintaining election books at county courthouses. This made Oregonians some of the first people in the nation, and Oregon women among the first women, to report detailed information about themselves in order to vote on cards stored and retrieved by counties. Legislators in the 1913

Oregon biennial session, the first since woman suffrage, passed a package of bills to overhaul, streamline, and simplify voting laws including permanent registration. Before 1913 voters had to enroll in their county of residence each biennium or be sworn in at the polls with several advocates as witnesses. With permanent registration voters would register once and that registration would be in force unless they changed their address.[44]

What many legislators hoped would be a way to make the process of voting more efficient became a confusing years-long muddle with the potential to suppress registration and discourage voting. All voters would have to register in 1913 to be able to vote in the spring and fall elections that year. But late in 1913, the Oregon Supreme Court declared the permanent registration law unconstitutional. The result was that everyone had to re-register to vote in 1914. The legislature crafted a new permanent registration law in the 1915 biennial session, which meant that everyone would have to re-register again in 1916. To vote consistently, voters had to register in 1913, 1914, and 1916, each time thinking that registration would be permanent. Confusion flourished. It was no wonder that during and after 1913 many voters were slow to register.[45]

Black women in Portland were particularly involved in voter registration in this period. Many registered to vote in 1913 for the spring and fall elections, eager to participate in this civic right after the successful woman suffrage ballot measure in November 1912.[46] The November 1914 election was the first general statewide election in which eligible Oregon women could vote, and it came in the midst of the confusing re-registration process. Lizzie Koontz Weeks, a social worker who would become the first Black woman parole officer in the Portland juvenile justice system in 1920, organized a voter registration drive on October 14, 1914, the day before the registration process closed for the November general election. Weeks facilitated a meeting at Portland's Central Library to form a Colored Women's Republican Club, in step with most Black Americans' post–Civil War political alignments. After the meeting the entire group went together to the nearby Multnomah County Courthouse so that those who were not yet registered could do so with their community around them. By the following spring, in advance of citywide elections, Weeks reported the club's ranks at 350 members, a large majority of Black women of voting age residing in the city.[47] Club members continued activities throughout the re-registration years and beyond with specific, concentrated work

INTRODUCTION / *11*

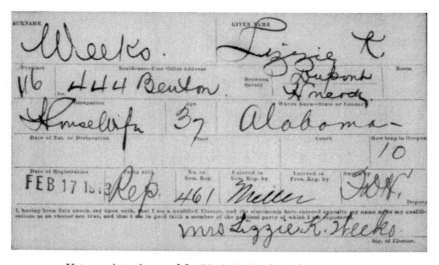

FIGURE 1 Voter registration card for Lizzie K. Weeks, February 17, 1913. Cancelled Voter Registration Cards, 1908–2010, Multnomah County Election Records, Multnomah County Archives, Portland, Oregon.

in advance of registration and election deadlines and held forums with speakers and candidates.[48]

White clubwomen lobbied the Oregon legislature's 1913 and 1915 sessions for legislation supporting teacher tenure, workplace safety, and the prohibition of alcohol, and in 1916 formed the Oregon Women's Legislative Council to advocate for laws that reflected what they believed were women's priorities and worked to establish the right to jury service for women by 1921.[49] The coalition represented the Oregon Federation of (White) Women's Clubs, the Woman's Christian Temperance Union, the Oregon Congress of Mothers and Parent Teacher Association, and, for several years, the Oregon Consumers' League. Members lobbied for more bills to support women and children, including wage-earning women, teachers, and students, but they also supported eugenic laws declaring some Oregonians to be unfit and mandating their sterilization.[50] Key leaders of the Oregon Women's Ku Klux Klan in 1923–1924 had been early registrants to vote in the state. Mae Gifford, Kristine Belt, and Nellie Hurd all registered to vote in Multnomah County in spring 1913, and Vora Sowers registered in Medford in 1914.[51] The Klan of the 1920s in Oregon and the nation was an engine for political organizing and activism. Thousands of Oregon

Klanswomen likely embraced the vote to elect legislators who would pass bills in service of White supremacy and anti-Catholicism, including the prohibition of religious attire in classrooms and the anti-Japanese land act and business licensing acts. The Klan used the initiative process to place an anti-Catholic Compulsory Education Bill, mandating students attend public schools, on the ballot in November 1922, and the measure passed, with many Klanswomen likely supporting it with their votes. Via a strong legal challenge, the US Supreme Court declared the Compulsory School Bill unconstitutional in 1925.[52]

Catholic Religious Sisters responded directly with voter registration and voting drives. They stood at the front lines of teaching and other Catholic community services that were under attack. The Sisters of the Holy Names was a registered Oregon corporation that owned and maintained a large network of educational institutions in the state in addition to the Marylhurst Convent in Lake Oswego. Provincial Superior Sister Alphonsus Mary, the corporation's president, sent a letter to all Sisters a month after the 1921 Oregon legislative session adjourned, encouraging them to register and to become active voters.[53] Sisters registered and voted and recorded their actions and motivations in their convent *Chronicles*. "All the Sisters at Marylhurst" who were qualified registered together on the afternoon of April 21, 1921, in Clackamas County. Sisters at St. Paul's Academy in St. Paul voted in the spring primary and fall general elections of 1922. "Because there are educational and religious issues involved," they noted, "we avail ourselves of the right of suffrage." The Sisters of the Sacred Heart Academy in Salem noted the election held "deeper interest than ever before" and were "anxiously awaiting the returns." Election day "holds a new significance for us," Sisters at St. Mary's Academy in The Dalles recorded, as they used "their right of suffrage by voting against the infamous so-called compulsory Education Bill" and went to the polls "in groups of two and three." Although averse to appearing at the polls for the November general election, the Sisters of St. Mary's Academy in southern Oregon's Jacksonville recorded: "we were glad, indeed, to cast our votes in the cause of that which closely touches our Catholic Schools and other institutions."[54]

Anne M. Butler demonstrated that Religious Sisters drew on "direct experience with democratic governance," including regular voting, within their institutions as they approached voting in electoral politics outside

INTRODUCTION / *13*

convent and school walls.[55] Across Oregon Catholic Religious Sisters' strategies about how they registered and how they voted, with some going all together as a visible unit, others in small groups of two or three, reveal their experience with the potential danger they faced in these very public actions. They knew best how to engage with the process in their specific community settings, whether there was protection in numbers or more security in going out in smaller groups over the course of the afternoon. The danger was tangible and visible. Robed and hooded Klansmen marched in the streets of various communities in the lead-up to the 1922 election. Sister Mary Etherlind of St. Mary's Academy in Portland, as Paula Abrams notes, walked school children from St. Mary's to Mass on Sundays and was "one of the many nuns regularly confronting hooded figures on horseback who rode onto the sidewalk to frighten the children" and who tried to intimidate the Sisters.[56]

OREGON FIRST BOOSTERISM AND ITS CONSEQUENCES

Oregon women achieved and used their voting rights in the midst of what Charles E. Rothwell called Oregon's achievement of "star state" status in the eyes of the nation that fostered an unrelenting Oregon First boosterism.[57] In 1914 sociologist William F. Ogburn declared Oregon to be "an experimental station in government" by virtue of the state's "Oregon System" of civic tools (including the initiative, referendum, and recall as well as permanent voter registration) that became a model for progressive structural change with the stated goal of bringing governance closer to the hands of the people.[58] The initiative was a key factor in the success of Oregon's woman suffrage movement and brought the attention of reform advocates from around the globe. Oregon was a leader in maximum-hour legislation for women that led to the landmark 1908 US Supreme Court decision in *Muller v. Oregon*; the first ten-hour-day law for all workers upheld by the US Supreme Court in *Bunting v. Oregon* in 1917; and the first enforceable minimum-wage law.[59] "Since Oregon achieved as a pioneer this long and varied list of governmental changes," Ogburn noted, "the world is watching to see what she will do next."[60]

The early movement for social hygiene in Oregon was another Oregon First. Anti–venereal disease campaigns and other antivice activities brought national attention to the state, and in turn advocates used that

14 / INTRODUCTION

acclaim to argue successfully for the expansion of their programs. The Oregon Social Hygiene Society (OSHS) was instrumental in organizing Portland's 1912–1913 Vice Commission, and Portland was among twenty US cities from 1910 to 1916, and the only city west of Denver, to fund a commission's work.[61] As this book shows, Oregon was an early and radical adopter of eugenics laws and policies, which dovetailed with the work of social hygiene in the state. Both added intensity and justifications for the identification and punishment of internal enemy "others."

The war accelerated the Oregon First trajectory and created an enhanced civic obligation for residents to contribute to "star state" results in a myriad of programs. During the conflict, when federal pressure on states to comply with wartime programs was immense and competitive, state and local leaders used the idea of Oregon's star state status to urge residents to even more achievements. As Rothwell observed in 1924, "Oregon was drawn immediately into the vortex of the war spirit," and residents "responded with a fervor" of action "as much if not more than any state in the union" under a "stupor of patriotism and intense nationalism."[62] In 1917 Oregon had the highest proportion of volunteers compared to its military draft quota of any state, and leaders used this first to urge more wartime achievements. The state's singular use of schools to enforce compliance with the Food Pledge conservation program was another early wartime first used to boost Oregon's record. And when Oregon became the first state to surpass its subscription quota in the Third Liberty Loan drive of 1918, leaders used that Oregon First to create the obligation to be first in everything concerning wartime registration and fundraising drives.[63]

In social hygiene work Portland's The Cedars was the first-in-the-nation detention home specifically created to incarcerate women with STIS, and the state expanded its national reputation in the wartime anti–venereal disease campaigns with "model" ordinances and legislation, including hotel licensing. When the War Department tallied statistics for the first million draftees in the conflict in December 1918 and found Oregon to have the lowest national rate of STIS in troops, it appeared to many to be confirmation that Oregon "set the pace" in the nation's social hygiene work.[64] Oregon's "star state" status became a reason for leaders to apply incredible pressure on residents to achieve other firsts related to wartime loyalty again and again. Oregon First acclaims and pressures continued in the postwar period. After the US Public Health Service published a

1920 survey declaring Portland to be the "cleanest" of all cities with a population of one hundred thousand to five hundred thousand by anti-venereal disease measures in place, Mayor George Baker featured the news in an advertisement for his reelection campaign published the next day in Portland newspapers. This Oregon First status created other political capital. The OSHS obtained additional state funding for its programs, as did the State Board of Health.[65]

Oregon veterans were among the first organizers and builders of the American Legion, a group that worked to exclude Japanese Americans and other immigrants and political and labor radicals. "Veteran organizations, fraternal orders, and secret societies" flourished in Oregon, Rothwell observed, making a "ripe field" for the Ku Klux Klan to reap "an early and rich harvest."[66] Local and national leaders touted Oregon's 1920 Survey of Mental Defect, Delinquency, and Dependency as another Oregon First achievement as the state deputized residents to surveil, identify, and report people they considered "feebleminded" and "insane."[67] Among other things, Oregon First sentiments created a blueprint for identifying, punishing, and excluding many people labeled as dangerous internal enemies.

SURVEILLANCE PROJECTS AND CRISIS PRODUCTS

During World War I and its aftermath, there were more agents of surveillance in American life than ever before. Arguably, Oregonians experienced more surveillance than residents of many other states during these years. The "price of vigilance" was a profound loss of civil liberties, as Joan Jensen tells us, and many people who scrutinized others turned from what Capozzola identifies as "vigilance" to "vigilantism," which included, as Jennifer Fronc demonstrates, surveillance by private agencies such as organizations concerned with morality and women's sexuality.[68] Residents of Oregon and the nation engaged increasingly with state bureaucracies through registration and documentation requirements during this period, such as birth certificates that expanded state scrutiny.[69] The 1918 registration of noncitizen "enemies" who had to carry photo identification, and whose Oregon story is chronicled in this book, followed by sixteen years the mass resistance in 1892 among Chinese Americans to the nation's first attempt at mass-photo-identification documents associated with Chinese Exclusion. It paralleled the widespread requirement of the passport as a

16 / INTRODUCTION

photo identification document and data file during and after the First World War. In criminal justice matters the Bertillon system of identification, including photographs, was giving way to fingerprinting, and Oregon officials used both for the registration of "enemy aliens."[70]

Oregon health officials created a new identity card for women incarcerated at The Cedars with STIs that carried their test results. Wartime registration of women for war service, the Food Pledge, and multiple registrations for fundraising such as Liberty Loans, all created a data archive for identification. Historian Harold Hyman has named these items "crisis products" that emerge from the "felt needs of authorities" during times of war and "periods of fear of subversion."[71] Food Pledge cards, registration for wartime service, "alien enemy" registration booklets, and loyalty oaths like the one imposed on workers after M. Louise Hunt refused to purchase a Liberty Bond in Portland are examples the many crisis products in action in Oregon during this period. Surveillance agencies enlisted people to police and enforce the loyalty of others and to suppress people's citizenship of dissent. Federal agencies included the Bureau of Investigation in the Justice Department, the Bureau of Immigration in the Labor Department, the Secret Service in Treasury, and postal employees throughout the nation authorized to inspect the mail and register and observe noncitizen enemies and dissenters and to assist other state agents in censorship and information gathering. The Bureau of Indian Affairs (BIA) conducted "industrial surveys" on reservations in the 1920s.

Wartime and postwar "vigilance" organizations of civilians such as the Portland Vigilantes and the Multnomah Home Guard augmented local law enforcement. Prohibition began statewide in Oregon in 1916, four years before the national ban on alcohol, expanding exponentially the agents of state surveillance.[72] Railroad yards and hotels and rooming houses were particular targets, as the cases of Portland railroad car cleaners, suspected sex workers, and Japanese American hotel managers in this book demonstrate. Social hygienists and members of other voluntary organizations policed sexuality and gender presentation based on Progressive-Era practices of private surveillance. In Oregon's nationally recognized system for detaining women suspected of STIs without due process, and in campaigns against radicals and dissenters, local groups worked with state and federal agencies, including the Bureau of Justice, the Military Intelligence Branch of the US Army, and the US Public Health

INTRODUCTION / 17

Service. Physicians at the Oregon State Hospital for the Insane worked with the Immigration Bureau to deport people who were not US citizens.

Surveillance projects often combined to create collateral scrutiny, the process by which agents interested in one objective of surveillance uncovered information related to other projects of state observation of residents. Oregon authorities repurposed the state's existing 1911 Vagrancy law for wartime and postwar use against noncitizens, dissenters, women at risk for STIs, and Oregonians they considered to be internal threats because of different abilities such as people identified as "feebleminded." The consequences ranged from incarceration and deportation to state-mandated sterilization, telling examples of Kerber's point that state agents punish individuals and groups for failure to fulfill their defined civic obligations. This book brings to the forefront the licensing laws Portland and Oregon officials used as tools for overlapping surveillance projects and exclusion in the anti–venereal disease campaigns to incarcerate women with STIs and against Japanese Oregonians who managed rooming houses and hotels. Oregon's eugenic surveillance cast a wide net, including the 1920 Oregon State Survey of Mental Defect, Delinquency, and Dependency and legislation designed to scrutinize all residents as potential internal enemies by reason of disability.

Canaday finds that officials and rank-and-file staff of the Bureau of Immigration, the War Department, and civilian organizations before, during, and after the war shared information and employed techniques of mass examination and scrutiny in what she terms the journey from "policing" to officially "regulating" gender-nonconforming people.[73] These actions and processes are evident in this book in the cases of gender-nonconforming Oregon residents Riedl and Teddy Gloss, caught up in the policing and regulating of "enemy aliens" and venereal disease during and after World War I, and Winnie Springer at the Oregon State Hospital.

THE CHAPTERS

The combined force of wartime and postwar campaigns for "100% Americanism" and loyalty coupled with Oregon's consequential eugenics movement with radical state-sterilization legislation defined an intense period of surveillance and scrutiny for internal enemy others in the state and a profound challenge to civil liberties. *Oregon's Others* analyzes this history in tandem with people's vital resistance in response to these destructive processes. The first chapter outlines Oregon's radical eugenics movement and policies, and the next three chapters analyze the wartime context for and practice of registration and surveillance. Three succeeding chapters analyze Oregon's social hygiene movement and the incarceration of women suspected of STIs, civil liberties and resistance at the Oregon State Hospital, and discrimination and resistance among Japanese American women in Oregon.

Chapter 1 establishes Oregon as a national leader in radical eugenics thought and policies, and outlines the alignment of wartime and postwar "patriotism" with eugenic thinking and actions in the state, including the 1920 Oregon State Survey of Mental Defect, Delinquency, and Dependency that focused on disabled Oregonians and Japanese and Chinese Oregonians as internal enemy others. An analysis of eugenic thinking and practices by federal Indian Affairs officials and reservation physicians suggests additional ways Indigenous people within Oregon were targeted as "unfit" others. Chapter 2 begins the analysis of wartime registrations, including war service registration for women, the enrollment of women in the Food Pledge army, and registration drives for wartime fundraising campaigns such as Liberty Bonds and War Savings Stamps (WSS). Many women in Oregon asserted their civic right to dissent, refusing to participate in a women's service registration for fear of a female draft, and several thousand challenged the Food Pledge, all after the Espionage Act went into effect in the spring of 1917. Their dissent in Oregon, combined with other people's challenges across the nation, hastened the passage of the more restrictive Sedition Act in June 1918. Supporters conducted most Liberty Bond and WSS drives in this incredibly restrictive climate where free speech and actions were severely curtailed in the name of patriotic loyalty. Registrations became a test and an obligation of patriotic womanhood and encouraged some women to police the lives and choices of other women who had a different view of citizenship and dissent and who became identified as internal enemies. Oregon First achievements and boosterism intensified the pressure. Some women welcomed and practiced patriotic womanhood through registrations, including many White clubwomen and some women in historically marginalized communities who participated as a way to build a more complete citizenship by engaging in the work of the nation.

Chapter 3 traces the stories of two women within these wartime drives who were surveilled and punished at their workplaces for dissent during the Liberty Loan and WSS campaigns. Portland librarian M. Louise Hunt was forced to resign her position at the Central Library for her refusal to purchase a Liberty Bond after a "patriotic inquisition" that included calls for her to lose her job, her voting rights, and to be deported. Pullman Company railroad car cleaner and second-generation German Anna Mary Weston was the first Oregon woman arrested for sedition in June 1918 for refusing to purchase a War Savings Stamp and criticizing the war effort while on the job. Weston worked in a multiethnic and likely mixed-race workplace at Portland's North Bank Railroad Station, and federal jurors acquitted her by reason of mental incapacity. Both cases reveal the pressures on workers with overlapping surveillance projects in place and the consequences of workplace surveillance on women in two very different workplaces. Weston was not committed to a state institution after her trial, and exploring possible reasons why helps to sharpen our understanding of the connections between ability and ideas about productive citizenship and the nation's work in an era of eugenic thinking and wartime loyalty campaigns.

Chapter 4 considers Oregonians who were required by federal policy to register as "enemy aliens" because they were German citizens—literal internal "enemy" others who faced a new system of wartime surveillance and restrictions on their civil liberties. Because the Expatriation Act of 1907 required women to take the citizenship of their husbands, federal "enemy alien" policy meant that women born in the United States who married German citizen men had to register. More than a quarter of women who registered in Oregon were born in the United States, raising questions about the nature of women's independent or dependent citizenship after the achievement of women's voting rights. Some Oregon women protested the registration process by direct action and self-representation in the face of registration. The surveillance of "enemy-alien" bodies resulted in the policing and punishment of gender-nonconforming Oregonian and German citizen resident Riedl, who registered as male but was interned as a "sexual pervert" for presenting in women's clothing. At the close of the war and internment, Riedl repatriated to Germany—an example of Goodman's coerced but "voluntary" deportation often hidden from history.

Chapter 5 builds an analysis of Oregon's leading role in the social hy-

20 / INTRODUCTION

giene movement and wartime and postwar incarceration of women with STIS at The Cedars. It traces the Oregon First developments in local and national policy, and identifies eugenic thinking behind the parallel movement to label sex workers and people engaged in nonsanctioned sexuality and gender presentation as "feebleminded" and "degenerate" people who should be subject to state-mandated sterilization as internal enemies, or, as in the case of Leonor Brunicardi, deportation to Mexico. Efforts to control "wayward girls" extended to Oregon's reservations and the Chemawa Indian Boarding School near Salem. Records of women paroled from The Cedars detention hospital provide a partial profile of people caught in the surveillance projects that supported antivenereal policies. Other records help to trace various acts of resistance, including Black Portlander Ruth Brown's 1921 habeas corpus suit. The Cedars inmates were also subjected to a "health parole" even when they had not been convicted of a crime, extending limits on their freedom, removing due process civil liberties protections, and expanding the surveillance against them. A decades-long "held for health" policy and the persistence of the examination of bodies during arrests—including the arrest, examination, and incarceration of gender-nonconforming Teddy Gloss in 1923—was one powerful legacy of the wartime programs to curtail civil liberties.

Chapter 6 brings the analysis of systems of eugenic thinking, gender and gender identity, race, ethnicity, and class to the Oregon State Hospital for the Insane with a sterilization policy in place after 1917. With the support of many Oregonians, including active endorsement by White clubwomen, the policy was under the direct leadership of physicians committed to radical eugenic policies. The chapter analyzes the experiences of Portlander Margarita Ojeda Wilcox, born in Mexico, whose husband was a US citizen, and Canadian Louise Burbank, who was a domestic worker in Portland. Both women experienced encounters with eugenic thinking, sterilization policy, and systems of deportation; both women resisted. Winnie Springer explored gender nonconformity in the face of eugenic thinking and policies while committed, and after release Springer sued the state for forced incarceration and cruel punishment in a case that went to the Oregon Supreme Court in 1919.

Chapter 7 explores the varieties of Japanese Oregonian women's resistance to growing systems of racial hatred and eugenic thinking that marked them as internal enemies. First-generation Issei women faced sys-

INTRODUCTION / *21*

temic and consequential barriers to their freedoms, safety, and well-being, including being labeled as internal enemy others because of their work building family businesses and bearing children born in Oregon who, by virtue of the Fourteenth Amendment, became US citizens at birth. State and federal surveillance projects targeted Issei residents, especially Issei women as workers and mothers. As their reproductive lives became politicized, Issei women made decisions about childbirth, including seeking care with Japanese midwives when and where they were available, and assuring that birth certificates were completed as evidence of their children's citizenship status. They engaged in consequential work to support their families. After the war Portland and Oregon business licensing laws became the urban equivalent to the anti-Japanese laws restricting land ownership to citizens. Mitsuyo Uyeto and Matsumi Kojima resisted these policies as rooming house managers in Portland's Japantown.

The book's conclusion draws together these case studies of the hunt for internal enemy others in this period to suggest the lasting impact of such policies and actions, the consequential challenges some Oregonians made to these campaigns, and the ongoing work of resistance and activism in movements for civil rights and social justice.

CHAPTER 1

Eugenics and
Internal Enemy Others

OREGON'S MOVEMENT to make eugenic sterilization statewide policy paralleled and expanded the wartime and postwar hunt for internal enemies. Many Oregonians embraced the "eugenic thinking" that permeated popular culture and influenced a constellation of other state policies, including expanded surveillance projects.[1] The Oregon eugenics movement was among the earliest in the nation, and by 1923 Oregon surpassed most other eugenic-policy states with laws that reached beyond institutional walls to police all Oregon residents as potentially "unfit" internal enemies. The eugenics crusade impacted all residents and influenced civil liberties questions during wartime registrations, in the social hygiene movement and the incarceration of women for sexually transmitted infections (STIS), at the Oregon State Hospital, and with a "New Patriotism" after the First World War that fueled anti-Japanese hatred and policies, nativism, immigration restriction, and the growth of the Ku Klux Klan.[2]

THE OREGON QUEST FOR RADICAL,
STATE-MANDATED STERILIZATION

Dr. Bethenia Owens-Adair was Oregon's foremost lobbyist for eugenic legislation.[3] By "preparing the public mind" with letters to the editors of newspapers across the state, giving countless presentations to women's clubs, religious, fraternal, and civic groups, and through relentless work with legislative sponsors and other supporters, Owens-Adair lobbied for forced state sterilization laws and other eugenic policies such as premarital physical examinations in biennial state legislative sessions from 1907 through 1923.[4] Her 1907 Oregon sterilization bill, proposed the same year as Indiana's first-in-the-nation sterilization law, did not survive the legislative session, but she "vowed to be on hand two years hence" and kept her promise.[5] Oregon legislators passed her bill in 1909, but Governor George Chamberlain vetoed it citing concerns about "abuse and discrimination."[6] After failing in 1911, Owens-Adair's 1913 bill passed with the support of Governor Oswald West, but opponents gained more than enough signatures to refer the bill to voters in a special election that November and they defeated it. Owens-Adair paused during the 1915 session to regroup after the referendum defeat and then built a coalition to pass Oregon's first successful sterilization bill in February 1917, less than two months before the United States entered World War I. The law survived an attempt to gather enough signatures for another referendum vote.[7]

Significantly, the 1917 legislation expanded who could be sterilized and why. The 1913 bill listed "habitual criminals, moral degenerates or sexual perverts" committed to state institutions such as the Oregon State Hospital or the State Penitentiary whose sterilization would be "for the best interests of the public peace, health and safety." Eugenicists and homophobic policymakers adopted these categories in the aftermath of Portland's 1912–1913 "Vice Scandal" involving gay men and also, as Portland Police Bureau's Women's Protective Division detective Lola Baldwin phrased it, "'because it applies to the female pervert as well as the male.'" The successful 1917 law retained these categories and added people who were considered "feeble minded, insane, [or] epileptic" to the list, as "persons potential to producing offspring who, because of inheritance of inferior or antisocial traits, would probably become a social menace or ward of the State." This expansive list with vague categories extended the possibility of sterilization to most anyone who was an inmate in an Oregon institution and in turn increased the categories local officials could use to commit people who could be sterilized.[8] Eugenic thinking and social hygiene programs linking sex workers with "feeblemindedness" made many more women vulnerable targets for sterilization measures. The 1917 legislation created a State Board of Eugenics comprising representatives from the State Board of Health and superintendents of the Oregon State Hospital, the Eastern Oregon State Hospital, the Penitentiary, and the State Institution for the Feeble-Minded. The board ruled on sterilization requests made by these same directors of the state institutions, creating a closed circle of power and control.[9]

Owens-Adair and her supporters next worked to expand Oregon's state-mandated sterilization beyond institutional walls. At the 1917 Oregon legislative session, Senator Robert Farrell (R-Multnomah) proposed an alternative sterilization bill via Owens-Adair's backing to include people who resided outside of state institutions. House members defeated that more extreme measure.[10] But at the next 1919 session, Oregon legislators embraced the radical outreach in a new sterilization section in the expansive 1919 overhaul of the Oregon State Board of Health. This section expanded state sterilization by investing the state health officer with the power to report all people who were or *might become* a "social menace" or "ward of the state" to the Eugenics Board. Owens-Adair advocated for the law as a "necessary" social measure and saw it as a legal strategy. The 1919 law, she wrote, included "all defectives and degenerates of the classes named, outside the state institutions as well as inside them." No one could object to the law "on the ground of its being class legislation" in violation of Fourteenth Amendment equal protection laws because it applied to all residents in Oregon. Harry H. Laughlin, superintendent of the US Eugenics Record Office, noted in 1923 that class legislation concerns made for the "principal legal difficulty" in getting sterilization bills to pass and to stay on the books without challenge.[11] But in 1921 the Marion County Circuit Court ruled the 1917 sterilization law unconstitutional as class legislation and declared the 1919 sterilization section in the Board of Health statute unconstitutional because it denied people rights to due process.[12]

In response to the court decision, Owens-Adair and her supporters crafted a new sterilization bill for the 1923 Oregon legislative session that addressed the court's objections to the former laws but kept the broad power to sterilize any resident identified as a potential "menace." Legislators addressed concerns from medical practitioners by including an individual's right to choose a physician to perform the sterilization procedure with approval of the Eugenics Board. They assured Christian Science adherents that the bill would provide for "medical freedom," but the final wording of the bill stated that this choice was possible only if it did not "interfere with the operation of this act, and the carrying out of its purposes." Governor Walter Pierce signed the bill into law in February 1923.[13] Oregon policymakers had created a state sterilization law that would withstand legal challenges and apply to all residents, and it was in effect until 1983. The *Eugenical News*, the official journal of the American Eugenics Society, praised Oregon's 1923 law as "the soundest and most satisfactory yet enacted" from the "eugenical point of view." The law provided "for [a] legally sound and constitutional procedure for preventing reproduction by the degenerate human family stocks of the state."[14] In 1927 the US Supreme Court upheld Virginia's sterilization law in *Buck v. Bell* and other states added sterilization measures to their codes. By 1937 Oregon was one of thirty-two states with a sterilization law. It was the only West Coast state and with Idaho the only Western state among the eight states with more radical legislation that policed all residents for possible state-sterilization beyond institutions.[15]

Owens-Adair also sponsored a series of premarital health examination bills in Oregon in 1909, 1913, 1921, and 1923 as part of her eugenic crusade with the hope of reaching all Oregonians as candidates for state steriliza-tion. Paul Lombardo demonstrates that marriage examination policies "fit readily within the goals and the conceptual frame of eugenics," and Mark Largent finds that across the nation state marriage examination laws were building blocks to state sterilization legislation.[16] Owens-Adair and her supporters certainly employed this "opening wedge" strategy to build acceptance for other sterilization laws but also worked to enact eugenic marriage policies as another way to extend state sterilization beyond the confines of institutions, to grasp for every Oregon resident they deemed "unfit." Marriage examinations highlighted premarital intimacy and sex-ual activity, and so created opposition among many residents. Governor Chamberlain vetoed the 1909 bill that required men to provide medical certification that they were free from sexually transmitted diseases as an "insult" to "the young men of Oregon," but Governor West signed a similar 1913 bill into law.[17]

Opponents tried to repeal the 1913 law in each successive biennial session without success, citing the ease with which prospective marriage partners could travel the ten miles to Vancouver, Washington (a "short streetcar ride" from Portland) to marry, the lax enforcement of the law, and its loopholes around obtaining certificates.[18] By 1921, Owens-Adair lobbied for a bill that would have expanded marriage legislation directly to state sterilization of people outside of institutions. Her proposed "hy-gienic marriage law," what *Oregon Voter* editor C. C. Chapman called a "sterilization bill," mandated a physical and mental examination for both prospective partners. If one or both failed the exam, no marriage could take place "unless one or both are rendered sterile." Representative Mary Strong Kinney (R-Clatsop) sponsored the bill in the Oregon House.[19]

Legislators passed the bill with a built-in referral to voters at a special election that June, and voters defeated it 53 to 46 percent.[20] In 1923, Owens-Adair proposed a similar hygienic marriage bill for both partners but provided an exemption for women aged forty-five and older, what Lombardo notes was a "common metric" for women past childbearing age in marriage legislation. The bill did not make it through the Senate, and one opponent called it "an insult to the young women of Oregon."[21] This appears to have been Owens-Adair's last attempt at legislation three years before her death in 1926.[22]

ORGANIZED WOMEN'S SUPPORT FOR EUGENICS

Prominent White clubwomen and other leaders in Oregon, and many thousands of their followers empowered with the vote, joined Owens-Adair in support of eugenic legislation. Not all members necessarily supported these bills, but the organizations endorsed the bills by formal vote and via the Oregon Women's Legislative Council, suggesting that many members voted for the measures and welcomed their club advocacy. Sarah A. Evans, president of the Oregon Federation of Women's Clubs from 1905 to 1915, urged her members to support state sterilization. In a talk titled "The Child That Should Never Have Been Born," and in her farewell address as outgoing president, Evans referred to the "human waste" of the "feeble minded" in the state and asked members to sponsor and vote for suitable sterilization legislation. Federation members, representing some thirty clubs around the state—including the Portland Woman's Club, the Portland Branch of the Council of Jewish Women, the Women's Political Study League of Portland, and the State Women's Press Club—agreed to sponsor both the extreme sterilization bill in 1917 that would have reached all residents in Oregon and the bill that did become law.

Federation president Ida Callahan of Corvallis urged all clubwomen in 1921 to support the marriage examination bill "to relieve us of the burden of feeble-mindedness and to decrease the spread of venereal diseases." Federation members endorsed Oregon's final sterilization bill of 1923, led by former Oregon state legislator Sylvia Thompson (D-The Dalles, Hood River, Wasco) and legislative committee members Margaret Bondurant and Bertha M. Buland.[23] Policewoman Lola Baldwin supported sterilization based on her work in the juvenile justice system and social hygiene movement from the early days of the eugenics movement.[24] Labor advocate Millie Trumbull, secretary of the Oregon Board of Child Labor Inspectors, executive secretary of the Industrial Welfare Commission, and a leader of the Oregon Consumers' League, believed there was "no menace greater" to industry "than the feeble-minded worker." Trumbull was the secretary for the Oregon Women's Legislative Council and principal lobbyist for the 1917 sterilization legislation when Owens-Adair could not attend the session in person. In letters to legislators, Trumbull claimed to represent the votes of thirty thousand clubwomen. She was also a strong supporter of the 1921 marriage examination bill and the 1923 sterilization law.[25]

Cornelia Marvin, the long-serving Oregon state librarian and state historian during and after the war, called Owens-Adair "Oregon's greatest woman and our most distinguished and useful citizen." Marvin's biographer, Cheryl Gunselman, notes that Marvin believed "her most important work outside of the library" was supporting Owens-Adair in her "long fight making possible the sterilization of the unfit" and the 1923 sterilization bill, signed into law by Governor Walter Pierce, who became Marvin's husband in 1928.[26] Mary Woodworth Patterson, one of the founders of Oregon's chapter of the Daughters of the American Revolution (DAR), urged DAR members to be "apostles" for the eugenic marriage bill of 1921. Her husband was Oregon state senator Isaac Lee Patterson (R-Salem, Benton, Polk), who would become governor in 1927.[27]

Eugenic thinking fit well with nativism, White supremacy, the hyper-loyalty of the war and its aftermath, and the growth of the surveillance state. It was part of the policies to incarcerate women with STIs in Oregon and the nation and embodied in anti-Japanese land and licensing laws and other nativist actions. Dividing the community and the state into productive, "fit" citizens and disabled, poor, immigrant, racial, and ethnic others who could be labeled as "feebleminded" and considered unworthy of full or partial citizenship, privileged some women over others. As Allison Carey notes, "middle class, morally 'fit' women" could claim and achieve "greater access to civic participation" when applying labels of "feeblemindedness" to racial, ethnic, class, and disabled others.[28]

Oregon Klanswomen embraced eugenic thinking and drew on propaganda imagery from the war for the mobilization of women "patriots" against internal and external enemies in their period of key strength in

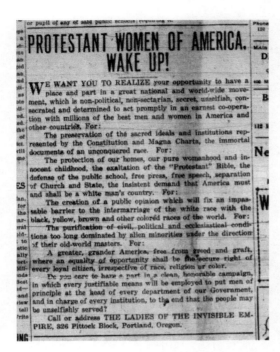

FIGURE 2 "Protestant Women of America, Wake Up!" *Western American*, June 7, 1923, 2.

the state in the early 1920s. Members of Oregon's Ladies of the Invisible Empire mobilized members with the image of a militant Joan of Arc, as did Klanswomen in other states.[29] The wartime Wilson administration had used Joan of Arc imagery five years before as a call to mobilize women to support the war effort. The Oregon Klan had a particularly strong link to wartime propaganda through Lem A. Dever, the publicity director for the state Klan and editor of the Klan's *Western American* newspaper. Dever had served with George Creel's Committee on Public Information, the chief propaganda arm of the wartime administration, as a journalist in the Russian campaign in Siberia and Vladivostok.[30] Dever drew on another wartime image of women called to patriotic action in a recruiting advertisement titled "Protestant Women of America, Wake Up!" published in several issues of the *Western American* in 1922 and 1923. James Montgomery Flagg's iconic poster image of wartime mobilization *Wake Up, America: Civilization Calls* was almost certainly Dever's model for recruiting Klanswomen to the postwar banner of the Klan's White supremacist Christian nationalism, which also embraced eugenics.

These connections demonstrate that Klan leaders sought to direct

FIGURE 3 James Montgomery Flagg, "Wake Up, America! Civilization Calls," The Hegeman Print, New York, 1917. Library of Congress Prints and Photographs Division, Washington, DC.

women's wartime loyalties to the postwar Klan cause and used messages similar to those about wartime "100% Americanism" and eugenic thinking to legitimize and popularize their own movement for White Protestant supremacy. The concept of the dangerous enemy other was embedded in Klan ritual that literally named Klan members as "citizens" and non-members as "aliens" in an induction ceremony known as a naturalization.[31] Thousands of Oregon Klanswomen likely used their votes to elect supportive legislators who would pass Oregon's radical sterilization laws in 1923 and other nativist and restrictionist policies.[32]

EUGENICS AND THE "NEW PATRIOTISM"

Owens-Adair and Trumbull used their versions of wartime lessons to promote eugenics as a "New Patriotism" in the years that followed, defining a contrived extended emergency that required "patriotic" responses. In a letter to Oregon legislators urging them to pass her eugenic marriage bill, Owens-Adair insisted that the war had accelerated the "curse" of "degeneracy" in Oregon and the nation. "When the call to arms came, your sons and the sons of other normal men rushed to its call and passed the test," but the "subnormal" failed and stayed home to reproduce. State-mandated sterilization was her remedy.[33] Trumbull praised Owens-Adair for giving eugenics "the emphasis of a patriotic duty" in the postwar world and expanded the argument to women. "If we continue to conscript the flower of our young manhood," she wrote, "and since women have entered the munition factories and every other activity which belongs to war," Trumbull expected conscription for "the best of our young womanhood," thus "leaving in the hands of the rejected, the scrubs of the human family, the breeding of the future generation."[34]

In the "New Patriotism" eugenics and nativism combined to define the obligation to punish internal enemies in an extended postwar period of artificial crisis. Mary Woodworth Patterson added White supremacy and anti-Japanese legislation to eugenics laws as the twin "reforms" of "Patriotism in Peace." America could not be conquered by another nation, she told assembled DAR members in 1921. "But an invisible war is being waged upon us with a force greater" than any hostile nation. "The insidious encroachment of the diseased mentally and physically [are] causing us to degenerate from within." Two reforms to end this "inner canker," Patterson insisted, were the eugenic marriage bill and restrictive anti-Asian land laws to help create a "white nation."[35] As part of her "New Patriotism," Owens-Adair suggested the forced sterilization of Japanese American women, whose very presence she believed was a threat to the nation.[36] And at the yearly convention of the Southern Oregon District of the State Federation of Women's Clubs in Ashland in May 1924, assembled White clubwomen endorsed the restrictive federal immigration act as an act of patriotic womanhood. "This is America's second Declaration of Independence," they resolved, to prevent "the idea that America is the asylum for the undesirables from all the rest of the world."[37] "America Must Clean House," Oregon Klanswomen read in the *Western American* in May 1923. "Freeborn white Americans are determined never to abdicate their rule, in every part of national life, to the unfit weaklings and half-baked 'Americans' that have flooded the country from Europe and Asia."[38]

THE OREGON STATE SURVEY OF MENTAL DEFECT, DELINQUENCY, AND DEPENDENCY, 1920

Another element of Oregon's "New Patriotism" in the postwar period was the eugenics-inspired 1920 Oregon State Survey of Mental Defect, Delinquency, and Dependency. With state approval, survey administrators deputized Oregonians to conduct eugenic surveillance in their communities to find and identify "unfit" internal enemies. Other states and counties were compiling statistics and surveys on the "insane" and "feebleminded" with professional, paid staff doing the work under the auspices of the National Committee for Mental Hygiene and the Rockefeller Foundation, some with additional state funding, part of a broad set of eugenics-based institutional studies in the war years and after.[39] But Oregon was unique, as the *American Journal of Public Health* reported: "For the first time in American history the citizens of a state, directed by a representative of the U.S. Public Health Service, are by voluntary service, with almost no money, carrying out a successful statewide investigation" of the "dependent, delinquent, and mentally deficient." The editors of the *Oregon Journal* expanded the description with the flourish of star state boosterism, describing the work of the survey as "the first citizen cooperative movement in mental hygiene in the history of the world."[40] Other states had partial surveys; for example, the California State Board of Charities and Corrections had employed people to survey representative samples of prisoners and institutional inmates and schoolchildren in 1916. But Oregon appears to have been the first to engage with a complete statewide and "citizen cooperative" effort to identify the "unfit."[41]

The reason for Oregon's "citizen cooperative" survey was that Oregon legislators supported the idea but would not appropriate funds. The US

Public Health Service detailed Chester L. Carlisle, MD, to work in cooperation with the University of Oregon to distribute, publicize, collect, and tally the results within existing federal and university funding and staff salaries.[42] Carlisle sent out certificates with the state seal and governor approval for people to serve "from a high sense of citizenship and patriotism" as a "Special Voluntary Assistant to the State Survey of Mental Defect, Delinquency, and Dependency." Special assistants were to fill out "statistical data cards" for all cases of "defect" they observed. Carlisle and university staff sent the commissions, instructions, and data cards to more than ten thousand residents, to "every physician, judge, lawyer, clergyman, nurse, educator, teacher," local and state officials, and every other "citizen known to be interested in community welfare work" and eventually opened the work to the general public.[43] The *American Journal of Psychiatry* commented favorably on the survey, and Carlisle published information about the study in the *Journal of the American Medical Association*.[44] Oregon's Henry Waldo Coe, MD, editor of the *Medical Sentinel*, praised state physicians for their support of the survey and the recognition they were receiving from the American Medical Association (AMA).[45]

The data registration card became a surveillance product. The card contained space for voluntary assistants to record an extensive amount of information, much of it subjective, about anyone they wished to report as "defective." There was no space for reporters to identify themselves, so the surveillance and specific information was officially anonymous. In addition to space for responses about demographic information, including "legitimate" or "illegitimate" birth, the card had sections for "physical" and "emotional" information, schooling, and symptoms of "mental defect (feeble minded)" on a sliding scale. Reporters were to record "all mental and nervous disorders *any* relative of the family ever developed," along with family citizenship and naturalization information in the "heredity" section. The personal history section asked if the person had been identified as a "sex pervert" or had "illicit consorts." The surveyors asked the voluntary assistants to make judgments about the person's "social record" including if they were a "steady worker," connecting concepts of the suitable, productive work of the nation from wartime to the postwar world. The sample card reprinted in the *Journal of the American Medical Association* and the "Summary of the Oregon State Survey" was for men, with the notation that the other cards for women had "minor changes."

These included listing a husband or father's occupation, how many "legitimate" children they had, and space to record "alias, if any," echoing the many references to sex workers adopting an assumed or alternative name in the records of The Cedars and Oregon Social Hygiene Society.[46]

Oregon's sterilization law magnified the destructive power and reach of the Mental Defect Survey. The 1919 state sterilization reporting policy gave anyone permission to report a person to the state board of health as "feebleminded" or otherwise "unfit" to reproduce, including people who were gender nonconforming or labeled as "sexual perverts." The data registration cards were a blueprint for reporting people considered internal enemy others, and the consequences could be state-forced sterilization. University of Oregon graduate students and staff, who conducted additional mental testing throughout the state, helped to complete the survey by December 1920. Carlisle published a first draft in spring 1921 as a forty-page report in the *University of Oregon Extension Monitor*. When it became clear that no additional funding was available to support the publication of all the data, the US Public Health Service published a ninety-nine-page version *Preliminary Statistical Report of the Oregon State Survey of Mental Defect, Delinquency, and Dependency* as *Public Health Bulletin No. 121* for December 1921. Carlisle framed both reports in a binary of "constructive" and "inadequate" citizenship when he analyzed who was "fit" and "unfit." Press reports showcased the Oregon First element of the survey process of "citizen cooperation."[47]

The Oregon State Survey found some sixty-five thousand Oregonians to be "inadequate citizens." Before providing a long list of specifics, Carlisle and Survey Committee members recommended a remedy. "Segregate the unfit. Treat the sick. Rehabilitate the handicapped. Educate and train the neglected and ignorant." And, in the context of Oregon's eugenics legislation, "protect the 96 percent of normal citizens from the inadequacy of the sub-normal 4 percent by adequate statutes which are enforced."[48] Carlisle distilled the survey findings into an exhibit for the Second International Congress of Eugenics held at the American Museum of Natural History in New York in fall 1922. The Oregon section provided survey findings about the "socially inadequate persons of all classes in the community," who were "essentially the insane, the mentally deficient without psychosis, the socially inadequate (frequently mentally abnormal) delinquent type, and the socially inadequate (especially the mentally defective) dependent type."[49]

34 / CHAPTER 1

Nested in the midst of a dozen other special reports included in the survey about schools and industry and tables with survey findings for Oregon institutions such as the Oregon State Hospital, Carlisle included a "special contribution" report titled "Chinese and Japanese in Oregon." The Oregon Bureau of Labor and Industries (BOLI) provided population figures and information on wages and land ownership for residents from the two groups, and Carlisle provided a brief paragraph to frame the data. "The Oregon State survey is fortunate in receiving these figures, as they make a valuable ethnological study in connection with our study as to the fundamental causes of dependency and social failure." In this chilling sentence, Carlisle suggested that being a Chinese American or Japanese American in Oregon was a "fundamental cause" of "social failure," disability, and inadequacy. He offered no other commentary except that "the number of individuals in State institutions from these races is shown in the nativity tables in each institution's report." But nowhere else in any of the pages or tables did any information about Japanese or Chinese Oregonians in institutions or any references to "nativity" appear. This "special contribution" reinforced the idea that to be Japanese or Chinese in Oregon signified "unfitness." The Oregon State Survey of Mental Defect, Delinquency, and Dependency, in addition to documenting the deputization of residents for the eugenic surveillance of all Oregonians and the eugenic thinking that labeled intellectually and developmentally disabled and gender-nonconforming Oregonians as "inadequate" citizens, provides a devastating example of the way officials could put "data" to work to support of the virulent currents of anti-Asian sentiment in the state and beyond in the context of eugenics.

The Oregon Survey of Mental Defect, Delinquency, and Dependency contributed directly to the adoption of Oregon's 1923 state sterilization law, in force until 1983, that provided for the sterilization of any resident deemed "feebleminded" or "deviant." There was a great deal of newspaper coverage about the survey in advance of the 1923 legislative session. Club and study groups discussed it.[50] Owens-Adair used the survey as evidence for the need for her 1923 sterilization bill and her "hygienic marriage" bill that same year. She devoted five pages of her 1922 *Human Sterilization* to discussion of the survey, and the opening words in her 1922 *Eugenic Marriage Law and Human Sterilization* pamphlet were about the survey's results with an emphasis on the costs to Oregon taxpayers to maintain institutions. "Shall we ask the normal people of our state, in addition to supporting themselves . . . to carry the burden of maintaining a disproportionate and *ever increasing* number of defectives and degenerates?" The survey provided the "proof" for Owens-Adair that "feebleminded" Oregonians were everywhere, and she advocated sterilization as the only answer. The proposed sterilization law for 1923 *"includes for its application all proper subjects,"* she wrote, *"whether in or out of institutions."*[51] Trumbull, then secretary of the Oregon Industrial Welfare Commission and Board of Child Labor Inspectors and a supporter and lobbyist for eugenic legislation, contributed a special report titled "The Mentally Defective Child in Industry" to the Oregon Survey of Mental Defect with the same information and arguments in her presentations to clubs and organizations. In addition to a suggested "psychological chart" for each person employed in Oregon industry, Trumbull insisted on legislative action to institutionalize "all those below a certain grade of mentality" with "sterilization as the price of freedom for all defectives in the communities."[52]

Clothed in the accolades of an Oregon First accomplishment, the 1920 Oregon State Survey of Mental Defect, Delinquency, and Dependency had a strong impact with great lasting harm. Here the postwar pursuit of internal enemies marched directly in step with eugenic thinking to empower all Oregonians to report people they considered to be "defective" citizens and residents. The Mental Defect Survey deputized all Oregonians to police and report on "defective" others with a new surveillance product and data card file. At the foundation of the survey was eugenic thinking and the binary of "unfit" and "fit" to define postwar internal enemies. This placed the gaze of the state, via "voluntary assistants," on anyone who might be considered different, disabled, or "defective," including people who did not conform with accepted gender roles and identities. Survey authors and supporters also equated simply being a Japanese or Chinese resident with "unfitness."

EUGENICS AND INDIGENOUS PEOPLE
ON RESERVATIONS IN OREGON

In addition to these state programs and policies to force or coerce eugenic sterilization in Oregon, the decades-long move toward hospitalization for illness and surgery and the medicalization of childbirth created the context

36 / CHAPTER 1

for physicians to have greater access to bodies and power in a medical setting that could lead to sterilization.[53] This meant physicians could act to sterilize people without their consent outside of state institutions or the Board of Health reporting process outlined by Oregon statute and policy. Given the nativism, racism, and ableism that permeated eugenic thought in the early twentieth century, and given the documented histories of the forced or coerced sterilization of women of color and poor women from the 1930s to today, it is likely that some physicians sterilized people against their knowledge or by coercion in the 1910s and 1920s.[54] This possible consequence of medicalization also underscores the importance of midwives in this period such as Addie Anderson in Portland's Black community, Agnes Thompson on the Siletz Indian Reservation, and the Japanese American midwives whose work is outlined in chapter 7.[55]

A consideration of Indigenous people and the policies and practices on reservations within Oregon during this period provides an important case in point. In the early twentieth century, federal Indian Affairs officials sought to "instill the hospital habit" among reservation residents. As Brianna Theobald and Christin Hancock demonstrate, officials described this as a process to address high rates of tuberculosis, trachoma, and infant mortality on reservations as part of a Progressive Era move to "scientific medicine" and the eugenics-inspired "better baby movement." The reservation field matron program, established in 1890, brought significant scrutiny over the bodies and lives of Indigenous women. Field matrons made regular home visit inspections into the details of households, health, relationships, and "morals" and reported their findings. Theobald has found for the national context, and Hancock for the Klamath Agency, that Native women engaged in significant negotiations with field matrons to seek and obtain health care they desired, including hospitalizations, making "intentional and often creative decisions" for themselves and their families. Theobald notes some Native women were more receptive to inviting White women health-care providers into their lives than male physicians employed by the federal Indian Service.[56]

Examples from health care on reservations in Oregon in the 1910s and 1920s suggest situations existed for coerced sterilizations and sterilization procedures without patient knowledge or consent. Theobald reported such conditions in the 1930s at the Crow Agency and beyond. Physicians, among other agency staff, "drew on eugenic logic in their assessment of social and economic problems on the reservation." Government doctors "who were so inclined" could be "well positioned to blur the lines between 'therapeutic' and 'eugenic' sterilizations" and to sterilize people for having STIs or other conditions.[57] As Theobald demonstrates in the case of Annie Walking Bear Yellowtail (Crow), Charles Nagel, head physician at the Crow Agency in Montana, sterilized Yellowtail in 1931 during surgery to remove an ovarian cyst following the birth of her third child. Yellowtail understood that the surgeon was "'just supposed to remove the cyst'" but sterilized, and she "'didn't even know it until he was through.'" Yellowtail, who had received her graduate nursing degree in Boston in 1927, had worked briefly in the Indian Health Service at the Crow Agency before this event, and her "later recollections suggest that she witnessed physicians performing unethical sterilizations" there. And "while Nagel sterilized Yellowtail in the midst of a gynecological procedure," Yellowtail noted that physicians intervened in other surgical situations and after childbirth without women's consent.[58]

Physicians at Oregon Indian agencies in this period who believed in eugenics had power over bodies in procedures that gave them the opportunity to perform sterilizations. In 1917 there were three full-time male physicians employed by the Medical Department of the US Indian Service on reservations within Oregon: Virgil M. Pinkley at the Siletz Agency, Thomas M. Henderson at the Umatilla Agency, and Clarence D. Fulkerson at Warm Springs.[59] Pinkley's tallies of medical and surgical treatments for the last six months of 1916 and the first six months of 1917 have been preserved. There is no specific evidence that Pinkley engaged in sterilization procedures, but his records suggest what may have been typical procedures at other Indian agency clinics and hospitals and document the potential opportunity for surgical sterilization in the hands of a physician who was so inclined. In the last six months of 1916, of the 135 procedures among 415 Siletz residents, Pinkley treated two cases of cystitis (urinary tract infection), two of dysmenorrhea (menstrual pain), three of dysuria (painful urination), one case of gonorrhea, one hernia, one hydatidiform mole (a uterine tumor of a nonviable pregnancy), and one case of "labor," presumably childbirth. In the first six months of 1917, of the 313 procedures among 422 residents, Pinkney attended one case of afterpains (postpartum cramps), two abortions, one case of amenorrhea (lack of menstruation), four cases of cystitis, one case of enuresis (urinary incontinence), three cases of gonorrhea, two of hemorrhage (perhaps associated with childbirth), two hernias, two cases of ovaritis (inflammation of the ovary), one case of salpingitis (inflammation of the fallopian tubes), and one ovarian cyst. In a separate section of the reports Pinkley recorded three births for the last six months of 1916 and seven for the first six months of 1917. It may be that he attended these births but did not record them in his medical and surgical list if they were uneventful, or that Agnes Thompson or another Siletz midwife or healer attended, or that birthing women and their circle were the only ones present for the birth.[60] All of these conditions held the opportunity for purposeful intervention resulting in sterilization if a physician had the belief and will to do so.

The war and its aftermath brought personnel changes as new contract and consulting physicians and surgeons took part in reservation health care in this age of eugenic thinking. Thomas A. Britten demonstrates that wartime inflation meant home-front medical supply costs "soared" as did the cost of infrastructure. The Bureau of Indian Affairs received no additional funding as Congress prioritized wartime spending. And medical and surgical personnel left reservation positions to work elsewhere as the war opened new opportunities in the field.[61] Pinkley left Siletz after 1917, and in his 1918 inspection report Indian commissioner William H. Ketcham noted the primary need at the Grand Ronde and Siletz Agency was "proper medical attention." Ketcham recommended a contract physician be hired," a less-costly alternative to a full-time doctor.[62] At the Klamath Agency, Klamath County health officer and Klamath Falls physician A. A. Soule worked on a contract basis in the early 1920s as the agency waited for the construction of a hospital. Soule provided treatments for syphilis for two agency residents in 1924 and indicated he would report the cases to the state board of health.[63] This meant local or new doctors were providing reservation health care with the potential for eugenic interventions.

Racialized eugenic thinking provided the broad foundation for the targeting and surveillance of tribal members in a series of "industrial surveys" that reported categories of "fit" and "unfit" individuals and households during the 1920s. The reservation surveys in Oregon and the nation had the stated goal of charting individual progress toward "civilization" via farming, industry, and "moral" behavior as the sanctioned work of assimilation. As Cathleen Cahill notes, Charles Burke, commissioner of Indian Affairs, harnessed Progressive Era techniques of the surveillance and information state as part of the "colonial drive to make conquered subjects legible."[64] Burke's instructions to local superintendents framed the industrial surveys in terms of medical, cultural, and economic assimilation and therefore reflected ideas about "fit" and "unfit" people and groups in the context of eugenic thinking. Burke instructed the superintendents to take the field matrons who provided home health-care visits and "wherever possible, the physicians" to assist with data collection "so that you and all the employees who should be cognizant of the home and farm conditions of the Indians may get the same impressions and facts" to implement follow-up plans "that may be outlined as a result of the visits."[65] Surveys survive for the Grand Ronde, Siletz, Klamath, and Umatilla Agencies. Officials reported on health matters, attendance or nonattendance at public or boarding schools, "behavior" and "morality," crime and imprisonment, whether a family was "nomadic" or settled, and general conditions of homes and acreage with photographs. The surveys reflect the idea of engaging in suitable labor as part of "fitness" and productive citizenship for membership in the civic community in the era of the Indian Citizenship (Snyder) Act of 1924. Grand Ronde canvassers, for example, described a sixty-year-old woman as "having had but little schooling but is bright and able to take care of herself."[66]

Oregon's sterilization laws and the eugenic thinking that framed them, alongside the eugenic sterilization practices in places such as Indigenous reservations, magnified the search for internal enemy others in this period and paralleled wartime and postwar calls for loyalty, patriotic womanhood, and community and state surveillance. Eugenics created civic binaries of the "fit" and "unfit" and defined the productive work of the nation. People who engaged in eugenic thinking are discussed in future chapters, but so, too, are many people who resisted and created survival strategies and advocacy that are part of the long movement for civil liberties and human rights in the early twentieth century.

CHAPTER 2

Patriotic Womanhood and Internal Enemies

FOR MANY OREGON WOMEN enfranchised in November 1912, the next steps in active civic participation were to register to vote, study the candidates, issues, and ballot measures, go to their precinct polling place, and vote in local, state, and national elections. Registration and voting were public acts with policy consequences and actions that made women citizens visible. During World War I, federal, state, and local officials and some women leaders repurposed registration as a form of civic participation. They created various enrollment projects to transform registration into an act of loyalty to the nation's war aims as part of the obligations of what Barbara Steinson and Kathleen Kennedy have identified as patriotic womanhood, what Christopher Capozzola calls coercive voluntarism, and what Lynn Dumenil refers to as gendered voluntarism within the "maternalist social reform" tradition.[1]

Registrations included wartime service registration for women, enrollment in the Food Pledge army, and registration drives for Liberty Bonds, War Savings Stamps (wss), and other fundraising campaigns. Oregon First boosterism and the need to maintain a national reputation for success fueled the pressure on state and local campaign leaders to produce rapid and widespread participation. These leaders distilled that urgent pressure on women residents. The war years coincided with the final stages of the campaigns for a federal amendment to protect women's voting rights, and registration organizers drew on the pageantry of suffrage parades and the mass advertising techniques of the modern votes for women movement to fuel public participation.[2] Registration drives accelerated state surveillance on people, with intrusion into and reporting about homes, businesses, and private lives. As the drives multiplied, leaders and supporters labeled people who chose not to engage as "slackers" and dangerous internal enemies. They created tremendous pressure on others to conform and discouraged any but the most restricted definitions of loyal citizenship and women's engagement in the work of the nation. Some women welcomed and practiced patriotic womanhood through registrations, including some women in historically marginalized communities who hoped for greater civic recognition and protection. Other women resisted and engaged in grassroots actions for civil liberties protections and a citizenship of dissent.

WARTIME SERVICE REGISTRATION FOR WOMEN

In the fall of 1917 women in various US states, acting under the guidance of the umbrella organization the Woman's Committee of the Council of National Defense (CND), tried to carry out a plan to register women across the nation for wartime service.[3] Women's registration came three months after the first compulsory military draft registration for men ages eighteen to thirty on June 5, 1917.[4] Some women considered wartime registration empowering. Penelope Brownell, the historian of the CND Woman's Committee, notes that "registration emphasized to women themselves their own contributions to family and community which often passed without remark" and drew attention to women's abilities to contribute to the nation's work in wartime.[5] Women physicians mounted a parallel campaign for wartime registration to demonstrate their fitness for service as many of them sought a place in the military medical corps.[6] But active opposition or lack of participation by the vast majority of women in Oregon and the nation suggested that many residents experienced the call for female registration as an intrusion of state scrutiny into their lives and an unwelcome test of loyalty and citizenship.

Oregon was one of forty states to have a formal female wartime registration program and one of fourteen to have a governor-proclaimed women's registration day on September 15, 1917. Many women leaders in the state equated female registration with the loyal wartime work of the nation. Therese Castner of Hood River, president of the Oregon Federation of Women's Clubs and chair of the Oregon Woman's Committee of the CND, oversaw the registration.[7] Statewide, clubwomen staffed four hundred local committees and established registration centers in spaces accessible and familiar to women at local schools, post offices, hotels, restaurants, public libraries, community centers, and at the State Capitol building in

42 / CHAPTER 2

Salem.[8] Portland women, representing some eighty organizations, divided the city into precincts for door-to-door canvassing to distribute registration cards, and leaders reserved city polling places for women to enroll on registration day. Castner reported sending out 125,000 cards across the state, well over half of the estimate of 198,114 adult women residing in Oregon.[9]

Three of Portland's four major newspapers published hopeful stories featuring women's patriotic enthusiasm for registration. The editors of the *Oregon Journal*, voice of the Democratic Party and supportive of the Wilson administration's war, noted a "steady" registration of large numbers of women representing "all classes, ages, and conditions." The paper featured stories of an eighty-six-year-old grandmother, stenographers and clerks, teachers, and businesswomen who signed up for various categories of war work.[10] The Republican-supporting *Oregonian* editors took a similarly optimistic tone, noting diversity among women registrants. Black activist Beatrice Cannady was the first to register in her Irvington district; two Jewish women of Turkish heritage enrolled together; and in general it was "surprising how many foreign speaking women registered."[11] Editors of the moderately Republican *Portland Evening Telegram* predicted a registration of ten thousand women in the city.[12] Significantly, the *Portland News*, a paper associated with the city's rank-and-file working class, and the smaller *Portland Labor Press*, did not report the registration.

Some Oregon women registered to be visible to the state and in their communities and linked registration to what they believed was women's civic obligation to work for the nation's war aims. White clubwoman Sadie Orr Dunbar, secretary of the Oregon Woman's Committee of the CND, believed the enrollment would represent "a great day in the lives of Portland women," to demonstrate that women's service to the state was of equal value with men's service.[13] But a great many other Oregon women worried that local and federal authorities would use the personal information women provided on the cards to assign them to compulsory national service. Press reports undoubtedly strengthened such fears of a female draft. Women read in central Oregon's *Bend Bulletin* that if they did not act, "compulsory registration may be adopted." The editors of the *Corvallis Gazette-Times* put the threat in a simple front-page headline: "Better Register Now Save Trouble Later."[14] Portland's registration took place at every polling place in the city's precincts, the same sites men had been required to visit to register for the first round of the male military draft three months earlier. The locations may have reinforced, for some, the civic links between the woman citizen's right to vote and women's wartime service. But other women may have felt considerable skepticism about enrolling at the very spaces in the city last used to register their brothers, partners, husbands, fathers, and sons for compulsory national military service.[15]

The registration card itself, published widely before the event in newspapers and distributed to many homes in advance of September 15, became a new surveillance product and suggests why many women were concerned about increased scrutiny and a possible women's draft. Registration organizers required women to list a great deal of personal information, including their employment and citizenship status. The card had space for women to note their strengths and training from among 119 skills in wage-earning occupations and voluntary work in categories ranging from agricultural, clerical, domestic, industrial, and professional to public and social service, with specific job categories ranging from janitress to stenographer, laundress, physician, nurse, and aviatrix. Could a woman speak or read another language? How well? Registrants were to complete a section on emergency service specifying that they would serve "anywhere," or "in the United States," or their "home town only," noting how soon they could begin. The card had a section for "contributions," suggesting that women could be scrutinized for what monetary or in-kind donations they might be willing to make—from funding an ambulance to sharing one's home "with widow or children."[16]

Despite these extensive preparations and press coverage, very few women registered across the state. The *Oregon Journal* reported that only 15 percent of women had actually turned in their cards in Portland in spite of enthusiastic predictions and reports on registration day. Some women said that "family duties" kept them at home, others that they had "given their husbands to the war and were now obliged to be both wage earners and mother" and could give no more.[17] Just fifty-five Bend women registered from the four hundred cards distributed.[18] Umatilla County in eastern Oregon had a light registration of 155 in a community of over twenty thousand people.[19] Editors in Ashland, Medford, Oregon City, and Salem cited fears of conscription to account for local registration rates at just 10 to 15 percent. The editors of the *Salem Capital Journal* concluded that women feared "that by signing the card," they would be "under obligation to the government and subject to call."[20] Only fourteen women registered in the working-class coastal town of North Bend out of some one thousand female residents. Many there worried that authorities had designed women's registration to discover which married women could support themselves, increasing the chances that their husbands would not receive exemptions from their local draft board.[21] Some women in Eugene signed up, but many reacted "with indifference, others with scorn," and some saw it "as a joke." One woman refused, saying: "Let the men do the work and fight the battles. It's all I can do to keep the family going."[22]

Castner and leaders of the Oregon State Woman's Committee followed national committee requests and kept registration open, with cards available at local libraries and women's clubs and occasional newspaper article reminders. The press underscored that registration was not a draft of women, not "designed to take women from their homes."[23] But resistance continued, as did various rumors of the purpose and consequences of women's registration. On October 31, 1917, an intelligence operative reported to William Bryon, Oregon field director of the Bureau of Investigation, that Levi Pennington, the president of Pacific College (now George Fox University), a Quaker institution in Newberg, had given a speech in nearby Springbrook describing women's registration as "merely a subterfuge on the part of the government to secure names of women who could be transported to France for illicit use by our soldiers." Bryon passed the case to the district attorney, who asked the local sheriff to investigate.[24] Later in life, Pennington recalled the visit clearly. He told the sheriff he had not been to Springbrook since women's wartime registration had been announced and had "never thought of such a thing" about the registration until the sheriff read the charges. "And if I had believed it," Pennington wrote, "I'd not have said it unless I was ready to go to federal prison."[25] In November the *Oregonian* editorialized that rumors continued to circulate that women "may be taken from their homes by force and even sent abroad at the whim of some official."[26]

Attempts by women leaders to complete a comprehensive registration of women for war service failed in Oregon and throughout the nation, the result of widespread grassroots resistance to the project. By May 1918, fewer than 3 percent of Oregon women registered, and nationwide the figure was 3.9 percent.[27] Emily Newell Blair reported 3,375,000 by the

Armistice in November 1918, and Penelope Brownell's tally of unpublished state summaries by the end of the conflict suggested some four million registrants, which would have been about 13 percent.[28] Women leaders stressed that registration was not intended to be a preparation for conscription. But the vast majority of women appeared not to agree, chose not to enroll, and many opposed the increased state scrutiny female registration placed on them and their families.

"ENROLLMENT IN THE CONSERVATION ARMY"

Just over a month after female registration day, women in Oregon and across the nation faced another kind of registration, this one a pledge to conserve food and by doing so to place themselves and their households in the service of the war effort. The Food Pledge drive was a canvass to convince "home managers"—most all of whom were women—to sign a voluntary pledge to conserve food with wheatless and meatless days according to the rules set down by Herbert Hoover and his staff of the United States Food Administration (USFA). Pledgers signified their wartime loyalty by posting a placard in the window of their home to show the community that they were an official member of the USFA engaged in directed food conservation. Federal and local officials considered the Food Pledge drive to be another method of registering women during the war, an "enrollment in the conservation army."[29] The Food Pledge card asked only for one's name and address, but administrators and workers and most potential registrants, it appears, understood that the cards would serve as a data archive of the contact information and pledge decision of those registering to participate. The Food Pledge window placard was tangible proof of women's patriotic citizenship, and its absence marked the home of a slacker who refused to engage in women's wartime and civic work for the nation—that is, a dangerous internal enemy. The process of registering women and their homes in the Food Pledge drive provided officials and community members with the opportunity to engage in scrutiny of women's lives far beyond their eating habits. And the significant and vocal opposition to the pledge in Oregon was another thread of grassroots resistance to registrations and state surveillance and a unilateral definition of women's citizenship as patriotic womanhood.

Food conservation registration politicized and strengthened women's

46 / CHAPTER 2

FIGURE 4 Member, United States Food Administration, Food Pledge window placard, 1917. Author's collection.

wartime roles as consumers and household managers, but the actual Food Pledge campaign marginalized women as civic leaders. The original national plan was for state Woman's Committees of the CND to oversee the drive, but when Congress authorized and funded the USFA in the summer of 1917, Hoover organized state units with male state leaders.[30] By August 1917 the Portland lumber magnate Winslow B. Ayer was on the job as the Oregon state food administrator preparing for the pledge drive for the week of October 28. Prominent White clubwomen Castner and Jennie Kemp were the only two women on the state board. Men served as key leaders at the local level, with women deputies who canvassed other women in their communities.[31] Some women embraced the opportunity to demonstrate their own civic credentials, loyalty, and participation in the wartime work of the nation by investigating and policing other women. They waged the Food Pledge campaign on the terrain of the American home. Unlike voter registration and war service registration, which depended on women choosing to come to courthouses, polling places, and other public spaces, Food Pledge canvassers carried food conservation

FIGURE 5 Tige Reynolds, "Uncle Sam Has 'A Bone to Pick' with Every Housewife This Week." *Oregonian*, October 29, 1917, 1.

registration directly to women's homes and onto the threshold of their private lives.

Federal, state, and local organizations were modeled on the military, with captains at the local level in charge of foot soldier canvassers. The pledge card campaign's *Organizer's Manual* designed to guide local committees gave careful instructions for approaching women in their homes to get them to sign the Food Pledge. "Timing of visits" was important, and "workers should select the portion of the day when they are most likely to find the women at home." This might be in the morning or afternoon "according to the neighborhood." Canvassers were to know the gendered rhythms of the neighborhoods assigned to them, which varied by class, race, ethnicity, and immigrant identity and involved childcare, shopping, work, and religious obligations. The *Organizer's Manual* authors suggested particular targeting of "War Mothers and Sisters" who have "felt the wrench of the heart strings" to "swell the ranks of the food conservation army."[32] *Oregonian* cartoonist Tige Reynolds and his newspaper supported the Food Pledge. His colossal Uncle Sam holding a woman and her home hostage and level with his investigative gaze suggests the intrusive power of the state to register women in the "food conservation army." Reynolds's signature tiger was happy to investigate the family's trash can for evidence of slacking.[33]

In Portland business leader Everett Ames chaired the local Food Pledge campaign executive committee of prominent male volunteers and organized the city by districts, with nineteen prominent men as district captains serving under the committee's authority. Women were the direct door-to-door canvassers, along with a few men.[34] In this city with a population of some 250,000, Ames set a goal for 45,000 signatures, about 95 percent of all estimated adult women residents, to be gathered by what proved to be a wildly optimistic estimate of an "army of 10,000 volunteer workers."[35] In a broadside titled "Wanted—Women Volunteers" printed in city newspapers, Ames echoed the USFA's *Organizer's Manual* and called on Portland women to join the canvassing army to be "put to the test" of loyalty as part of the work of the nation. "To carry such a message, to secure such pledges, is a woman's work," he noted. "We hope the response will be immediate and overwhelming and will prove that the appeal to the womanhood of Portland has not been made in vain."[36]

Fearful of low return rates, Oregon Food Pledge leaders harnessed the influence and extensive networks of schools to reach into homes for the pledge drive, placing teachers, who were predominately women, in the role of local canvass supervisors across the state. It appears that Oregon was singular among other states in using schools for this purpose. Arthur Churchill was both the state chair of the Food Pledge campaign and the state superintendent of public instruction, and he enlisted all Oregon schools and teachers in the Food Pledge canvass.[37] In every Oregon county the school superintendent became a member of the state executive board, and many county administrators appointed one teacher to direct the pledge drive in the school district.[38] "School work may suffer if need be," the county school superintendent for southern Oregon's Jackson County told teachers, "but our immediate or first duty is in the service of our country."[39] Rather than printing cards in languages other than English, administrators depended on children of first-generation immigrant parents to "prepare" their parents to sign the Food Pledge when the parents were "not familiar with the language."[40] Father Edwin V. O'Hara, the superintendent of schools for Oregon's Catholic Diocese, directed teachers, most often Religious Sisters, to facilitate the Food Pledge work among twenty-six hundred Catholic families in Portland with thirty-seven hundred students in the city's twenty-six Catholic schools.[41] Outside Portland, local Catholic committees organized religious and private schools with O'Hara assuring statewide cooperation.[42] Certainly many teachers may have been enthusiastic supporters of the Food Pledge campaign and saw their work as a way to build their civic credentials or to support the community. But those who did not believe in the registration efforts faced negative consequences and risked their jobs if they acted on their views.

As with other wartime registrations and loyalty campaigns, many women who faced systemic barriers to equality and civic access saw patriotic support of Food Pledge enrollment as a way to assert more complete citizenship rights by engaging in the wartime work of the nation and demonstrating loyalty. Food administrators at the national and local levels worked within existing networks of religious congregations and women's clubs to urge participation by women as canvassers and pledgers. They wanted to draw women's local identities and connections and their desire for civic visibility into the wider campaign. State food administrator Ayer distributed pledge cards to Portland religious leaders and asked them to have women sign when they attended services.[43] Food Administration leaders reached out to Katherine Gray, chair of the State Federation of Colored Women's Clubs, part of the National Association of Colored Women's Clubs. The Colored Women's Council in Portland, chaired in this period by Emma K. Griffin Stanley, "passed resolutions conforming with the food conservation movement" and pledged to encourage other women in the community to conserve. With support from the National Council of Jewish Women, Portland branch president Salome Solis-Cohen Bernstein appointed a committee of women to distribute cards and take part in the city canvass.[44]

Food Pledge leaders defined registration for food conservation as the work of the wartime nation. They devised strategies to reward those who enrolled and to punish resisters and dissenters as internal enemies. Public reporting and competition among Oregon cities and counties and a deluge of every sort of mass media propaganda added to the pressure. Newspa-

50 / CHAPTER 2

pers reached local readers with countless cartoons, posters, and editorials.[45] City and county leaders developed canvassing strategies designed to place maximum public pressure and scrutiny on home managers to sign and to display the Food Pledge card in their window, an act that would put pressure on other residents to "get in line."[46] In Eugene and Lane County, if residents failed to respond to high school students coming door-to-door, "a special committee of business and professional men will be sent out" to "make another attempt to get the signature."[47] Pledge refusers, the *Baker Herald* reported, would be given several chances to change their minds: "After that persons refusing will be assumed to be pro-German and their names will be made public through the local newspapers."[48]

Oregon's food administrator, Ayer, had a final step to discourage dissent: a special printed sheet designated for reporting daily totals for "Home Managers Not Seen or Declining to Sign" for each precinct or subdivision such as a school district. The main portion of the sheet provided blank, lined spaces for canvassers to record the name, address, and specific reasons a person refused the pledge.[49] Newspaper readers across the state learned that personal contact information for the "traitors" and their reasons for refusing would be detailed and "reported directly to government officials."[50] Attorney Lawrence A. Liljeqvist, Coos County Food Pledge chair, believed the threat was potent and effective. As quoted in the *Portland Evening Telegram*: "'The report sheets of those who have not been seen or refused to sign,'" he concluded, "'was a master stroke in bringing in the unwilling.'"[51]

This sustained and fierce pressure to enroll households underscores the significance of the resistance of several thousand Oregon women who did not participate in the Food Pledge registration. Some refusers spoke directly against the pledge and the Wilson administration at a time when the Espionage Act of June 1917 criminalized speech that interfered with military matters and imposed $10,000 in fines and thirty years of imprisonment.[52] At least eight Oregon men had been arrested for violating the Espionage Act when the Food Pledge canvassing started.[53] Portland had 1,905 households listed on the forms as refusing to pledge or avoiding the workers altogether, some 4 percent of those canvassed. Because organizers instructed canvassers to make a complete record of the opposition they encountered on the "Declining to Sign" sheets, and because many workers were apparently furious with those who refused to participate, the sheets offer brief but specific information about why some people refused the Food Pledge, often with direct quotes.[54] One hundred thirty-two residents made explicitly political comments in opposition to the Food Pledge and the US involvement in the war; seventy-eight voiced religious objections to the conflict; and 696, the largest group, simply refused or gave no reason for declining. Another 112 told canvassers they were already conserving but didn't want the government to force them to do so. Dozens of entries noted "thinks registration is silly" or "knows her own business," or "Hoover and his bunch could go to the dickens."[55] Well over a thousand residents of Portland, the vast majority of them rank-and-file women household managers, facing powerful pressure, would not go against their beliefs to do what the government and canvassers wanted them to do for the war work of the nation. And some of them explained why with claims of a citizenship of dissent.[56]

In Portland some precinct captains considered certain respondents to be so dangerous that they stood out among those declining to sign and used capital letters, exclamation points, and blue-and-red markings to highlight the information about their responses. Johanna R. received a blue notation. "Thinks this Country should not have entered the war. She apparently has no friendly feeling for our cause."[57] Socialist Geraldine Kite, an "agitator" arrested in the Portland free speech protest in 1913, told canvassers: "only people of wealth should be compelled to sign such cards." Kite, born in Washington State, lost her US citizenship when she married Arthur Q. Kite, a British citizen, because of the federal Expatriation Act of 1907. "I'm a woman without a country," she told workers.[58] Rose P. a blacksmith's wife, told block workers she would "have nothing to do with capitalists, press, or government at this time," and canvassers labeled her "SOCIALIST: Anti-war."[59] Emma R. would not sign, and canvassers evidently called on neighbors for more information about her. They said she was affiliated with the radical Industrial Workers of the World and engaged in "secret meetings" above "vacant stores."[60] Even women who expressed opposition but decided to sign were marked to invite additional scrutiny. Louella C., whose husband Russell was a railway conductor, signed "under protest." The workers added that she was "bitter against our government. Predicting open Rebellion here. Remarks were very Anarchistic."[61]

Discrimination by race and ethnicity characterized many of the notations. Anti-German sentiment was pronounced. Workers used the negative label "Pro German" to denote everything from political opposition to speaking German-accented English. Social prominence was no protection for Milla Wessinger Hart, who could trace her life through the Society pages of Portland's newspapers as part of the Weinhard Brewery family dynasty. Block workers noted that Hart "refused angrily," and they reported her family connections and called for additional investigation of her case.[62] Other reports targeted rank-and-file refusers. "Refused to talk. German accent."[63] "Scared foreigner. Would not give name."[64] A number of entries noted language barriers, often with dismissal: "Several Chinese could not understand." Three "Japanese families; did not understand English."[65] "Italian. Do not understand English."[66] Unlike the Liberty Loan and Stamp drives that followed, leaders appear not to have employed translators to assist in the canvassing.

The "Declining to Sign" sheets make the intense surveillance and fervor of the canvassers come to life, highlighting their repeated efforts to gather information and innuendo from neighbors. Mrs. C. first told the block workers that she "saves but signs no pledges," but the workers returned and left a card with her. A neighbor was watching and later told the workers "Mrs C. burned [the card] and boasted that she would have meat 3 times a day."[67] Kate N. "repeatedly refused to open [the] door or see [the] ladies who called." Canvassers "saw her through the window and even went to a neighbor's house and had her phoned and she answered the telephone call."[68] Viola G. Tilden and her partner canvassed the home of Lillian B. three times and "we knew she was there." When Lillian refused to answer the door on their fourth visit, Tilden "called her on the phone [and] told her I was sorry she did not see us." Lillian "said she would not sign a pledge for any one."[69]

The drive for 100 percent enrollment in the Food Pledge led to increased scrutiny of private lives and additional vulnerability for some residents. Food administrators in the nation and in Oregon extended the pledge drive for another week through November 10 because of continuing resistance, and they stepped up efforts to gain signatures at every household to expand compliance. One consequence was an increased focus on residents who were not married, broadening the net for surveillance of same-sex partnerships at a time when same-sex intimacy was criminalized and medicalized as deviant "sex perversion." "Bachelors, spinsters, and other people living in rooming houses are to receive special attention," the editors of the *Oregon Journal* noted. The *Baker Herald* in eastern Oregon described Portland's campaign this way: "Pledge Campaign Now Centers on Spinsters: Campaigners Concentrate on Unmarried People."[70] The *Journal* account also referenced targeting "hall-room girls," a term that referred to women living in the cheapest accommodations, often implying that they were sex workers or vulnerable to becoming "hardened prostitutes."[71] The extended Food Pledge week coincided with coordinated police raids on "disorderly houses" in Portland that targeted women as part of Portland's anti–venereal disease campaign. Police arrested some one hundred women in these sweeps.[72] Sex workers, women who engaged in heterosexual intimacy outside of marriage, gender-nonconforming people, and people who had same-sex intimate relationships were vulnerable targets.

Newspaper coverage provides evidence of surveillance and resistance in other cities and counties in the state. "Are Local Families Slacking?" editors of Pendleton's *East Oregonian* asked and answered in the affirmative. By November 15 only 769 of 1,270 homes in the city, some 60 percent, had pledged.[73] Editors of the *Evening Observer* in La Grande reported on eastern Oregon's Union County results. About 2 percent of 248 householders refused to pledge. Some respondents voiced a direct concern about government surveillance or opposition to the government. One woman "was angry at President Wilson for not supporting woman suffrage" and would not sign. "It is well remembered," the editors warned, "that the reason for every refusal is sent to Washington to be investigated."[74] The editor of the *Oregon City Courier* was "shamed to record the fact that many persons in this county have absolutely refused to sign food pledges." When "a housewife tells us that she is 'against all things American,'" and another "'I hope the Kaiser wins the war,' it is time to investigate officially."[75]

Some local leaders believed in more punitive measures to promote compliance. Oregon progressive William S. U'Ren believed those who did not sign the pledge should be "delivered" to Germany, or "if that cannot be done, why not put them in concentration camps as the next best thing?"[76] George R. Funk, elected Portland city auditor that summer and one of the nineteen prominent Portland men who served as Food Pledge district captains, left a paper trail of his outrage at the refusers in his precincts. Canvassers reported numerous instances of residents who believed the Food Pledge was all "humbug," labeled many of them "Pro German," and noted rumors of pro-German meetings and literature.[77] In a number of cases, Funk added his own comments in a large, distinctive hand. "Worker reports [this person] may have a son who is a slacker. Investigate," he wrote about one. "These last two need looking after," he said about cases on another block.[78]

It appears that the words and actions of the Food Pledge refusers served as a catalyst for Funk to engage in deeper surveillance and reporting of dissenters. At a January 1918 organizing meeting, the forty people attending elected Funk president of the Portland Vigilantes. The new group's aim was to engage in an "active crusade against sedition" by investigating and receiving reports of disloyal speech or actions and to pass those reports to federal authorities for investigation of violation of the Espionage Act. Two months later, the group claimed twelve hundred members in Portland.[79] Funk organized a Vigilante dance at Portland's Public Auditorium on April 17 with the assistance of several committees of men and women members including his wife Maude to raise funds for their "war on sedition" and to "stamp out pro-Germanism."[80] The dance coincided with press reports of an unnamed member of the Vigilantes taking credit for vandalism at the offices of the city's publisher of German-language newspapers, painting over German words on the plate glass window with yellow paint and threatening to break windows. After the publisher removed the German words, Funk issued a press release disavowing anyone who would use violence and affirming the "law-abiding" work of the Vigilantes "to assist the constituted authorities in the work of stamping out sedition, to secure information, and make reports of seditious acts or utterances."[81] Thereafter the Portland Vigilantes moved their organizing behind the scenes in the city.

U'Ren, Funk and the Portland Vigilantes, Oregon newspaper editors, and other community leaders joined a chorus of voices nationwide calling for more drastic action. They believed speaking out against the war or the Food Pledge should be specifically and directly criminalized beyond the 1917 Espionage Act to make sure that the refusers and other dissenters would be liable to prosecution. The Espionage Act "did not reach the individual, casual, or impulsive disloyal utterances," free speech scholar Zechariah Chafee Jr. later noted. And as US attorney general Thomas Gregory reported, "individual disloyal utterances" that "occurred with considerable frequency throughout the country" led to a "demand for such an amendment as would cover these cases." Congress obliged with an amendment to the Espionage Act popularly known as the Sedition Act of May 1918, making a criminal of anyone who "shall willfully utter, print, write or publish any disloyal, profane, scurrilous, or abusive language" about the government or the war effort. Enforced loyalty and participation in the designated work of the nation without the freedom of expression now had the force of federal law.[82]

LIBERTY LOAN AND OTHER WARTIME
FUNDRAISING REGISTRATION DRIVES

Women's registration for war service and the Food Pledge overlapped with the first of five nationwide Liberty Loan drives from 1917 to 1919 and numerous other fundraising enterprises such as War Savings Stamp (wss) and Thrift Stamp campaigns. The Wilson administration and local leaders financed the war by "mobilizing emotions" for campaigns for bond sales rather than engaging in other methods, such as taxation, to finance the conflict. The purchase of a Liberty Bond or a Thrift Stamp was a "loan" to the federal government to be repaid after the war. Banks handled installment payments. As Treasury Secretary William McAdoo phrased it, the Wilson administration "capitalized [meaning monetized] the profound impulse called patriotism," raising some $21.5 billion across the five Liberty Loan campaigns alone. Like Liberty Bonds, but created to be affordable for the masses including schoolchildren and wage earners, Thrift Stamps and War Savings Stamps were designed to secure wartime funding from residents regardless of age or economic status. Beginning in December 1917, the government issued War Savings Stamps in twenty-five-cent and five-dollar denominations that would grow in value by one cent each month; saving successive Thrift Stamps could equal a War Savings Stamp.[83] Purchasing a Liberty Bond or a War Savings Stamp became a requirement for loyalty and a badge of wartime citizenship signifying active participation in the wartime nation's work. People who did not participate became dangerous internal enemies.

The participation of women in Oregon and the nation was vital to the success of wartime and postwar Liberty Loan drives. The Wilson administration harnessed the power of women and their organizations to assist with Loan campaigns by creating the National Woman's Liberty Loan

56 / CHAPTER 2

Committee (NWLLC) in May 1917, just over a month after the United States entered the conflict. The organization was in force until the final Victory Loan drive ended in spring 1919. Headed by Eleanor Wilson McAdoo, daughter of the president and wife of the secretary of the Treasury, the NWLLC was housed in the Treasury Department. National NWLCC leaders connected with established women's organizations in the states to administer local efforts and work with male state, county, and city committees already in place.[84] Clubwoman and suffragist Sarah A. Evans chaired all of the Oregon Woman's Liberty Loan drives, with local city and county women working under her direction. The Oregon State Federation of Women's Clubs, the umbrella organization of the state's White women's clubs that Evans directed from 1905 to 1915, was part of the NWLLC advisory board. Evans attended the national NWLLC conference in Chicago in July 1918 to represent the state and report on state activities. Oregon Liberty Loan director Edward Cookingham appointed Evans to the state Liberty Loan executive board and instructed county chairs to include women "wherever they can be used to the best advantage."[85]

The bond and stamp drives deepened the surveillance by neighbors and law enforcement agents on residents and sharpened the hunt for internal enemy others. National and local leaders used increasingly brutal public propaganda campaigns to persuade Americans to purchase millions of dollars in bonds and stamps again and again with posters, speakers, rallies, public shaming, intimidation, surveillance, and violence. After the war Portland physician Thomas Ross noted that "the patriotic dollars in the Liberty Loans were very few as compared to the ones which were wrenched from the public through fear."[86] The federal government reached into homes, rooming houses, and apartments by mobilizing local residents, especially women, as canvassers and agents. Campaign administrators created special pins, window cards, and placards for those who contributed so that they could display tangible evidence of engagement in the nation's work.

By the Third Liberty Loan in April 1918, local Oregon committees used a "pre-campaign household questionnaire" to discover and document very personal information for each individual in their districts to be sent to a state "ratings committee" to determine how much each person should pay. The city of Medford's committee recruited bank employees to scrutinize financial records, and Salem and Grants Pass committees used county

FIGURE 6
"Let your Quarters Help Win the War," War Savings Stamp poster, 1917. Library of Congress Prints and Photographs Division, Washington, DC.

FIGURE 7
C. R. Macauley, "You Buy a Liberty Bond, Lest I Perish," 1917. Library of Congress Prints and Photographs Division, Washington, DC.

property tax records.[87] State officials rated residents on a color-coded card signifying financial status with a specific donation amount they were expected to pledge, and they distributed the completed cards to district supervisors who sent them on to canvassers. As with the Food Pledge, if residents declined to subscribe, workers were to write down the reasons why in detail. The completed forms would "constitute a card index census" of each district "for future use," and yellow cards for slackers would be sent to the US Bureau of Investigation for individual investigation.[88]

Editors printed the names of subscribers for each successive loan campaign in local papers with the dollar amounts they pledged. Some printed the names and sometimes the addresses of the refusers for public inspection.[89] Eugene workers constructed an imposing dial outside the city train station to measure contributions.[90] Zealous Portland boosters constructed a "Liberty Temple" on Southwest Sixth Avenue in the heart of the city as a stage on which to present and perform the city's Third Liberty Loan drive and all subsequent Liberty Loan activities. A banner with running totals for bond purchases topped the Liberty Temple as a constant reminder of the need to participate and the pressure to meet expectations.[91] Tillamook residents dedicated their Liberty Temple in April, and Bend residents in November 1918.[92] The state achieved another Oregon First during the Third Liberty Loan as the first in the nation to surpass its subscription quota, garnering national attention and an "honor flag." But this achievement also increased the pressure to attain the same or better results as a star state in subsequent drives.[93] By the Fourth Liberty Loan campaign in fall 1918, state Liberty Loan officials pressured everyone to commit to public pledges before the official start, with "I Am Pledged" ribbons to be worn as rewards for supporters and public scorn for those who had no ribbon. The Portland Vigilantes pledged to "hunt down" the "slackers and shirkers" who had not subscribed or those residents they believed could afford to take on more bonds to save Oregon's reputation. They mobilized the Multnomah Guard, a paramilitary group, as a force of "special solicitors" to go door to door to pressure residents to donate.[94]

For Native residents of reservations there were additional layers of complications and control during the Liberty Loan drives. Across the United States, Bureau of Indian Affairs officials and local Liberty Bond organizers established programs and publicity to encourage Liberty Bond purchases by tribal members. By June 1917, Interior Secretary Franklin Lane "in an effort to boost sales even more" took steps to allow him to invest tribal funds and estates in Liberty Bonds, more than $5 million by his estimate. Congress empowered Lane to take control over these investments if he believed it would "benefit" tribal members and the United States. Lane had individual bonds put into his own name for this purpose, but individuals were "entitled" to subscribe in their own names if the BIA determined they were "competent." Voluntary contributions and funds from tribal accounts amounted to $25 million in Liberty Bonds across the nation for the five bond campaigns. And, as Thomas Britten demonstrates, Lane often refused individual requests to cash in the bonds after the war for the bonds in his name, or made the process complicated for people who had bonds in their own.[95]

At the Klamath Agency, BIA superintendent J. M. Johnson and his staff worked with Klamath County committee members to determine amounts Klamath residents should be asked to pay based on their finances and anticipated revenues from timber and herd prices. Johnson told the head of the Klamath County Liberty Loan drives that "the Indian money invested in Liberty Bonds [from the Klamath Agency] consists mostly of funds to the credit of individuals under the control of this agency. Much of it belongs to minors," he wrote, "and has been derived from the sale of land and timber." Some was in the name of Secretary Lane and some in individual subscribers' names. Johnson noted that many residents were interested in the 4.25 percent interest paid on Liberty Bonds instead of deposits in banks at 3 and 4 percent. For the Third Liberty Loan in spring 1918, Klamath reservation residents subscribed a total of $48,450. Six of the fourteen adults investing their separate funds were women; Annie Bright Jim had the largest purchase of $2000 worth of bonds. Of the twenty-one minor children whose funds were used to invest $31,400 on their behalf, six were girls or young women, and funds from six men's estates became part of the total invested. The Klamath records do not provide information about direct challenges from individual investors, but the many bureaucratic snarls noted in the correspondence suggest these policies deprived Klamath investors of their full interest during this period.[96]

Many Oregon women embraced the wartime fundraising drives to demonstrate their equal service with men and to engage in what they believed was the proper wartime work of women citizens. Women sub-

60 / CHAPTER 2

scribed to Liberty Loans as individuals and enhanced the visibility of their organizations by subscribing as a club or workplace group. Members of the Dallas and St. Helens Woman's Clubs as well as the Portland Woman's Christian Temperance Union (WCTU) purchased $50 bonds, the smallest amount available. Members of the Portland Woman's Club and Portland's American Association of University Women (AAUW) each invested $300 as organizations. The Portland Derthick Music Club voted to tax each member sixty cents to purchase one club Liberty Bond of $50.[97] Cleaners and laundry workers at the Hotel Multnomah and loom operators at the Portland Woolen Mills bought bonds on installment. The six-hundred-member strong Portland Grade Teachers' Association pledged $1,000 of their organization's budget for bonds, and their individual subscriptions equaled 100 percent of the membership.[98]

Liberty Loan director Sarah Evans believed participation increased women's claims to a citizenship of shared experience, rights, and duties with Oregon men. At the beginning of the drives, Evans emphasized "what has been growing since the women of Oregon began work of this nature; that is, the respect that the men have come to have for women's work" and the "feeling [men] have that a movement of this kind is benefitted by the cooperation of the work of men and women."[99] Evans called on members of the Oregon Equal Suffrage Alliance to participate, and Alliance members held key administrative roles in all of the subsequent Loan campaigns.[100] By the time of the Third Liberty Loan, Evans had established committees for work among clubwomen, women of color, religious congregations, women in immigrant communities, wage-earning women, and teachers. Katherine Gray headed the committee representing the State Federation of Colored Women's Clubs.[101] Council of Jewish Women member Julia Swett chaired the organization committee.[102] Irma Mentz Sears, a second-generation Austrian American married to a prominent Portland physician, was in charge of the Third Loan work among immigrant women.[103] Sears enlisted first- and second-generation immigrant women and also US-born clubwomen with second-language skills to work with her as translators and mediators. Her corps visited Japanese, Chinese, Spanish-speaking, Italian, Armenian, Syrian, French, and Scandinavian women in door-to-door canvasses of their homes.[104] Hazel Cartozian, who had come to Portland with her Armenian parents from Turkey, canvassed among the small but visible community of Armenian Portlanders for the Third Liberty Loan with notable success.[105]

Under Gray's direction, members of the Oregon Federation of Colored Women's Clubs canvassed in the Liberty Loan drives but also took specific action within their communities, part of a national movement of many Black women to build civil rights progress into women's support for home-front programs.[106] In April 1918, Gray organized and chaired a Black women's Patriotic Drive Association to centralize and support Black community participation and staffing for the dozens of Portland's wartime projects.[107] Scores of women marchers represented Black Oregonians in an August 1918 parade and public reception at Portland's Public Auditorium to send off fifty Black men from Portland and eight others from around Oregon to army service at Camp Lewis. For the occasion representatives of the Rosebud Study Group dressed in the white uniforms of the Red Cross reminiscent of woman suffrage parades.[108]

Like the Rosebud Study Group's march, the Liberty Loan and War Stamp drives drew on a tradition of patriotic parades and pageants in Oregon and the nation, such as celebrations of the Fourth of July, votes-for-women parades, and community events. Portland's annual Rose Festival parade, first held in 1907, created additional public traditions and spaces for a wide variety of residents to claim civic inclusion including among immigrant communities. And in the 1918 Portland Labor Day parade, women telephone and telegraph operators, garment and laundry workers, and waitresses linked their claims for workplace justice with support for the war effort.[109] The Liberty Loan and Stamp drives were part of a heightened politicization of other fundraising and philanthropy for the war effort, including work for the Red Cross, sponsorship of French and Belgian orphans, and contributions to groups such as the American Fund for the French Wounded. As the war years sharpened the call for a public demonstration of loyalty and "100% Americanism," some women used the heightened connections linking public space, pageantry, and politicized philanthropy to enhance their claims to civic inclusion.

Women whose families came from nations among the Allied cause or national groups persecuted by nations at war with the United States could build on the citizenship of shared experience in their claims for more complete civic recognition. Cartozian, who canvassed her Ottoman Armenian community in Portland for the Third Liberty Loan with such success in spring 1918, participated in a variety of civic projects beyond

62 / CHAPTER 2

the loan drives. After attending classes in the commerce department at Portland's Franklin High, Cartozian worked as a bookkeeper at the family's Cartozian Brothers Oriental Rug company in the city.[110] She represented Armenia in Portland's 1918 Fourth of July pageant. Organized as a "Panorama of Nations" with some ten thousand participants, the pageant featured sections comprised of marchers who were immigrants from Allied and neutral countries.[111] Cartozian also represented Armenia for "All Nations Day" at the Oregon State Fair in Salem in September 1918 and in a "Pageant of Nations" at Portland's Star Theater during "Victory Week" immediately after the Armistice.[112] She took a visible role in Armenian refugee and relief efforts in Portland during and after the war.[113]

Cartozian's work for Near East Relief took place when Armenian Americans were "on the boundary of White" in American society, part of what Michel Trouillot characterized as the shifting "ideologies of ethnicity" in this period.[114] The 1909 *Halladjian* decision in Massachusetts had determined that Armenians were ethnically White and could become naturalized citizens, but policymakers challenged that right through denial of first naturalization papers to Ottoman Armenian applicants. The Oregon District US Court challenged Hazel's father T. O. Cartozian's eligibility for naturalization and Whiteness in 1924. She was one of the defense witnesses called to establish that Armenian Americans "are generally considered white and mingle on terms of social equality with Americans" and to emphasize Armenian women's progressivism. The court granted Cartozian's right to naturalized citizenship.[115]

Pearl Moy, who shared the stage with Cartozian at the Oregon State Fair's "All Nation's Day" and the "Pageant of Nations" at the Star Theater, worked to build an image of patriotic Chinese American womanhood and emphasized the citizenship of shared experience in support of the recognition of Chinese Americans.[116] The Oregon-born daughter of Moy Back Hin, successful Portland business owner and honorary consul for China in the Pacific Northwest, Moy graduated from Lincoln High School in 1920 and thereafter worked as a stenographer in the family's Eastern Trading Company.[117] Moy participated in Portland's canvassing for a nationwide campaign of famine relief for northern China in 1921, modeled after community mobilization strategies of the Liberty Loan and Near East Relief drives, and took part in benefit concerts for the cause.[118] At a time when immigration exclusion was US policy toward China, Moy and her friends helped to establish a Chinese Student Association within Portland's Young Women's Christian Association (YWCA), part of the "Girl Reserves" movement for high school and young women graduates, and joined other young women in the city in various programs during and after the conflict. Advocates within this Chinese student group and the Chinese American community of Portland worked to change the policy of the Portland YWCA to give the women "the same privileges of the pool as other members have" in fall 1919 as one small measure of integration into the dominant White community.[119] In April 1922 the *Oregonian* ran a full-page article with photographs of Moy and four other Chinese American women of Portland on the front page of the women's section of the Sunday edition, noting that Moy and her friends were "some of the finest types of citizens."[120]

Oregon and national leaders made women's wartime registrations pageants for the public enactment of patriotic womanhood. Engagement in war service registration for women, the enrollment of women as household managers in the Food Pledge, and registration drives for wartime fundraising campaigns became sanctioned women's wartime work for the nation. Some women participated as a way to build a stronger civic identity, including White women and some women who were part of historically marginalized communities seeking respect and inclusion in civic life. If many Oregon women supported the wartime Liberty Loan and Stamp registration drives as their civic duty as patriotic women citizens, others opposed the campaigns and the tactics associated with them as violations of privacy and civil liberties, tactics they believed were based on a narrow definition of female citizenship. Supporters policed dissenters with increasing vigor in Oregon as the state's Oregon First boosterism combined with the federal Espionage Act and, by June 1918, the Sedition Act to criminalize dissenting speech.

The cases of M. Louise Hunt and Anna Mary Weston, detailed in the next chapter, provide two examples of women's resistance and claims for a citizenship of dissent. Their experiences suggest particular ways that wartime surveillance reached into women's workplaces to police wartime loyalty and abilities in performing the nation's work during the conflict.

64 / CHAPTER 2

CHAPTER 3

Trouble at Work

IF SOME WOMEN ENGAGED with registrations and drives as the wartime work of the nation, others declined to enroll, and they did so in an increasingly dangerous climate of pressure to participate that intensified with both the Espionage Act of June 1917 and the much more punitive Sedition Act in force by May 1918. Liberty Loan and Savings Stamp drive canvassers took their campaigns directly to people's workplaces, accelerating the public pressure to engage and intensifying the surveillance on workers. Like the teachers enlisted by Oregon leaders to oversee the Food Pledge registration, many other wage-earning women faced losing their jobs and economic security if they spoke out in dissent. The pressure and scrutiny of registration drives combined with other surveillance projects such as the prohibition of alcohol to create overlapping layers of observation and encouraged coworkers to police and inform on one another for their own security and safety.

This chapter examines two cases of accusations of disloyalty among women wage earners on the job during Portland's wartime registration drives. M. Louise Hunt was a rising star in the feminized profession of librarianship who refused to purchase a Liberty Bond. She was forced to resign her position under a storm of publicity that challenged her morality, professional identity, and citizenship and designated her as a dangerous internal enemy who some leaders and rank-and-file Oregonians believed should be deported for disloyalty. Second-generation German Anna Mary Weston spoke out against the war at her multiethnic and likely mixed-race workplace as a Pullman railroad car cleaner at Portland's North Bank Station; she became the first woman in Oregon to be tried under the Sedition Act. A federal jury found Weston not guilty by reason of mental incapacity, and her experience suggests ways that ideas about ability, eugenics, work, and gender may have impacted her in this most vulnerable of situations on the wartime home front. Comparing the cases of Hunt and Weston helps us frame and analyze some of the consequences that resulted from linking women's workplaces and identities to the pressures to conform with patriotic womanhood during the intense civic scrutiny of wartime registrations, eugenic thinking, and the hunt for internal enemy others.

HUNT'S REFUSAL TO PURCHASE A LIBERTY BOND

In the midst of the Third Liberty Loan drive, on Friday, April 12, 1918, the *Portland Evening Telegram* broke the story that M. Louise Hunt, a librarian at Portland's Central Library, refused to purchase a Liberty Bond; a flood of coverage from other papers in Portland and around the state followed.[1] The librarians at the Central Library were paid and directed by a separate library board but were generally considered part of the Multnomah County workforce. The situation started with an anonymous letter, a "most base and cowardly device," library board vice president and progressive Portland attorney Richard W. Montague later recalled. Montague and board president Winslow B. Ayer, who was also food administrator for Oregon, immediately met to discuss Hunt's case. They concluded that Hunt's situation did not warrant any additional action and considered the incident closed.[2]

But that afternoon Portland's local Liberty Loan committee detailed two "special officers" to come to Hunt's workplace at the library to interrogate her in view of coworkers and library patrons. The men tried to convince Hunt to purchase a bond. When she refused, they reported her to Bert Haney, US attorney for Oregon. William Bryon, Bureau of Investigation special agent for Portland, called Hunt into his office for additional questioning.[3] Montague provided legal advice and went with Hunt to the interrogation.[4] Ayer convened a special meeting of the library board the evening the story broke in the press to hear Hunt's side of the story. Hunt confirmed that she would not purchase a bond, concluding in her official statement: "I merely wish to claim the constitutional right privately to hold a minority opinion." Library board members gave way to pressure from a torrent of angry Liberty Loan officials, editors, members of city organizations and clubs, including many White clubwomen, residents writing letters to newspapers, and condemnation from Governor James Withycombe and Mayor George Baker. They accepted Hunt's resignation at another meeting on April 15. At that meeting, board members William Woodward and Rufus Holman, who were particularly hostile to Hunt,

66 / CHAPTER 3

escalated tensions with heated exchanges, table pounding, and charges of disloyalty against other board members.[5] Hunt was the target of relentless negative press reports and editorials; she received anonymous letters containing death threats.[6] The reactions to Hunt's refusal to purchase a Liberty Bond were powerful examples of what Lewis Mumford would call, a year later, a "'patriotic' inquisition."[7]

When newspapers broke the story, editors included a "sworn statement" about Hunt's interrogation by the two special agents who asked Hunt "if she realized what the Huns were doing and had done in France and Belgium, the cruelties they had practiced and were practicing, and women being ravished," using a common slur for the German enemy and with "ravish" being a euphemism for rape that the newspapers could print. Did Hunt not "think that she should support our boys who were fighting to protect her from the same fate?" The agents insisted Hunt was "ready to suffer anything rather than to buy a bond" and said this meant that she would rather be raped by German soldiers than purchase a Liberty Loan Bond.[8] Hunt denied that she had responded in this way, but the special agents' account became a touchstone for protests across the state. The editors of the *Eugene Daily Guard* believed Hunt's "claim" that she would "sooner be ravished by a Hun than contribute to the support of America" to be "the most amazing incident that has occurred in the state of Oregon since the United States entered the war."[9] The editors of the *Oregon Journal* insisted that the world war was "a war to make the world safe for women," to secure them against the "horrors that have befallen captive women in Belgium and other women who have fallen to the mercy of Hun soldiers."[10]

These accounts cast Hunt as a woman who would rather be raped than purchase a Liberty Bond, or as a prostitute betraying her country with the enemy. These representations linked Hunt with the sex workers targeted by anti-prostitution campaigns as destructive internal enemies and translated her act of civil liberty into a sexual transgression that violated the tenets of patriotic womanhood. Hunt became the antithesis of a properly practicing woman citizen, a dangerous internal enemy in a "war to make the world safe for women."[11] Her opponents believed she should lose her job for refusing to engage in the nation's wartime work of purchasing Liberty Bonds. White Portland clubwomen joined the "storm of patriotic wrath" and condemned Hunt at the monthly meeting of the

Portland Federation of Women's Clubs in the midst of the controversy. Some 150 delegates representing the fifty member organizations voted unanimously to "protest against any exoneration" for Hunt and "against the retention of any person in the library service who displayed disloyalty to the government" or the nation's "war policies."[12] Some clubwomen were almost certainly among the Liberty Loan workers protesting at Portland's Liberty Temple "indignation meeting" that culminated in a resolution against Hunt. Fury turned to "great anxiety" when Liberty Loan supporters realized that the Hunt controversy might damage the Third Loan drive still in process and threaten Oregon's star state status and reputation.[13] Railroad attorney Arthur Spencer put it this way: "the ownership of a Liberty Bond by every person not in the military service . . . who can possibly afford to buy one is the only acceptable evidence of good citizenship. No person should be continued in public office or employment who does not possess this badge of citizenship."[14]

Locating Hunt's citizenship at her workplace had important consequences for her and for her library colleagues. Hunt engaged with librarianship as a positive force for community support and civic engagement. Born in Portland, Maine, in 1876, Hunt graduated from Philadelphia's Drexel Institute Library School in 1901, and after several posts came to Portland, Oregon, in 1910. Within the year she became the assistant city librarian in the administration of respected library director Mary Frances Isom.[15] With the support of women's clubs and a strong reform coalition in the city, Hunt and Isom worked to make the library a community center and agent of social justice in the vibrant new building dedicated in the heart of the city in 1913.[16] Dozens of local organizations held meetings and talks at the library, and in the library year ending in October 1917, 30 percent of Portlanders had a library card, some eighty-four thousand residents, and the library hosted eight hundred lectures and university extension classes, and almost two thousand meetings of various community groups.[17] Hunt's detailed assistant librarian reports reflect pride in building collections across several languages for patrons in Portland's immigrant communities.[18]

Hunt was involved in progressive and peace activism in Portland before the war. She was an active member of the Oregon Social Workers Association and a member of the Congressional Union for Woman Suffrage, the more radical wing of the votes-for-women movement. And in 1916,

68 / CHAPTER 3

when intellectual, cultural, and political interest was strong in the "prewar heyday of Socialism" and fairly mainstream among the city's activists, Hunt served as president and then secretary of the Portland Alumni branch of the Intercollegiate Socialist Society. She took a leave of absence from the library from August 1916 to August 1917 for postgraduate work at Columbia University and represented the Oregon Peace League at the Mass Meeting for Peace on April 2, 1917, in Washington, DC. Her socialist and peace activities soon flagged her as a person to be scrutinized during the Liberty Loan drives.[19]

Many women librarians in Oregon and at Portland's Central Library, with others across the nation, saw themselves engaged in a carefully calibrated project for the professionalization of librarianship and an increase in salaries comparable with men in similar positions—that is, equal pay for equal work and economic citizenship.[20] The Multnomah County library system employed women exclusively in library and assistant positions. After Hunt's refusal, accusations of disloyalty expanded to chief librarian Isom and then to the entire staff, although no one else was forced to resign. Some colleagues viewed Hunt's case, even Hunt herself, as threatening the fragile reputation they were constructing. Cornelia Marvin, the Oregon state librarian in Salem, privately expressed great anger with Hunt, as did other colleagues.[21] Later in life, Hunt recalled that Isom had made it clear, without saying it "in so many words, that she wanted me to resign."[22]

Hunt's case had a powerful impact on her colleagues because it led directly to a loyalty oath for employees of the library board and Multnomah County workers. On April 15, just three days after Hunt's story appeared in the newspapers, Rufus Holman, one of Hunt's primary antagonists on the library board and a Multnomah County commissioner, proposed a loyalty oath; commissioners approved it immediately.[23] According to the *Oregon Journal*, the entire Central Library staff arranged to go before county judges the morning after Hunt's resignation. They were the first among other workers to take the oath, and it appears that county and library association workers signed the oath with only a very few exceptions.[24] In the wake of Hunt's refusal to purchase a bond, Multnomah County officials made loyalty the literal price of employment for all county workers. While the federal Espionage and Sedition Acts of 1917 and 1918 provided punishment for people who were discovered to be speaking or acting in opposition to the government's war aims, the employee loyalty oath instead required someone to actively affirm and commit to supporting the government and war policies amid public scrutiny and in front of managers and coworkers with a document on file at their workplace.

Holman and the Multnomah County commissioners took the county loyalty oath to another destructive level by creating a special oath for employees who had declared their intention to become citizens but had not completed the naturalization process, people known as "declarants" or holders of "first papers." In addition to the standard language of allegiance, the oath required noncitizen declarants to swear they would "absolutely and entirely renounce and abjure all allegiance and fidelity to any foreign prince, potentate, state, or sovereignty" and then to fill in the specific name of the leader of that nation.[25] This was the same language of the Oath of Naturalization for US citizenship, but Multnomah County's oath obviously did not confer citizenship status. This meant that the commissioners made noncitizen employees *stateless* by requiring them to renounce their allegiance to their nation of citizenship in order to keep their employment with the county. In the relentless search for internal enemies, Holman's special loyalty oath placed noncitizen workers who signed in the vulnerable limbo of statelessness.

M. Louise Hunt had the status of a citizen but was considered a dangerous internal enemy, the citizen's antithesis, for refusing to engage in the sanctioned wartime work of the home front. Some opponents felt that she should not only forfeit her job, but all of her civic rights as a result. Most Oregon women had gained the right to vote in 1912, and the editors of the *Corvallis Gazette* argued for passage of a special law to disqualify Hunt from voting to prevent her from exercising this right of citizenship.[26] Before Hunt's resignation, Oregon governor James Withycombe declared: "Not only should she be summarily dismissed, but if she continues her anti-war propaganda she should be interned during the course of the war, like any other disloyal citizen or alien enemy."[27] That same month Oregon senator George Chamberlain sponsored a bill that would have considered civilians on the home front who challenged the war to be spies subject to trial in military courts, defining the entire nation as a military zone for the suppression of dissent.[28] "We would like to see Miss Hunt and her type of women turned over to the Kaiser for a term," the editors of the *Hillsboro Argus* proclaimed.[29] Mrs. Kantner, the mother of a soldier, wrote a letter

70 / CHAPTER 3

FIGURE 8
"Why Not?"
Portland Evening Telegram, April 17, 1918, 6.

to the *Oregonian*: "I think there are enough loyal women in Portland to see that transportation be given [Hunt] to the land of the Hûn. I will start the subscription with $1."[30]

The *Portland Evening Telegram* editors asked: "Why Not?" in a cartoon depicting Uncle Sam hammering shut a crate sending Hunt and other "Liberty Bond Slackers" to "Kaiser Bill, Berlin, Germany." Deportation itself is an act of violence; the *Telegram* enhanced this by adding a sign on the deportation crate with instructions to "Handle Roughly." From sending death threats to advocating Hunt's forced deportation, many members of the "'patriotic' inquisition" did not hesitate to use violence toward Hunt as a tool to try to force her compliance and conformity and to intimidate others at her workplace and beyond.

Hunt found work on the East Coast after her resignation, including serving as librarian and research secretary for the progressive magazine

TROUBLE AT WORK / 71

The Nation in New York; she later became the long-serving and respected head librarian at the Racine, Wisconsin, public library until her retirement in 1940. Hunt persisted in her commitment to social justice and pacifism. She was a member of the American Civil Liberties Union at least as early as 1921, a year after the organization was founded. She returned to her birthplace in Portland, Maine, upon retirement and in the aftermath of World War II served as the active executive secretary of Maine's Progressive Party. Hunt was a dynamic participant in pacifist and antinuclear organizations including the Committee for Peaceful Alternatives and one of ten Maine residents signing the 1949 petition to President Harry Truman to outlaw the atomic bomb and to press for disarmament. She was a member of the American Continental Congress for Peace and a sponsor and supporter of the Stockholm Appeal to ban atomic warfare in 1950. Hunt died in Portland, Maine, in 1960.[31]

WESTON, ABILITY, AND WORKPLACE SURVEILLANCE

On June 26, 1918, in a very different Portland workplace just over two months after Hunt's resignation, federal authorities took Anna Mary Weston into custody while she was on the job as a Pullman railroad car cleaner at Portland's North Bank Railroad Depot near Union Station. A divorced wage worker and second-generation daughter of German immigrant parents supporting herself in Portland, Weston spoke negatively about the war and President Woodrow Wilson and positively about Germany in the presence of coworkers several times over the month of June during Thrift Stamp canvassing campaigns at her workplace.[32] Weston had a war job keeping railroad cars clean and ready for passengers, but she refused to engage with the nation's other home-front work of purchasing Thrift Stamps and maintaining loyal speech.

Understanding the pressures on the small but significant multiethnic and likely mixed-race workplace of railroad car cleaners at the North Bank yards and the impact of overlapping wartime surveillance projects on their lives can help us analyze the circumstances of Weston's arrest and some of the broader implications of wartime registration drives for working-class women. Weston became the first woman in Oregon tried for violating the wartime Sedition Act and was found not guilty of sedition by reason of mental incompetency, but authorities did not commit her to an institution.

Other members of Weston's family were institutionalized, including her sister Lena, who was committed to the Oregon State Hospital just two months after Weston's trial.[33] Weston's case demonstrates the importance of considering ability and disability as categories of identity as Oregon's program of eugenic sterilization of the "unfit," the wartime hunt for internal enemies, and the question of useful work for the wartime nation all came together at the North Bank Station of the Portland railroad yards.

Labor shortages in the essential wartime railroad industry meant higher pay for wage-earning women who left prewar jobs to fill a variety of railroad positions—from clerks, stenographers, telegraphers, and machinist helpers to seamstresses and laundresses and the cleaners of the inside and outside of railroad cars. They fueled the 47.2 percent increase in the number of women employed by the nation's railroads in 1918, bringing the total number of women railroad workers to more than one hundred thousand. As Maurine Greenwald has demonstrated, before the war most of the women newly employed in the yards like car cleaners had worked in "laundries, hotels, restaurants, and private households." They were wage-earning women who changed jobs in search of better wartime working conditions; only a minority of railroad women workers entered the job market for the first time during the war.[34] The Oregon Bureau of Labor estimated that women and children comprised 10 percent of the state's railroad workers in July 1918.[35] By October 1, 1918, there were 3,747 women who cleaned the inside of railroad cars across the nation—1,176 of them in the western United States, and 87 in Oregon.[36]

Women railroad car cleaners at Portland's North Bank yard were multiethnic White workers and likely Black workers. During the Thrift Stamp drives in the railroad yards, canvassers needed interpreters and they spoke with people who were of "seven or eight different nationalities," identifying Italian American and Bulgarian American women specifically.[37] The US Railroad Commission did not keep consistent statistics by race for this period, but historian Robin Dearmon Muhammad's research demonstrates that Black women were the "single largest group of railroad car cleaners" across the nation during the war. Railroads employed thousands of Black women across the stations under federal control, especially in southern railroad hubs like Atlanta and in Great Migration destination cities such as Philadelphia, Chicago, and Cleveland. Black women worked to challenge segregation, poor facilities, and low wages, "determined to strengthen [their] tenuous foothold" in railroad work.[38] Greenwald notes that railroad work "constituted a high point in the graph of black women workers' wages during the war."[39]

Pullman Company records for car cleaners at Portland's North Bank yards in this period are sparse and do not tell us how many women worked there and whether Black women were part of the workforce. But the railroads were consistent employers of Black men in Portland and in Oregon, the West, and the nation; Black railroad porters and other male workers on the rails were a core part of Black communities. William Toll found that about 20 percent of Black men residing in Portland were employed by the railroad from 1910 to 1920.[40] The 1920 census helps us locate eight Black women who were car cleaners, suggesting that perhaps some of them may have worked at the North Bank Station with Weston in the summer of 1918. In 1920, Sadie Baker worked as a car cleaner and her husband Elijah was a Pullman car porter. Louisa Waddy's husband, William, had died as a result of a railroad accident from his work as a Pullman car porter in 1919, and she is listed in the 1920 census as a car cleaner.[41] Lucile Simalton supported herself as a car cleaner; recently widowed Alice Edmundson lived with her sister, mother, and niece; Belle Gallagher lived with a nephew; Lena Rogers had a lodger living with her in addition to her car cleaning work; J. Elizabeth Smith was a single parent supporting two teenage children; and Louise Rhodes lived with her husband and daughter.[42] Family and community connections were likely gateways for these eight and perhaps more Black women to gain employment as railroad car cleaners during and after the war.

Muhammad's vivid description sets the stage for understanding the work of railroad car cleaning. Passenger cars had "many of the accoutrements of a middle-class house," including "cushioned seating, carpets, curtains, bathroom fixtures and paned glass windows"—all of which needed dusting, vacuuming, and polishing to prepare for the next leg of the train's journey. The on-train toilets needed emptying and disinfecting. And "all the work was done by hand and women were expected to scrub floors on their hands and knees if necessary." Expectations and standards of cleanliness were "perhaps higher than in private households or even hotels."[43] This was true especially for the Pullman parlor cars and sleeping cars, first-class accommodations travelers reserved for an additional fee. Railroad car cleaners engaged in many of the same tasks as domestic workers in private homes or janitors and cleaners at businesses and government buildings.

Women began work as car cleaners in Portland in May 1917, just weeks after the United States entered the war, and their workplace was covered by overlapping layers of surveillance, increasing the scrutiny on and making more likely the arrest of Anna Mary Weston for sedition just over a year later.[44] During the war and its immediate aftermath, the federal government took over the management of the nation's railroads, deemed an essential industry, through the US Railroad Administration. This brought federal observers into the yards. The Railroad Administration equalized many fares, but passengers in regular Pullman cars and Pullman sleeper cars continued to pay a higher rate for the business-class accommodations and the standards of cleanliness sold with the price of a Pullman ticket. The company had to work to maintain public trust and confidence to ensure ridership.[45] This gave supervisors additional reasons to keep a watchful eye on Pullman car cleaners and other railroad workers.

Staff members of city employment bureaus added another layer of scrutiny as they monitored working conditions and worker behavior. When the war started, Portland had more than a dozen free employment bureaus to connect job-seekers with paid work. These included The People's Institute, a community welfare organization and settlement house, the Portland Women's Union offering support for wage-earning women, and the Portland Young Women's Christian Association.[46] The city had operated a free public employment bureau since 1906.[47] The voluntary and municipal bureaus charged no fees to workers or employers, in contrast to the often predatory commercial employment agencies that Oregonians voted to regulate and license in 1915.[48] During the war the employees of the city bureau worked cooperatively with local staff of the wartime US Employment Service in shared offices with separate men's and women's departments. The Pullman Company worked directly with the city bureau to hire women as car cleaners, and employment bureau staff members were active in placing and reporting on women in the railroad yards.[49]

Oregon's Industrial Welfare Commission and the Portland Police Bureau Women's Protective Division, two agencies tasked with protecting women workers, added other layers of scrutiny at the railroad yards. And employers and supervisors had reason to cooperate with these organizations. Members of the Industrial Welfare Commission enforced Oregon's minimum wage law for women and had the authority to inspect workplaces and working conditions for women. The welfare commissioners included the new work category of railroad car cleaner in their April 1918 lists, placing car cleaners in "public housekeeping" along with waitresses, cooks, and janitors.[50] Women's Protective Division agents provided additional surveillance in the railroad yards, which in turn strengthened management's own scrutiny of workers. A Protective Bureau officer investigating the Northern Pacific Terminal work site in May 1918 praised supervisors who gave "good information" about a missing car cleaner that included many details beyond her work record. They had "watched closely her associations in their yard and elsewhere." A women car cleaner told the Protective Division officer that "the foreman keeps a pretty sharp supervision over us, but I guess it is for our own good."[51]

These observers offered women railroad car cleaners a double-edged sword of support and increased scrutiny. Employment Bureau staff represented the city's interest in linking dependable workers with wartime employment, and other voluntary agency staff wanted the same outcome. As third parties to the worker/employer relationship, they had an interest in keeping track of women and the goings-on at their workplaces. Industrial Welfare Commission representatives, Women's Protective Bureau agents, and company welfare officials hoped to enforce decent working conditions and pay, but also made it their business to monitor employee behavior. Seeing to it that women followed the rules, especially high-profile wartime restrictions on free speech in the Espionage and Sedition Acts and the purchase of War Savings Stamps or Liberty Bonds, would have been top priority for employers, supervisors, and social welfare staff members. And women in a multiethnic and likely multiracial workplace like the Pullman car cleaners at the North Bank yards may have experienced particular attention.

The illicit alcohol trade focused a great deal of additional scrutiny on the railroad yards. Pullman cars, with their cushions and compartments and passenger luggage, were excellent places to hide bottles of liquor when the state prohibition of alcohol was in effect beginning in 1916, before national prohibition took effect in January 1920. There was a thriving illicit market in alcohol on the railroad lines between San Francisco, where the purchase of alcohol was still legal, and Portland. Vigorous surveillance and searches for liquor by law enforcement exposed car cleaners to addi-

76 / CHAPTER 3

tional observation from local and state prohibition enforcement officers, whose eyes and ears would also be open to violations of the Espionage and Sedition Acts and other "disloyal" behavior. Prohibition enforcement was so persistent and sustained on the railroad lines and in the yards that in August 1918, just over a month after Weston's arrest, the Pullman Company issued a circular "instructing employees to use 'every effort short of physical force' to protect the passengers and baggage carried on Pullman cars from the investigation of officials engaged in the work of ferreting out bootleggers between Portland and San Francisco."[52]

In the ensuing press and legal debate, Multnomah County sheriff Thomas Hurlburt revealed that he had issued "nearly 1,000 special deputy commissions" to guards and watchmen at work sites in Portland and Multnomah County since the beginning of the war, including the Pullman car yard, greatly expanding the law enforcement and prohibition surveillance effort and capacity with an astonishing number of deputies. Oregon law required a search warrant for a railroad car until it arrived in the yards, but after trains entered the yards, where railroad car cleaners worked, officers and special deputies could search a railroad car at will without a warrant.[53] The persistent presence of law enforcement agents and other deputies with license to surveil and search railroad workers for potential alcohol violations increased the targeted scrutiny on the Pullman car cleaners' workplace.

The nationwide War Savings Stamp (wss) and Thrift Stamp drive the week of June 24, 1918, and the quest by leaders to keep Oregon's star status, added another layer of surveillance on the workers at the railroad yards. By June 1918, wss drives were regular features of the wartime culture of Portland and around the state, and as with the Liberty Bond and food drives, many residents were very weary of them. The *Oregonian* reported that canvassers and wss administrators were "stung by the unresponsive attitude in Portland" that week, and they vowed an unrelenting, continuing campaign until they had raised the quota of $6 million in pledges.[54] wss managers in cooperation with Portland's Central Labor Council targeted railroad yard employees during the drive, and *Oregon Journal* reporters and photographers came along to record their efforts. wss speakers held meetings at the North Bank Depot and Union Station among employees. Canvassing teams worked individual job sites, including among women railroad car cleaners.[55]

Within this context of overlapping layers of surveillance and incredible pressure to conform to the rules, some railroad car cleaner coworkers either chose to report or were coerced into providing information about Weston to their superiors for her "disloyal remarks" while at work. On June 26 the Wednesday of the WSS drive, Charles R. Grisim, a Portland police detective on assignment as a special officer for the Justice Department, went to the North Bank yards to follow up on reports the Portland DOJ had received about Weston. Grisim used the Pullman Company office to interview six women car cleaners about what they heard Weston say on June 10. This suggests that the eyes of coworkers and managers were on the six women as they came to the office and participated in the interviews.

According to later testimony, head cleaner Mary Murphy heard Weston insist she would not purchase any Liberty Bonds or War Savings Stamps. Laura Sutton, Lucinda (Mrs. Reuben A.) Conlee, and Marie K. Day all reported Weston said that "she hoped Germany would win the war," and that President Wilson "caused hard times" in a rich country. Two other coworkers reported words they heard Weston say the day of Grisim's visit, June 26, in the midst of the Thrift Stamp drive. Anna Murphy stated that "today" Weston said she would not salute the flag "and no one could make her." Madeline Hoffert also heard Weston make these statements and "heard her say that it was not Germany's fault that we were in war; that the United States had no business in this war." Weston's alleged statements echoed the words Food Pledge refusers used in the fall 1917, but now the Sedition Act was in force to criminalize Weston's statements more directly. Grisim brought Weston in for questioning, but she would only reveal minimal personal information. He took the reluctant Weston to the Portland DOJ, where Grisim and Bureau of Investigation agents William R. Bryon and Charles W. Robison questioned her "about her pro-German remarks." Weston's response was that "she had a perfect right to stand up for her own nationality; further than that, she absolutely refused to talk." Bryon told Grisim to take Weston to Portland Police headquarters "and book her to be held for the Department of Justice."[56]

On Weston's journey to a federal trial for violating the Sedition Act that October, officials questioned her "mental capacity" several times, and jurors eventually acquitted her by reason of being "mentally incompetent."[57] Her possible disabilities may have created yet another layer of scrutiny at the North Bank Station. Oregonians were engaged in eugenic thinking, observing people's mental capacities, looking for "feeble minds" via surveillance. Coworkers may have believed that Weston made their workplace vulnerable in the campaigns for eugenic scrutiny and the wartime imperatives for unquestioning loyalty.

The forces at work on the railroad car cleaners at North Bank Station were enormous and layered. Weston's trial transcript is devastatingly brief, yielding the statements of Weston's coworkers and a verdict and nothing more. But the sustained pressure appears to have threatened coworkers, as authorities undoubtedly hoped it would. Employment records are available for two of Weston's accusers. Head cleaner Mary Murphy had a great deal to lose by problems on her watch, including her place as head cleaner and the additional salary that came with it. Married, with three children to provide for, Murphy had started in the yards in 1914 and continued as head cleaner until transferring to the Los Angeles yards in 1925. Madeline Hoffert started her job as a car cleaner with Pullman in May 1917. Railroad work was a family vocation, and Hoffert continued her work as a foreperson in the yards and as a continuous Pullman employee until her retirement.[58] We cannot know the reasons why the six women talked with Grisim and testified at Weston's federal trial, but we can certainly see the way that overlapping surveillance projects and threats to their own employment and safety may have created the pressure to do so.

Weston was in legal, physical, and psychological limbo at Portland police headquarters the day of her questioning, not yet under arrest, but being "held for the Department of Justice" with her liberties at risk. By holding Weston "for investigation," officers were engaged in what Portland attorney David Robinson termed the "pernicious police system of holding persons incommunicado, not permitting them to get in touch with family, friends, or counsel" in violation of civil liberties.[59] And by directing Grisim's actions, Agent Bryon was colluding with the Portland police in the practice on behalf of the Justice Department. Officials did not formally arrest Weston for violating the Sedition Act until Friday, June 28, and so it appears she spent two days and nights at the jail without support or advice while being questioned.[60] Weston's preliminary hearing on Wednesday, July 3, was conducted by US Commissioner Fred H. Drake and Assistant US Attorney John C. Veatch. Because violation of the Sedition Act was a federal offense, Weston came under the control of the US attorney's office and the jurisdiction of the US commissioner, who served as a committing magistrate for federal crimes.[61]

There is no evidence that Weston had any counsel for her preliminary hearing with federal officials. Portland mayor George Baker had suspended the short-lived office of Public Defender in July 1917, three months after the United States entered the war. In the summer of 1918 there were lawyers who volunteered their time to represent accused people who were not connected to counsel, some on staff with social welfare agencies. The Multnomah County Bar Association had a Public Welfare Bureau to provide legal aid, but their work was overwhelming in the absence of the Public Defender.[62] Weston does not appear to have had representation until her US District Court federal trial on October 21, 1918.

At the close of Weston's preliminary hearing, Veatch and Drake ordered that she be "held until her mental condition can be investigated" and scheduled an examination for that afternoon.[63] Weston's federal file contains no information about the preliminary hearing nor the sanity investigation, and the press did not follow up on the sanity hearing. Because her case went forward to the grand jury, the doctor or doctors evidently judged her to be mentally capable to stand trial, but it is significant that Drake and Veatch were concerned about Weston's ability.[64] Weston moved through the legal system over the next several months until her trial that October. The members of the grand jury indicted Weston for violation of the Sedition Act on September 18, 1918, with bail set at $1,000. Weston appeared without counsel opposite Assistant US Attorney Veatch on October 5 and plead not guilty to the charges.[65]

At her October 21 trial, District Court judge Robert S. Bean presided, Veatch represented the United States, and Andrew Hansen represented Weston as her counsel. Available sources do not permit us to know how Weston connected with Hansen at this stage of her case, whether she or supporters had the financial resources to hire him, or whether he volunteered to work with her without cost. Hansen's later advocacy for an end to capital punishment and his legal defense of a conscientious objector suggests he likely defended Weston's civil liberties by responsibility and by inclination.[66] The official trial records comprise one page and provide only brief details. Both sides produced evidence and made closing arguments, and the twelve male jurors found Weston not guilty, all within the day.[67] The *Portland Evening Telegram* reported "by reason of what the jury believed to be her impaired mental condition," they declared her to be "mentally incompetent" and acquitted her. Authorities held Weston

80 / CHAPTER 3

for another mental competency examination but did not commit her to an institution.[68]

Weston was the second of three Oregon women who were arrested for violating wartime loyalty legislation and the first Oregon woman to be tried for sedition during the war.[69] Federal officials charged southern Oregon dressmaker and socialist Anna Blachly with violating the Espionage Act on May 11, 1918, several days before the Sedition Act amendments were passed on May 16. Klamath Falls Home Defense League members accused Blachly of disloyalty at a vigilante court with a jury they convened on May 7, 1918, after wss canvassers visiting her Main Street shop reported that Blachly declined to purchase stamps because she believed they would prolong the war by funding it. Blachly affirmed that she was a socialist but denied disloyalty and wanted to clear her name. Klamath Falls had an active local party chapter before the United States entered the conflict.[70] US commissioner Bert Thomas arrested Blachly on Saturday, May 11, but Blachly and her husband could not raise the collateral for a $10,000 bond. Someone sent an anonymous note calling for her to leave town, and Blachly "became the center of so violent public excitement" that fearing "mob violence," the sheriff took the couple to Ashland in the dark of night. Federal officials met them there and escorted the couple to Portland for examination.[71] Assistant US attorney Robert Rankin found that the "zeal of the citizens exceeded the evidence at hand" and declined to prosecute.[72] The Blachlys relocated in Portland to start their lives again.[73]

Portland physician Marie Equi was celebrated by many Oregonians and notorious among others for her advocacy for workers, women, reproductive freedom, and for her open same-sex relationships. Equi was taken into custody on Sunday June 30, 1918, after a speech at Portland's Industrial Workers of the World Hall that military intelligence officers considered to be in violation of the Sedition Act, two days after Weston's arrest. Equi's sensational November 1918 trial in Portland featured supporters and detractors, accusations of radicalism, slurs and denunciations regarding Equi's same-sex partnerships, and physical violence toward Equi by federal agent William R. Bryon outside the courtroom. A jury convicted Equi, and she served ten months in San Quentin prison.[74]

There were important differences between Weston's case and the actions against Blachly and Equi. The latter were both socialists and branded as "agitators." They confronted hostile community members in vocal, open proceedings, and each faced physical violence. Both had a very high bail of $10,000, ten times the amount of Weston's.[75] All three were White working women, but there were class and workplace differences. Blachly, a successful dressmaker, and Equi, a well-known physician, lived in worlds different from Weston's and her work as a railroad car cleaner, although both Equi and Blachly engaged in direct movements for working people. It's also significant that there is no evidence that law enforcement or the courts requested an examination for mental competency for either Equi or Blachly. Authorities had questioned Equi's sanity during Portland's 1913 cannery strikes, but apparently not at her arrest or trial for sedition.[76] This suggests that an insanity or mental incapacity charge was not an automatic strategy for prosecuting women on trial in Oregon for violating the Espionage or Sedition Acts, which sets Weston's case apart.

Weston had several siblings, including her sister Lena, who were committed to institutions with a diagnosis of developmental or intellectual disability. This did not necessarily mean she was someone who experienced similar conditions, and institutionalization of some siblings could create scrutiny of other family members.[77] But Weston may indeed have experienced psychological, intellectual, or developmental disabilities. Her younger sister Lena was married at age twenty-two in 1910 in Washington County, Oregon, and gave birth to six children in the eight years of her marriage before her commitment. Lena's fifth child died at three months in September 1917, and her sixth was born in August 1918. Four months later, Lena's husband had her committed to the Oregon State Hospital, two months after Weston's acquittal on the charge of sedition. The examining physician diagnosed Lena with "imbecility" and a "mental capacity below normal." Lena had "borne children rather rapidly," and "six children in eight (8) years . . . has no doubt sapped her vitality." The physician considered frequent childbirth to be a contributing cause to her present condition. For the last year Lena had "no interest in her family" and would go to her neighbors' houses, saying that she did not have any children and refusing to return home. State Hospital physicians recommended that she be sterilized by the state under the provisions of Oregon's 1917 eugenics law because she was "very prolific" but "unable to care" for her children "let alone more" due to "imbecility." But, they wrote, she was "quiet and could be of some help to her family if protected against future pregnancies."[78]

82 / CHAPTER 3

The eugenics board recommended sterilization on April 18, 1919, and surgeons removed both of Lena's ovaries on June 12. Doctors discharged her on July 2, 1919, "as not insane but feebleminded." She healed from surgery, placed in the care of her husband. When Lena returned home, she found her children gone because her husband had sent all five of them to state care two weeks after Lena's own commitment.[79] Three months after her discharge, Lena's husband had her committed to the Oregon State Institution for the Feeble-Minded (later Fairview Training Center) in Salem. He was active in selling and purchasing properties at the time and petitioned successfully to act as Lena's guardian with control over her estate. In 1920 he sold the house Lena owned to support his business enterprises, which he continued to develop until his death in 1926. Lena was paroled to live with her brother Louis in 1921, readmitted in 1923, paroled to live with her sister Anna Mary in Portland in 1925, readmitted, then sent to the Columbia Park Hospital and Training Center for geriatric residents in The Dalles; she lived the last four years of her life in a nursing facility in Sandy, Oregon, until her death in 1966.[80]

Understanding the intertwining threads of ideas about ability, the productive work of the nation, and eugenic thinking and policy in this period may help to explain why Weston was never committed to an institution despite her high-profile case and the verdict of an impaired mental condition, and her sister Lena was institutionalized for most of her life. It appears that medical and judicial authorities believed that Weston engaged in useful, productive work and was not a dangerous internal enemy or a threat to her community. But they believed Lena had become a threat given her "failure" to engage in useful work and her capacity to bear children. Before her state-ordered sterilization, Lena had reportedly "no interest in her family" and was "unable to care" for her children and home. She had evidently stopped being a "proper" mother and housewife, her civically suitable work, and so authorities ordered her sterilization. But the sterilization surgery was to pave the way for Lena's return to useful work at home, as she was deemed "quiet and could be of some help to her family if protected against future pregnancies."

Henry Waldo Coe, MD, director of Portland's Morningside Psychiatric Hospital and editor of the *Medical Sentinel*, expressed this view in a 1913 editorial in support of eugenics legislation. The basis of the eugenics law, he wrote, was that after sterilization "such feeble-minded as may be able to make a livelihood" could "go out from the state institutions and become producers instead of charges upon the state." The "greatest danger" in the case of women who were "feeble-minded" was the "propagation of a line of like persons," Coe wrote. Many "feeble-minded" women, he believed, "while mentally defective, are otherwise physically strong types, well built specimens of womankind, and when married make, in truth, helpmates for their husbands." He continued: the "robust, well-formed female mental defective is quite often, if not in most cases where at large, taken by some man as a wife."[81]

Lena was sterilized at the OSH and, according to the physicians who discharged her, ready to return to useful work. But her husband had removed their children from their home and placed them in the care of the state. Lena was either unable to engage in such labor, or her husband's dissolution of the family and desire to sell her property made it impossible for Lena to do so, and her husband had her recommitted. The court's willingness to parole her to her brother in 1921 and to her sister in 1925 suggests that authorities believed in Lena's ability to be part of the working life of a household when provided the opportunity, one of the elements of release and productive citizenship. A 1951 entry in her Fairview file noted useful labor indeed: "She is still very active, enjoying her many routine jobs on the cottage. She never needs to be told what to do next and is always busy washing dishes or clothes, making beds, or caring for sick patients."[82]

By contrast, Anna Mary—acquitted of sedition charges because of mental incapacity by a federal jury in October 1918—was not institutionalized. Like many women in history, we have only the records and reports made by others about Weston's life and family. But taken together, these sources offer some important clues and possibilities for analyzing Anna Mary's escape from commitment in the context of gendered eugenic policies operating during the wartime search for internal enemies. David Weston's version of Anna Mary's actions in his complaint for divorce in 1914 is the only public account that appears to survive of their relationship. He alleged that Anna Mary had sex with other men and exposed him to sexually transmitted infections across several years. David claimed that Anna Mary slapped, struck, and cursed at him regularly and refused to engage in household tasks even though she was a "strong able-bodied woman and well able" to do the work. By October 1912, David asserted, he was humiliated, and his life was "unbearable." According to his complaint,

84 / CHAPTER 3

David gave all the "household furnishings and property" to Anna Mary and left her. In December 1913 he began divorce proceedings against her.[83] His divorce complaint might have been describing Anna Mary accurately as someone who was experiencing intellectual or developmental disabilities or who otherwise behaved erratically or violently. Or his description could have been a way to build a case against a woman who spoke her mind and acted with physical force against traditional expectations. Anna Mary did not appear in court to contest the divorce.

When the sheriff tried to serve a summons for Anna Mary, her half-brother told the sheriff he could reach Anna Mary by "her post office address at 255 Harvard Street in Los Angeles." There does not appear to have been a 255 Harvard Street in 1914, but 255 Harvard Boulevard was the residence and offices of Robert A. Campbell, MD, a homeopathic physician and surgeon with an additional professional suite in the Mason Building in downtown Los Angeles. Campbell specialized in obstetrics and gynecology, including treatments for STIs.[84] It appears that in 1914, thirty-seven-year-old Anna Mary Weston was likely Campbell's patient, giving his address as one to which mail could be forwarded during her time there. She could possibly have been in treatment for an STI, having surgery to remove ovaries or a uterus infected by an STI, a surgical procedure such as an abortion or tubal ligation, experiencing pregnancy or childbirth, or perhaps a combination of several of these possible treatments or procedures.[85] It is very possible that when Weston was examined by physicians for mental competency during her arrest and trial five years later, doctors learned that she could not have children. This may have been a deciding factor in the decision not to commit her to the Oregon State Hospital or the Institution for the Feeble-Minded with a goal of eugenic sterilization and release on parole.

David Weston's divorce complaint described Anna Mary Weston as a "strong able-bodied woman and well able" to work but someone who chose not to do so, the very definition of a slacker and internal enemy during the war. This, of course, was only David Weston's side of the story. But at the time of her arrest in 1918 Anna Mary was working in an essential wartime industry as a Pullman car cleaner and supporting herself. This may have been another possible reason she escaped commitment, as she was engaged in the wartime work of the nation. There is no evidence that Anna Mary faced commitment to the Oregon State Hospital or the

State Institution for the Feeble-Minded at any time after her 1918 arrest and trial. It appears that her civically suitable work and ability to support herself, and perhaps evidence that she could not bear children and would not be a candidate for state-forced sterilization, were reasons why she escaped commitment when her mental abilities had been questioned. Anna Mary's file is not among the surviving Pullman Company records and so we don't know whether managers fired her from her North Bank Station job cleaning Pullman cars when she was arrested. By 1920 she was working as a laundress and until her death supported herself as a laundress and domestic worker in Portland. In 1923 Anna Mary married John Durkin, a carpenter, and the two had enough collateral (likely her home) to post a surety bond for $1,000 so that her sister Lena could be paroled to them. After her second divorce, Anna Mary married David Cohen, a worker in Portland's street cleaning department. They divorced before her death in 1938.[86]

Anna Mary Weston did have a final encounter with another kind of institutionalization in Oregon. She was admitted to the Multnomah County Poor Farm on December 7, 1938. The Poor Farm provided medical attention and a residence for the county's poor who were unable to work. At sixty-two, living singly, for several months she had suffered with an infected toe that developed gangrene and became a medical emergency. She died at the Poor Farm six days later and was buried by family members at Portland's Greenwood Hills cemetery.[87]

Workplace surveillance to promote loyalty and punish wartime dissent was sustained, deep, and consequential in Oregon and the nation. Multiple surveillance projects for loyal citizenship and engagement with the suitable work of the nation impacted all workers at a site, whether at a library or railroad yard. This was particularly true with Oregon First pressures at hand. M. Louise Hunt's refusal to purchase a Liberty Loan Bond touched off a firestorm of protest, led to her demonization as a woman prostituting herself with the enemy and calls for her to be fired, lose her voting rights, and be deported as an internal enemy. Her status as a professional woman in public service, critics argued, required her to be even more loyal in thought and in the work of the nation than people of other classes.

German American Pullman railroad car cleaner Anna Mary Weston's comments against the war and Wilson resulted in her arrest under the

Sedition Act, the first of an Oregon woman during the war. Women workers in Portland's railroad yards experienced relentless scrutiny from employers, social welfare workers, Liberty Loan and Stamp drive canvassers, and prohibition officers and deputies. Questions about Weston's abilities in the context of eugenic surveillance for "unfit" others and her acquittal by reason of mental incapacity suggest the interconnected strands of "fitness" and engagement with the nation's work. Her ability to support herself and her possible inability to have children may have been factors in the state's decision not to commit her. Weston's sister Lena's case and her forced sterilization highlights views about "feebleminded" women, childbearing, and work that contrast profoundly with Weston's escape from institutionalization.

CHAPTER 4

"Alien" Enemies

WOMEN'S WAR SERVICE REGISTRATION, the Food Pledge enrollment, and the Liberty Loan and War Stamp drives pressured women in Oregon and the nation to engage with the practice of patriotic womanhood as the work of the nation to prove their wartime citizenship or risk being labeled and treated harshly as internal enemies. These wartime registration projects were technically voluntary, but as the war continued, there were increasing penalties, including the Sedition Act by May 1918, for women like Anna Mary Weston who dissented. By contrast, the compulsory registration of wartime noncitizen "enemies" put the full force of federal prosecution and possible internment behind the process of wartime enrollment. And rather than providing a path for demonstrating loyalty and conformity with gendered citizenship ideals, "enemy alien" registration for women automatically defined the people enrolled as dangerous internal enemies, without due process.

During World War I the United States, along with other combatant nations and some neutral nations and colonies, registered, restricted, policed, and interned residents who were citizens of enemy nations.[1] For the first year of US involvement in the conflict only men who were citizens of Germany could be designated as "enemy aliens." But after April 1918 and through December 1918, federal legislation, presidential proclamations, and local policies included women as noncitizen enemies, requiring them to register, adding restrictions to their civil liberties, and increasing surveillance upon them. The complexities of this wartime registration for women were compounded dramatically by the Expatriation Act of 1907, federal legislation mandating that US-born women who married noncitizen men lost their own citizenship and took the citizenship of their husband.[2] In Oregon more than one-fourth (404) of the 1,567 women who registered as noncitizen enemies were born in the United States and had been US citizens before marriage.[3] An analysis of "enemy alien" registration with questions of gender in mind illustrates another layer of wartime enrollment, competing ideas about women's citizenship, and whether women could be political actors and subjects independent of husbands and family members. The registration of German-citizen residents expanded the reach of the surveillance state to the policing of "enemy" and "alien" bodies, including the actions that resulted in the internment of Riedl, a gender-nonconforming Oregonian. People resisted noncitizen enemy surveillance and labeling in significant ways, including by direct protest and efforts at self-representation.

Anti-German and nativist sentiment often merged with misogyny and gendered stereotypes in the registration and surveillance of German-citizen women. The front-page headline of the *Oregonian* "Claws of Teuton Women Clipped" described and dehumanized women registrants as monstrous and violent, defining them as dangerous enemy others. All "enemy aliens in skirts," they wrote, would be "dealt with same as men."[4] Female "enemy alien" registration, the editors of the *St. Johns Review* asserted, meant that men must "pause" any chivalrous feelings they had toward women and warned the "female species is often more dangerous than the male." Women who were German-citizen residents, according to these sources, had forfeited any claims to being "protected" and therefore were to be treated with the same harsh measures as those for German-citizen men.[5] Editors drew on negative cultural stereotypes about all women in their descriptions. "It is a matter of congratulation that the woman alien enemy now can be interned," the *Oregonian*'s editors insisted. "Her spiteful tongue has been a cause of wrath in many small communities."[6]

REGISTRATION OF "ENEMY ALIEN" MEN

Government policies regarding the scrutiny and eventual registration of "enemy alien" men beginning in April 1917 established a framework for the rules and modes of surveillance put in place for women a year later. When President Wilson issued his "Presidential Proclamation of War Against Germany" on April 6, 1917, three-quarters of the document addressed the topic of noncitizen enemies. The administration defined "alien enemies" specifically as male citizens of Germany fourteen years and older "residing within the United States and not actually naturalized," including those who had taken out "first papers" but had not completed the citizenship naturalization process. Women and men born in Germany were the largest group of residents in Oregon born outside the United States as measured by the 1910 census, some 18,000 people in a total state population of 672,765.[7] Oregon had allowed qualified residents who had declared their intention to become citizens with "first papers" to vote until 1914, and because of that policy, many people had not completed the naturalization process by the time the United States entered the war. And once the war began, federal law prevented those noncitizens considered to be "enemy aliens" who had "first papers" from completing the naturalization process. As in the case of Multnomah County loyalty oaths, this combination of state and federal policies certainly contributed to the number of noncitizen residents in Oregon, and in this case residents who were citizens of Germany now declared "enemy aliens."[8]

Free speech, movement, work, and travel could all be restricted. Noncitizen Germans could not "write, print, or publish" threats or attacks against all levels of government or the military.[9] Noncitizen German men had to turn in any weapons, ammunition or explosives, wireless or signaling devices, or any "paper, document, or book written or printed in cipher, or in which there may be invisible writing" to police or sheriffs within twenty-four hours or face immediate arrest.[10] Wilson's proclamation also barred noncitizen German men from being within a half mile of an armory or other military installation unless they carried a special permit.[11] From the distance of more than a century this may not seem overly restrictive, but armories and other military sites were located close to city center business and shopping districts, hotels, railroad stations, courts, and post offices. Oregon had eight official state armories: one each in Portland, Salem, and Eugene, and five located in the smaller communities of Albany, Ashland, Dallas, Roseburg, and Woodburn.[12] Justice Department officials included smaller facilities such as those in Cottage Grove, Hood River, and the national guard headquarters and rifle range in Clackamas County as part of the barred zones.[13] In smaller towns the entire city would be off limits.[14] A November 1917 presidential proclamation expanded the barred zones to include being within a hundred yards of a freight railroad yard or dock. And "enemy" noncitizens could not travel on bridges, lifelines in cities like Portland, except when on a train or streetcar. Travel on foot or by any other vehicle on a bridge was prohibited.[15]

In practical terms, creating the barred zones was a quick method of severely restricting the movement, business, transactions, and employment

90 / CHAPTER 4

of those deemed noncitizen enemies, threatening their economic security. The requisite permit facilitated the gathering of information about citizenship status and other private details about individuals in advance of a more rigorous registration process to come.[16] The nationwide deadline for men considered "alien enemies" to secure a permit was June 1, 1917. The document carried a photograph of the bearer and required either an employer signature or three written character references, information on employment since the war began in 1914 in Europe, birthplace, and a detailed personal description. The local US attorney had discretion to require collateral for a bond in order to issue a permit. Those found within barred zones without a permit could be arrested and convicted without a trial or due process.[17] Some men took their chances and did not apply for permits because to do so would shine a light on their nationality status. But noncitizen men were also required to register for the military draft on June 5, 1917, giving the government information about nationality and citizenship status that could be cross-checked. Thereafter, police officers could ask anyone appearing to be a man between twenty-one and thirty years of age to show their draft registration card without any other cause.[18] Police made dozens of arrests across the state, and by the end of November 1917 one hundred Portland men deemed "enemy aliens" had lost their jobs near the docks because they did not have permits.[19]

Wilson's November proclamation also established a registration process for all noncitizen German men, which took place February 4–9, 1918. Across the nation some 260,000 men registered, 2,245 of them in Oregon, at local police stations and, in communities of less than 5,000, at local post offices. They filled out a four-page registration form and were required to keep the official registration booklet, which included a photograph, with them at all times. Those who violated the regulations circumscribing behavior and movement were arrested and investigated. Thousands found themselves in this vulnerable situation at local jails or military installations such as the Pacific Northwest's Vancouver Barracks in Washington State. Nationwide, the Department of Justice considered twenty-three hundred civilian men dangerous enough to be interned in two regional camps: Fort Douglas, Utah, and Fort Oglethorpe, Georgia. This included ninety men from Oregon.[20] Officials in the Pacific Northwest targeted particularly men who were members of the Socialist Party and the Industrial Workers of the World, considered radical "undesirables" as well as "enemy aliens."[21]

In addition to these official surveillance policies, Oregonians engaged in more secretive methods to observe noncitizens and measure loyalties. Clarence Reames, US attorney for Oregon, and Oregon attorney general George Brown sent confidential letters to all district attorneys just after the United States entered the war, emphasizing legislation they could use immediately to suppress dissent and control noncitizens. They outlined Oregon's capacious Vagrancy Law of 1911 that included "every idle or dissolute person . . . who wanders about the streets or highways, at late or unusual hours of the night," or who used "abusive or obscene language in any street, highway, house or place," to disturb the peace. Such laws, they instructed, could be used "in a manner which might not ordinarily and readily occur to the average county prosecutor" to address loyalty issues and to police dissenters and enemy noncitizens.[22] Reames and Brown suggested that county officials step up their surveillance capacity by hiring Secret Service officers, special investigators, or additional deputy sheriffs.[23] Business owners scrutinized employees and customers by racial or ethnic profiling. For example, Pacific Steamship Company officials required agents to check the papers of everyone with German-sounding or "Austrian, Hungarian, Turkish, or Bulgarian names" (nations among the Central Powers allied with Germany) who wished to purchase tickets.[24] Other local residents banded together to engage in extra-legal observation of neighbors, including the Portland Vigilantes, who watched and reported on suspected noncitizens and dissenters.[25]

Many women were affected by these regulations and practices monitoring and penalizing fathers, brothers, partners, husbands, and sons even before the government decided to include women as "enemy aliens" in January 1918. They and their families were under increased scrutiny and publicity, and in the anti-German climate they faced violence. Businesses and employment and household budgets were at risk. Other government agencies acted to bring policies in line with federal aims. For example, Oregon State Fish and Game officials responded by denying fishing licenses to "alien enemies" unless they had special permission from the Department of Justice. "'We wouldn't be doing right to issue licenses to aliens that would allow them to go where they are not permitted to go,'" an official stated. Such licenses would have been important for food provisioning in some family economies and in business enterprises.[26]

The US Congress declared war on the Austro-Hungarian Empire on

92 / CHAPTER 4

December 7, 1917, and Wilson issued a proclamation four days later that did not impose registration and residential restrictions on citizens of Austria-Hungary living in the United States. The vast linguistic and ethnic diversity of the group—including those with German, Hungarian, Czech, Moravian, Slovak, Polish, Ruthenian, Slovenian, Serbian, Croatian, Bulgarian, Romanian, and Italian heritage—combined with economic and corporate considerations, led to this decision. Attorney General Gregory noted that "representatives of the largest industries of the country," including coal, steel, and shipyards, approached the Wilson administration as soon as war was declared with Austria-Hungary expressing fears that they would experience "serious labor dislocation and disorder" if their workers were declared "enemy aliens." Given this, and "the general state of good order theretofore observed by this class of alien enemies," Gregory reported, "it was determined to interfere with them as little as possible." Wilson called on all Austrian-Hungarian men over fourteen to "preserve the peace" and "refrain from crime," and if they did so, they would be "undisturbed in the peaceful pursuits of their lives and occupations." They could not leave or reenter the country without a permit. If convicted of a crime or found "about to aid the enemy," they could be detained or interned.[27]

REGISTRATION OF WOMEN AS "ENEMY ALIENS"

A month before the registration of noncitizen German men the first week of February 1918, the Wilson administration announced plans to register women under the same terms, but congressional authorization for the process did not pass in time to include women in the February enrollment.[28] Registration for women took place June 17–26, 1918. Across the nation some 220,000 women registered under the same policies and procedures for male registration.[29] In Oregon 1,567 women registered. Almost half lived in Portland, but women registered in all other regions of the state. The oldest was eighty-one and the youngest seventeen, most were in their thirties and forties.[30] Women had to register at police headquarters, places associated with criminality, if they lived in communities with five thousand or more residents such as Portland, Salem, and Eugene; in smaller communities registration took place under the direction of post office staff.[31] Women who did not register locally during the designated days would have to travel to Portland at their own expense to do so or be subject to arrest.[32]

Registrants would have to keep their identity booklets with them at all times or be subject to search and arrest. Women needed permits for a change of residence and for any work in restricted zones such as ports, and they were now included in the many restrictions on freedom of speech and movement and possession of such items as firearms, wireless sets, and suspicious documents. The new US attorney for Oregon, Bert Haney, warned: "German women will be arrested and interned as quickly as male subjects if they are believed to be dangerous to the government."[33] But as Matthew Stibbe notes, "although scores of women were arrested" as noncitizen enemies in the United States, "most were quickly released and only fifteen were held indefinitely."[34] There is no record of an arrest of a noncitizen "enemy" woman in Oregon.

Federal, state, and local authorities understood that female "enemy alien" registration would be complicated exponentially by the 1907 Expatriation Law making US-born women married to German-citizen men German citizens themselves, and therefore classified as "enemy aliens" who needed to register. This was true in Oregon, where more than a quarter of the women who registered had been born in the United States. There were additional intricate provisions contained in the fifteen separate definitions of women's naturalization and nationality in the president's proclamation. Women born in Germany now residing in the United States who were married to men of another nationality—such as Denmark, for example— would also have to register. These provisions, and questions stemming from separation, divorce, and death of a husband, made an accurate female registration appear overwhelming.[35] Newspaper editors around the state published the complicated regulations in advance, and some included additional articles emphasizing the details of the Expatriation Law. The editors of the *Eugene Morning Register* framed it this way: "Woman Belongs to Her Husband's Own Country."[36] Portland officials held an information session for women at the federal courtroom the Friday evening before registration began. George F. Alexander, US marshal, met with a "room packed with women and some few men" who listened carefully to his "long reading" of the rules and process. He then "received a volley of questions from women who were in doubt as to whether they should register and were uncertain as to what streets they had to keep off."[37]

94 / CHAPTER 4

Federal and local officials used the registration of German-citizen residents to expand the wartime state with new surveillance products. First, they created a form and filing system that required extensive, detailed personal information and made it readily available to local and federal officials. Women registrants had to list their birthplace and date, marital status, the name and citizenship status of their husband(s), separation or divorce documentation, names and residence details about children, parents, and siblings, where they had lived and worked since 1914 when the war in Europe began, whether any relative was fighting "for or against" the United States or its Allies and to name that person, to list their personal citizenship and naturalization process details, whether they had been "arrested or detained on any charge," and all languages spoken or read.[38] At the time the Bertillon visual system of identification was still in strong use but was giving way to fingerprinting as a tool for law enforcement. The registration forms required both. The Bertillon system asked for a description for specific physical characteristics, any distinctive marks, and a photograph, and registrars took fingerprints. Bertillon information and fingerprints were part of a global system of data creation, storage, and sharing across law enforcement agencies for the identification of criminals. "Wanted" and "Reward" posters and letters with images and Bertillon descriptions circulated widely across state and international agencies in this period. The use of Bertillon and fingerprinting data on the registration forms expanded state scrutiny of noncitizen German women as it had men months earlier and imposed the stigma of criminality upon them.

Women had to bring four copies of a photograph of themselves to register. Workers attached photos to three separate copies of the entire registration form, kept one copy locally at the police station or post office, sent another to the US marshal for Oregon's office, and sent a third to the DOJ in Washington, DC.[39] The fourth photograph became part of an "identification booklet" registrants had to keep on their person at all times. Local law enforcement personnel could require anyone they suspected of being a noncitizen enemy to produce their card and could search that person to find it. Those noncitizen Germans who failed to produce the booklet would be arrested. The booklet included the Bertillon information, a photograph, address, the date and place of registration, and the name of the police officer or post office employee in charge. Blank pages with spaces for official changes of address completed the booklet. Registrants had to return to the police station or post office to pick up the booklet and at that time provide a signature and left thumb print. The booklet warned registrants that they must comply with "any and all laws and regulations now existing or hereafter made concerning the conduct of alien enemies." Registrants had to agree to abide by laws and policies that *had not yet been created*, about which, the booklet made clear, there was to be no dissent.[40]

These policies established an ongoing system of scrutiny of noncitizen "enemy" Germans and the US-born wives of noncitizen German men supervised by the attorney general and the Department of Justice in tandem with law enforcement and post office staff in every community. Women's registration took place a month after Congress passed the Sedition Act in May 1918. Section 4 of the act expanded the powers of post office staff to read and report mail that might violate the law. Postal workers were now registering "enemy alien" women in towns of fewer than five thousand people, which meant they could increase their scrutiny of registrants' mail as persons of interest. Law enforcement and post office personnel in Oregon expanded and enhanced community surveillance even more by sharing names and often addresses with local newspapers for publication. This included people who had registered or had not registered, and sometimes both those who had not returned to pick up their registration cards and those who had changed their residence. Some newspapers provided workplace information.[41] When challenged about making personal information public, the Department of Justice ordered US marshals to keep the "affidavits . . . strictly confidential," but they could choose to publish information from a "Marshal's summary sheet" if "local conditions or the attitude of the aliens themselves may make it advisable to give full publicity to the registration."[42] Local officials also used data from the previous registration of noncitizen German men and military draft registration records to cross-check women's registration responses as part of extended families. "Officials have a check on the women through the registration of the men," the *Oregon Journal* reported, "and they expect to make use of this information soon after the registration offices close."[43]

Most newspaper editors reported slow registration in the early days in large and small communities. "Roseburg either has few alien women, or else they are very slow about registering," the editors of the *Roseburg Evening News* reported on June 21.[44] Registration was proceeding "very slowly" in Salem.[45] Only four women had registered in Medford by June

96 / CHAPTER 4

21, and "all the others must do so" by the June 26 deadline if they "desire to avoid trouble with the government."[46] Bend women read of "consequences of a serious nature," if they did not complete the process.[47] By the end of the first week, only 440 women (about half) had registered in Portland.[48] Police captain Leo Harms worried his office would be "swamped on the last few days."[49] He tried to frighten women into compliance. "A few minutes neglected effort may result in internment for the period of the war," he warned. "Promptly at 8 o'clock on June 26 the doors will shut and those women who should register but do not will face internment."[50]

Many women associated the police station and the required photographing and fingerprinting with criminality and "WANTED" posters, and threats of internment only increased these anxieties. The *Oregonian* reported the women registrants seemed "to have a horror of the registration." Many feared "they might never see the light of day again, once they are within the four walls of the police station."[51] One Portland woman declared that "it was bad enough having my picture taken," but the fingerprinting was "far worse" and she did not want to do it.[52] Portland police set women volunteers like clubwoman and Liberty Loan chair Sarah Evans to work directly with the registrants, but the two German/English interpreters were male police officers John Schum and John Wallbrook. This meant that women who needed translation assistance faced two uniformed men who represented the state that threatened to intern them.[53] "Morose and sullen" women, the editors of the *Portland Telegram* reported, registered by "force rather than choice."[54]

The laborious bureaucratic process combined with some women's particular needs and responses created additional complexities. Most wage-earning women on the day shift could come in only during their lunch hour.[55] Many women were not prepared with photographs. Others did not have all of the information required for the form and had to return on another day with the necessary documents. On the second registration day in Portland, 145 women came but only 29 completed the registration because they lacked these materials.[56] In Portland registration staff were "besieged hourly" by advocates for registrants "in the hope that some loophole may be found to evade registration."[57] At the Portland police station the two German/English interpreters were "kept busy all day." And the work was not limited to the spoken word. Some of the documents women brought with them were in German; some women completed

FIGURE 9 Volunteer Sarah Evans, *far right*, and Portland police captain Leo Harms, *far left*, work to register noncitizen "enemy" women at the Portland Police Station on the first day of female "enemy alien" registration, June 17, 1918. "German Alien Women Appear for Registry," *Oregon Journal*, June 17, 1918, 1.

the registration forms in "half German and half English," and these had to be rewritten.[58] A deaf woman at the Portland police station required additional interpreting assistance through the use of fingerspelling in addition to the German/English translation.[59] Captain Harms requested and received additional funding for the larger-than-imagined price tag "on account of the unexpected large number of registrants and extra work in registering these Alien Females." Portland had "nearly as many females registered as males during the recent registration," he said, "and [it was] much more complicated."[60]

Mapping the dates women registered certainly reflects these challenges with the paperwork and perhaps also the persistence of women and their advocates looking for the loopholes. Registration patterns suggest that in the calculus of fear and force, the published names and addresses and threats of arrest and internment after the process was under way may have motivated reluctant women to act. Women not born in the United States and those born in the United States who had lost their citizenship upon marriage to German citizen men all were slow to begin registering, with stronger activity just before the final deadline.

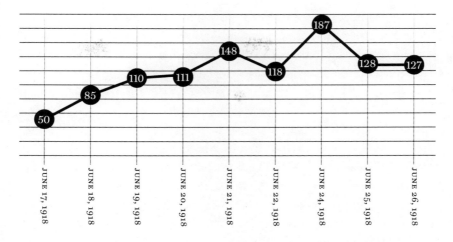

FIGURE 10 Oregon women not born in the United States by registration days. World War I Alien Registration Forms, MSS 1540, Oregon Historical Society Research Library, Portland.

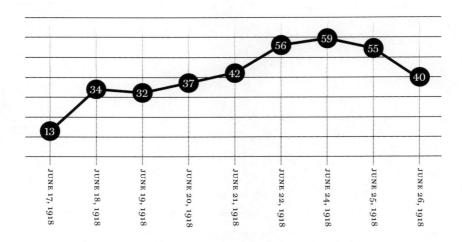

FIGURE 11 Oregon women born in the United States by registration days. World War I Alien Registration Forms, MSS 1540, Oregon Historical Society Research Library, Portland.

Many women chose to resist registration in a variety of ways. Some made direct protests in person when they came to register. One Portland woman asked why she was forced to register when she had been born in the United States. "If I had any pro-German tendencies," she said, "to have to register and have my thumb prints taken, will not less[en] any such tendency. I declare it is an outrage and uncalled for."[61] Another Portland woman, born in Germany, with two sons in the US Army, brought photographs of her sons in uniform with her to show that by virtue of their service she need not register. When told she would still need to enroll, the woman protested: "I think that it is just a money-making scheme between the police and the photographers."[62] About half of the US-born women resisted by reframing the registration form itself. The DOJ constructed the form without accounting for US-born women who had lost their US citizenship upon marriage to German-citizen men. Line 8 asked registrants to complete the phase "I arrived in the United States" and to give the date and asked for other information about entry points and the specific ship on which they took passage. Almost half of the US-born women chose to make statements emphasizing their US birth rather than leave these areas blank. Some wrote "Born Here" or "Born in the United States" in the space for the arrival date. Maggie Kiss wrote that she had arrived in the United States "on August 3, 1886," which was the date of her birth. Several other women followed suit.[63]

Many of the photographs for the forms and identity booklets suggest additional ways women challenged "alien enemy" registration and their designation as dangerous internal enemies by local and national authorities. Noncitizen enemy registration took place in the midst of a large-scale popularization and vigorous promotion of studio and amateur photography in the United States. In 1918, Portland had fifty-four photography studios; Astoria, four; The Dalles, five; Salem, six.[64] Millions of Americans had their own cameras: they were affordable, portable, and easy to use.[65] Advertisements in newspapers across Oregon in urban areas and rural counties—from drug stores, opticians, jewelers, department stores, and professional studios—emphasized the ease of use and the affordability of cameras, film, and development.[66] This meant that many Oregonians took and developed their own photographs. The Portland registrant who believed the process was no more than a "money-making scheme between the police and the photographers" may indeed have observed opportu-

100 / CHAPTER 4

FIGURE 12 Eugenie Kromminga, Reedsport, Oregon, 1918. World War I Alien Registration Forms, Oregon, MSS 1540, Oregon Historical Society Research Library, Portland.

nistic amateur or professional photographers hoping for business on the path to the police station. But many women and their friends and families also had ready access to cameras and film.

Registration file photographs demonstrate that some of the women required to register as noncitizen enemies exercised a measure of control and creativity in defining how they would represent themselves. Some registrants created photographs emphasizing their individuality rather than conforming to expectations of how an "enemy alien" woman might appear, and some challenged the requirement the image should contain just the head and shoulders with the head uncovered.[67] Twenty-three-year-old Meta Koehring of Salem chose a smiling picture of herself in her nurses' uniform at her job at the Oregon State Hospital, perhaps to emphasize her role as a contributing worker in the state. It may also have been an image taken previously as part of her employment.[68] Anna Bertha Neureither, whose husband was a butcher, wore a formal dress and jewelry and gazed

"ALIEN" ENEMIES / 101

FIGURE 13
Sister Mary Stanislaus (Victoria Schindler), Cook at St. Benedict's School, Woodburn, Oregon. World War I Alien Registration Forms, Oregon, MSS 1540, Oregon Historical Society Research Library, Portland.

out the window of her Roseburg home.[69] Mathilde Schafer, wife of a gold mine owner in Kerby, near the California border, chose to have her photograph taken behind a desk with a blotter and stack of books, holding a sheaf of papers in her hand in a scholar's pose. Her daughter, Pauline Elsbeth, used the same desk and book stack and held a pen and paper.[70] Reedsport resident Eugenie Kromminga was lead hand at P. Reed's farm near the southern Oregon Coast, living with a second husband and eight children. Kromminga presented in trousers, a long-sleeved shirt, and a tie with hair cut short, standing in front of a farmhouse porch with a white sheet as a backdrop.[71]

Thirty-six other photographs of Catholic Religious Sisters in Oregon registering as noncitizen "enemies" represent a successful challenge to part of the regulations. On the eve of registration, Attorney General Gregory "recognized the claims of many religious sects which make it imperative for female members" to wear head coverings. He "modified the ruling" that required women to be photographed with heads uncovered.[72] In Oregon the thirty-six Catholic sisters who registered with photographs in their complete habits were teachers, nurses, administrators, seamstresses, laundry workers, cooks, cleaners, and a typesetter in hospitals, academies, and convents across the state in Portland, Beaverton, Mt. Angel, Woodburn, Baker, Pendleton, La Grande, and Ontario.[73]

Noncitizen enemy registration collided with other complicated life situations. Grace Crocker Reimers, born in the United States, had to redefine the state's classification of her as an "enemy alien" in divorce proceedings. Reimers's German-citizen husband, Paul, left Portland on August 3, 1914, after Germany declared war on Russia and France, to join the German military. Reimers had a son just over a month old to support. That November, when the United States was still a neutral nation, the *Sunday Oregonian* featured Reimers in a sympathetic story about "war-widows" in Portland whose husbands were serving in the various combatant armies. But by May 1918, having not had word from Paul and facing the question of her need to register as a noncitizen enemy, Reimers filed for divorce. At the same time, she complied with regulations and registered as a noncitizen German on June 25, 1918, the second-to-last day. Reimers and her lawyers were successful in having her status placed on hold while waiting for her divorce decree, which came on September 5. Reimers identified herself in divorce and registration proceedings as a loyal American woman supporting a child, abandoned by a husband loyal to Germany. This was particularly important because Reimers worked as a clerk with the Oregon and Washington Railway and Navigation Company located in the waterfront zone prohibited to noncitizen Germans without a permit. Her livelihood and support of her family was at stake.[74]

Hattie Burbank Dahrens felt the power of community and family scrutiny over her marriage to a German noncitizen amplified by the surveillance of local and state officials. Born in rural Airlie, in the Willamette Valley's Polk County in 1899, Hattie was the eleventh child in a family of thirteen whose parents had both been born in Oregon. Her father was a dairy farmer and cattle rancher, and the extended Burbank family was prominent in local community life.[75] In the prewar years Hattie kept house for her older brothers near home and also engaged in the seasonal work of harvesting cascara bark in Sherwood, Oregon, west of Portland.[76] Somewhere in or around this work in the woods, Hattie met Adolph Dahrens, whose jobs as a logger with various companies had taken him across forests in Oregon and southwestern Washington. The couple married on July 12 and resided in Sandy, in rural Clackamas County east of Portland. Adolph, born in Germany in 1890, had come to the United States in 1895 and had applied for his "first papers" in 1916 and was thus not yet a US citizen. From Sandy he had registered for the draft in June 1917, and as a

German noncitizen "enemy" in February 1918, so information about his citizenship status was on file. Their marriage on July 12 therefore followed female German noncitizen registration at the end of June. Hattie became an unregistered "alien enemy" the moment she wed because of the federal Expatriation Act of 1907.[77]

Postal employees, in charge of registration in small towns and rural areas and in a position to monitor local gossip and the mail, and with more surveillance power after Congress passed the Sedition Act, were conduits for information about Hattie and Adolph. Twelve days after their marriage, Sherwood, Oregon, postmaster M. M. Fitch wrote to Frank S. Myers, the Portland postmaster assigned the job of "Chief Registrar" for noncitizen Germans in the aftermath of the registrations. "This case was reported to the Carrier on route No. 4 by the [woman's] own people who had strongly objected to the marriage. I am also given to understand the young lady has stated that she would not register as an Alien Enemy." US Marshal Alexander cross-checked Adolph's draft and German noncitizen enemy registrations and then drew upon the postal service network to contact Charles D. Purcell, postmaster for Sandy. Alexander provided the particulars, including the date Adolph registered with Purcell as an "enemy alien," asked Purcell to investigate and to "advise Mrs. Dahrens that she must register with you as a German alien" because of her marriage. Hattie, facing family and state scrutiny and with a penalty of imprisonment at stake, capitulated, filled out the forms, and provided the affidavit.[78] After the war Dahrens regained her US citizenship when Adolph completed the requirements for naturalization in December 1920.[79]

POLICING GENDER IDENTITY
THROUGH "ENEMY ALIEN" REGISTRATION

The stated purpose of registering and surveilling noncitizen German residents was to protect the wartime nation from disloyalty and dangerous internal enemies. But the case of a gender-nonconforming person known to authorities as Thomas Riedl demonstrates how representatives of the state could take surveillance policies far beyond their stated scope to police gender identity. In Riedl's case, officials used penalties designed to punish "enemy aliens" to instead persecute what they considered gender

FIGURE 14 Thomas Riedl, Oregon City, Oregon, 1918. World War I Alien Registration Forms, Oregon, MSS 1540, Oregon Historical Society Research Library, Portland.

transgression. Born in Germany in 1891, Riedl came to the United States in 1913 presenting officially as a man, applied for first citizenship papers in New York in 1915, and registered for the draft in San Francisco on the first Selective Service day on June 5, 1917. By that November, Riedl had found work in a paper mill in Oregon City, some twenty miles from Portland. Riedl registered with the Oregon City postmaster as an "enemy alien" on February 7, 1918, during the period for men's registration. Riedl was among thirty-one individuals the newspaper identified publicly as German "enemy alien" men in Oregon City, a town of some forty-five hundred people.[80]

Two months later, on April 14, 1918, the Oregon City sheriff and a deputy US attorney were hunting for another suspect on the suspension bridge that crossed the Willamette River connecting Oregon City with the town of West Linn. They noted that Riedl, walking on the same bridge, seemed nervous. The men took Riedl to the police station for questioning and discovered Riedl's noncitizen German "enemy" registration papers. Because regulations stated no "alien enemy" was to walk on a bridge, the sheriff used this information to raid Riedl's room in the city's Electric Hotel. Officers found "several complete female outfits," including "wigs, corsets, skirts, etc." Riedl initially denied owning the clothing and claimed it had been left by a previous tenant but "later admitted" to purchasing

"ALIEN" ENEMIES / 105

"part of the outfit in Oregon City," a detail corroborated by the store owner. Authorities brought the clothing and other items to the jail, forced Riedl to "dress up," and concluded Riedl "could easily pass for a female."[81]

On the afternoon of April 16 district attorney Gilbert Hedges and E. C. Latourette, special assistant US attorney, escorted Riedl to Portland to face US attorney Bert Haney.[82] During his 1918–1920 tenure Haney initiated the surveillance and prosecution of Portland physician and labor activist Marie Equi, other socialists, and political radicals in Oregon.[83] Just one month into his tenure, Haney's handling of the Riedl case demonstrated that he was willing to use penalties designed to punish noncitizen Germans to persecute a person who broke the sanctioned rules of gender presentation. Newspaper editors and Haney took two different paths designed to define and punish Riedl. Editors cast Riedl as a cross-dressing spy, discounting the possibility that a "man" would present as a woman for any other reason. Haney saw Riedl as a "sexual pervert," acknowledged Riedl's gender boundary crossing, and punished Riedl with incarceration in a camp for "alien enemy" men at Fort Douglas, Utah, for the duration of the war.

The editors of the *Oregon City Courier*, the *Oregon City Enterprise*, and the Portland *Oregonian* all concluded that Riedl was a German spy whose "female impersonation" was no more than a clever strategic disguise. Their coverage of the story included lengthy details of "incriminating" items at Riedl's residence at Oregon City's Electric Hotel in addition to the "complete female outfits." All of these items, the editors surmised, pointed to espionage. Investigators found maps, "crayons suitable for sketching," flashlights, correspondence in German, evidence that Riedl had served in the German military, a mysterious badge "similar to those issued to employees at the aviation fields," several passports, cash, and a loaded revolver. The editors of the *Oregon City Courier* referred to Riedl as a "Wilhelm Agent," a spy for Kaiser Wilhelm II of Germany, and the editors of the *Oregon City Enterprise* and the *Oregonian* called Riedl a "German spy suspect." All three newspapers reported that it was after the discovery of the "complete female outfits" in Riedl's room that authorities found Riedl to be a "female impersonator," suggesting that Riedl was not presenting as a woman when meeting authorities on the Oregon City suspension bridge.[84]

In his official report on the Riedl case dated April 22, 1918, Haney told Attorney General Gregory that people in Oregon City had jumped to conclusions about espionage. "Being an alien enemy and found in women's attire, the rumor at once spread that there was a German spy in the toils," he wrote. Here Haney suggested that authorities had encountered Riedl in women's clothing on the bridge, not that they had only discovered "female impersonation" after the room search. Haney sent a special agent to Oregon City to investigate "and after a thorough investigation of [Riedl's] effects, came to the conclusion that [Riedl] was nothing but a plain pervert." Haney confirmed this verdict with his subsequent investigation and in his own interview with Riedl in Portland. Documentation showed that Riedl had been in the German army for only ten weeks before coming to the States and had complied with both the US Selective Service draft registration and noncitizen German "enemy" registration requirements. Riedl had come to Oregon City after "working at odd jobs in different parts of the country." Riedl had a revolver, had been discovered crossing a bridge on foot, had been in Portland several times, and had probably come within a half mile of the Portland Armory without a permit—all of which were against federal policy regulating noncitizen enemies. But Haney believed Riedl's claim not to have known that these were regulations.[85]

With these pieces of circumstantial evidence plus the loaded revolver, Haney could have requested a federal order of internment for Riedl based on violations of the president's Alien Enemy Proclamation. Others were interned for less. But Haney chose to use the "enemy alien" policy as a path to punish Riedl for crossing gender presentation boundaries. "In a personal interview with him, he impressed me as being of a low, immoral type," Haney informed the attorney general. "I am of the opinion that he would be a dangerous man to be at large." Haney did not feel that Riedl had really violated enemy alien policy but named Riedl a dangerous internal enemy and ordered Riedl's internment for the duration of the war "for the best interests of the community as well as for [Riedl's] own protection" because Riedl was a "degenerate and addicted to wearing female clothes."[86] On May 11, 1918, less than a month after Oregon City authorities detained Riedl on the suspension bridge, the *Oregonian* reported that authorities had taken Riedl and two other German citizen "enemies" to Vancouver Barracks in Washington State, "on the first lap of their journey to Fort

Douglas, Utah, where they will be detained until the close of the war."[87] Riedl survived this wartime incarceration and appears on a May 29, 1919, list of internees at Fort Douglas requesting repatriation to Germany.[88]

The Armistice ending the war came on November 11, 1918, and on December 23, 1918, President Wilson, in preliminary peace talks in Paris and at the recommendation of Attorney General Gregory, issued a proclamation rescinding the orders for registration of noncitizen enemies, including all regulations relating to women registrants. The federal government retained some restrictions on noncitizen "enemy" travel and for those who had been incarcerated. Gregory sent detailed instructions to US Attorney Haney and US Marshal Alexander making the change effective December 25, 1918. The Department of Justice issued a press release explaining the situation to residents: "On Christmas day the permit and pass system . . . will be abolished all over the country and . . . all prohibited areas and restricted zones will go out of existence. All registration regulations will likewise cease." No change of residence permits would be required moving forward. Former noncitizen "enemies" would now be "freed of all restrictions affecting places of residence and employment."[89]

Rescinding regulations about noncitizen "enemy" registration did not repair the damage to people and civil liberties in Oregon and the nation. Policymakers and people invested in extending wartime fears and discrimination continued to treat many German Americans as dangerous internal enemies following the war. Individuals, their families, and communities lived with the consequences. And noncitizen "enemy" registration during the First World War provided context and lessons for the registration of noncitizen "enemies" of combatant nations during the Second World War. In the United States the Alien Registration Act of 1940 required every noncitizen to register, and Japanese Americans who were noncitizens and citizens alike were designated as dangerous internal enemies and incarcerated during the conflict.[90]

The registration of noncitizen "enemies" in Oregon and the nation was a powerful example of the official naming and policing of people considered dangerous internal enemies by their status as a group rather than by any actions on their part. "Enemy alien" policy went beyond the requirement to register to be visible to law enforcement and included restrictions on civil liberties and everyday life for registrants. "Enemy alien" registration was also a central process in the growth of the wartime surveillance state.

Registration created a new surveillance product with the extensive details in the registration file and the photo identification booklet required to be on one's person and producible on demand. The May 1918 Sedition Act enhanced the power of post office staff who registered and policed noncitizen enemy women. Law enforcement in Oregon and the nation expanded to increase scrutiny and manage the "enemy alien" bureaucracy. Newspaper editors cooperated by publishing names and addresses of those who registered and those who did not. And the fact that more than one-fourth of the Oregon women who registered had been born in the United States but had lost their citizenship upon marriage to German citizen men underscored the double standard of women's achievement of independent voting rights as citizens but having that citizenship tied specifically to a husband's nationality if married. Resistance included speaking against the registration at enrollment sites, subverting the registration form in ways to gain some agency and identity in the process, and finding ways through the six months of living within the restrictions until they were lifted at the end of 1918.

Riedl's detention and incarceration for challenging sanctioned gender roles and gender presentation is an important example of the way that policing for "enemy aliens" created parallel scrutiny for gender-noncon-forming people. Margot Canaday demonstrates that immigration and military officials were policing immigrants, draftees, and enlistees for "perverse practices" and for having "perverse bodies" at a time when the "sex pervert" as a type was entering medical, legal, and eugenical thinking and systems of policing.[91] Eugenic thinking and policies in Oregon also identified "sexual perverts" as enemies to be excluded or punished with sterilization. And Riedl was among the noncitizen enemies interned at Fort Douglas who asked to be repatriated to Germany at the close of their incarceration, an example of the "voluntary" deportation Adam Goodman makes visible in the long history of deportation from the nation.[92]

CHAPTER 5

Held for Health

US PARTICIPATION IN THE FIRST WORLD WAR created a new urgency about controlling the home front that made women's bodies and projects against sexually transmitted infections (STIS) vital national security matters with campaigns that labeled women with STIS and prostitutes as dangerous internal enemies.[1] Wartime fears and opportunities created an emergency to add urgency and funding to ongoing programs about social hygiene and expanded the reach of federal, state, and local surveillance systems against women far beyond the war years. Oregon had significant firsts in social hygiene and anti–venereal disease campaigns during and after the war, and diverse Oregonians were caught up on all sides of these movements. Social hygienists created a coalition to work against venereal disease, prostitution, gambling, alcohol consumption, and to support eugenic measures and sex education.[2]

Oregon's distinctive developments included an early social hygiene movement with statewide and local funding that led to the establishment of The Cedars, the nation's first detention home specifically for women with STIS. Portland and Oregon ordinances and laws directed against the people Portland policewoman Lola Baldwin referred to as the "Venereal Girls" became models for other national anti-STI and anti-prostitution legislation.[3] Oregon policymakers developed a long-standing "hold for health" tool for law enforcement and a "health parole" outside of due process protections that impacted Oregon women through the 1970s. And the links between Oregon's early and active state sterilization policies and anti–venereal disease social hygiene campaigns provide insights into how eugenic thinking influenced multiple state projects targeting women considered to be internal enemies. The story of the violations of civil liberties of incarcerated women is also a record of resistance, including legal challenges, escapes from incarceration, and everyday defiance and survival.

Many thoughtful scholars have outlined the contours of the "American Plan" to detain women during the conflict and beyond. In the early twentieth century the scientific view competed with a "moral" view of sexually transmitted diseases in public policy: were syphilis and gonorrhea contagious diseases to be treated, or "immoral" conditions for which their sufferers should be punished? What were the public health and civil liberties questions about individuals versus the needs of communities to be healthy and safe? Anti–venereal disease campaigns targeted women in these campaigns with powerful double standards. Before sulpha drugs and penicillin, Wassermann blood tests and the new syphilis treatment Neosalvarsan were not always reliably administered nor standardized, and with false positives all raised the question of reliability. Complicated tests for gonorrhea made cures elusive. Public health officials and physicians struggled with the social, medical, and legal question of reporting the "medical secret."[4] An analysis of the Oregon experience in anti–venereal disease campaigns provides important details in the broader national story as it deepens our understanding of the many comparative elements of civil liberties and citizenship questions developing in the state and nation in this period.

"VENEREAL GIRLS" AND SOCIAL HYGIENE IN OREGON

In the early twentieth century, many women in Portland and other Oregon cities including Salem and Astoria, like their counterparts across the nation, navigated a new world of popular amusements such as dance and pool halls, parks, roadhouses, and movie theaters. Here young women found space away from adult chaperonage. Some negotiated new rules of "treating" by providing intimacy or intercourse in exchange for a partner's paying for a day at the amusement park or evening out, especially because most young women were living on low wages. Others welcomed the chance to explore same-sex or heterosexual intimacy in the new world of the industrial city that brought workers from around the state and across national borders. People engaged in nonsanctioned sex for a variety of reasons in both urban and rural areas. Some sexual activity was coercive, demanded by employers, coworkers, or partners. Pregnancy could have served as a strategy for marriage and even greater economic stability, perhaps over family objections. These developments often caused intergenerational conflicts in immigrant and working-class families and strengthened elite and middle-class reformers' goals to control diverse women's sexuality. And reformers joined with "medical and psychiatric experts" to turn "single working women's leisure habits into a social problem."[5]

Portland and Oregon were at the forefront of work associated with social hygiene and anti–venereal disease programs in this period. Organizers established the Oregon Social Hygiene Society (OSHS) several years in advance of the national organization. William T. Foster, president of both the state society and Reed College, publicized the work to the rest of the nation early in the movement, helping to establish Oregon's social hygiene reputation and lay the groundwork for wartime action.[6] With support from and energized by OSHS campaigns, Portland was among twenty US cities from 1910 to 1916, and the only city west of Denver, to fund a commission to investigate the causes of and the remedies for vice in the community. Portland's vice commissioners produced six separate reports in 1912 formally published together in January 1913 with subcommittee reports to follow. Gloria Myers notes that at least a third of the members of the various Portland vice committees were affiliated directly with the OSHS.[7] Much of the what the commissioners reported and recommended targeted women's sexuality. Commissioners placed Portland women who engaged in unsanctioned sexual activity on a scale of declining "moral delinquency" from heterosexual experimentation to prostitution that mirrored the national conversation on vice matters.[8] Portland's vice commissioners confined their discussion of same-sex intimacy to several paragraphs concerning "sex perversion" among men with reference to Portland's 1912–1913 vice scandal.[9] But beyond the report, "female perverts"—women who loved other women, and other gender-nonconforming people—were also on the minds of social hygienists in Oregon.[10]

Women's bodies were under surveillance, and city officials believed women were responsible for that scrutiny and for any violence that might happen as a result. In the summer of 1913, Portland was apparently experiencing an epidemic of "mashers"—that is, men who stalked women on the streets and in shops and on streetcars. In July, Portland police chief John Clark announced that "Mashers Must Go" and instructed officers to be on the lookout for men following women and making sexual advances toward them. Clark and others believed that "the evil seems to have increased with the prevailing spectacular style of dress adopted by many women."[11] Mayor H. Russell Albee agreed, and on August 19, he issued a

112 / CHAPTER 5

citywide ban on women wearing "scanty or suggestive attire" on the city streets, particularly a sheer "X-ray gown" then being popularized. Police had instructions to observe all women in the city to determine the legality of their dress. Albee noted that although the order was "a rather drastic one," he had done it to protect "the young men and women of Portland, in an effort to uphold the morals of the city. The matter had gone so far," Albee said, "that young boys and men would congregate on the street and make obscene remarks about the dresses worn by some of the women passing." These forms of women's dress, he concluded, came from prostitutes of the vice "underworld," and "their object will be apparent to all at first thought." For Albee, any woman who dressed in the banned clothing could be considered a prostitute and, like the chief of police, he felt that she was responsible for violence against her.[12] The dress ban on the X-ray gown and punishment of women wearing it suggests powerful ways in which many people saw women's bodies and sexuality as a threat to the community at the time of Portland's Vice Commission report.

The Vice Commission's work led to the later creation of The Cedars, the nation's first detention home specifically for incarcerating women with STIS via quarantine that became a national wartime model. Reformers called for an end to the system of arrest, fining, release, and rearresting prostitutes with the consecutive fines enriching the city's coffers and advocated for the detention and rehabilitation of women who engaged in sex work. Vice commissioners hoped city officials would invest quickly in detention facilities, but The Cedars was not completed until August 1918, when the urgency of the wartime "American Plan" campaign against women with STIS provided funding. Yet the same blueprint for the incarceration of "Venereal Girls" was part of the Portland plan from the beginning: in July 1913 a separate Detention Home Subcommittee of the Vice Commission created plans for the women's facility that would eventually become The Cedars.[13]

Many women in Oregon and the nation embraced social hygiene as one of the various reform programs of the Progressive Era. One of the appeals of anti-vice projects across the nation, as Mara Keire demonstrates, was that activists crafted a message about a broad "vice trust" that fit in with larger Progressive Era reform challenges to industrial capitalism with similar legislative strategies.[14] In her study of San Antonio, Courtney Shah found that anti-vice crusades "reconfirmed divisions among women" as

HELD FOR HEALTH / 113

"middle-class white reformers" sought "greater political power, [and] in so doing they denied the same right and privileges to working-class and nonwhite women."[15] White medical women in Oregon had a limited relationship with the OSHS. Some male physicians participated in the OSHS, but most women doctors did not, and those who did engaged primarily in talks with women and girls around the state at workplaces, schools, and clubs, as did a few White clubwomen. Women could only join the OSHS in a separate category of membership, still paying full membership dues, "but this class of members" was "not entitled to sit on the executive committee or hold office."[16] Portland policewoman Lola Baldwin served on a short-lived OSHS women's committee in 1916–1917 and was a vice commissioner for just two months before resigning because of time commitments. However, her work kept her in constant touch with incarcerated women, including at The Cedars. Labor advocate Millie Trumbull was the only woman to serve for the entire length of the Vice Commission's tenure through 1913. Three women joined Trumbull and six men on the commission's Detention Home and Venereal Disease Hospital Subcommittee: clubwoman Aristina Felts, Portland society leader Gretchen Hoyt Corbett, and Portland physician Sarah Whiteside.[17] After the creation of The Cedars for interning women, White clubwomen advocated for seats for women on the managing board, and OSHS social worker Anna Murphy lobbied women's organizations across the city for donations and placements for women paroled from The Cedars until it closed in 1923.[18]

Members of Portland's Colored Women's Council mirrored the concerns of Black clubwomen across the nation about the intersection of racism and gender discrimination within the justice system and in the anti-vice and anti–venereal disease campaigns. In the fall of 1917, when Portland began incarcerating women for STIs, Black women formed a Colored Women's Protective Association to work with Judge George Rossman of the Portland Municipal Court to support Black women in the system, including women suspected of venereal disease and prostitution. Members of the Portland Colored Women's Council, led by Emma K. Griffin Stanley, worked with OSHS social worker Anna Murphy beginning in 1918, continuing what Murphy called the "committee to care for their girls in court."[19] And activist Lizzie K. Weeks won and held a position at the

114 / CHAPTER 5

Portland Court of Domestic Relations, which had the power to sentence women to The Cedars, as a probation officer in 1920.[20]

"PORTLANDIZING" WOMEN

When the United States entered the war, the War Department's Commission on Training Camp Activities (CTCA) took a major role in policing sex work, alcohol sale and consumption, and other "vice" activities near home front army and navy training centers, enforcing the War Department's imperative to keep soldiers "fit to fight" and out of danger from sexually transmitted infections. Authorities focused blame on women for transmitting STIs and treated but did not exempt men with STIs from military duty fearing "they might otherwise deliberately secure infections to avoid service." The War Department and CTCA were empowered and funded in this work by the rules legislators wrote directly into the Selective Service Act of May 1917. The CTCA and a coalition of other reform and wartime organizations worked to pressure communities to target and remove women sex workers. Portland—unlike the other West Coast ports of Seattle, San Francisco, and San Diego—did not have an army or navy cantonment. But Oregonians and Portlanders were caught up in the need to demonstrate loyal patriotism. Many calculated the potential profits a strong relationship with the military could bring with shipbuilding, lumber mills, and other wartime sources of federal dollars in addition to the spending money of soldiers on leave from Camp Lewis and Vancouver Barracks in Washington State just north of Portland. The CTCA urged cities to act locally and proactively to comply in vice control but also threatened to make a noncompliant city off-limits to soldiers and their pay packets, a public shaming the CTCA gave to Seattle briefly in late 1917 and early 1918.[21]

Portland officials responded directly to the CTCA anti-prostitution and anti–venereal disease program beginning in early November 1917 with a series of "cleanup raids" by the Portland police in the city's North End to "make the city safe for soldiers." Police arrested over one hundred women suspected of prostitution for violating Oregon's extensive 1911 Vagrancy Act in coordinated raids that November—sixty-six on the first night alone. Police took women to the station for booking and to be tested for STIs at the city's Emergency Hospital located on the fourth floor of the police station, staffed by the city health officer and two medical student interns. Bail was set at $100 per person, a sum nearly all except several Black women arrested were able to raise.[22] The *Oregon Journal* reported that the "general rumor at police headquarters" attributed the raids to "threats from the commanding officers at Vancouver barracks that if the city was not cleaned up, Portland would be blacklisted the same as Seattle as far as soldiers were concerned."[23]

At the same time, a coalition of Oregon officials and reformers were on hand with a ready-made plan for interning the women caught up in the raids, reviving the blueprints for a detention jail and hospital for women near Portland that had been stalled for lack of funds since the 1913 Vice Commission recommendations. The timing of the vice raids was no accident. After the "cleanup" the *Portland Evening Telegram* reported the "first problem confronting the authorities is what to do with the women who are afflicted with disease and are a menace." And "if the work is to continue," it was clear that "an internment camp or quarantine station will have to be provided." Oregon attorney John McCourt represented the CTCA in the region and joined members of the OSHS, including David Robinson (the society's new counsel for law enforcement and prostitution control), in pressing for meetings and action. They were poised with the public knowledge of the unfolding raids against sex workers, unconfirmed but widely circulated press reports that 40 percent of the women arrested tested positively for syphilis, and the certainty that local officials would want to work with the CTCA to boost Portland's economy and reputation as a loyal, patriotic city rather than face negative consequences for inaction. Before the end of November, city, county, and social hygiene leaders brokered a deal for funding a women's detention home to be constructed in Multnomah County with funding from the city and county. Women would be detained in temporary facilities at Kelly Butte, the county's "rock pile" stockade jail, until the permanent facility could be constructed.[24] The "war on vice" was "a patriotic duty," the editors of the *Oregonian* declared in Oregon First language. "Portland has shown the way and it is up to other cities to follow."[25]

Observing from his vantage point in Seattle, Horace R. Clayton, editor of the city's weekly Black newspaper, voiced his concerns about civil liberties violations in Portland's new plan of action and adopted a phrase that underscored the city's leading role in wartime detention of women. "To

116 / CHAPTER 5

intern or Portlandize fallen women," he wrote, "means the corralling of them on acre tracts, where comfortable quarters are prepared and then all of them put at gainful occupations." And "whether the constitutions of the various states are sufficiently elastic to intern women who are guilty of no crime save that of immorality, is a question for the courts to determine." Clayton had "little or no faith in this interning proposition," in Portland, he wrote, nor in the "cleanups" the CTCA was ordering in cities like Portland and Seattle all around the country.[26]

Two Portland city ordinances, passed in record time, provided the legal machinery for officials to "Portlandize" women and became model policies for the region and nation. The first was Ordinance 33510 Providing for the Suppression of Venereal Diseases passed by the city council on November 23, 1917. The ordinance declared venereal disease dangerous to the public health, added syphilis and gonorrhea to the list of mandatory reported diseases, and gave health officers power to examine all "persons reasonably suspected" of carrying syphilis or gonorrhea. And "owing to the prevalence of such diseases among prostitutes," anyone officials could label a possible prostitute was automatically "reasonably suspected." City officials were to "use all proper means of suppressing" prostitution. Significantly, exposing someone else to an STI became a crime—an "unlawful" act. The ordinance defined detention as "isolation" for quarantine and decreed that no one other than medical personnel could "enter or leave the area of isolation" without specific permission from the city health officer, including legal system advocates. Persons with permission from the mayor could post a $1,000 bond and engage in private treatment with physicians. Portland officials adopted the elements of "reasonable suspicion," and considering all prostitutes as suspects from the California law passed a month earlier in October 1917. But the Portland provision that the act of spreading venereal disease was unlawful seems to have been a singular development, one that other cities and states adopted beginning in 1918.[27]

The Suppression of Venereal Disease ordinance was based on a series of civic double standards. Even though much of the language was gender-neutral, in practice persecution and prosecution focused on women. The model became one of free or reduced treatment for men with STIs and the surveillance of women suspected of venereal disease because of their appearance or behavior, and their subsequent incarceration. The ordinance contained a powerful class bias with the provision for posting

HELD FOR HEALTH / 117

a $1,000 bond. But the ability to post bond did not mean authorities accepted it. Cultural assumptions about working-class women and women of color as more likely to engage in unsanctioned sexual behavior and prostitution were embedded in these civic double standards. Throughout the war and postwar years the city council added teeth to the ordinance, with these basic premises at the foundation of policy and practice moving forward.

Next, Portland City Council members established an innovative way to control prostitution and unsanctioned sex activity by passing Ordinance 33649 Providing for the Regulation of Hotels, Rooming Houses, and Lodging Houses on January 2, 1918. The ordinance required anyone operating a hotel, rooming house, or lodging house to have an annual license from the city, and all applicants had to be "of good moral character." License holders could not permit their property to be used "as a house of ill-fame, brothel, bawdy house or disorderly house, for the purpose of prostitution, fornication, or lewdness; or suffer any lascivious cohabitation, adultery, fornication, or other immoral practice to be carried on therein." Managers had to keep a register and were prohibited from assigning a room to persons of the opposite sex unless they were husband and wife or were siblings accompanied by parents or guardians. The register was to be "open at all times for inspection" by police or city officials or by "any guest of the house," who presumably could be another agent of surveillance. The long list of prohibited practices made virtually any hotel or rooming house owner at risk and assured that residents or guests engaged in sex outside of heterosexual marriage were vulnerable to prosecution for vagrancy or other charges, including the "unlawful act" of spreading an STI from the November 1917 ordinance. The hotel ordinance empowered the city and police to "examine into and investigate the character and qualifications of applicants for licenses within the meaning of this ordinance" and report findings to the city council for approval of or to revoke a license.[28]

Astoria, a city of ten thousand at the mouth of the Columbia River with the army's Fort Stevens ten miles away, had its own "cleanup" on a smaller scale. The city council had pressure from the army but also Portland's models to follow. Members debated "closing all gambling and houses of prostitution, and ordering the inmates of such places out of the city limits of Astoria" in May 1917, a month after the United States entered the war. That October, Fort Stevens officials contacted the city with worries about "moral conditions" and called for a stricter curfew ordinance enforcement. At the request of Fort Stevens leaders in November, Clatsop County health officer Nellie Vernon worked with the city council to establish a detention hospital for women with STIs at the County Poor Farm. By April 2, 1918, the city and county had worked out a funding plan, with Clatsop County providing twenty-five dollars a month for each woman detained, and the City of Astoria sharing the salary of a matron with the county and funding the cost of medicine. In January 1918, Astoria city councilors passed both Portland's venereal disease suppression and hotel ordinances just weeks after their Portland counterparts placed them on the books.[29]

OREGON FIRSTS AND THE MACHINERY OF VENEREAL SURVEILLANCE

Portland and Oregon had considerable influence on the next steps in federal action for detention homes and in the administration of national wartime venereal disease policy, particularly with two well-placed social hygiene advocates who relocated to work in Washington, DC: Harry Moore and David Robinson. Leaders in the CTCA and War Department, the Council of National Defense, and the US Public Health Service worked with Oregon senator George E. Chamberlain (D) and California representative Julius Kahn (R) to attach a venereal disease funding package (designated Chapter 15) to the Army Appropriations Act of 1918. Moore, OSHS executive secretary, went to Washington, DC, in December 1917 to accept a position as secretary of the recently formed Civilian Committee to Combat Venereal Disease of the Council of National Defense. He was the central facilitator and author of Chapter 15 of the Chamberlain-Kahn Act, with heavy direct and indirect lobbying from the OSHS. Chamberlain-Kahn passed both houses unanimously in July 1918 and made available over $4 million during the war and postwar periods disbursed to states through the US Public Health Service. Chamberlain-Kahn facilitated the formation of a federal anti–venereal disease bureaucracy with the Interdepartmental Social Hygiene Board and the Division of Venereal Diseases of the US Public Health Service to administer policies and state funding.[30] Robinson, former Portland public defender and legal counsel for the OSHS, left Portland in December 1918 for Washington, DC, to serve as law enforcement director of the Public Health Service and legal liaison with the CTCA with particular focus on venereal disease matters. He also provided counsel to the Interdepartmental Social Hygiene Board.[31] Moore and Robinson were in place to promote Portland and Oregon's social hygiene vision for detention homes and venereal disease control in federal policy.

The journey of the Portland hotel and rooming house licensing ordinance from the city's Vice Commission recommendation to national policy model provides a strong case in point. Portland reformers had been trying to get a city hotel licensing ordinance to stick on the books since the 1912–1913 Vice Commission recommendations. Before the twentieth century, most states had laws against houses of prostitution based on their common law definition as a nuisance, and by 1915 eighteen states, including Oregon in 1913, had passed injunction and abatement laws based on Iowa's innovative 1907 statute that allowed residents to bring legal action against owners of properties where they believed sex workers were operating.[32] The Portland City Council passed two anti-prostitution ordinances in the fall of 1912 in the wake of the Vice Commission study and recommendations based on the connections commissioners made between sex work and hotels and rooming houses.

The first ordinance, known as the Tin Plate Law, was based on the Iowa statute requiring owners of hotels, boarding houses, and saloons to post their name and address on a readily visible sign or plate for public inspection. The second, the hotel bonding ordinance, required permission from the city council via a permit and a $1,000 bond to operate a hotel or other similar business. Portland became famous for the Tin Plate Law, even though permit holders found many loopholes.[33] But a group of Portland hotel owners filed suit against the hotel bonding ordinance just over a month after the city council approved it, and in March 1914 circuit court judge Robert G. Morrow voided three sections of the ordinance as unconstitutional. Additional protests by members of the Oregon Hotel Association and their attorneys effectively ended the enforcement of the rest of the ordinance and any additional legal action. Significantly, Judge Morrow noted that the provisions in Section 5 giving the city council the power to "revoke at pleasure" any permit to operate a hotel or rooming house constituted "a deprivation of property without due process of law" and "an arbitrary denial of the equal protection of the laws."[34]

But in the fall of 1917, OSHS legal counsel Robinson found a way to introduce a new kind of licensing ordinance, building on the old foundation

120 / CHAPTER 5

and capitalizing on the wartime imperatives of loyalty and the growing consensus about anti-prostitution strategies. Robinson explained how he did it in a December 1917 letter to Moore, who had already relocated in DC with the Council of National Defense's anti-venereal disease section. "In studying the Vice Commission's report," Robinson wrote, "I came across the suggestion of a license scheme for hotels and rooming houses." He found out about the Hotel Association's fight and Judge Morrow's voiding of the provisions that effectively ended the ordinance in 1914. In consultation with Portland mayor George Baker, Robinson reworked the ordinance: no one could get a license "unless of good moral character," and the city council could revoke a license "by showing improper conditions to exist." Baker had Robinson meet with members of the Hotel Association to gain their support. Robinson negotiated a replacement of the $1000 bond requirement from the 1912 ordinance with a five-dollar annual license fee. That change, the need to cooperate with the War Department and city officials, and the opportunity to shine a light on hotel owner wartime loyalty caused Hotel Association members to approve the ordinance unanimously. The ordinance passed the city council on January 2, 1918.[35]

Portland's 1918 hotel and rooming house ordinance became, quite literally, the model for venereal disease control policy for the nation's cities during and after the war. The new hotel ordinance had only smoothed the surface of the violations of due process and equal protection of the laws to which Judge Morrow had objected in his 1914 ruling. A revealing note appended to a copy of the ordinance and the license application sent by Moore and circulated by Robinson in the law enforcement section of the Public Health Department's Venereal Disease Division makes this clear. "This is a cracker-jack way of repressing prostitution in assignation houses and disorderly hotels," another staff member wrote. "The particularly good feature is the power vested in the Council to revoke a license *after the violation of any provision of the ordinance*. Trial and conviction in court is not necessary for revocation. Much more informal evidence can be successfully used in a hearing before the Council than a court of law requires. Evidentiary technicalities frequently defeat conviction in legal trials."[36] By December 1918, Robinson had moved to DC to direct the law enforcement section of the US Public Health Service. He recommended Portland's hotel ordinance widely and included it as the model hotel ordinance in various pamphlets, including *Venereal Disease Ordinances*, he edited for the US Public Health Service. Robinson also included the Portland anti–venereal disease ordinance making the act of spreading an STI unlawful as a model provision.[37]

In Portland, in Oregon, and across the nation wartime and postwar cultural shifts widened the net for targeting women as potential inmates of the detention home from "hardened" prostitutes to potentially any woman who engaged in unsanctioned sex or who contracted an STI—all in the name of the war effort. Authorities used information being gathered showing high STI rates among the nation's draftees to argue that men were exposed to venereal disease in their home communities before entering military service. This meant that targeting sex workers around military training camps was not nearly enough, so a comprehensive plan of finding and detaining all women suspected of carrying venereal disease no matter where they lived would be the only way to keep men "fit to fight."[38]

Three Oregon developments helped fuel this expansion. Maintaining that the venereal disease danger to men was from local women, in April 1918 social hygiene reformers, war department officials, and local and state authorities expanded the reach of Kelly Butte/The Cedars beyond Portland and Multnomah County. Now authorities from around the state could "Portlandize" women by sending them directly to the detention home and thereby "purify" their communities.[39] In a second development, beginning in December 1918, boosters of all sorts touted another Oregon First when Surgeon General Rupert Blue announced that among the first million soldiers drafted, Oregon's men had the lowest rate of STIs of any state. The OSHS, the press, and local and state leaders celebrated the publicity and what they considered the validation of Oregon's social hygiene activities and local and state policies; they vowed to continue a statewide hunt for women carrying STIs.[40] A third development came in February 1919, when members of the Oregon legislature passed significant revisions to state laws regarding venereal disease quarantine and the authority of the State Board of Health. The changes included the power to hold and test those people "reasonably suspected" of being carriers of venereal disease based on the Portland ordinances, now vetted nationwide. The revisions gave the Oregon State Board of Health the blanket authority to "make such rules and regulations as shall in its judgement be necessary for the carrying out of the provisions of this act, including rules and regulations providing for the control of persons isolated or quarantined" and "concerning venereal

122 / CHAPTER 5

diseases." They would soon use this power to expand a new "health parole" that challenged the civil liberties of women detained at The Cedars in a new way. This overhaul also included a state-sterilization section with reporting of anyone to the state health officer who appeared to be "unfit" expanding the reach of eugenic policies to inmates of The Cedars and beyond.[41]

Local, state, and federal authorities paired the new detention laws that opened people's bodies, homes, and businesses to inspection with stronger tools and more agents of surveillance. Undercover CTCA operatives joined military intelligence officers, and the OSHS employed undercover agents to surveil and report about neighborhoods, hotels, and people suspected of prostitution.[42] Attorney Herman F. McInturff served as special law enforcement officer for the State Board of Health and the US Public Health Service, detailed specifically to investigate venereal disease cases statewide.[43] Portland policewoman Lola Baldwin, tapped for wartime federal service as Pacific Northwest field supervisor for the CTCA Division on Women and Girls, expanded surveillance including working with local postal workers to intercept and inspect mail women received from soldiers. Baldwin created a file of photographs of detained women to "more easily trace venereal cases from city to city" as "names mean very little" because of the widespread use of aliases. Portland police targeted Black women in particular for mug shots.[44]

In January 1918, Portland police chief N. F. Johnson created a new division, the War Emergency Squad (WES), with eight officers to "sift the entire population" of the city to "protect soldiers from undesirable persons." WES detectives continued "aggressive clean-ups" of areas of suspected prostitution. The Police Bureau expanded the Women's Protective Division with additional operatives for the period of the conflict and demobilization.[45] Portland Police Investigative Reports from November 1917 to the end of 1919 provide some details for 183 calls for investigation of women suspected of prostitution or experiencing STIs. A full 70 percent of the calls for investigation came from neighbors, family members, angry husbands and partners, property managers, and those who wrote letters or telephoned anonymous tips to headquarters; the rest came from the local police, Women's Protective Bureau workers, the State Board of Health, the Federal Bureau of Investigation, and US Military Intelligence. Eighteen detentions occurred as the result of collateral surveillance by prohibition agents.[46]

FROM KELLY BUTTE TO THE CEDARS

Until construction of The Cedars could be completed, Portland and Multnomah County officials agreed to incarcerate women at the Kelly Butte jail adjacent to the city's rock pile and quarry in Multnomah County east of Portland. Kelly Butte was infamous as a rough place for harsh punishment, where guards put men to work with sledgehammers to break rock into small enough pieces to enter the huge rock crusher located on site. The facility was in and out of use by the city and county for prison labor and sometimes paid labor when there was a pressing need for crushed stone for road construction, for public works employment of men during times of high unemployment, and when the mayor wanted to intimidate protesters such as members of the Industrial Workers of the World.[47]

Press coverage of the dramatic escape by twelve male inmates in March 1916 provided information about the layout of the jail in which a hundred or more "Portlandized" women would live from December 1917 through August 1918. The jail had room for about fifty people in a "large stone cell house" and cells "heavily barred" with iron positioned in the center of a large room circled completely by an observation corridor. Outside, a thirty-foot perimeter enclosed by a wooden stockade with barbed wire on top surrounded the entire jail.[48] In November 1917 a county emergency appropriation of $10,000 paid for new furnishings, medical supplies and laboratory facilities, repair of the stockade fence, and ongoing expenses such as food and salaries for a matron, nurses, a cook, and a guard. County commissioners "reserved the right to increase the number of guards from one to as many as may be necessary" to provide strict security for the sixty to one hundred women they anticipated would be incarcerated there. Under the thin veneer of hopeful promises that Kelly Butte would be a "haven" and not a "real" prison were the very real plans for few if any visitors and armed guards watching. "Extra guards will probably be appointed," the *Portland News* declared, "as the authorities are anticipating trouble."[49]

Meanwhile local and state authorities placed high hopes in The Cedars as construction moved forward but were anxious to please federal wartime officials and go beyond simple compliance to stand out and retain the glow of Oregon First star state acclaim.[50] Some twelve miles from Kelly Butte and twenty from Portland city center in Troutdale, Multnomah

124 / CHAPTER 5

FIGURE 15 "New Women's Detention Home, 'The Cedars' Is Completed." *Sunday Oregonian*, August 11, 1918, Section 1, 12.

County, The Cedars was built on five acres of land adjacent to the Multnomah County Poor Farm and the small county quarantine "pesthouse" for smallpox patients.[51] Policymakers took pains to characterize The Cedars as a wholesome and recuperative home and farm and chose the name for "a group of stately cedar trees" that graced the grounds.[52] The initial goal of an April 1918 opening snagged on construction delays and new concerns about capacity as Kelly Butte began to take on women detained from across the state due to the new policy. By June, with fifty-seven women interned at Kelly Butte, the plan for The Cedars to have a capacity of forty-three women with single rooms in cottage-style buildings soon evolved to wards and women sleeping in the attic and basement of the main administrative building and under a screened sleeping porch. City officials inspected army barracks at Fort Vancouver in Washington State as a model in case additional quarters were needed.[53] On August 9, 1918, fifty

HELD FOR HEALTH / 125

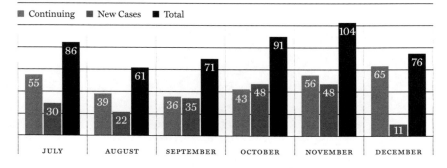

FIGURE 16 Inmates at The Cedars, July–December 1918. Figures from Detention Hospital Report for "The Cedars," July–December 1918, Division of Venereal Diseases, US Public Health Service, Folder 235.4.1 Reports, Box 90, RG 90, Records of the Public Health Service, 1912–1968, 90.3.5 General Records of the Venereal Disease Division, 1918–1936, National Archives and Records Administration, College Park, Maryland.

women transferred from Kelly Butte to The Cedars. The *Oregon Journal* reported "the patients are provided with individual rooms, lockers for clothes, and hot and cold water bathing, including a shower bath." Images of one of the cottages and the administration building published in the *Oregonian* suggest that "individual rooms" for fifty or more people would have been very small indeed.[54]

Reports about The Cedars documented poor conditions and overcrowding as officials, often in strident conflict with one another over funding and authority, tried to keep the institution afloat and plan for expansion until its defunding and closure in 1923. The official report to the Public Health Service Division of Venereal Diseases for the second half of 1918 showed consistent overcrowding and a surge of new detainees in October and November as the war concluded.[55]

On November 19, 1918, a week after the Armistice, Rabbi Jonah Wise, chair of the OSHS Committee on The Cedars, was concerned that "the 70 girls there now are housed like animals." And by that date the discharge of over 30 inmates had reduced the November high of 104 to 70. "There are no sitting rooms, sewing rooms or other places where the girls may find normal recreation," Wise maintained. "The effort should be to make better women of them, not criminals. If the women who go there now are not morally deficient they soon will be in such quarters."[56] Roseburg physician A. C. Seeley, serving as acting assistant surgeon for Oregon in the Public Health Service and chair of the State Board of Health, wrote to Surgeon General Blue several weeks later on December 3, 1918. Buildings were "badly planned and lacking in capacity" with unfinished grounds around them, he reported, and the water supply had been condemned. The inmates were "crowded far beyond capacity." The death of The Cedars chief nurse, Maud Myrick, that December during the influenza pandemic underscored the danger of overcrowding and poor sanitary conditions for staff and detainees alike.[57]

CIVIL LIBERTIES QUESTIONS

The detention of women at Kelly Butte/The Cedars added a new dimension to the Portland law enforcement "held for investigation" practice that ensnared Anna Mary Weston when she was suspected of sedition in 1918. Authorities implemented an indefinite "held for health" policy for STI testing, circumventing due process and civil liberties, based on the Portland venereal disease ordinance of November 1917. Women could be arrested and held for health or held for health alone without any charge based on a "reasonable suspicion" of a venereal infection. Margaret Mathews's April 1918 letter to Portland's Mayor Baker is a powerful illustration of the practice. "I am held a prisoner in the City Jail for the last four weeks," she wrote. Arrested and tried on a charge of disorderly conduct, the court fined Mathews ten dollars and sentenced her to a day in jail. She paid and served the time so she should have been released on March 18 with her sentence complete. But authorities told Mathews she would have to have a physical examination for STIs before she could be released. Mathews's attorney advised her not to submit to the examination, and she told the mayor, "I have not the money to take it into the courts at present." Four weeks in, being held at the jail without any criminal charge against her and without funds, Mathews asked the mayor for help.[58] The *Oregon Journal* in December 1918 reported an average of three to four days for women to be held at the city jail for STI testing before being sent to The Cedars or released.[59]

Many layers of surveillance agents, including War Emergency Squad and Women's Protective Bureau officers, targeted women to be held for health, and other agents such as prohibition officers engaged in collateral scrutiny while searching for illicit alcohol. Portland WES officers alone held forty-two people for health in the month of October 1918. The policy targeted working people and people of color, and Portland press reports underscore the gendered double standard often found *within* the class and racial bias of the health hold. In a March 1918 raid police officers held four Black women for health and arrested two Black men who were with them without a health hold. In September 1918 WES officers arrested three White men, one Black man, and two White women for vagrancy, maintaining a nuisance, and violation of prohibition laws but only held the two women for health. In October 1918 WES officers looking for alcohol arrested two Native Hawai'ian men and a White woman for violating prohibition laws. Detectives held the woman for health but not the two men; officers took the "great quantities" of whiskey they discovered on the premises to the police station "as evidence."[60]

Lawmakers created an opening for women with resources and connections to post a $1,000 bond to avoid incarceration at The Cedars. By 1918, Portland and other Oregon cities modeling ordinances on the Portland prototype required the chief of police, the mayor, and a judge all to sign off on permission for the health bond. Applicants had to swear under oath that they were not prostitutes.[61] It was difficult to prove a negative, and the process invited additional scrutiny over women's lives. The cost was beyond the reach of most working women when the Oregon minimum wage for an experienced adult woman in industry was $52.80 per month.[62] But even with resources, the process was stacked against women applicants. The partial documentation of Margaret McKie's experience provides a strong illustration. Police arrested twenty-six-year-old McKie, a second-generation Irish American domestic worker, in Portland in April 1918, tested her for STIs, and released her until the test results came in. McKie "promised to return, which she did not do," and the lab reported her test was positive for gonorrhea. Police located and detained McKie six months later in November, retested her and kept her in detention, and the results were again positive for gonorrhea. On November 8, five days after her arrest, McKie completed the paperwork for a bond assisted by her uncle, a clerk in a Portland shoe store, who agreed to post his house as collateral. She swore that she was "not now nor have I ever been a prostitute." While police investigated, the bond application process added nine

128 / CHAPTER 5

days to McKie's held-for-health detention. Police Chief Johnson recounted McKie's failure to return in April, the positive gonorrhea tests, and reported "the arresting officers in this case are quite thoroughly convinced that the woman was sporting," meaning engaging in sex work. Johnson provided no evidence for the assertion, but recommended against the bond, and the mayor denied her application. McKie was incarcerated at The Cedars.[63]

Opposition to gendered double standards and violations of civil liberties generated by the Portland and Oregon licensing, hold for health, and other venereal disease detention policies came from many sides and increased at the war's end and until The Cedars closed in 1923. Women escaped from The Cedars with frequency. In December 1918 matron Elizabeth Rogers requested a transfer due to overwork; Lola Baldwin suggested she was being pushed out because of the many escapes on her watch.[64] At least seven women applied for writs of habeas corpus to challenge their incarceration at Kelly Butte or The Cedars from November 1917 through April 1921.[65] All of this resistance appears to have had an impact. As early as February 1919, Baldwin reported "an epidemic of fear" among "judges and police officials to insist on medical examinations unless the woman has been convicted as a vagrant or a prostitute." They "seem to be afraid to move lest they be prosecuted personally."[66]

In July 1919, citing the changing postwar climate and increasing criticism for keeping a wartime practice, Mayor Baker ordered authorities to discontinue the hold-for-health policy. Now women would not be held for testing for venereal disease "unless convicted on charges of immoral conduct." When he heard the news, Surgeon General Blue sent Baker an urgent message asking him to reconsider. Portland and Oregon, he said, were pioneers—the first to enact laws that allowed for women to be held for health without being convicted of a crime, models the rest of the country followed with success. Therefore it would be disastrous for Portland to "relax" its "vigilance," and the "disease spreading element" would undoubtedly rejoice. Blue hoped that Portland would "retain its enviable position and not permit demoralization of the legal fabric so carefully constructed" against women with venereal disease during the war. Baker responded to Blue after convening a coalition of health and law enforcement representatives to craft a response that would allow Oregon to keep the health hold, and the state and city's national reputation, but to calm opponents and resisters. Since the war, Baker wrote, "it has been necessary for us to adopt methods involving more care" because "the element of patriotism and cooperation with the Army and Navy is eliminated." Oregon and Portland officials now had to guard against more lawsuits. But they had a revised plan and hold for health was back. "The precaution we have adopted in our new method," Baker wrote, was to have a trusted "woman operative" overseeing each woman brought to the police station. "If she finds circumstances that give rise to a reasonable indication of infection the suspect is held for examination regardless of the criminal charges in the case." The practice of "holding all women indiscriminately for examination has been discontinued because the plan was abused," he told Blue. "When policemen had no other grounds for holding a woman in jail they did so by holding her for the Health Department." There had been "several unfortunate mixups and it is certain," Baker told Blue, that if they had continued, "we would have brought trouble to ourselves and the city." The new policy meant authorities could "exercise care without taking long chances" and "accomplish must as much good as heretofore."[67]

Martha Randall, recently returned from wartime nursing service in France and experienced in venereal disease police work in Oregon before the conflict, went to work for the Portland Police Bureau with the rank of deputy state health officer with authority to investigate and hold women all across Oregon. Randall was empowered to investigate "every woman brought before the Court," and she alone determined if they would be held for a health test. Lola Baldwin told assistant surgeon general C. C. Pierce, head of the Venereal Disease Division, "this will prevent the carrying out of the orders that were given when no one was to be examined unless first convicted in court as a prostitute." Baldwin told the press about Randall's new role, insisting it was in accord with the state's 1919 legislation about examining persons suspected of carrying venereal disease. Baldwin and other social hygiene leaders had preserved Blue's carefully constructed legal fabric and walked back Baker's promise to discontinue the practice unless a woman was convicted "for immoral conduct." This made "all women who came into the hands of the police" vulnerable to detention.[68] The social hygiene coalition found a way to give a new set of clothes to the hold-for-health policy in the postwar world to please the federal government, maintain the Oregon and Portland First reputations, and deflect liability.

130 / CHAPTER 5

In practice, Randall did not wait for others to report cases to her as the policy suggested. Portland Police Investigative Reports contain several examples of Randall directing police officers to pick women up for health holds who were not under arrest, and there were some twenty-five requests for hold-for-health actions by the police and board of health officers.[69] Black women were specific targets. In September 1919, for example, Portland police authorities directed officers to arrest two Black women in particular and hold them for health and "all other colored prostitutes that have been arrested and convicted in the last two weeks." In November 1920, officers reported: "Pursuant to instructions we worked on Colored Prostitutes. Arrested eight of them."[70]

Black Portlander Ruth Brown's April 1921 application for a writ of habeas corpus to secure her civil liberties and release from The Cedars provides powerful details about the hold-for-health and bond application practices. Arrested on April 3 for vagrancy, Brown paid her twenty-five-dollar fine but was tested for STIs, sent to The Cedars, and detained incommunicado. Her advocate, Black porter and Portland resident Walter O. Prime, "being a friend of the said Ruth Brown, and knowing the facts," worked with experienced White attorneys J. J. Fitzgerald and Lou Wagner to prepare the application for the writ, filed on Saturday, April 9. Wagner and Fitzgerald may have been acting pro bono as opponents to the double standard.[71] According to their petition, Brown was tested for STIs without her consent, and health officials "forcibly seized" Brown and "conducted her against her will" to The Cedars without due process. Brown then followed procedure outlined by city ordinance and applied for a $1,000 bond to secure her release, posting sufficient collateral. Health officers refused to accept the bond, stating in writing that unless someone was "oked" by Martha Randall, their bond would not be accepted, showing that Randall had gathered additional power over the process of detention and incarceration. Brown and her advocates argued that the city was enforcing the provision for posting bond arbitrarily, "not against the public generally, but only against certain individuals, and that none but women are selected and subjected to these decisions, and to incarceration in this institution known as the Cedars." Now she was incommunicado and could not sign papers or see her attorneys, an additional violation of her civil liberties. Brown and her advocates challenged due process matters as had other women and their advocates in Oregon and the nation without success, but these arguments went to the heart of the gendered double standard in detention practice and policy and the violations of civil liberties in the entire process.[72]

Brown's attorneys, Wagner and Fitzgerald, appear to have calculated an opportunity for wider and favorable hearing of the case. Wagner, an experienced municipal court defender, and Fitzgerald, a former city and district attorney known for his support of Oregon's Chinese American community, filed the application for Brown's writ of habeas corpus with circuit court judge William Gatens rather than presiding circuit court judge John Kavanaugh.[73] Gatens released Brown on her bond that Saturday afternoon and filed a temporary application for the writ, taking the opportunity to share his strong opposition to The Cedars and the gendered double standard with the assembled press. "I'm opposed to the whole system and I don't care who knows it," Gatens said. "I cannot see the justice of the double standard it supports." Why "a woman who has been arrested for vagrancy or some minor offense should be compelled to submit to a blood test and then be isolated at The Cedars if she is shown to have a disease, and men arrested for similar offenses and not examined has never been clear to me." Gatens had no objection to "The Cedars for women," he concluded, "if the city would be fair and establish The Pines for men."[74]

That Monday, April 11, Judge Kavanaugh heard the case and gave the city until Wednesday to provide rebuttal evidence. The city attorneys and health board assembled copies of complaints and results of Brown's April 3 arrest and a prior arrest and fine for vagrancy in May 1920 as well as copies of the STI tests and results. They also produced a copy of Brown's admittance card to The Cedars, documenting yet another form of state identification specifically created for the "Venereal Girls" at The Cedars. In Brown's case some of the crucial information and signatures were missing, and full authority rested with Randall as "jurisdictional health officer." The city's evidence was enough for Kavanaugh, and he ordered Brown remanded to The Cedars. Her attorneys decided not to contest the decision.[75]

Leonor Zambrano Brunicardi's 1922 case demonstrates how local and federal authorities combined hold-for-health and detention policies at The Cedars with deportation to Mexico. Her case suggests how popular culture messages framed racialized and gendered ideas about a young

132 / CHAPTER 5

ADMITTANCE CARD, CEDARS DETENTION HOSPITAL

Admit, quarantine and treat.... *Ruth Brown*

(Name of Patient)

For venereal disease..., to wit: *Syphilis 4 + - g.c. sus*

(Character of Disease)

Diagnosis has been confirmed, as provided in subdivision "C", Section 49 of the rules and regulations of the Oregon State Board of Health, and results checked and approved by

....

(Head of Laboratory or Chief Pathologist)

Source of Infection ....

Date of Onset of Disease ....

Blood drawn by .... *Dr. Woolley* ....

Slide taken by *Dr. Stanard + Mr. Evans* ....

Examination performed by ....

Exhibit E .... *Signed Martha Randall* ....

(Jurisdictional Health Officer)

FIGURE 17 Exhibit E, Ruth Brown Admittance Card, Cedars Detention Hospital, 1921. "In the matter of the Petition of Ruth Brown for Writ of Habeas Corpus," Rendered April 15, 1921, Filed May 11, 1921, Judgment #84069, Reel 00-1146, Multnomah County Circuit Court Files, Multnomah County Courthouse, Portland, Oregon.

Mexican American woman in Portland and her sexuality in the midst of anti–venereal disease campaigns. The 1920 census counted just 569 residents of Oregon who had been born in Mexico and categorized them as "foreign born white."[76] But White anxieties about Mexican immigration in the context of the Mexican Revolution and postwar fears about labor competition and nativism combined to define Mexican Americans in Oregon as racial others distinct and distant from White residents and their privileges. According to newspaper accounts, Leonor was working as a telephone operator in Mexico City when she met Anselmo Brunicardi, an Italian citizen. The two married in Texas in 1920 and by 1922 were living in Portland. Leonor came to law enforcement attention in a September 1922 anti-venereal "cleanup" raid in the North End.[77] With instructions from assistant US attorney Allan Bynon, Portland police arrested Anselmo for trafficking Leonor and violating the 1910 Mann Act, which criminalized taking women across state lines for purposes deemed to be "immoral." Bynon had Leonor held for health, and after testing she was detained at The Cedars. A grand jury failed to indict Anselmo, and he was released.

HELD FOR HEALTH / *133*

Early reports cast Leonor as a victim, first suggesting she was a maid, then that she had been forced into prostitution, then as a "hardened" prostitute who "openly practiced her disreputable profession."[78] Press coverage labeled Leonor on a spectrum of Latina identity: as a "Spanish woman," a "comely young Mexican girl," a "Latin Beauty."[79]

Bynon located Inez Fernandez, whose testimony he hoped would bring new evidence to convict Anselmo, and he brought Leonor from The Cedars to his office so that he could question them both.[80] The Portland press framed what happened next following cues from popular new films featuring Latin lovers in the first "Latin wave" of silent film of the early 1920s.[81] Many Portlanders considered such films to be dangerous, especially because they often challenged ideas about respectable womanhood. Portland had a motion picture censor board, and many women's clubs in Portland and Oregon had film censorship committees, charged with protecting their communities from "films detrimental to public morals."[82] The press reported a physical fight in the US attorney's office between Leonor and Inez as two "Latin Beauties" fighting for the affections of their Latin lover Anselmo Brunicardi, who was Italian-born, as was that most famous of the cinema's Latin lovers, Rudolph Valentino. The *Oregonian* described "jealousy, hot latin blood, and a battle" worthy of a "first rate movie scenario." It took two "husky federal agents" to separate Leonor and Inez, and Bynon had Leonor returned to The Cedars. Federal legislation in place made any woman who was not a citizen vulnerable to deportation if accused of immorality, and Bynon invoked the law to deport her to Mexico.[83] These were policies to which all women were vulnerable, but the process of representing and constructing Leonor as a sexualized Latin beauty who "lacked morals" may certainly have marked her for incarceration at The Cedars and for deportation to Mexico, all without trial. Mexican Oregonians were in a transition from being categorized as "foreign born whites" to the racial category of "Mexican" by the 1930s, when their large-scale deportations from the United States followed the Great Depression.[84]

The Cedars closed at the end of March 1923, but the held-for-health and STI examination policy lived on as a legacy of the anti–venereal disease campaign, and authorities connected the policy to other parts of the criminal justice system in the state. The case of gender-nonconforming Oregonian Teddy Gloss is a powerful example. Assigned female at birth and named Sarah with a twin sister, the fifteen-year-old Gloss "always

134 / CHAPTER 5

deeply resented the fact that she was a girl" and "hate[d] women's clothing." Gloss worked the family ranch at Aurora, Oregon, advocated for animals, competed in rodeos including riding "some of the wildest horses at the Pendleton Round-up," and hoped to become a Western film star.[85] Gloss presented as male, wore male clothing, and signed letters as "Ted Gloss." *Oregonian* reporter Ernest Potts described Gloss as an "Amazon" with a masculine nature who "craves the life" of a cowboy, a "Buckaroo" with the "restless nature of a boy, cast in the mold of a girl."[86] In February 1923, just as The Cedars was closing, Gloss was caring for the rural Clackamas County farm and animals of a neighbor on jury duty. Two young boys went with Gloss to the property and they all began to fool around. A window and several bottles broke. Authorities apprehended Gloss and one other boy and brought them to Oregon City for arraignment. "Before being taken into court," the *Oregon Journal* reported, Gloss "was subjected to [a medical] examination required by law, which so outraged" Gloss that they "could not restrain" their anger. "Handled and humiliated," the *Oregonian* related, "led back from a physician's office into court," Gloss kicked the judge and ran from the building. When sheriff's deputies gave chase, Gloss hit several of them before being restrained.[87] For Gloss a pelvic examination for STIS designated their body as female in addition to being an intrusive act of medical surveillance committed on a person apprehended for breaking a window.

The Oregon City judge sentenced Gloss to a year's incarceration at the Oregon State Industrial School for Girls in Salem, part of the juvenile justice system, further designating Gloss as female, a status they rejected. The Cedars was soon to close, and judges had been sentencing many defendants who tested positively for STIS to the Industrial School. The sentence carried the potential for Gloss to remain detained until they were twenty-one years old. "Strapped" to two deputy sheriffs for the automobile trip to Salem, Gloss continued to resist upon arrival and intake, refused to wear the institutional women's clothing provided, and hunger-struck for four days. After an escape attempt, attendants placed Gloss in a straitjacket, and the marks of restraint were still visible over a month later.[88] Family and community advocates' lobbying efforts succeeded when the State Board of Control and Governor Walter Pierce paroled Gloss on March 22, 1923, for work at the Humane Society over the objections of the Industrial School matron.[89]

HELD FOR HEALTH / *135*

Gloss was free, but the case was an example of the extreme excesses of the anti–venereal disease campaign that continued far beyond the war and how the held-for-health policy could be used to police bodies, gender presentation, and gender identity. In Portland the hold-for-health policy for women suspected of prostitution lasted for more than fifty years, until the reorganization and closure of the Portland city jail facility in 1972.[90]

THE INCARCERATED AT THE CEDARS

A complete set of records for people incarcerated at The Cedars does not appear to exist, but we can draw together materials from reports and other sources to try to understand more about how diverse Oregonians experienced The Cedars, ways in which they resisted, and the impact of detention on their lives thereafter. An early list of fifty individuals at the Kelly Butte detention home in its first months of operation from December 6, 1917, to February 8, 1918, shows they were confined for an average of five weeks (34.86 days) before their release. Thirty-six federally supported detention homes from April 1918 to January 1921 averaged 9.8 weeks of detention, almost twice the time of the early Portland women's experiences.[91] Most in this first group were likely sex workers caught up in the waves of police "cleanups" designed to arrest women suspected of prostitution. Many were likely women of color, including the Black women who could not raise the initial bail after the raids. The list also includes names of twenty-five other individuals detained February 8 through March 25 with only a handful of release dates recorded. Among them was Buster Taylor, incarcerated on March 12, 1918. An August 1918 press report from Rogue River, in southern Oregon's Jackson County, noted that "Mrs. Higgins, better known as 'Buster Taylor,'" had been detained at the county jail and would be taken back to The Cedars, apparently after a successful escape. Taylor's presentation with a male-identified name is compelling, as is the recording of that name in The Cedars list of detainees, suggesting persistence and resistance on Taylor's part.[92]

The 1920 census for Troutdale, Oregon, lists twenty-nine women between the ages of sixteen and twenty-one incarcerated at The Cedars in January 1920.[93] All were listed as White. Their young ages conform to many of the stereotypes of publicity reports: nine of the twenty-nine were sixteen, seven were seventeen years of age. But the detainees did

136 / CHAPTER 5

not conform to the reformers' message about young, inexperienced "girls" with "khaki fever." The census taker categorized more than half (fifteen) as being married or divorced, and some women listed as single could have been previously married or divorced. A September 1920 Oregon State Board of Health report found twenty-eight women in detention, sixteen from Portland and twelve who had been sent from other state locations. Since June 1920, ninety-eight women had been released, fifty-eight Portland residents and thirty-five from elsewhere in Oregon.[94] A December 1920 article in the *Oregon Journal* suggests that cities did not always send women to The Cedars for incarceration while being treated. Bend city nurse Anna Day and Jessie (Mrs. Emerson) Stockwall, head of the city's Women's Protective Bureau, visited The Cedars for an inspection. "The city of Bend has had many venereal cases to cope with," the *Journal* noted, "and several patients from that city have been cared for at The Cedars."[95]

Case notes made by Anna E. Murphy, The Cedars rehabilitation and parole officer, provide a unique contribution to the historical record and more information about what happened to inmates after incarceration. The case notes are incomplete, often brief, and arranged by date rather than by case, designated as numbers or initials without other identification. Murphy documented 234 cases during two years of her work from April 1918 to April 1920. Within these limitations the collated case notes offer some powerful insights into the experiences of people at The Cedars and during parole.[96] The OSHS hired Murphy in February 1918, in part to "remove the opportunity for some criticism" about women's detention, and with the social hygienist rehabilitation model in mind.[97] Her job was to transition women from The Cedars with employment, housing, and reintegration in partnership with other community organizations.

Murphy exemplified the model of an accomplished female social worker of the period. She was the daughter of a successful Idaho rancher, a 1904 graduate of Boise's St. Teresa's Academy for Girls, a former milliner who, in 1912 at age twenty-nine, chose a new career path in social work with Portland's Catholic Women's League. Murphy took a leave of absence to attend the winter 1913 term of courses at the Chicago School of Civics and Philanthropy, with financial support from the League. The school was a magnet for students of social work from around the nation and beyond with links to the Hull House settlement, a pilgrimage site for credentialing, networking, and extensive field work experience. Luminaries of the

FIGURE 18 Anna E. Murphy. Folder 8, Richard B. Dillehunt Photograph Album, 2004 001, Special Collections & Archives, Oregon Health & Science University, Portland.

nation's female reform community, including Jane Addams, Edith Abbott, Julia Lathrop, and Sophonisba Breckinridge, were among the instructors that term. Murphy also completed field work with the Juvenile Court of Chicago and the United Charities.[98] Back in Portland by the summer of 1913, Murphy accepted a position at the new North Portland Branch of the Catholic Women's League, represented the League in the umbrella interdenominational organization of the Big Sisterhood, and was employed by the Associated Charities as a social worker for the greater Portland area.[99]

Murphy's work connected her with the vibrant Portland world of social work and settlement houses: with labor reformer and minimum wage activist Caroline Gleason; social worker Miriam Van Waters, then on staff at the Frazer Home and soon to enter the national stage of women's prison reform; Ida Lowenberg of the Neighborhood House settlement of the Portland branch of the National Council of Jewish Women; and Valentine Prichard of the People's Institute Settlement and Free Dispensary.[100] Two years into her tenure with the OSHS, Dr. Henry Waldo Coe described Murphy as never giving up "the basic idea that there is some good in most of her charges," contrasting her with "square-toed, third

138 / CHAPTER 5

degree, municipal" women detectives who thrived on "the convictions, arrests, and harassments they are able to inflict on their weaker sisters."[101]

Murphy built her new position with the tools of social work and her previous experience—visiting, networking, mentoring with Big Sisters, finding employment, room, and board for the women in her charge—all with broad powers of surveillance. The anonymous case notes suggest that the majority of parolees were from urban or rural working-class backgrounds. But not all. Murphy noted the marriage announcement of one of the women with whom she had worked in the Society section of the *Sunday Oregonian*.[102] Murphy did not give details on work placements for most of the women in the case notes, but for those with workplaces listed, most labored as domestics in private homes. Some were able to return to jobs they had held before incarceration or used their own contacts to get employment. Several worked as waitresses, others as nurses with private families, in hospitals, and at the Waverly Baby Home. Six managed boarding houses or small hotels.[103] A few worked in factories, in department stores, as dressmakers and in tailor shops, at offices, and two as theater ushers. One parolee was "anxiously seeking" the opportunity "to do boy's work," perhaps for higher wages, or to link their work to gender identity, or both. Murphy found a position for them at a lumber company and furnished work shoes and clothing for the job.[104] In other cases Murphy provided work clothing, shoes, and coats, sometimes on credit, sometimes from her own account. One woman would only take a position in a workplace represented by a union.[105] Another engaged in seasonal work in hop fields, another in Hood River apple orchards.[106]

Of the 234 women paroled from The Cedars, 1 in 4 went to live with extended family members, some outside of Portland. Of the 234, 49 (21 percent) were married before their incarceration and parole. Just 2 women experienced divorce, and several others were considering ending their marriages as they reported to Murphy as part of their parole. And 26 of 234 (11 percent) married during or after their parole. Of the women Murphy supervised, 16 were sent back The Cedars during their parole, and 2 were returned an additional time. Almost 1 in 4 (56 of them) broke their parole in some way. And 34 disappeared from the city or escaped from supervision when in an institution such as the Multnomah County Hospital. Of the 234 parolees, 40 (17 percent) had illnesses other than STIs, and the sporadic nature of the case notes and large number of contacts by

HELD FOR HEALTH / *139*

mail or phone call certainly underestimate women's health experiences. The case notes span the influenza pandemic and at least a dozen women contracted the flu. One woman was hospitalized after complications from an abortion, another for appendicitis, others were hospitalized for unnamed operations and conditions. Murphy reported mumps, troubles with eyesight, tooth problems. One woman attempted suicide. Murphy sometimes connected parolees with private physicians and free care at the Multnomah County hospital; in other cases, women were on their own to seek treatment.

Murphy's almost complete silence in the case notes about the race and ethnicity of the women she supervised doesn't seem to have an obvious explanation. Other records indicate that women of color, especially Black women, were particular targets of the anti–venereal disease campaign. Perhaps Murphy wished to make the notes as anonymous as possible. Throughout the case notes, she referred to just four women specifically as being Black, and all received support from other women in the Black community. Emma K. Griffin Stanley, president of Portland's Colored Women's Council, worked to assist a woman on parole from The Cedars whom Murphy had placed as a domestic. Living and working with a private family, she had to board out her baby. The woman who boarded the child was asking "an exorbitant price" and was holding the child until her bill was paid. Stanley worked with Murphy to make alternative arrangements with the city's Waverly Baby Home.[107] Colored Women's Council members worked with Murphy on another case to enable a parolee to have her baby live with her; Murphy paroled a third Black woman released from The Cedars directly to the care and responsibility of council member Louise Thomas; and a fourth she released directly to the young woman's mother.[108] Council members understood that most Black women were wage earners who needed strong childcare support, and advocacy for mothers incarcerated at The Cedars or on parole was part of these larger community projects.[109]

Overall, Murphy referred to twenty-six women who were mothers, including the four Black women supported by their community, in her case notes. The number of women with children was likely higher, as Murphy only wrote about children if she helped to arrange care or helped to resolve a custody dispute. This is a significant exception to what was

140 / CHAPTER 5

otherwise an almost perfect silence about incarcerated mothers and their children and the challenges they faced under STI detention policy across the nation. The detailed analysis of six thousand women detained in the anti–venereal disease campaigns in twenty-eight states by the Inter-departmental Social Hygiene Board listed marital status but provided no information about children. And Mary Macey Dietzler, in her 1922 study of detention homes, discussed "babies born of infected mothers" briefly, but acknowledged that most institutions did not keep records about children.[110] Silences concerning detained women as mothers hid the ways that anti–venereal campaigns hurt children and their mothers and divided families. Wage-earning women in Portland employed many strategies for childcare, including care by extended family members and neighbors, day nurseries, Portland's Fruit and Flower Mission, the Waverly Baby Home, and private caregivers. In step with national trends, Portland began a licensing requirement for home care providers in 1920 to address standards of care. Detention at The Cedars interrupted women's ability to earn a wage and for mothers, to support their children.[111]

Some women held at The Cedars struggled with custody and childcare issues before their incarceration and detention magnified their struggles. Margaret McKie, whose application for a $1,000 bond was denied in November 1918, had a five-year-old daughter when she was arrested and detained at The Cedars. Married in 1913, she left her husband in 1915, taking their daughter Margaret Jennie with her and working as a domestic in Portland to support them both. McKie sued her husband for nonsupport, and he was arrested in Corvallis and brought to Portland. He countersued for custody in 1916, claiming McKie was not able to care for their daughter properly in Portland. McKie responded that he had never provided any support for Margaret Jennie and won a sum for support and to prepare for a legal response to the suit. When McKie was held for health, denied bond, and sent to The Cedars in November 1918, she was in the middle of preparing her divorce suit. After her release, she continued her legal challenges and secured a divorce from her husband in 1919; she supported her daughter by working in a Portland office, and they lived with McKie's aunt and uncle. In April 1920, McKie "in poor health" attempted suicide at the home they all shared, apparently overwhelmed by the many events and encounters with systems of the law and detention.[112]

HELD FOR HEALTH / 141

"HEALTH PAROLE" AND PRODUCTIVE LABOR

Murphy's case notes offer a window into the development of health parole as a significant new tool for surveillance against women in the anti–venereal disease campaign. From the start, some women were "paroled" to Murphy, or to family members or responsible others, when released from The Cedars without formal arrest; Murphy served as a court parole officer for some women who had been convicted of a crime in addition to being detained at The Cedars.[113] Seven months into her work and frustrated by women who were not keeping contact with her or following her advice, Murphy started promoting "the need for a definite parole system with all girls released from The Cedars" to the OSHS and took steps to strengthen her authority and to extend the duration of parole.[114] Murphy's informal system of support and surveillance was not yielding desired rehabilitation results: according to the Oregon State Board of Health, only 30 percent of women were "reformed" after release from The Cedars in 1920.

In response, the health board formalized and strengthened Murphy's informal practices by dictating a yearlong, mandatory health parole for any person being treated for venereal disease "at the public expense" beginning in 1921. The board cited authority from the 1919 state law giving the health board broad powers to make "necessary" rules and regulations in the anti–venereal disease campaign that would carry "the force and effect of law."[115] The language the Oregon State Board of Health chose included "persons" and "men and women," but women released from The Cedars were the particular targets. The yearlong health parole applied to a woman regardless of whether she had been tried and convicted, plead guilty, or was incarcerated without trial for STIs. It was separate from any criminal parole a woman might also face, meaning that women who were convicted of a crime would have a double parole. Health parole officers, Murphy for Portland residents and a local person responsible for reporting for detained women who returned home or to reside outside of Portland, were to administer a system of weekly visits reported to the Oregon State Board of Health.[116]

Oregon's health parole had four important features as a new instrument of surveillance against women. The health parole officer controlled where a woman lived and if a woman could change residence or leave her community for any reason. Health parolees had to be employed in

142 / CHAPTER 5

a job approved by the health probation officer and the work had to be a "useful occupation," reflecting the importance of civically suitable labor for reformers and also class biases about wage work. Women who were on parole were not to break the law, but the rules of health probation went beyond this to give the officer the subjective power to control a woman's "moral well-being." A woman on health parole could not be "on the street at unreasonably late hours" or frequent "dangerous" places of amusement and could not "keep company" with anyone the health parole officer had "good reason to disapprove." And finally, health parolees had to keep a health parole card with them at all times to be produced upon request, another new surveillance product. A person who violated any of these terms of health parole could be charged with a misdemeanor, fined up to $1,000, and sentenced to a year in prison.[117]

Murphy called on law enforcement officers to assist in finding health parole violators. For example, a woman on health parole in 1921 left Portland without permission, and Murphy put out a "be on the lookout" request with law enforcement across the state. Albany city police and Linn County sheriff's office personnel worked with rooming house managers to locate the woman, who was living and working under an assumed name and made the mistake of claiming a letter addressed to her real name at the post office. They held her in the city jail until Murphy arrived to escort her back to Portland.[118]

Authorities scrutinized women detained at The Cedars and on health parole for useful labor as a measure of their ability to move toward release, and this unpaid work served the institution and the families with whom paroled women were placed. In his December 1918 report to the surgeon general about The Cedars, A. C. Seeley noted "the dress, toilet and adornment, both personal and of rooms of inmates, differs but little" from what one might see in "the usual 'red light'" districts of prostitution. "The inmates have no useful employment," he noted, "though plans are maturing to remedy this." Seen in this light, Seeley and many others considered women who were carriers or suspected carriers of STIs to be "hardened prostitutes" engaged in sex as work. For Seeley and others this was labor that went far beyond useless or "unfit" employment to work that was positively destructive to the state. In this view women with STIs were keeping men from being soldiers, keeping men from doing the work defined by the wartime nation as their civic duty, the work of being "fit to fight," and were thus dangerous internal enemies. Seeley described inmates' rooms at The Cedars as a "red light" workplace and their personal appearance, their "dress, toilet and adornment," as the uniform and demeanor of women who engaged in sex as work to the destruction of the community and national security.[119]

The *Oregonian* and the *Oregon Journal* featured images and descriptions about the work of the "Venereal Girls" at The Cedars in 1920, framing their before and after transition to useful employment in visually appealing Sunday Magazine sections that circulated among a wide audience. In the *Oregonian* in May 1920, young White women appeared eagerly engaged in sewing, food preparation, work in the barn, with the dairy cows and chickens, and "at the plow" in what Claudia Malacrida has called institutional "performances of happiness and productivity." In the *Oregon Journal* feature in August 1920, assistant city editor Earl C. Brownlee emphasized the rehabilitative work at The Cedars. He used clothing and dress as a symbol of work, as Seeley had in his 1918 report, but a year and a half later described a success story of women who were transitioning to useful citizenship. He described The Cedars attic holding the discarded clothing of sex workers, with a "rack of fragile, high-heeled shoes, all sadly worn," and "shoddy, soiled dresses of a sometimes sensational pattern." Residents had exchanged these clothes for "modest, sturdy uniforms." The "discard of itself," Brownlee noted, "tells a big part of the story of The Cedars." After abandoning the uniforms of sex workers, the inmates now engaged in sanctioned and useful labor: farm work, needlepoint, "attending chores in the spotless, sanitary and modern milkhouse," or working in the "modern, electrically equipped laundry." Former "Venereal Girls" in the process of rehabilitation now occupied "their time with worthy tasks." Their work was a "health restorer" in both the physical and the civic sense.[120]

THE CEDARS AND EUGENIC THINKING

Concepts of ability versus disability and internal enemies linked to Oregon's state sterilization policies were at the heart of the creation of The Cedars and the hold-for-health policy targeting women. In Oregon and across the nation, policymakers and reformers equated sex work with intellectual and developmental disabilities.[121] Sarah Evans told assembled White clubwomen attending the Oregon Federation of Women's Clubs an-

144 / CHAPTER 5

nual conference in 1915 that every vice commission in the nation reported "that fully 50 per cent of the prostitutes are mentally defective, and still society goes on treating them as though they possessed a normal mental balance."[122] Portland Vice Commission Detention Home Subcommittee members concluded "little" could be done for "defective" women "except to cure them of [venereal] disease and restrain them from being a constant menace to society" (a code for state sterilization) "and to make them as self-supporting as possible."[123]

Vice subcommittee chair George A. Thacher was a prominent eugenicist. An influential advocate for the identification, segregation, and sterilization of people considered "feeble-minded," he shaped the subcommittee's report and built momentum for these policies as an author and public campaigner. A lawyer, criminologist, and eugenicist, active in social work, and soon to be president of the Oregon Prisoners' Aid Society, Thacher was a frequent community speaker and author who gained a national reputation with his article "Feeble-mindedness and Crime in Oregon," published in 1917 in the *Journal of Delinquency*, and the book *Why Some Men Kill*, published just before his death in 1919.[124] Thacher believed adamantly that Oregon and the nation should sterilize and segregate the "feeble-minded" rather than bring intellectually disabled residents to trial and imprisonment. He made this cause his life's work. But as Thacher and many others with him fought against the injustice of prison terms for intellectually and developmentally disabled offenders, they created new assaults on civil liberties by embracing the detention and sterilization of the "defective."

A 1914 article by eugenics-supporter Millie Trumbull suggests that one of the reasons the OSHS hired Anna Murphy in 1918 as a social worker for detained women may have been because of her experience with addressing the needs of developmentally and intellectually disabled people. Workers connected with women's employment issues from the Catholic Women's League, the YWCA Employment Bureau, the Associated Charities, and the Municipal Free Employment Bureau shared cases of women they identified as "different." For women "definitely below the line of normal action," they worked with the superintendent of the Oregon State Hospital to have the women committed. Women "on the border line" would be referred to the Associated Charities," which would serve as a clearinghouse for other resources. "All cases of female delinquents so far as possible are to be referred to a worker who has made a special study of cases of delinquent girls"—likely Murphy, who worked with both the Associated Charities and Catholic Women's League.[125]

By the time Portland officials began to incarcerate women at Kelly Butte/The Cedars, people at various points in the system screened individuals for "feeblemindedness," ability, and psychological issues.[126] This included the period before they reached The Cedars, throughout their incarceration, and during health parole that followed. Local police, the courts, representatives of the city and state boards of health, individuals working with the OSHS, and private physicians conducted tests for mental ability and sanity on women bound for The Cedars. In 1918 the OSHS created a special committee to study and recommend detention measures for "feebleminded" women who were going to be discharged from The Cedars. Reed College psychology professor Samuel Kohs served as the examining psychologist for the Portland Court of Domestic Relations during the war and represented the OSHS by conducting intelligence testing of women before and during their incarceration at The Cedars. Emma Maki Wickstrom, MD, had studied psychoanalysis during postgraduate studies in Europe and had been involved with the Oregon social hygiene movement before the war. In 1920 she joined Kohs as a medical and psychological examiner for the Court of Domestic Relations.[127] Natalie Lira has shown that intelligence testers could use "deviant behavior" to "label someone 'borderline' or 'feebleminded' if their IQ score was higher than [the] test administrator expected." This meant that some testers used "poverty, gender, deviance, and nonwhite racial status" to "calibrate IQ scores" to a lower level.[128]

After 1919 incarceration of women at The Cedars combined with Oregon's new state sterilization policy that reached residents beyond specific institutions, meaning that women suspected of STIS were vulnerable to reporting for state sterilization across the entire process of arrest, holding for health, incarceration, and health parole. As Trumbull's report suggests, it's likely Murphy brought prior specific experience with women identified as intellectually or developmentally challenged from her prewar work to her job at The Cedars. Part of the description for her position with the OSHS was "assisting other agencies in special cases (Border line girls)."[129] Murphy consulted both Wickstrom and Kohs for testing and treatment of women on health parole. Her case notes provide specific evidence for

146 / CHAPTER 5

thirteen women who had additional mental and intellectual screening while on health parole, with at least one woman bound to the Oregon Institute for the Feeble-Minded. These screenings would have been after the other points of examination before and during a woman's commitment to The Cedars, suggesting workers identified even more women as "defective" in the entire process. And at a statewide meeting of health officers, Murphy included testing and institutionalization in her larger plan for rehabilitation and civically suited work.[130] These actions coordinated and concentrated eugenic surveillance of women and made them vulnerable to commitment and sterilization and also subject to sterilization outside of institutions in Oregon. Because Murphy's case notes are anonymous and other record connections sporadic, we can't know the extent of the commitments or the sterilizations. But we can certainly say that the ideology permeated many people's engagement with anti–venereal disease campaigns and that the threat of state sterilization was ever present for the "Venereal Girls."

During the war years and after, Indian Affairs officials often employed eugenic thinking, language, and actions as they addressed the "problem" of "wayward girls." Some local and federal reservation officials tried to persuade state juvenile facility directors to accept Indigenous women from reservations into their facilities. In 1923, Klamath Agency superintendent Fred Baker was working with BIA officials to convince state officials to have young Klamath women committed to the Oregon Industrial School for Girls so that they could "receive proper corrective training and punishment." Baker referred to the two young Klamath women arrested for theft in 1923 he was trying to send there as being of "low mentality" as he advocated for their placement in the school.[131] At the end of the 1923 school year, Chemawa Indian School superintendent Harwood Hall responded to a query about the status of mental testing at Oregon's boarding school just outside of Salem. Staff had made "a few tests" that academic year, but "next year we expect to use the tests in our work."[132]

Staff closed the doors and locked the stockade perimeter gates at The Cedars in March 1923. Contributing factors were long-standing conflicts about state, county, and city funding; the evaporation of federal dollars as the wartime anti-venereal national security issue waned; opposition to the gendered double standard of detention; and continuing opposition by many physicians to reporting STIS. In May 1922 district court judge

Richard Deich joined the chorus of criticism for the gendered double standard of the detention policy when six women who had escaped from The Cedars came before his court. "The women themselves feel the unfairness of the situation and the general public believes it to be unjust," Deich noted.[133] A series of exposés by *Oregon Journal* reporters in January 1923 during the biennial legislative session summarized these issues and revealed widespread problems of funding, job patronage and nepotism, and failures of therapy and rehabilitation that even Anna Murphy, Martha Randall, and other Board of Health and OSHS officials admitted when interviewed.[134] "The Cedars is not reducing the social evil, it is not curing its inmates, it is not providing after-care either in reformed living or institutional restraint," the *Oregon Journal* editors concluded, "and it is costing the taxpayers far more than value received."[135] The legislature did not fund The Cedars after these revelations, and state health officer Frederick Stricker issued instructions to city and county officials that they would need to provide care for treatment of women with STIs locally after the March closing.[136]

Other coercive agencies and voluntary organizations that had been engaging in the work of policing women and sexuality stepped into the space left vacant with the closing of The Cedars. The Pacific Coast Rescue and Protective Society, headquartered in Portland, had traveling women agents to cover the region and expanded its reach. In 1924, for example, agents worked with Edwin Chalcraft, superintendent of the Siletz Indian Agency, to apprehend and have the court sentence two young Siletz women to Portland's House of the Good Shepherd.[137] Teddy Gloss was among many individuals committed to the State Industrial School for Girls with hold-for-health policies in place. By 1920 state officials financed routine "mental testing" for inmates there. And after numerous requests, in 1929 Oregon legislators added the State Industrial School for Girls as one of the state institutions with the "duty" to report people for eugenic sterilization.[138] The longevity of these policies, including the hold-for-health policy through the 1970s in Portland, the health parole, and the continuing eugenic surveillance and control of "Venereal Girls" had powerfully destructive consequences on people's lives and on civil liberties—a long history that continued the work of The Cedars well into the twentieth century.

Oregon's policies toward the "Venereal Girls" comprise a significant chapter in the destructive power of both wartime and postwar crisis thinking and eugenic thinking in the hunt for and punishment of internal enemy others. People targeted by this hunt engaged in significant resistance. Incarceration at Kelly Butte and then The Cedars, or in local facilities in cities and towns like Astoria or Bend, placed women in a quarantine that could prevent advocates from reaching them, as Ruth Brown's habeas corpus case demonstrated. Health workers and other officials surveilled bodies and tested minds, and the women were outside of the legal system's due process protections when "held for health," when confined, and during "health probation." The association of "feeblemindedness" with sexuality that was out of bounds meant that the inmates risked state-forced sterilization at all points along their journey through the system. Their stories parallel the experiences of people held in the Oregon State Hospital for the Insane in chapter 6.

CHAPTER 6

"Insane" or "Unfit"

IN THE 1910S AND 1920S the Oregon State Hospital (OSH) in Salem was a place where people with a variety of mental and physical conditions resided, some with the support of family, friends, or advocates, others alone and vulnerable in a powerful system of control. After 1917, Oregon's eugenics policies became part of the very fabric of the hospital bureaucracy and defined how the hospital functioned every day. Eugenic thinking and practice combined with chronic underfunding and overcrowding meant that staff decisions about committed people flowed with parallel currents of sanctioned gender roles and identities, White privilege, and nativism as well as class, racial, and ethnic prejudice. Some people found healing or respite at OSH, but the hospital was also the location of surveillance and powerful violations of civil liberties and human rights. These violations included forced sterilization, unlawful arrest and lack of due process, deportation, cruel and unusual punishment, invasions of privacy and property rights, and censorship. Residents who were among the many Oregon women enfranchised in 1912 lost their voting rights because the 1859 Oregon Constitution declared "no idiot or insane person shall be entitled to the privileges of an elector." They could vote again only after they were officially discharged by OSH staff after a period of parole that lasted about a year.[1]

The OSH was also a site of resistance to these policies and actions during this period, including by women and gender-nonconforming people—from daily defiance and endurance to negotiations for release with the support of advocates, resistance to deportation, resistance to sterilization, and civil suits such as *Springer v. Steiner,* which brought civil liberties violations at the OSH to the Oregon Supreme Court in 1919.

THE OREGON STATE HOSPITAL FOR THE INSANE

The year 1913 was one of expansion and reorganization for Oregon's carceral and custodial institutions. In response to growing numbers of commitments and overcrowding, voters approved the construction of a second state asylum for the insane, and Eastern Oregon State Hospital in Pendleton opened its doors in January 1913 with a transfer of some three hundred patients and staff from Salem. That same January, at the request of Governor Oswald West, Oregon legislators consolidated prisons, asylums, and other state custodial institutions under the authority of a single state Board of Control, removing individual institutional boards of trustees. West hoped this move would provide cost savings in management and efficiency and would avoid individual institutions being used as "political footballs" each legislative session. The Board of Control comprised the Oregon governor, secretary of state, and state treasurer, and they placed institutions on strict and uniform systems of accounting and reporting.[2] Perhaps the most poignant element of the consolidation policy was additional 1913 legislation providing for the construction of a crematorium on the osh grounds for unclaimed bodies of the dead from osh and from all state institutions. In addition, legislators evacuated and closed the osh cemetery, ordering the exhumation and cremation of the bodies of those who had died and been buried at osh before 1913.[3]

Family, friends, community members, members of law enforcement, and physicians could commit Oregonians to the osh by means of a sanity hearing before "one or more competent physicians" and a county judge.[4] There were many small, private sanitaria in the state as well as private duty nurses for people with the means to afford them, but the osh was a large institution into which people with many and varying conditions were gathered, including patients in the last neurological phases of syphilis, those with dementia or epilepsy, people experiencing developmental and intellectual disabilities, or those with physical conditions such as cancer, as well as a host of conditions under the rubric of "insanity." Some people were there because they held views or behaved in ways contrary to community and family expectations or disrupted community standards. Experts and the public held many conflicting views about what constituted "insanity" and how best to provide treatment. The osh was like a small city on the outskirts of Salem, an employer of hundreds, a place where goods were produced and consumed, where some two thousand staff and residents lived and worked. Residents were patients seeking treatment and health but also inmates who were confined, who received "restraint" and punishment, who might have visits with friends and family restricted or prevented, and whose incoming and outgoing mail was censored by institutional policy. After 1917 sterilization was often a requirement for patients to be released. OSH managers deported and attempted to deport OSH inmates who were residents of other states or who were not US citizens.[5]

For the 1913–1922 period the daily patient population average at OSH expanded from fifteen hundred to about two thousand, and facilities continued to be severely overcrowded, even after the construction of the second hospital in Pendleton.[6] According to OSH reports, women made up a consistent 36 to 37 percent of new admissions until 1920, rising to 41 percent of new admissions in 1921–1922. About 50 to 55 percent of women were admitted from Portland and its surrounding Multnomah County. Most women OSH residents, from 70 to 80 percent, were born in the United States, and those who were first-generation immigrants came almost exclusively from Canada, Great Britain, and Europe. By 1917–1918, OSH began to report the category of race for residents, and from 1917 to 1922 staff counted eleven Black women, two South Asian Americans, one Chinese American, and one Indigenous woman.[7] Oregon residents were overwhelmingly White in this period, and the very small numbers of women of color at OSH certainly reflect these population figures. Errors in record keeping are apparent from a study of some patient files. For example, Margarita Ojeta Wilcox, born in Mexico, does not appear in these figures as having been born there.[8] Native people committed from reservations, including the single Indigenous woman who came to OSH during these years, were officially wards of the federal government and could not remain permanently at a state institution. They would be committed permanently to the federal Asylum for Insane Indians at Canton, South Dakota.[9]

By virtue of their commitment, the state considered patients to be "unfit" citizens who through productive work might reenter civic life and regain their civic and mental health. The same 1913 legislation that created the Board of Control affirmed the practice of using inmate labor "in the production and manufacture of articles for the use of, and in the performance of labor for the State."[10] When people were committed,

152 / CHAPTER 6

they were often considered "insane" or "deficient" because they were not engaged in suitable work. Thus productive work was part of the systems of most institutions and asylums across the country. Doctors considered it therapeutic, and administrators knew it helped pay the bills and keep overcrowded institutions solvent.[11] In 1915–1916, OSH employed women "each day in preparing vegetables for the kitchen and in assisting with the various housekeeping details of the many wards" as well as engaging in seasonal harvesting of farm and orchard crops. "Basketry, rug-making, needlework and fancy sewing" in the industrial room resulted in hundreds of products offered for sale to benefit state institutions. Fifty patients, most likely women, worked in the laundry under the direction of four staff members, doing "all the washing, ironing and sterilizing for the entire institution, turning out approximately 10,000,000 pieces of work during the biennium," in addition to making all of the soap for OSH and other institutions.[12] Some fifty women worked in the sewing room and produced thousands of articles of clothing, linens, and surgical gear and supplies for patients and staff each year. They sewed articles related to the life cycle including sanitary napkins, cloth diapers when inmates gave birth, and burial shrouds. Women workers mended more than ten thousand articles within the hospital each year for reuse by patients and staff. OSH officials purchased commercially-made restraints but also had women patients in the sewing room produce them for institutional use, including 462 straitjackets and over five hundred waist belt restraints from 1913 to 1922.[13] Women's engagement in this civically suitable productive work at the OSH meant that they were sewing the very articles that staff used to restrain them as part of their treatment.

The OSH was a medical and surgical hospital in addition to an institution for people considered insane or incapacitated. After 1917 the possibility of state-ordered sterilization in the OSH operating room was a direct part of the lives of most inmates, for men at most any age and for women before menopause. We cannot calculate the impact of sterilization or the threat of sterilization on people's lives. Mark Largent, in his compilation of statistics from Board of Eugenics reports found that 60 percent (302 of 509) of the sterilizations at OSH between 1918 and 1941 were surgeries on women; the vast majority were salpingectomies to remove all or part of the fallopian tube, with other women having ovaries removed. From 1913 through 1922 the core period examined in this book, the Oregon State

Eugenics Board reported thirty-six salpingectomies and six ovariectomies at OSH. The female patient files and other reports suggest those numbers underestimate the number of state-ordered or state-coerced sterilization surgeries on women.[14]

The OSH was also equipped for other medical, surgical, and dental procedures. Many patients had limited access to hospitals and medical care because of poverty and other systemic restrictions due to class, ethnicity, and race as well as second-language and regional circumstances. The hospital expanded laboratory, medical, surgical, and dental facilities across the 1910s and 1920s. Each patient received "a thorough physical, neurological and mental examination, including laboratory tests of the blood [for syphilis] and urine, dental inspection, usually including X-ray examination." Because of lack of funds and access, most women admitted to OSH did not have "the means to secure even the most urgently needed dental work or surgical operation."[15]

Most female patients at OSH and individuals in this chapter shared a key experience: being evaluated and treated by Lewis Frank Griffith, MD, first assistant physician and assistant superintendent of OSH. Griffith was arguably the most significant practitioner of radical eugenic sterilization in Oregon in the early twentieth century. Bethenia Owens-Adair, MD, was certainly the most active lobbyist for eugenics laws in the state and had a wide audience. Robert E. Lee Steiner, MD, superintendent of the OSH from 1908 to 1937, was a visible and successful bureaucrat who favored sterilization but was active principally as hospital administrator.[16] Griffith's influence stemmed from his work as a teaching professor, academic, and expert witness, as a popularizer of radical sterilization theory and practice, and via his direct control of patients at the OSH for more than three decades. Born in 1868 to a White settler farming family on substantial acreage east of Salem, Griffith attended Willamette University and graduated with high honors from Vanderbilt University Medical Department in 1890. His 1897 marriage to Julia Metschan, daughter of state treasurer Phil Metschan, expanded his social and political horizons.[17]

Griffith began his long term of service at the OSH in 1891 and served as first assistant superintendent and physician, with a 1919–1920 interlude as acting superintendent, until his death in 1930. A member of the teaching faculty at the Willamette University Medical College until its merger with the University of Oregon Medical Department in 1913, Griffith held the

154 / CHAPTER 6

chair of obstetrics and a professorship in the "diseases of women."[18] Following the merger, he lectured and supervised clinics on mental disease and diseases of women as a clinical lecturer in psychiatry until his death.[19] Griffith often served as an expert witness in trials and commitment hearings, expanding his reputation in the new field of psychiatry.[20] Griffith's reach across the medical and medical-legal community—as a teaching professor, in his role in popularizing eugenics as a legislative public health measure, as an administrator who implemented eugenic policy, and in his daily work as the surgeon who operated on people at OSH—meant that his impact on inmates' lives was immense and consequential.

In medical and legal circles, and as a popular public speaker for the Oregon Social Hygiene Society whose presentations were reprinted by newspaper editors, Griffith voiced a specifically Oregonian eugenics of settler colonialism and advocated surgical sterilization for all persons deemed insane or "feebleminded," a radical position in step with Owens-Adair's furthest-reaching sterilization and eugenic marriage legislation.[21] Griffith embraced this view as early as 1913, placing him at odds with other leading Oregon physicians who specialized in psychiatric and developmental disabilities and accepted sterilization for some but not all persons in institutions at that time.[22] Combining eugenic thinking with nativism and settler colonialism, Griffith argued that the conditions and nature of immigration had changed by the early twentieth century, resulting in increased insanity and disabilities in Oregon and the Pacific West specifically.[23] He wrote: "Our own state and the Pacific Coast generally may proudly boast that the strongest and most intrepid offspring of the sturdy New England stock toiled through months of hardships, privation, and danger, across desert plains to reach this far shore, obeying the instinct that 'Westward the Course of Empire Takes Its Way,'" to build the "last and greatest empire of man." This "dream might have worked out if all who came" had to undergo the challenging passage West, Griffith said, "which would test their fitness more thoroughly than the most skillful immigration official."[24]

But by the 1910s he believed the "survival of the fittest" in Oregon was no longer possible. "Conditions have changed, transportation facilities invite the neurotic, the restless fanatic, the criminal whose native surroundings have become untenable, the invalid seeking change, all to come to the Golden West." The result was, Griffith concluded, "our pure stock

[is] becoming polluted" with "unfit stock." These conditions, combined with stressful modern life and the transmission of syphilis, were bringing "insanity," "mental inferiority," and "degeneration" to Oregon in large numbers, perhaps some 30 percent of the state's population. This "state of affairs," Griffith believed, left Oregonians with only one recourse: the sterilization of every person who might possibly be "insane" or "mentally inferior." Even the "insane who recover," he insisted, "breed disaster to the coming generations." Griffith believed in sterilization for all of Oregon's "defective classes."[25]

Most women committed to the OSH during this period encountered Griffith in some capacity. Many faced him in the most intimate inspections of their bodies and had to deal with him daily as a medical gatekeeper with control over them and their treatment. He made decisions about sterilization, parole, and release. Griffith controlled women's ability to see and communicate with family, friends, and advocates. The system they entered was ordered on his views. Griffith and others on the medical staff at the OSH had the power to sterilize residents in large part because of the advocacy of many White clubwomen across the state who supported eugenic legislation and embraced the eugenic concepts of the fit and unfit and the policing of bodies behind the state's eugenic laws. They supported Griffith's and Owens-Adair's radical view of the sterilization of all "unfit" Oregonians, a policy in force for sixty years.

MARGARITA OJEDA WILCOX

Given Griffith's racialized and nativist ideas about eugenics and "degeneracy," it is not surprising that he worked to deport some OSH residents who were not US citizens as unfit internal enemies of the state. Thirty-two-year-old Portlander Margarita Ojeda Wilcox was committed to the OSH in December 1919 at the request of her husband, Walter, via the proscribed process of a court hearing and physicians' examination. Born in Mexico in 1887, Margarita was sixteen in 1904 when she married Walter in Arizona; Walter was a US citizen employed in Mexico as an engineer working with machinery, likely in mining. The couple resided in the Mexican state of Sonora and came to the United States for periodic stays; those stays lengthened with the increasing turbulence of the Mexican Revolution after 1910 and eventually led to their full-time residence in

156 / CHAPTER 6

FIGURE 19 Margarita Ojeda Wilcox, 1919. Oregon State Hospital Female Patient Files, Oregon State Archives, Salem.

Oregon. Walter requested commitment because Margarita had become acutely fearful of others and at times violent toward him, and he hoped the hospital could be of help to her. She had no physical injury, he said, but during the Revolution she had experienced "plenty of fright," with a "revolver in her face, threatened with death, shot at, old friends killed." For months, Walter said, "we did not know what minute we would be killed." If Ojeda Wilcox saw "anyone digging anywhere," she believed it was for her grave.[26] Her circumstances reveal what we today would call post-traumatic stress and point to the long trauma of wartime violence in people's lives, including noncombatants.

Federal immigration law, Oregon state legislation, and OSH policy all came into play as officials examined Ojeda Wilcox's case, and her patient file became a document for and a record of surveillance against her. Griffith and OSH staff flagged her case because she had been born in Mexico, and they believed she was not a US citizen. Federal immigration law from 1891 excluded persons likely to become a public charge, which could include those committed to a state asylum, and stipulated that immigration officials could deport people who became dependent on public funds for a period of a year after their arrival. Legislation later expanded this deportation window to two and then three years. The federal Immigration Act of 1917 targeted "insane persons" specifically and expanded deportability to five years of residency.[27] At the urging of OSH officials, the state legislature appropriated $8,000 at the 1917 biennial session "for transporting the non-resident insane out of the State of Oregon" and continued funding thereafter.[28] The practice in Oregon, as Alexandra Minna Stern found for California, was nativist but "couched in fiscal terms."[29] Legislators and immigration administrators and staff spent "considerable resources to single out people likely to become public charges," as Adam Goodman's research demonstrates, and the policy was gendered with more women deported as likely to become public charges because officials treated women as "male breadwinners' dependents rather than economic actors in their own right."[30] OSH biennial reports emphasized and documented the cost savings but did not provide reliable statistics. During the 1913–1920 period, OSH reported deporting 680 "non-residents" but did not always distinguish whether this was to other US states or to countries outside the United States. After 1920 OSH stopped providing direct numbers and reported merely that "with the assistance of the United States Immigration officers we have deported residents of foreign countries whenever possible."[31]

Court commitment documents for Ojeda Wilcox specify that she had been in the United States for seven and a half years, listing the date she entered the country as July 2, 1912, which would place her safely outside the five-year window for deportation if found to be insane. We don't have an account directly from Ojeda Wilcox herself, but the first medical notes of her file, likely written by or with the supervision of Griffith, specify that she stated she had "been in the U.S. continuously" for seven and a half years. "This statement is doubted," Griffith wrote, questioning her residency statements and status directly in the medical notes of her file with no additional evidence.[32] Across the next several weeks Griffith worked hand in hand with Ralph P. Bonham, director of the Oregon Bureau of the US Immigration office in Portland, to check Ojeda Wilcox's immigration and citizenship status. In this postwar period of nativism, anti-immigrant, and antiradical fervor, Bonham was known for "combing the penitentiary, insane asylum and other institutions at Salem for subjects who might properly be shown out through the country's back door." Like other immigration officials nationwide, Bonham "enjoyed tremendous discretionary power" to obtain deportations.[33]

In a December 23 letter, Griffith wrote to Bonham that he suspected Ojeda Wilcox, born in Mexico, could be deported. Griffith had contacted her husband, Walter, in Portland for additional information and enclosed a letter written by Walter "which states that he took her to her people in Mexico about the year 1917." Such a visit would mean Ojeda Wilcox had not been in the United States continuously for the required five years and could in fact be deported via the 1917 Immigration Act. Griffith gave Bonham the Portland contact information so that he could question Walter directly and check additional documentation.[34] Alerted by questions concerning their US residency and travel to Mexico, it appears that Walter took steps to have his wife released, and he was successful. The file is silent about the process, however, and it is not clear if they knew that the 1907 Expatriation Act made Ojeda Wilcox a US citizen because of their marriage. The couple may not have trusted the immigration system to work in their favor, and they apparently had some legal advice or knowledge about the need to demonstrate at least five years' residence in the United States for a person not born in the United States who was committed. Ojeda Wilcox's release may have been possible because OSH physicians could not seem to make a definitive diagnosis: at thirty-two, she was "well physically," but they could not determine her "mental state." Griffith noted she was "large and strong and her body is well nourished," signaling that doctors believed Ojeda Wilcox would be capable of productive labor if released. Intake information indicated she had never been pregnant, and her relatively short commitment time meant there was no window for an application to the Eugenics Board for her sterilization. Her Wassermann test, administered to all patients on intake to test for syphilis, came back with a negative result.[35] For all or some of these reasons, hospital staff paroled Ojeda Wilcox to her husband's care on January 5, 1920, one month and a day after her commitment. She left the hospital "much improved," they reported.[36]

Almost two weeks later, on January 17, 1920, Bonham wrote to Griffith. He had investigated the case and found that Walter was a US citizen. Because of the 1907 Federal Expatriation Act, Ojeda Wilcox took the US citizenship of her husband when they married and therefore she could not be deported.[37] The same act that required US-born women married to German-citizen men to register as "enemy aliens" during the war made Ojeda Wilcox a US citizen who could not be deported for insanity. She was already paroled with her husband, but now Bonham's letter about her citizenship status ended the threat of deportation should she be readmitted. Per process, Walter wrote to Griffith a year from Ojeda Wilcox's parole, indicating that she was "doing fine" and he had had "no trouble with her since she left the hospital." Griffith discharged her permanently.[38] The couple relocated to Nevada, where Walter worked with the Union Pacific Railroad. He was killed in a car crash in 1926; Ojeda Wilcox was a passenger, sustained injuries, and died in 1928.[39]

LOUISE BURBANK

Margarita Ojeda Wilcox avoided deportation, but OSH and immigration officials deported twenty-one-year-old Canadian-born Portland domestic worker Louise Burbank in 1925. Burbank decided on deportation as part of a coordinated plan with friends and advocates to escape state ordered-sterilization at OSH. She came to Portland in January 1924 to work as a maid for Florence and William Holford and their three children at their home in the affluent Riverdale neighborhood. William was a noted Portland architect who had designed the University of Oregon Medical School building in Portland among other landmarks as a partner in the prominent architectural firm of Lawrence & Holford.[40] In October, when Burbank "rather suddenly became excited, and disturbed in mind," she received some care in a private sanitarium and was admitted to Portland's St. Vincent's Hospital under the supervision of Dr. George N. Pease. By the end of October, William Holford petitioned for a sanity hearing for Burbank, and after an examination by Dr. William House, Judge George Tazwell committed her to the OSH. Burbank arrived on November 1, 1924.[41]

Florence Holford took an active interest in the progress of Burbank's case and advocated for her care. As the daughter of an influential Brooklyn, New York, surgeon, sister to two physicians, and wife of a prominent Portlander who had designed the city's newest medical building, she was confident and persistent in her correspondence with OSH physicians.[42] Burbank "has been a fine maid and a lovely girl," Holford wrote to Steiner, superintendent of the OSH. When Holford wanted to send Burbank a holiday gift basket, Griffith discouraged the act of kindness and support. "In her present condition I think she would give no heed to a Christmas box," he wrote. Holford asked about Burbank's condition in a July 1925 letter

160 / CHAPTER 6

to Steiner and wanted to know when she could be released.[43] Holford was conversant in the medical world with a prominent family and status. Her advocacy for Burbank was a reminder to OSH doctors and directors that she was watching from outside the walls with the social power to expect reports and results.

Louise Burbank resisted her commitment and sterilization with daily defiance and by engaging in a series of negotiations about sterilization and deportation with the help of outside advocates. Burbank was "noisy and much disposed to resist," Griffith told Holford in a letter soon after Burbank arrived at OSH. "Since coming to my ward she has been so disobedient that I have not undertaken to talk with her," assistant physician Walter W. Looney wrote to Holford in January 1925. And by July, nine months into her commitment, Looney reported Burbank still needed restraints to "keep her out of mischief."[44] Diagnosed with manic depression, in February 1925 the State Board of Eugenics authorized Burbank's sterilization after just three months of commitment. OSH staff made the request because "this young woman is of child-bearing age and because of her mental condition it is thought wise to recommend her case for sterilization to prevent procreation, in the event she should leave the hospital."[45] Here was Griffith's radical eugenics in action to sterilize the "insane who recover" to prevent them from "breed[ing] disaster to the coming generations." But Burbank did not want to be sterilized and initially did not provide her consent for the operation. By mid-March the board had received permission from Burbank's sister in Canada for the procedure as a legal alternative to Burbank's own consent.[46]

Burbank's friends Marguerite Romacly and Lillian Lafferty, bank clerks in Portland, became effective advocates opposing her sterilization. After they visited the OSH in August 1925, Lafferty wrote to request that Burbank be paroled to their care as they were in a position to provide support for her until she was stronger and "capable of caring for herself." The attending nurse had told them Burbank "would soon be well enough to go home." In response, Looney wrote that Burbank "no doubt will be able to leave the hospital in the near future." It was, he said, "a little early for her to be released as she might have a relapse." He informed Burbank's friends that physicians had "presented her case to the State Board of Eugenics and they have granted us permission to sterilize her." OSH surgeons would operate "within a week or so," and after recovering, Burbank "should be

FIGURE 20 Louise Burbank, 1925. Oregon State Hospital Female Patient Files, Oregon State Archives, Salem.

in a condition to leave the hospital." This was shocking news to Burbank's friends, and Lafferty wrote expressing urgent concern and asking if Burbank had given permission. Lafferty felt "sure if [Burbank] realized fully what it means, she would not wish it." Please "with hold this operation until you could mail us the full data," Lafferty concluded.[47]

Within days, Portland attorney Junius Ohmart agreed to represent Lafferty and Romacly in their quest to intercede to prevent Louise Burbank's sterilization and have her released from OSH to their care. A graduate of the University of Michigan Law School and a Christian Scientist, Ohmart had authored an unsuccessful 1920 statewide ballot measure opposing compulsory vaccination in schools and appeared to oppose state sterilization based on similar religious principles.[48] Ohmart contacted Steiner on behalf of his two clients, recounting their correspondence with Looney. Ohmart told Steiner that his clients had informed him that Burbank wanted to be discharged but that Looney had informed her she "could not leave until she signed a statement giving her written consent to such an operation." Trapped, fearful, and confined, Burbank had succumbed to the pressure and signed the consent form "in her anxiety to leave the hospital." Burbank's friends knew that she was "very much opposed to such an operation," Ohmart wrote, and they "were concerned about her welfare

162 / CHAPTER 6

and would look after her upon her release." Ohmart did not disclose his own spiritual beliefs to Steiner, but reported that Burbank was "interested in Christian Science and has been receiving helpful treatments in that respect." Ohmart requested a cancellation of the sterilization order based on the religious exemption in the 1923 law. He provided strong character references for Lafferty, employed at Portland's Bates Bank, and Romacly, at Portland's First National Bank, and requested Burbank be released to their care without being sterilized.[49]

When Steiner received Ohmart's letter and requests, he took immediate action. First, he "went over the matter" of sterilization with Burbank, telling her that he knew her friends believed it to be unnecessary. "But after going over the various phases of the case with her," Steiner reported, "she felt that her interests could be best protected by having this done." After this coercive discussion without any advocate present, Steiner had Burbank sign another consent form to replace the one her friends said she had signed earlier under duress. Louise Burbank's signature on that coerced sterilization consent form is shaky with contorted letters, different from other signatures she provided while at OSH, poignant direct evidence of her reaction to the conversation, the pressure, and the life-altering implications of Steiner's "consultation" with her. Next Steiner reported Burbank to Oregon Immigration Bureau director Ralph Bonham for deportation after asking additional questions about her citizenship status and Canadian birth during their "talk." Steiner asked Bonham to expedite the deportation process. Burbank was "in very good physical and mental condition," he wrote, "and we are anxious to have her case acted upon at your earliest convenience" because "we fear that by the time her case might be passed upon she would be so disturbed that we would have trouble getting her back [to Canada]." Steiner wrote to Ohmart, insisting that Burbank's sterilization order had been "handled in the regular manner," and he had a "definite Order" by the State Eugenics Board. Steiner outlined his "consultation" with Burbank, noted that she had consented to sterilization after his session with her, and announced that he had initiated deportation proceedings against her because she was "a foreigner and a public charge." In their ongoing correspondence, Ohmart notified Steiner he would be on vacation until September 12 and asked that Steiner take "no action whatsoever" until his return. Armed with Burbank's "consent" and with deportation orders in motion, Steiner told

Ohmart he would not act to sterilize her before Ohmart's return "unless some circumstance arises warranting this to be done and that does not seem probable to me now."[50]

Burbank and her advocates responded to Steiner's actions by raising consent questions relating to her case and by turning the citizenship and deportation question back on Steiner and OSH to try to prevent her sterilization. Lafferty and Romacly visited Burbank at OSH and found her in "good condition." She told them she had only given Steiner consent for her sterilization "under pressure of desire to leave the institution." Ohmart wrote: "Inasmuch as [Burbank] is not a citizen of the United States but is a foreigner and a citizen of Canada," she could be deported to her sister in Alberta "without the necessity of having any operation." Her lack of citizenship made sterilization legally questionable. "It would appear to me," Ohmart told Steiner, "that inasmuch as she is not a citizen of this country that such an operation should not be performed." It's possible that Ohmart knew no Canadian province had yet legislated state sterilization; this meant that Burbank would be safe from the procedure if somehow she was institutionalized after her deportation to Canada.[51] Griffith responded on behalf of OSH the next day. They would be willing to work with Burbank's sister to have her returned to Canada. "There will be no disposition to insist upon her being sterilized," Griffith wrote, "if she or her probable progeny are not to be charges upon this state."[52] Fiscal considerations and the possible legal challenges of sterilizing a Canadian citizen eclipsed Griffith's and Steiner's desire to sterilize Louise Burbank as an "insane" person.

Over the next several weeks, with the question of sterilization apparently resolved, Lafferty, Romacly, and Ohmart tried to have OSH physicians parole Burbank to their care in an effort to protect her from deportation. Arrangements for Burbank's deportation would take a few days, Romacly and Lafferty wrote to Steiner, and "we would appreciate it if you can arrange for us to have her" in our care. Griffith responded that patients must be deported directly from the hospital because in the past staff had "a great deal of trouble" with "the matter getting out of our hands and the arrangements not being carried out." My clients will provide for Louise Burbank, Ohmart informed Steiner. Burbank was healthy and did not want to return to Canada. She "would rather remain here, and obtain employment, [and] it would seem to me that would be the rea-

164 / CHAPTER 6

sonable thing to do to, rather than to force her deportation." This would all relieve OSH, immigration, and Burbank's sister from "a burden and expense." If Burbank relapsed, which he and his clients believed would not happen, "then the question of the operation could be taken up." No, Griffith responded. Burbank's case was "in the hands" of immigration, and he referred them directly to Bonham. It would be a "serious mistake" not to deport her because "it is most likely that eventually she will become a public charge. The same is true of any of her possible progeny." Griffith wrote to Bonham that same day, alerting him that Ohmart, Lafferty, and Romacly were trying to free Burbank and to "keep her in this country." We are "sending the photographs" of Burbank to you, he said, presumably so that Bonham would have her image for identification and apprehension in case Burbank and her advocates tried to free her by other means or if Burbank tried to escape en route to Canada.[53]

On October 3, OSH staff released Louise Burbank to immigration custody with a formal discharge from the institution. Bonham reported to OSH that immigration officers "checked [her] out" of the United States at Eastport, Idaho, on October 13, 1925. Burbank carried her handbag and a suitcase with the possessions she had brought with her when committed: clothing, outerwear, gloves and hat, bracelets, earrings, personal care items, and a Red Cross pin.[54] Burbank's situation and strategies place her among the thousands of people who "voluntarily" agreed to deportation in Adam Goodman's study of this period, including increasing numbers of people born in Canada or Mexico.[55] And for Burbank, who did not wish to return to Canada, deportation was the alternative to the far more destructive act of sterilization. The threat, the certainty of sterilization if she remained, was a powerful incentive to cooperate with this voluntary deportation from the OSH, Oregon, and the United States.

Louise Burbank, her employer, her friends, and the attorney that represented them engaged in strategic, multilayered, persistent negotiations with the doctors at OSH. They prevented OSH physicians from sterilizing her by state order but the cost was deportation. Ohmart's position on state sterilization and vaccination as a Christian Scientist was likely one reason he agreed to represent Burbank's interests, and he reported that Burbank herself had received Christian Science treatments. It's not clear whether Lafferty and Romacly were also Christian Scientists, but Rolf Swensen's research into early twentieth-century adherents in Portland and other

Pacific Coast cities demonstrates strong participation from wage-earning women in a movement "on the cutting edge of new assumptions about health, religion, and the roles of the sexes."[56] It's less likely that Florence Holford was connected to Christian Science as the daughter and sister of regular medical practitioners. But her social prominence and advocacy through frequent inquiries about Burbank signaled that she was keeping watch on her progress at OSH. Holford, Lafferty, and Romacly all provided written evidence of their support for Louise Burbank to show that she would have a place to live and could find employment after her release so that she would not be a "public charge." Griffith, Steiner, and Bonham, however, professed a certainty that Burbank and her "probable progeny" would become public charges despite evidence to the contrary. These assumptions without evidence were the basis for both her sterilization order and her deportation. As Goodman notes, the "likely to become a public charge" clause in immigration regulations was "capacious and difficult to refute."[57]

Louise Burbank and her advocates engaged in one final act of resistance to the policies and practices of the Oregon State Hospital and federal immigration authorities. By some means she returned to Portland and worked again as a maid in the home of her former employers, Florence and William Holford, from 1927 to at least 1930.[58]

WINNIE HULL SPRINGER

If Margarita Ojeda Wilcox and Louise Burbank experienced commitments and attempts at deportations among a circle of family, friends, and advocates, Winnie Hull Springer engaged in resistance to both policy and family during her commitment to the OSH and its aftermath. The circumstances that brought the teacher and woman suffrage activist to OSH and then to become an advocate for patient rights comprised a public strand and a more private strand of experiences. The public strand led to legal action and courtroom testimony about citizenship and civil liberties abuses that roiled the institutional world of Oregon and the region in a case that went to the Oregon Supreme Court in 1919. The more private strand was a process of conflict, inquiry, self-discovery, and self-determination. Winnie identified as female but was struggling with questions about her nonbinary body in a world that insisted on male and female.[59] Born in

166 / CHAPTER 6

Washington State in 1879, Winnie came with her parents to a Benton County, Oregon, farm as a child. Educated at Philomath College and at Monmouth Normal School for her teaching certificate, she taught school with husband Clare G. Springer in Umatilla in eastern Oregon and Mill City in Marion County. She was a votes-for-women activist and organizer during the final 1912 Oregon campaign and authored a popular "Ballots for Women" song and several weekly installments of a woman suffrage column in the *Corvallis Gazette Times*.[60]

The public strand of events about Winnie's OSH commitment showcased contrasting viewpoints held by Winnie herself and by family, medical, and judicial "experts" about alternative healing versus traditional medical expertise, the rights to due process and safety in one's person versus "necessary" restraint and institutionalization, and the impact of the label of "insanity" on useful employment. Trial transcripts, newspaper articles, and other documentation of the conflicting views scripted a public version of the case. Winnie had experienced painful menstruation since adolescence. In 1914, Winnie's brother-in-law, Dr. Emil Washington Howard, had recommended to then thirty-five-year-old Winnie an operation for a tipped uterus to relieve the pain and perhaps other surgery. Winnie "refused, determinedly, to go on the operating table" and came to Portland in December 1914 to pursue alternative healing methods, including Christian Science and New Thought.[61] Winnie studied with Dr. Perry Joseph Green of Portland's New Thought Temple of Truth and believed her condition to be cured by the first week of January 1915.[62] She contacted her father, William Hull, in Benton County, thinking he could find relief for his own medical problems in sessions with Green. Thereafter Hull, Dr. Howard, and Winnie's sister Tena Howard, his wife, came to Portland to try to convince Winnie to return home. Soon law enforcement officers apprehended Winnie at the Portland YMCA and transported her to the Multnomah County jail against her will. They held Winnie there while her father brought commitment proceedings before Multnomah County judge T. J. Cleeton and Drs. Curtis Holcomb and Sanford Whiting, on January 8, 1915. Winnie was transported and admitted to OSH, where she resided for five months until paroled to her sister Tena on May 31, 1915. During Winnie's time at OSH, administrators put her to unpaid work sweeping ward floors and producing baskets in the industrial room.[63] Winnie returned to live with her husband, Clare, on their Benton County property that fall and was fully discharged from the OSH in March 1916.[64] Winnie's release was eleven months before the Oregon legislature passed its 1917 sterilization law, so her experience did not include the threat of forced sterilization by the state.

After release Winnie built a case to challenge her commitment to the OSH and the treatment she experienced there. She wrote to Oregon attorney general George Brown and to Dr. Griffith at OSH in November 1915 and sent numerous letters to Griffith thereafter through the end of 1916 with questions and requests to see her hospital files, including the many letters she had written.[65] Winnie hired Portland attorney Wilson T. Hume to represent her in a series of civil suits. They succeeded in having her official commitment papers voided and cancelled by a Multnomah County judge in January 1917. Then in circuit court they sued Steiner and Griffith, Winnie's brother-in-law, Dr. Howard, and examining physicians Holcomb and Whiting for wrongful imprisonment and requested $10,000 in damages. Winnie won the suit in May 1917 with an award of $2,500 and took satisfaction in the public hearing of the case details and the unanimous jury verdict.[66] Before the trial the court had eliminated Steiner and Griffith as defendants, maintaining that public officials could not be the objects of civil damage suits.[67] Winnie turned to the Marion County Court with jurisdiction over Salem, where the hospital was located. With attorney Grant Corby, a friend from Philomath college days, she brought a new suit against Steiner and Griffith, which was eventually dismissed.[68] Howard and Holcomb appealed the judgment against them, and the Oregon Supreme Court reversed the lower court's decision and dismissed the suit in February 1919.[69]

Winnie's legal proceedings and courtroom testimony revealed a long list of violations of civil liberties in the treatment and institutionalization of someone labeled as an insane person. Her challenges addressed due process rights, protections against false imprisonment and cruel and unusual punishment, property rights including control over letters to be mailed and received, economic citizenship, and the civic implications of a verdict of insanity. Winnie argued she had come to Portland in part to find an alternative means of healing chronic painful menstruation and had found a cure in New Thought healing techniques. Family members, especially her brother-in-law, Dr. Howard, believed that Winnie's choice to pursue New Thought instead of following mainstream medical advice

FIGURE 21 Winnie Springer. *Salem Capital Journal*, June 29, 1912, 5.

(and having the operation Howard recommended) constituted insanity. Howard, Winnie's sister Tena, and their father Hull tried to get Winnie to return home. They came to Portland and met with Perry Green to convince him to tell Winnie to return, and Howard sent Green a letter threatening him with the police if he did not comply.

Hull was staying at the YMCA, and when Winnie went to see her father there, he told her she was "not going to have anything more to do" with Green. As Winnie saw her father speaking with someone in the lobby, Multnomah County jail matron Elizabeth Rogers and two sheriff's deputies detained Winnie forcefully without explanation. They had no warrant and did not disclose any charges, seized Winnie "violently" and "restrained her of her liberty in a public place," and "forcibly and unlawfully conveyed [her] through the public streets," violating her rights of due process.[70] At the county jail, Winnie testified, staff did not allow her to contact other family members or friends. Drs. Holcomb and Whiting came to the cell, she testified, and "I answered their questions until I got indignant, when I thought they asked me questions they had no business to, and then I would not answer any more." None of the questions, Winnie testified, addressed her mental condition. Her father signed the complaint, but the other paperwork was incomplete and, attorney Hume argued, Judge Cleeton's name was typed on the commitment document without his signature.[71]

Charges of false imprisonment and religious freedom led to an extensive discussion of violations of additional civil liberties while Winnie was committed at the OSH. Winnie testified that she had been denied access to a lawyer and that the OSH had censored her mail as it was hospital policy for staff to intercept all mail written by inmates. In his testimony Griffith said Winnie had the "privilege of writing" to lawyers, family, and friends, but it was his decision whether to send any of that mail. The court allowed the introduction of seven letters between Winnie, her husband, her mother, and Griffith into evidence but did not have them read publicly. Counsel and the court read them for the appeal.[72] Winnie objected to violations of her right to be protected from cruel and unusual punishment. On her second day at the OSH, she said, after an initial intake, she objected when Griffith subjected her to a complete physical examination. "I considered it was an outrage," she testified, because she believed she was completely healed from painful menstruation. She questioned how a physical examination connected to mental competency. "If I had been ailing and saying that I had been, the doctor might have had some excuse for putting me thru that sort of examination."[73]

Winnie spoke of the use of an electric bath during her menstrual period that caused peeling and burns on her skin, combined with staff pouring water down her body for hours and trying to force her to drink water again and again. "They pour water down you like you have read about in the water cure in the Philippines," she testified, referencing war crimes committed by the United States in the recent Spanish-American-Philippine War.[74] Winnie described the use of waist and hand restraints for most of her three-month residence in the receiving ward. And when transferred to the main hospital ward, she said, staff compelled her to wear a straitjacket on many nights and once for a seventy-two-hour stretch. "It is not very long after one is in that position until one is aching all over," she testified, "and at the end of 72 hours I could not raise my right arm, the one that was drawn over, they drew my right arm over the left, so that it was nothing more nor less than torture."[75]

In addition to questions of punishment, Winnie addressed her right to economic citizenship in her suit. She and her attorney argued that even with her discharge from the OSH and the restoration of her civic rights,

170 / CHAPTER 6

including voting, she would have difficulty in finding employment as a teacher because of the record of her insanity. This was a key point: if the record remained, Hume told the court, it would be "a constant menace" to Winnie, "threatening to prevent her from earning her livelihood or exercising her rights under a life diploma as a teacher in the public schools of Oregon."[76] Oregon teachers had achieved a major economic rights victory in the 1913 legislative session, the first after woman suffrage, with the passage of a teacher tenure bill, which provided more job security with procedural steps and due process to prevent dismissal without cause.[77] But Springer and Hume contended that the record of commitment for insanity might be used as a cause for dismissal or even as a reason for not hiring her in the first place, even though she had secured a life-certificate to teach in the state.

When Winnie won the lower court judgment in May 1917 and the award of $2,500 by a unanimous jury, state and OSH officials and their attorneys were alarmed and worried. The three-person Oregon State Board of Control, consisting of the governor and the secretaries of state and treasury with administrative power over state institutions like the OSH, asked Oregon attorney general George M. Brown to take personal charge of the state's response to Winnie's suits. Brown succeeded in having OSH physicians Steiner and Griffith removed from the case, but state officials remained at vital attention as the case made its way to the Oregon Supreme Court.[78] Thad Vreeland, lead attorney for Dr. Curtis Holcomb, wrote to Griffith of his immediate plans for appeal. "If this case is affirmed there is not a legal commitment at the present time for any patient at the Oregon State Asylum," and "if the result before this last jury is a criterion of what may happen in the future it is a hard row of stumps for the defendant."[79]

The next day OSH superintendent Steiner wrote to Brown in light of the Springer decision to ask for his legal opinion on seven points relating to OSH operations and policies. Two of the seven points addressed censoring mails, including the right to open and censor the incoming and outgoing mail of inmates and the right to destroy mail without its being read or sent.[80] Brown was evidently waiting to respond publicly until the outcome of the appeal, as he issued no opinion and the practices continued. But Winnie's questions raised important civil liberties concerns. The Oregon Supreme Court reversed the $2,500 judgment for Winnie, noting that perhaps Dr. Holcomb's examination "was not so thorough as it might have been," but that he and Dr. Whiting were part of an established legislated process for commitment. The doctors were not responsible for OSH policies and practices. And since Attorney General Brown and his staff had been able to have Steiner and Griffith removed from the suit, they and the OSH were not on trial. The legal process ultimately exonerated all of the defendants.[81]

The public strand of the case revealed some, but not all, of a more private strand of Winnie's experiences. Sometime in 1913, Winnie's husband, Clare, decided that the couple should quit their teaching posts in Mill City on the North Santiam River some thirty miles from Salem and live on land they purchased near Philomath in Benton County. The property would require substantial repair and construction work, and he wanted them to take that on themselves. Winnie liked the community and her work in Mill City and wanted to stay; the district had offered them both raises and wanted them to continue teaching. But Clare prevailed and they left at the end of the school year. Isolated and unhappy, Winnie described a "life of oblivion" at the "backwoods ranch, a regular hole in the ground, where we sunk most of the money we saved when we were teachers." She didn't even have a horse "to get away with when I wanted to." Her mother later recalled that when Winnie visited her after the move to the Benton County ranch, she was poorly dressed. Winnie had scrimped on things "to save money to pay for the place" and felt "too shabby" to visit her sister. Clare made threats of physical violence against Winnie and threatened to harm himself, leading her mother and sister to try to bring her home to separate Winnie from Clare for her physical safety and "so that she would not lose her mind."[82] Winnie wrote during her commitment: "I have never lived hardly a happy day with that man. For if he chanced to be pleasant I was still sad because of some recent abuse."[83]

Winnie was also grappling with identity, sexuality, and questions about bodies. In a later letter to her mother, she wrote of her 1879 birth with her twin brother Willie: "There was no doctor to welcome me into the world and no nurse," and "you have told me that you could scarcely determine my sex. 'I looked as much like a boy as a girl.' I said I wished I had grown to be a boy. You said I developed into a girl." Later "you told me that you suspicioned that I was a hermaphrodite and was built wrong and that was why I had such pain. After I was married you again told me of this and held out the idea that I 'could not have a child if I wanted to.' I never truly *wanted* to."[84] In other letters, Winnie indicated she was attracted to

172 / CHAPTER 6

many men sexually beyond her husband Clare. Her brother-in-law, Dr. Howard, advised an operation for a tipped uterus to relieve menstrual pain; Winnie's aversion to an operation could also have included a fear of some additional or alternative operative procedure that might alter or remove external or internal genitalia.

Sometime before the end of 1914, Winnie took steps to break free from her marriage and other family expectations about her life. A voracious reader, she consulted with Oregon state librarian Cornelia Marvin to check out books on New Thought and self-help from the Oregon State Library and also discovered the New Thought magazine *Nautilus* at around this time, published by former Portlander Elizabeth Towne.[85] Winnie testified at her civil suit trial that "the family had been talking in the idea that an operation was the best thing to do," but Dr. Howard was at the Mayo Clinic for postgraduate studies and would not be returning until "after Thanksgiving time, and the operation had been postponed until after his return."[86] This window seemed to be an opportunity and a catalyst for action. By December 1914, Winnie decided to separate from her husband. But instead of going to stay with her sister Tena Howard in Brownsville as planned, she took the train to Portland and got a room at the YWCA. "I came to Portland for several purposes," she testified. Her brother-in-law's recommended operation "had a great deal to do" with her decision to come to the city to explore New Thought methods of alternative healing. Winnie also met with Mary Frances Isom, head librarian of Portland's Central Library, because she had "been considering the matter of taking a library training course" as a new career and life direction.[87]

By 1914, Portland's New Thought community was a well-established enclave of alternative healing and spirituality that in the decades before Springer's arrival had attracted women activists such as Eleanor Baldwin, Elizabeth Towne, Abigail Scott Duniway, Millie Trumbull, Clara Colby, and Lucy Rose Mallory. New Thought had many crosscurrents and schools of thought regarding gender roles and women's rights, but, as Lawrence Lipin demonstrates in his biography of Eleanor Baldwin, many Portlanders were drawn to New Thought views about the cultural and social construction of women's health and illness and the belief that people should take their health, their bodies, and their lives into their own capable hands.[88] Dr. Perry Joseph Green was a rising star in Portland's New Thought community, and it was to Green that Springer went for healing education and support. Green had established the New Thought Temple of Truth in 1911, and his weekly Sunday lectures and midweek entertainment nights had expanded membership and interest and made New Thought a visible presence in the city. A major thread of his messages was "Mind Power" and "Heal Thyself Through Realization and Knowledge." Green had been a vocal opponent of Oregon's 1913 Eugenic Sterilization bill, insisting it was wrong for medical authorities "to have this power over the bodies of insane persons or prisoners."[89]

After attending one of Green's lectures the day after Winnie arrived in Portland, she engaged in daily sessions until her arrest and considered herself cured and pain-free.[90] Her excitement about the experience of healing with Green prompted her to contact her father, William Hull, who was in "poor health" and "physically incapacitated beyond most," with a spinal condition, to invite him to come to Portland from Benton County to take treatments.[91] This was apparently the first word the family had from Winnie since her arrival in Portland. Her contact reignited family conflicts and conflicts between mainstream medicine—embodied by Winnie's brother-in-law, Dr. Howard, and her sister Tena, his wife and a trained nurse—with Winnie's new belief in self-empowered healing and New Thought teachings. Hull arrived on January 2, 1915; the Howards arrived on January 5, and they engaged in a series of negotiations to have Winnie return home.[92]

The apparent final catalyst for Winnie's commitment, silenced in the courtroom versions of the case, was that at some point Winnie requested a room at the Portland Young Men's Christian Association, rooms that were reserved for men only. A letter her mother, Eleanor Hull, wrote to Winnie while she was committed at the OSH, a letter staff apparently never delivered, provides a key to unlock other references to the YMCA in this part of the story. Eleanor wrote: "when you wanted to take rooms among the men (which was against their law) they thought you were crazy."[93] William Hull, whose civil suit testimony was unclear in many places because he was trying to avoid being a defendant, said his daughter Winnie "caused herself" to be arrested. He told Emil and Tena that "she was unruly and they could not take care of her" at the YMCA.[94] Multnomah County jail matron Elizabeth Rogers recalled being summoned to the lobby of the YMCA and a clerk there asked her to "'try to get [Winnie] out as quiet as possible and not raise a disturbance or excite the other parties.'"[95]

Peter Boag's study of what became known as the Portland Vice Scandal of 1912–1913 helps us think about some possible meanings of Winnie's bid to get a room at the male YMCA and her subsequent arrest. Portland's YMCA was one site of an emerging gay men's culture and what we today might refer to as a queer cultural space in the city. The Portland Y, like other Ys across the nation, provided temporary rooms for men visiting the city like Winnie's father and also more permanent lodging for men working in the city, especially young, lower-white-collar workers, as longer-term tenants, some 160 residents in 1910. And it was a place where some men pursued same-sex intimacy and relationships. Starting in 1912, a "vice scandal" involving dozens of men in allegations of same-sex acts of intimacy, then against the law, unfolded with six of the men implicated associated with the Portland Y. Press coverage "ignited a citywide controversy over go-ings-on at the Y" that resulted in financial losses and a "considerable reduction" in membership.[96]

If Winnie insisted on a room, apparently presenting in the clothing of a woman given the record of what she was wearing when admitted to the OSH, and if she raised strong objections when told she could not have a room, then staff may have been particularly concerned about adverse publicity in the financial and reputational crunch following the 1912–1913 "scandal." They would have wanted to remove Winnie without disturbance or publicity.[97] Press coverage of Portland's "vice scandal" over a year before Winnie's journey to the city in December 1914 would likely have put the Portland Y on the map for her. In any case, it was a distinctly male space, with rooms for men only. The YMCA was directly next to the YWCA, where Winnie had been staying, and her father had a temporary room at the Y. We can't know whether Winnie's request for a room at the Portland Y was an effort to present her body as male, an attempt to find a way as a non-binary person to break gendered boundaries, or a more general attempt to shake up gendered conventions by requesting a room at the male Y while presenting as a woman. But in any case, Winnie's action created the reaction that led to commitment.

Winnie's quest to understand a nonbinary body and identity and sex-ual desire continued at the OSH. She explored questions and concerns frankly in her correspondence. "She wrote voluminous communications to me and to her people, many of which were quite obscene and during all of her periods of excitement here she talked mostly about sex matters," Griffith recalled.[98] Winnie feared that Griffith and Howard were in communication about an operation and that Griffith would make such an operation a requirement for her release. "For some time I was much worried with the fear [Griffith] would not rest easy or pronounce me as well, without *practicing* surgery on me," she wrote to OSH director Steiner in March 1915.[99] It is also possible that Griffith, who believed all "insane" people should be sterilized, was proposing a hysterectomy or some form of sterilization as an operative procedure, even before the successful 1917 legislation. No record exists of a surgery in Winnie's file, and her release happened before the creation of the State Board of Eugenics.

Winnie cataloged many of her concerns on a lengthy "Question List" addressed to Griffith sometime during her commitment. One area of focus was Griffith's physical exam on intake. Speaking of herself in the third person, Winnie asked: "What is the record of her physical examination when you first examined her?" When she challenged him and tried to stop the examination by declaring "'right here is where I draw the line,'" Griffith answered: "'I won't dispute a Lady.'" Winnie asked if he made that statement "in a spirit of sarcasm or irony?" This suggests Winnie had an intersex body, and Griffith observed this during the exam. Was he being sarcastic or ironic, Winnie asked after the fact, by referring to her as a lady? Winnie asked Griffith: "Is Winnifred a woman or a man or a go-between called a hermaphrodite? Is that the reason she has never had any children? Do you know what her mother thought about her sex when she first saw her own little naked kiddies? . . . . Is menstruation dishonorable? Do men menstruate?"[100]

In a long letter to her mother anticipating her release, Winnie discussed some of the lessons of her commitment experience. "The bird has indeed been captured and caged and is caged yet. God only knows the bruises of the lattice. No one else can. Truth is what I wish to know. I can rejoice I have had this experience. It has taught me a great many things," she wrote. "One thing I've learned, I guess I'm queer. I never knew it before." But "I don't feel queer, or past anyone's understanding that is, as near as one person can understand another. I *have been* just myself, Mamma."[101] "Queer" was a term with many meanings in 1915. It could refer to someone or something different or unexpected, but the word "queer" was also in use to refer to someone who experienced same-sex desire or to describe gender nonbinary people in some way. Michael Helquist, Peter Boag, and

176 / CHAPTER 6

Amy Sueyoshi, among others, have located and identified people using the word "queer" in Oregon and the West prior to and during this period as an affirming self-reference to people who experienced same-sex attraction or nonbinary gender identity or gender presentation, and also as an outside term of derision referring to people who expressed gender differently.[102] We can't know just how Winnie was using this term, but we can take note of her explanation: she felt "queer" but insisted that did not mean that she was beyond human understanding. Indeed, it meant that she was affirming her humanity on her own terms: she was, she wrote, "just myself."

Winnie drew a line between her life before the OSH and after her release from the institution with as many conditions of her own making as possible. She was paroled in 1915 and worked to gain a full discharge by 1916 so that she could exercise her rights of citizenship and voting.[103] She divorced her husband Clare in 1919 soon after the Oregon Supreme Court decision against her suit that February and supported herself by teaching in the public schools in Portland's Mount Scott neighborhood.[104] Early in 1919, she helped organize a Portland Mental Hygiene Society, served as secretary and became involved in patients' rights issues. Her experiences helped shape the agenda: legislation to confine people deemed insane in the county hospital rather than the county jail as well as policy changes at the OSH and elsewhere to end the use of restraints for confined and committed people.[105] But the Portland Mental Hygiene Society seems to soon have been eclipsed by a new state mental hygiene society in which she did not participate, chaired by Rabbi Jonah Wise with Reed College psychologist Samuel C. Kohs and Dr. J. Allen Gilbert as officers and supported by Dr. Griffith and others at the OSH.[106]

Winnie continued her own advocacy for OSH patients and work for legal aid for prisoners. Sometime in October 1920, after a complaint against her for "butting in" at cases in the county municipal court, the judge ordered a sanity hearing. Officials paroled her to an aunt in Portland. In December 1920, after becoming involved as an advocate in a high-profile murder case, and after leaving the jurisdiction of her parole to attend the funeral of her father in Benton County, the court recommitted Winnie to the State Hospital in Pendleton because the OSH was too crowded to accept her. She was released in February 1921.[107] Winnie taught school in Arizona, moved to California where she was a patient at the Napa State Psychiatric Hospital in early 1932, married, was widowed, and married again, with another stay at the Patton State Hospital beginning in 1949. She died in San Gabriel, California, in May 1952, survived by her husband Charles Pierson, her twin brother Willie, and her sister Tena Howard, who had Winnie's remains buried in the Bellfountain Cemetery in Benton County.[108]

These examples of resistance at the Oregon State Hospital suggest the importance of studying civil liberties at the local and institutional level as part of the long history of the movement for civil liberties in Oregon and the nation. L. F. Griffith's long reach as an advocate for and practitioner of radical sterilization policy combined eugenic thinking with nativism and settler colonialism. Griffith and his colleagues made the OSH a site of "stern restrictions" on the bodies and liberties of inmates. The confusion about Margarita Ojeda Wilcox's citizenship and residency status suggests the incomplete information many medical and legal professionals alike had about the intricacies of immigration law and the danger that posed to individuals and families. Louise Burbank's case demonstrates that deportation from the OSH was bound up in the dangerous and destructive politics and policy of sterilization. For Burbank and her advocates, deportation became the only alternative to escape surgery. The deportation or threat of deportation of patients at the OSH raises powerful questions of medical ethics, immigration law, and civil liberties. Managers of institutions were willing to default on their obligation to care if they could deport those committed—a violation of basic human rights to safety in one's person. And for both Ojeda Wilcox and Burbank, medical case files became tools in the process of surveillance, including Burbank's intake photograph distributed to immigration officials.

Winnie Springer challenged policies and laws that violated individual freedoms and safety in the name of treatment. Her civil suits exposing the lack of due process in the commitment process shook Oregon's legal and institutional administrators with the seriousness of her threat to current practice. She used her trial and its publicity to name civil liberties violations and give voice to the experience of commitment and engaged in patient rights advocacy after her case was overturned by the Oregon Supreme Court. Her more private path to gain understanding of a nonbinary body in a hospital that policed bodies and minds suggests ways that gender identity and actions for civil liberties protections merged inside and outside the Oregon State Hospital during this period.

CHAPTER 7

Japanese Oregonian Women's Resistance

MANY OREGON POLICYMAKERS AND RESIDENTS, like their western state counterparts, responded negatively and fearfully to the economic success of Japanese Oregonians in the early twentieth century by targeting them with race-based, exclusionary policies and actions linked to eugenic thinking. Government scrutiny during the war and its aftermath, fueled by anti-immigrant nativism, expanded and deepened community surveillance of Japanese Oregonians and threatened their civil liberties and safety. Many White policymakers identified first-generation Issei women as a key part of a "Japanese Problem" in need of a solution, labeling them as dangerous internal enemy "others." In the case of Issei wives and mothers, racial hatred and fear turned the gendered formula for constructive citizenship and productive membership in society on its head. Issei women's successful and useful labor in fields and family businesses as well as their work to raise children born in the United States who were therefore citizens, all part of women's traditional civic responsibilities, were precisely what anti-Japanese opponents mobilized to try and destroy.

Policymakers and anti-Japanese community members called for exclusion, restriction, discrimination, and even one Oregon-specific appeal for the eugenic sterilization of all Issei women as "solutions" to the so-called "Japanese Problem" in the state and nation. Across hop fields, strawberry orchards, and market gardens, in railroad line and cannery boarding houses, at urban laundries, restaurants, barbershops, and hotels, and within communities of their own making, Issei women in differing circumstances resisted these actions. They attended to reproductive health care and birthing choices and engaged with the state via birth certificates for their citizen children. They contributed vital paid and unpaid work for their families. Mitsuyo Uyeto and Matsumi Kojima, who managed hotels in Portland's Nihonmachi, or Japantown, challenged the city's restrictive and exclusionary hotel licensing practices and surveillance projects that threatened their homes and livelihoods. This chapter expands our understanding of many Oregonians' efforts to identify and punish Japanese Americans as internal enemies and builds our understanding of vital acts of Issei resistance.

ISSEI WOMEN AS INTERNAL ENEMY OTHERS

Anti-Japanese ideas and actions in the United States and in Oregon in the early twentieth century followed the exclusion of Chinese immigrants. As Erika Lee notes, White Americans often saw both groups as "inassimilable cheap laborers who were threats to white workers and to existing race relations." People who opposed Japanese migration in this era viewed Japanese immigrants "as both superior to and more threatening than other Asians [as] Japan had modern industries and a powerful military." And "unlike Chinese immigrant communities," Japanese American communities "included a substantial number of women and an increasing number of children, meaning that the Japanese were likely in the U.S. to stay."[1] Susan Smith demonstrates that anti-Japanese opponents "politicized" the birth of US citizen children to Issei parents "as an imperial threat."[2]

Members of the Oregon legislature and the Portland City Council took vigorous steps to restrict Japanese Oregonians during the war and after, actions that dovetailed with a national movement for exclusions and limits to Japanese Americans' movement, work, and civil liberties. In 1922, when Takao Ozawa challenged the basis of restrictions against naturalization placed on Issei immigrants, the US Supreme Court denied his petition and upheld the long-standing practice of classifying first-generation Japanese Americans as "ineligible for citizenship" and "unassimilable."[3] Oregon legislators introduced bills preventing noncitizens "ineligible for citizenship" from owning land, targeting Japanese immigrants specifically from 1917 until the state "Anti-alien" Land Act passed in 1923, part of the broader noncitizen land act movement in western states.[4] Policymakers, city council members, and legislators mounted a parallel campaign to prevent Japanese Oregonians from obtaining required licenses to operate their businesses in Portland and throughout the state from 1921 through 1925, the urban equivalent of the land acts.

Some Oregon policymakers also joined the postwar movement to amend the citizenship clause of the Fourteenth Amendment granting citizenship to persons born in the United States with second-generation Japanese Oregonians in mind.[5] In the special legislative session of January 1920 the members of the Oregon legislature passed Senate Joint Memorial No. 1 urging the US Congress to modify the citizenship clause of the Fourteenth Amendment.[6] A year later, Oregon's US Senator Charles McNary and Representative Nicholas J. Sinnott, both Republicans, represented the state on the newly formed Western Congressional Delegation on the Japanese Question chaired by Senator Hiram Johnson (D-California). The group promoted the triple goals of passing state-level anti-Japanese legislation, calling for federal action to exclude Japanese immigrants, and amending the Fourteenth Amendment birthright citizenship clause.[7] The Federal Immigration Act passed in 1924 was a culmination of these activities and effectively barred immigration from Japan until the McCarran-Walter Act of 1952.[8]

In 1920, Oregonians of Japanese descent numbered just over four thousand.[9] As Issei gained economic success in Oregon and the Pacific Northwest, many White residents expressed fears of economic competition. These fears often focused on the shift toward settled families as opposed to sojourner men. Women comprised 4 percent of Japanese American communities in Oregon in 1900, and by 1920 they were over a third of Japanese Oregonian residents.[10] This growth was due in large part to the "Gentlemen's Agreement" of 1907 that barred new immigration by Japanese laborers but allowed wives and family members to migrate, including via so-called "picture bride" marriages arranged by families, a policy in effect until 1924.[11] First-generation Issei could not become citizens, confirmed by the US Supreme Court in the *Ozawa* decision of 1922, but their children, Nisei, born in the United States, were citizens by virtue of the Fourteenth Amendment. Surveys, covert intelligence and surveillance information, data gathered for state biennial reports and congressional studies, and press reports often focused on Japanese Oregon women as threatening internal enemies who as racial others engaged in both productive labor in family businesses and reproductive labor as the mothers of second-generation birthright citizens.

Most scholars of the Progressive Era and beyond know Oregon's Bureau of Labor and Industry (BOLI) for its enforcement of child labor laws and protective labor legislation for women. But when the members of the Oregon legislature created BOLI in 1903, they included detailed requirements for the specific surveillance of Japanese and Chinese Oregonians. The statute required the state labor commissioner to make a detailed biennial report regarding "the number and condition of the Japanese and Chinese in the State, their social and sanitary habits; number of married, and of those single, the number employed, and the nature of their employment," their wages and expenses, how much they spent in Oregon and how much for "foreign" imported products, and "to what extent their employment comes in competition with the white industrial classes of the state."[12] These specific reporting categories went far beyond requirements for any other group of workers in Oregon. BOLI's charge required gathering quantitative data about demographics and wages but also subjective observations about "social and sanitary habits." And the Oregon legislature mandated an analysis of the level of competition with White industrial workers in the report. BOLI reports during this period chronicled the declining Chinese American population and the growing Japanese American population in Oregon and a state increasingly concerned with surveilling Issei mothers and the rising birth rate among them.[13]

Japanese Oregonians had their own reasons to seek and share information about the demographics of their growing communities. The Japanese consulate in Portland held the diplomatic responsibility to maintain current vital statistics for Japanese Oregonians.[14] Consular staff also maintained strong ties with the Oregon Japanese Association.[15] The secretary of the Oregon Japanese Association, Iwao Oyama, a journalism graduate from Waseda University in Tokyo, connected Japanese Oregonians with news and information first as a contributor to and then as the editor of the region's Japanese-language newspaper, *Oshu Nippo* (*Oregon Daily News*).[16] Oyama published statistics about population growth and communities in the pages of the *Oshu Nippo*, and the Japanese Association published an annual Japanese-language *Guide Book* drawn from consular and Japanese Association figures.[17]

Federal officials expanded the scrutiny and surveillance of Japanese Oregonians in 1920 with the US House Committee on Immigration and Naturalization hearings and investigations of West Coast Japanese Americans.[18] The committee held hearings in several major California and Washington cities that received constant press attention. There were no public hearings in Oregon, but legislators visited Portland and the Hood

River Valley, home to Oregon's largest Japanese American farming community, to investigate local conditions. Oregon officials including Toyoji Abe, president of the Oregon Japanese Association and publisher of the *Oshu Nippo*, collected data and forwarded reports to the committee.[19] Special agents for the Federal Bureau of Investigation continued the work of surveillance and reporting on Japanese Oregonians in 1921, and in turn Department of Justice staff shared their reports with the Military Intelligence Division.[20] Governor Ben Olcott commissioned former legislator and newspaper editor Frank Davey to investigate Japanese Oregonians, and Davey published *Report of the Japanese Situation in Oregon* in August 1920.[21] Olcott shared the report with the House Committee, the state published the report as a pamphlet, and newspaper editors circulated major excerpts and findings widely. As Barbara Yasui notes, Davey's choice of the word "situation" identified Japanese Oregonians as a problem, casting them, their families, work, and businesses as being in conflict with Whites in the state, a problem to be resolved.[22] Davey included data on Issei land ownership, business success, and his perspective about loyalty to the nation of Japan, all of which fueled Oregon's drive for an "Anti-alien" Land Act to match the one California passed in 1913.

A major theme in Davey's report was the recent transformation of enclaves of working men to successful communities of homes and farms with Japanese "picture brides" and American-born, US-citizen children. Describing coastal Astoria and Clatsop County, Davey noted men working in the sawmills and canneries, and a few in Astoria "operating some soft drink places, cheap eating houses, and lodgings." Some 40 women lived among the 455 men in the county; almost half had arrived during the previous eighteen months from Japan as "picture brides." The real danger, Davey emphasized, was that "these movements take place so quietly that the general public knows nothing about it." This led to "much surprise all at once in such communities when Japanese women and babies begin to appear on the streets and there is wonder as to where they all came from."[23] In Multnomah County east of the Portland city limits, he wrote, "there are said to be nearly 300 Japanese, a good many having families, the crop of children being numerous and regular."[24] In Hood River, Davey noted that anti-Japanese White residents "point to the birth rate of the past few years to illustrate the results to be expected in the near future."[25] In Gresham, east of Portland, Davey reported that nine-tenths of the land Japanese Oregonians worked was planted in vegetables and berries. "There crops require a stooping posture" not "favored" by White workers but, he claimed, "the Japanese are particularly adapted to it on account of their short stature." Willingness to assume such "tiresome postures," he wrote, and "the fact that men, women, and children work in the fields, all combine to give them a decided advantage over an American family." Consequently, many Oregonians believed White "Americans cannot possibly compete with Japanese in agricultural production."[26]

Taken together, these reports engendered many dozens of newspaper accounts that were equal parts statistical summaries, muckraking news exposés, and travel narratives. Davey focused the attention of his readers on Japanese women in the Oregon landscape, portraying them literally as embodying a dangerous threat to the state and nation. They labored alongside their husbands in the fields with bodies "adapted" to "stooped postures" and were simultaneously prolific in bearing children who worked alongside them, children born in the United States who were empowered with US citizenship. Natalie Molina identifies California policymakers' same concerns as they cast Japanese American women as a "double threat" as mothers and workers.[27] The frequent claim that Japanese Americans were unassimilable was based in part on representations of Japanese women's productive and reproductive labor as "alien," threatening, and dangerous to Oregon and the nation.

Issei women living in cities and towns faced additional scrutiny and negative stereotypes. In Portland, where some five hundred Issei women were living in 1919, one of the two Nihonmachi neighborhoods was located in the city's North End long associated with prostitution and vice and singled out by the Portland Vice Commission as an "immoral" location where prostitution flourished.[28] As Kazuhiro Oharazeki has demonstrated, Japanese women who engaged in sex work were part of the complex transnational history of migrations in the late nineteenth and early twentieth centuries in the North American West. They faced scorn and attention from anti-prostitution reformers and critics in Japan, from members of Japanese migrant communities in the Pacific Northwest anxious to avert criticism, and from critics and reformers from the dominant White community. Transformations in immigration and federal enforcement laws by 1910 and the crackdown on prostitution and sexually transmitted infections meant a decrease in the number of Japanese sex workers in Oregon and other western states.[29]

But the stigma was still strong, and all Japanese Oregonian women were vulnerable to scrutiny and innuendo, especially those living and working in cities. Writing in the *Oshu Nippo* in 1922, Teruko Takeshi lamented the "cold eyes of contempt and ridicule poured over the Japanese working women."[30] The stakes for Issei women working in barbershops and as rooming house and hotel managers and partners could be even higher. At least twenty Issei women worked as barbers or barber apprentices in Portland in the 1920s.[31] All women working in barbershops faced the insinuation that they were available sexually to clients and others in that quintessential male space.[32] The *Oregonian* referred to the "'lady barbers' in the North End," meaning prostitutes.[33] The 1913 Portland Vice Commission listed Japanese American hotel and rooming house managers and residents as being engaged in prostitution, gambling, and selling liquor and narcotics.[34]

Dr. Bethenia Owens-Adair envisioned an additional "solution" to the Japanese "problem" as state-sponsored eugenic sterilization of all Issei women. She discussed this possibility when speaking with reporters just before the opening of the 1921 Oregon legislative session in Salem. She was lobbying for her "hygienic marriage" bill that would have mandated a physical and mental examination of all prospective partners to eliminate the "unfit" and make them liable for sterilization. Owens-Adair characterized Oregon's sterilization law as "just a wedge to things to come," a first step for more extensive uses of eugenic sterilization. One of those uses, she suggested, would be "a solution of the Japanese problem" by the "sterilization of all the Japanese women admitted to the country."[35] Several weeks later, Owens-Adair responded to questions about her plan to "settle" the "Japanese question by sterilization" in a letter she sent to the editors of the *Oregon Statesman* the *Salem Capital Journal*. She had "not as yet advocated" a specific plan, she wrote, but "it is a question that must be settled and when the time comes we must and we will find a way to meet it."[36] Owens-Adair also reprinted her letter in her book *Human Sterilization*, published in 1922, evidently to expose her ideas about Issei women's sterilization to a wider audience.[37]

Leaders in the Japanese Oregonian community experienced the anti-

Japanese scrutiny, rhetoric, and acts of violence and disrespect firsthand. Many advised assimilation and Americanization as a solution and directed advice to women in their urban and rural communities, often with a cultural and class-based vision of correct behavior. Community leaders' assimilation strategies dovetailed with traditional Japanese expectations for women to be "dutiful wives and intelligent mothers."[38] Iwao Oyama, Japanese Association secretary and *Oshu Nippo* editor, emphasized Issei women's roles in the creation of "good homes" and in the "remodeling" of Issei society in Oregon with their "beautiful, noble, and gentle emotions." He believed such "remodeling" had a purpose within Issei communities but also a vital role in challenging anti-Japanese hatred and discrimination. "I hope that they will demonstrate the characteristics of Japanese ladies," he concluded, "for the sake of harmony between Japanese and Caucasian people."[39] Hood River's Masuo Yasui echoed these sentiments, applying them to rural communities, with a list of "Requests to Japanese Ladies." Issei wives were diplomats representing "all Japanese women" with "greater influence than the Japanese government officials." He urged them to guard the images they presented to White Oregonians.[40]

REPRODUCTIVE HEALTH CARE AND BIRTH REPORTING

Issei women in Oregon built their lives, resisted anti-Japanese surveillance, ideas, and actions, and worked within or challenged community leaders' expectations in a variety of ways within the possibilities and limits of their circumstances. Two major elements of their resistance—(1) reproductive health care and bureaucratic matters surrounding childbirth reporting, and (2) engagement in wage work and building family farms and businesses—are powerful examples of the enduring consequences of Oregon Issei women's resistance to being designated as internal enemy others.

If White Americans politicized Issei reproduction, Issei women attended to birth and reproductive health care by making the political personal as best they could. Birthing choices reflected what was possible in any given community: attention to cultural practices, second-language concerns, and responses to and protections from anti-Japanese ideas and violence. For Issei in Oregon, birth registration provided positive and tangible evidence of the citizenship of their US-born children and the protection of that citizenship in bureaucratic systems of evidence.[41]

186 / CHAPTER 7

Issei needed to connect and comply with birth reporting for both US and Japanese citizenship and record-keeping via the State of Oregon and the Japanese Consular Office in Portland. Before 1924, Nisei children became citizens of Japan at birth by virtue of their parents' citizenship. After 1924, Issei had to register the birth of their children with the Japanese consulate in Portland within fourteen days of birth.[42] Childbirth options were shaped by location, but all births linked Issei women, their husbands, and children to the bureaucracy of US citizenship.

Implementation of standardized birth certificates and requirements for reporting by birthing women and their families, midwives, and physicians was part of the growth of the modern information-based state of the early twentieth century.[43] When the Oregon legislature created a State Board of Health in 1903, lawmakers established a general process for registering births and, at the urging of state health officials, medical professionals, and women's and civic organizations, updated the process in 1915 to align with a national "model law" and census requirements for recording and reporting vital statistics. After 1915, Oregon required midwives, physicians, family members, or householders to complete a birth report on a standardized birth certificate within ten days of the birth. Failing to comply or providing false information was a misdemeanor with possible fines and imprisonment after the first offense. The law required midwives and physicians to register with local registrars who were usually physicians in their communities.[44]

A close reading of Oregon birth certificates from 1917 and 1918 enables us to analyze some Issei women's birthing choices and actions in the context of these important personal and political matters in both rural and urban communities.[45] Birth records indicate that rural Issei women and Issei women in smaller towns most often gave birth at home, with some exceptions to be noted here. Their births were attended by family, or by local doctors who were willing to attend and who, in most cases, were vetted by Issei community members. Portland Issei women, and some women in areas of rural Multnomah and Clackamas Counties, in Clatsop County, and in Polk County, had the option of securing the services of Issei midwives. Less frequently Japanese American male physicians were available. Across communities, Issei women and their families worked to assure that the birth reporting for their children was accurate and filed with the proper authorities by the deadline to confirm that citizenship requirements for their children were met and that the birth experience was as supportive as possible.

In 1917–1918, Issei women in the Hood River Valley, the state's largest Japanese Oregonian farming community, exercised one of two birthing options in this period where no midwife-assisted deliveries were recorded. One option was to engage the services of a White physician who was trusted and recommended by other Issei community members. Hood River's small, sixteen-bed Cottage Hospital was a general hospital at which physicians attended some of the community's deliveries.[46] But Issei women like Tei Endow found the prospect of a hospital birth "worrisome" because they would have been uncomfortable and concerned about communicating in English.[47] In California's San Gabriel Valley, Michiko Tanaka noted that when doctors were available, "they would not treat us [Japanese] or their services were too expensive," and Hood River conditions were likely very similar.[48] In this two-year period in Hood River, Issei women and their husbands engaged White physicians for about half of all births (twenty-seven of a total of fifty-two).

Howard L. Dumble, MD, delivered the vast majority, twenty-five of those twenty-seven physician-attended births. Dumble was willing to work with Issei families and known in the Issei community.[49] His experience with attending births, some fifteen hundred by 1923, recommended him. He was the mayor of Hood River during this period, and his leadership role and connections with how the city worked would likely have instilled confidence in his abilities.[50] Marcus Thrane, MD, and Edgar O. Dutro, MD, attended one birth each during this period.[51] Some Issei couples who may have hoped to deliver at home among family may certainly have sought the services of a White physician because of challenging pregnancies or birth situations. But Issei community vetting appears clear given how many families selected Dumble. Dumble, Thrane, and Dutro were among fourteen doctors active in Hood River in 1918, all of whom were White. Given these numbers, it is likely that many of the other doctors did not treat Japanese Oregonians due to anti-Japanese prejudice.[52]

A second option for Hood River Issei women was to deliver at home with husbands, family, and friends in attendance. Tei Endow recalled that most Issei women in the valley "learned birthing through friends" and delivered at home.[53] Birth records for 1917 and 1918 indicate just fewer than half (twenty-five of the fifty-two total) of Issei births there occurred at home with family. In these circumstances Issei families relied almost exclusively on a trusted community leader with strong English skills to assist with reporting the births of their children. Dr. Homer Yasui recalled that his father Masuo Yasui used his fluent English skills and position of leadership to help community members with translations and bureaucratic tasks.[54] This was certainly the case for birth certificates in 1917 and 1918, as Yasui reported twenty-one of the twenty-five births that occurred at home with family to the health office on behalf of another household. Yasui reported the birth of his own daughter on another certificate. Kay Yamahiro, who managed a market farm cooperative, reported one other birth for a household, and fathers representing their own households reported the two other births at home with family.[55]

In Portland the vital work of seven Issei midwives during this period created an important additional option for birthing Issei women and their families living in or near the city. In 1917 and 1918 within the Portland city limits, midwives attended 71 percent (123) of the 174 Issei births recorded. Midwife Takako Urakami assisted with fifty-two births across these two years from her residence at 85 North 9th Street, delivering the children of laborers, hotel managers, florists, grocers, storekeepers, shoemakers, and elite families including jewelers and newspaper editors. Riki Kariya engaged in practice from her residence at 46 North 9th Street and worked with forty birthing Issei women from January 1917 through May 1918 among the working families of Nihonmachi whose husbands were janitors, cooks and restaurant workers, sawmill hands, clerks, and hotel keepers. Natsu Sato delivered fifteen babies in this two-year period, especially among elite Issei merchants and hotel keepers in Portland. Ko Sasaki, at 127 North 12th Street, attended seven births; Tora Mirayasu, at 50 ½ North Third, and Kimi Uchida, at 66 North 11th Street, delivered four babies each; and Masaye Yamaguchi, at 51 North 12th, delivered one child. All the Portland midwives except Uchida offered space in their residences for deliveries in this period; all except Yamaguchi, whose single delivery in this period took place at her residence, also assisted birthing women in their own homes.[56]

Issei midwives offered women and their families culturally specific and familiar care and at the same time connected them with state bureaucracies via their official roles and experience with birth reporting. Issei midwives in Portland likely offered services matching their Seattle counterparts: frequent prenatal appointments and after-birth visits including mentoring for baby care and wellness checks, with the comfort of communication in Japanese during these intimate experiences. Rin Miura, who gave birth to her son in Portland's Japantown in May 1922, received this type of care. She had prenatal visits, and her son Taro was born at the midwife's house. Miura and her son "stayed there for about a week. We went home after we recovered." The midwife, she noted, "constantly had two or three Japanese babies to take care of."[57] Issei midwives also provided specific traditions of care, likely including the hara obi, or pregnancy sash, that gave back support and warmth, and the involvement of women in the community in the birth process. The seven Portland Issei midwives offered a bridge to American requirements and bureaucracies. They were registered with health authorities and connected to other health care providers and services. They knew the rules of Oregon state law and how to file an accurate birth report that would secure US citizenship and its benefits for second-generation children. And, as Susan Smith notes, at home or at the midwife's residence, "the midwives and their clients retained authority over the childbirth process."[58] The relationship between Issei birthing mothers and midwives was one form of resistance to the anti-Japanese surveillance and discrimination that could permeate the world outside those walls.

The importance of Japanese American midwives in the context of anti-Japanese racism and hostility is underscored by other birth and medical statistics in Portland from this period. Householders and White physicians reported the other 29 percent of Issei births in Portland in 1917–1918, with fathers, and in two cases neighbors, reporting 12 percent (21) of those births. White physicians attended 17 percent (30) births. The greater Portland area had 523 physicians listed in 1918, and just ten of them attended those 30 Issei births, indicating some combination of Issei community vetting and anti-Japanese views among some or most of those physicians not involved in Issei care.[59] Three of those ten doctors attended most of the births. Charles Zeebuyth, MD, with twelve deliveries, was based in the Montavilla neighborhood and worked with city couples and among farm couples in more rural southeastern Portland. Two of the deliveries he supervised with Issei women were in the Portland Sanitarium hospital near Montavilla.[60] Ralph S. Fisher, MD, with six deliveries, lived in the Benson Hotel and served as house physician there, and was "one of Portland's well-known physicians" with a thriving practice.[61] Jessie McGavin, MD, with five deliveries in the Issei community in this two-year period, was active in Portland's women's medical community and civic affairs. She engaged with Japanese and Chinese American women and children as patients across her practice.[62] Several of the other seven White physicians who attended one birth each may likely have been called in to assist with birthing complications. Two of their number, Joseph Pettit and Alvin Baird, were on the surgical faculty at the University of Oregon Medical School.[63]

The segregation of Japanese American patients during the 1918–1919 influenza pandemic in Portland provides additional evidence of the impact of anti-Japanese sentiment on medical care and public health in this period. This demonstrates the vital need for Japanese American and supportive White medical practitioners in the community. State health administrators and city officials used the Portland Auditorium as an emergency hospital to provide care and quarantine facilities for Portlanders at the height of the epidemic beginning in mid-October 1918. On November 5 administrators created a separate ward for Japanese American patients with Japanese American doctors and nurses on staff. An initial group of twenty patients were transferred to the ward, and city records name ten patients with accounts for medical services provided, including three women. It appears that Japanese Americans were the only influenza patients segregated officially by race or ethnicity in Portland in this major medical event of 1918–1919.[64]

Some midwives strengthened the links between White physicians who did engage in community care and Portland's Issei community. Natsu Sato worked with Dr. Jessie McGavin on at least two deliveries. McGavin listed Sato's address as the location for a June 1918 delivery and for another in August 1918. For the latter, Sato filled out the birth certificate information.[65] Sato may have been the person who placed the notice of a "Young Japanese Midwife Wants Position with Lady Physician" in the "Situations Wanted—Female" classified section of the *Oregonian* in early January 1917.[66] Joseph Pettit, MD, delivered a daughter by cesarean section for a Portland Issei couple at St. Vincent's Hospital and listed their address as Sato's, suggesting Sato was working with the mother and called Pettit or arranged for the mother's transport to the hospital.[67] And Dr. Ralph Fisher delivered midwife Riki Kariya's son at her home in September 1917.[68]

Widening the lens outside of Portland for 1917–1918 birth certificates reflects the importance of location for birthing options.[69] In rural Multnomah County, Charles Zeebuyth delivered more than half of the children of farm couples in East Portland. Jessie McGavin and Florence Manion, MD, attended one delivery each. Gresham physicians Herbert H. Hughes, MD, and George Inglis, MD, attended five and three deliveries respectively in this period.[70] Midwives Takako Urakami and Ko Sasaki attended two birthing Issei women, and two additional midwives, Sui Ito and Natsu Shiraishi, delivered one baby each. Tokuji Hirata, MD, a 1916 graduate of the University of Oregon Medical School, delivered two Issei babies in Gresham in 1917 before he relocated to Los Angeles.[71] Four other midwives attended one birth each in other parts of the state: Kariki Ninomiya in Polk County and Koyo Hayashi, Yoshino Tanimoto, and Take Uyesugi in Clatsop County.[72] The single Issei couple giving birth in Bend worked with Anna Ries Finley, MD, the only woman physician in town.[73] Charles Ballard, MD, attended the two births among the two Issei families in Lakeview, in central Oregon's Lake County, at the laundry at which the couples lived and worked.[74]

LABOR IN FAMILY ENTERPRISES AND WAGE WORK

Issei women's wage work and labor in family enterprises provided another form of resistance to anti-Japanese ideas and surveillance. Women's paid and unpaid labor sustained families, provided educational and cultural opportunities for their children, and helped to build communities. In many cases Issei women's ability to adapt to new work roles was crucial for family success and safety. Yuji Ichioka observed that "ideally, Japanese women were supposed to confine themselves to the home as 'dutiful wives and intelligent mothers'" but "economic realities forced the majority to assume a third role as workers whose labor was indispensable." Most Issei women worked arduous, long hours whether on berry or hop farms, in urban shops and boarding houses, coastal canneries, or railroad camps, and those who were mothers engaged with housework, meal production, and childcare in the evenings, mornings, and throughout the day.[75]

Linda Tamura learned from conducting oral history interviews that Issei mothers were "burdened by the feeling that work prevented them from properly attending to the needs of their precious children." The

192 / CHAPTER 7

"education of our children was our foremost goal," Tei Endow recalled. White people "may have felt that we spent our lifetimes working," she noted, acknowledging the negative stereotypes she had faced. "But we felt that education was so important that nothing else mattered."[76] Given migration patterns and immigration restrictions, most Issei mothers did not have extended family with them to provide childcare and other support.[77] But as Kelli Nakamura argues, the third role of worker created possibilities for some leverage and power for Issei women because their labor was vital to family and community economies and businesses. Nakamura's conclusions about Issei women in Hawaii in this period mirror the Oregon experience. "Issei women endured great sacrifices, such as long work hours and the lack of proper child care," Nakamura points out. "But they still worked a 'double day' to advance their independence" and build family and community.[78] As workers, Issei women experienced increased scrutiny from outside the community but also engaged in elements of resistance and empowerment.

In rural Oregon in this period Issei mothers worked in orchards and fields as they cared for children and homes east of Portland in Montavilla, Gresham, and Troutdale, in the Hood River Valley, in the Brooks/Labish Meadows river land outside of Salem, around Independence hop farms along the Willamette River in Polk County, and in rural Benton County.[79] Miyoshi Noyori recalled the "exhausting work" of farming. "We had to work at it very hard. We were determined to work at it, because we had to, we had to also raise children . . . because we worked right alongside with the men, even though we took a baby out in the field in a small apple box close by where we were working." Just the "same as the men, I worked until 6:00 p.m.," Hatsumi Nishimoto of Pine Grove recalled. "When I came home [from the fields] I had to cook too. After dinner during harvest, we boxed the fruit. Then when everyone went to bed, I cleaned the house" and on Sundays "had laundry and housecleaning."[80] Poet Shizue Iwatsuki, who came to the Hood River Valley from Japan in 1916, recalled: "'Helping my husband, I worked so hard that I was amazed at myself. If we didn't work, we couldn't go on living.'"[81] In 1920, her sixth year in America, Sowa Uchimada was managing a household with three children under five and assisting her husband, Gonzyo, with the family poultry farm at Kings Valley in rural Benton County.[82] Hatsuno Fukai came to Oregon in 1915 at age twenty to marry farmer Misao Yada. Ten years later, she had five young children and the family leased land for market farming in Labish Meadows in the Willamette Valley, where in addition to the family farm work, her husband Misao served on the board of the cooperative Japanese Oregon Growers' Exchange and then on the board of the twenty-nine-family-strong cooperative Labish Meadows Celery Union. With direct seeding and greenhouse planting for two crops per year, household tasks, and childcare, "everything was hand labor, from early morning to dark," Hatsuno's eldest son Tats recalled.[83]

Work in the forests and on railroad lines and highways of Oregon often meant just one or two Japanese American families in residence in a community with a few single men on a work crew in need of board and room. This meant that in addition to other household and childcare tasks women worked to feed and care for male boarders, providing essential services for their small working communities. After the war Kino Fujii's husband, Chiyogi, began work on a crew constructing the Pacific Highway in rural communities around Grants Pass in Josephine County near the California border. In 1920 she was managing a household of four children under five and occupied with the work of boarding two single men who were on the highway crew with her husband.[84] In Bend, Ito Takehara and Kiyono Takeichi lived a block away from one another on Division and Franklin Streets, adjacent to the Oregon Trunk Line Railroad, in 1920. Kiyono's husband, Riheiji, was a section foreman for the railroad, and Ito's husband, Sueji, was a section hand. Kiyono cared for her one-year-old son Masao and housed and fed two male boarders on the railroad crew; Ito's daughter Kimiko was seven, and she also had two male crew workers as boarders.[85] Also that year, Sumino Fujii earned wages as a cook for a boarding house for the Corvallis Logging Company in Bellfountain in rural Benton County. Her husband, Seiichi, was a logging crew member, and the couple and their one-year-old daughter Yoshimi lived with Seiichi's uncle, father, two brothers, and three boarders.[86]

Issei women residing in urban areas in Portland's Old Town Nihonmachi, the newer Japanese community in the city's southwest section, and Salem's Japanese American community labored long hours to build their family economies. Many wives and mothers worked alongside their husbands managing and maintaining boarding houses, restaurants, and shops and then engaged with childcare and household work at their family residence.[87] In 1920, Satsuki Azumano cleaned and maintained the rooms

194 / CHAPTER 7

FIGURE 22 Three Issei women and their children by the Japanese Hand Laundry delivery van, 445 Ferry Street, Salem, Oregon, ca. 1926–1927. Photo via Stephanie Knowlton, "Beyond Barbed Wire," *Statesman Journal*, June 3, 2007, 4A–5A.

of nine male boarders at the family's Panama Hotel on Front Street managed by her husband, Hatsutaro, while caring for her toddler son Ichiro and giving birth to her daughter Reiko.[88] Some women administered rooming houses independently. In the 1920s Suzu Yamada managed a rooming house on Everett Street, then another on Second Street as she cared for her growing family of three daughters. Her husband, Kho Tagae Yamada, was a respected physician. The family lived in the rooming house Suzu managed, and Tagae had a separate office nearby for his medical practice.[89] Suge Teshima worked alongside her husband, Ariyoshi, at their barbershop on First Street in Nihonmachi while caring for her young daughter.[90] Portland barbers Tomo Kiyohiro and her husband, Junichi, sent their children to live in Japan for their early schooling as they built their shop and customer base and welcomed the children back as they reached their later teens.[91] Natsu Sato cared for her son and daughter, ages five and three in 1918, while engaging with her busy practice as a Portland midwife.[92]

The Japanese Hand Laundry became a thriving business on Ferry

FIGURE 23 Japanese Hand Laundry, Salem, Oregon, ca. 1918–1919. Print from Trover Negative from State Library of Oregon, Salem, Willamette Heritage Center Collections X2011.003.0072, Salem.

Street in Salem's business district and a center for the extended Japanese American community in the mid-Willamette Valley. Issei women worked in the laundry, which was the residence for workers and their families. In the 1920s Shiyo and Matazo Nakamura along with Ume and Ichizo Tsukamoto, with two young children, co-managed the business. Ichizo's cousin, Hisakichi, and his wife, Kiku Tsukamoto, lived and worked with them and were raising their own three young children. Ichi and Dangiro Takagi also lived and worked at the laundry. Ichi was raising their three young children as well as Dangiro's teen daughters from his first marriage.[93] Publicity and family photographs represent the women of these families as both workers and mothers in front of the laundry. The image of three women and their children is likely from around 1926, when the *Oregon Statesman* announced the laundry had a new 1926 Ford delivery van.

The Japanese Hand Laundry appears to have been a community gathering place for the Salem/Independence Issei and their children, especially for the extended Tsukamoto, Nakamura, and Mitoma families. Some are in this World War I–era photograph in front of the laundry.[94] Towa Nakamura, wife of Independence hop farmer Torakichi Nakamura, is seated under the words "Dry Cleaning" on the sign with her daughter Teruko on her lap.[95] Hisa Mitoma, wife of Independence hop contractor and grower Jentaro Mitoma, is seated to the left of the door, with her daughter Chiyono on the bicycle and an infant in arms.[96] Koshizu Susie Mitoma, wife of hop grower and Independence entrepreneur Cho Frank Mitoma, is seated at the right with her children, including twin girls Hotsco and Cotsco in their matching coats, born in 1916.[97]

Flexibility and adaptability in meeting changing work roles and labor conditions was another element of Issei women's resistance to anti-Japanese conditions. This pattern of moving within and from various kinds of wage work to managing family enterprises such as hotels or shops held true for many Issei couples.[98] Kikuno Hirabayashi's experience provides a poignant example. Arriving in Portland in 1921 to be the wife of grocer Kichisaburo Hirabayashi, Kikuno found wage work as a typesetter at the *Oshu Nippo* newspaper and printing offices.[99] By 1925 she became a teacher at the Japanese School on Everett and 16th Streets as her husband moved from managing a soft drink establishment to hotel management.[100] The *Oshu Nippo* editors featured the Hirabayashis as part of a special 1925 edition of the paper dedicated to Japanese-owned and -managed hotels. After noting Kichisaburo's hotel management accomplishments, the editors wrote: "His wife presently braves the educating of children at the private academy for very little pay. She holds most of the responsibility of promoting the education of our children, and, more so than some guardians, she is adored like a loving mother [by her students]." Kikuno received additional praise for her work in a poem:

> The Wife for the Children's Education
> Exhausts herself, like a loving mother
> Honorably idolized.[101]

Kikuno appears to have joined her husband Kichisaburo in managing the Hart Hotel on Burnside Street by 1927 or 1928.[102] She may have had a direct reason for leaving her teaching position. In August 1927 a dozen White boys and young men vandalized the Japanese School, causing $2,300 in damages, equivalent to more than $40,000 today, and leaving

a violent trail behind them. The "interior of the school was quite generally smashed up," an *Oregonian* reporter noted. The vandals attacked
the piano, desks, bookcases, maps, tablets, even toys used at the school.
"Scarcely an object of value was left undamaged." After wrecking the
school interior and smashing windows, the attackers "donned Japanese
straw hats and marched up Everett street to Eighteenth street in a grand
parade swinging Japanese lanterns and loot as if [they] were pillaging
troops."[103] As a symbol of Japanese culture and heritage in Portland, the
Japanese School, its teachers, and pupils, were receiving an additional
level of scrutiny that led directly to violence. Kikuno Hirabayashi may
have made the move from teaching to hotel management for her own
safety and the safety of her family.

HOTEL LICENSING, SURVEILLANCE, AND RESISTANCE

The experiences of Mitsuyo Uyeto and Matsumi Kojima, two Issei women
hotel managers in early 1920s Portland, illustrate the perfect storm of
anti-Japanese hatred, overlapping surveillance projects, and exclusionary policies and legislation in a time of economic competition during the
postwar recession in Oregon. Both businesswomen engaged in resistance
to protect their livelihoods, their families, and the residents in their family
hotels. Both left the city after repeated challenges to their businesses and
lives. Portland City officials used the same 1918 hotel licensing ordinance
that became a model for anti–venereal disease and anti-prostitution policies nationwide during the war to try to exclude Japanese Portlanders from
operating hotels and rooming houses. By 1923, Oregon legislators passed
a statewide law that barred noncitizens from obtaining certain licenses to
conduct business, a law that targeted Japanese Oregonians specifically.
These were all efforts by city and state officials to make exclusionary
licensing policies the urban equivalent of "anti-Alien" land laws directed
at residents they considered internal enemy others.[104]

In 1914 twenty-two-year-old Mitsuyo Suginato came to the United
States from Hiroshima, Japan, and married Katsutaro Uyeto. Katsutaro, thirty-seven, had come to the United States from Japan as a teen-
ager and was living in Portland, where the couple settled. By 1917 they
were taking in lodgers at the Villa House in the heart of North Portland's

198 / CHAPTER 7

Nihonmachi.[105] The community grew steadily from the 1890s through the war as a central labor contracting hub for Japanese men to gain work in the Oregon fields and forests and with the railroads and also served as a "temporary home to which they returned when they completed seasonal work." After the 1907 Gentlemen's Agreement created a means for Japanese women to immigrate to the United States, Nihonmachi grew as a location for urban family life. By 1920 lodgings like the Villa House were part of a vibrant four blocks of the city along with grocery stores, restaurants, barbershops, and baths for Japanese American patrons. Rooming houses and other service-oriented businesses "also served non-Japanese retirees and pensioners who needed low-rent housing and modestly priced services." Villa House was among the latter group, with the 1920 census listing the six men who roomed there as born in Finland, England, Sweden, and Armenia, along with the Uyetos who made their home on site.[106]

The influx of workers during the war boosted the hotel and boarding house business substantially, but the postwar recession created conflict and increased scrutiny upon Issei business owners, managers, and workers. The *Oshu Nippo* reported a wartime increase from ten cents to fifty cents to a dollar "for a bed in a two-bed room" in a Portland boarding house or hotel from before the war to the beginning of 1918.[107] Community leader Senichi Tomihiro identified the war years as a "golden age" in Portland when "over 40,000 people came together and livened up the center of the city." Hotels and rooming house investments "became splendidly energetic," he observed. This spurred additional expansion: in 1919 the number of Japanese hotels and boarding houses rose from fifty to ninety in Portland. Wartime food shortages boosted agriculture, and wartime wages for jobs in industry, shops, farms, sawmills, railroads, and canneries rose. But by 1920 the postwar recession had reached Issei businesses across the state and in Nihonmachi. This in turn reduced the funds available in mutual aid societies and through cooperative investing. During the war, Tomihiro noted, "if someone wanted to purchase a hotel priced at four or five hundred dollars, they could easily raise the money by gathering funds from two or three friends." But by 1922 "our brotherly business world's cash loaning" gradually became "stringent." And as wages fell, there were fewer occupants paying rent.[108]

Agents with Portland's Morals Squad and the War Emergency Squad tasked with protecting soldiers from "vice" and looking for violations of

Oregon's prohibition laws had broad surveillance powers that did not include search warrants and used other strategies to entrap people.[109] Their activities continued with vigor after the war and with the onset of national prohibition. Emergency Squad agents, including Lieutenant Harvey Thatcher, a sergeant, and twenty patrol officers, targeted Nihonmachi among other areas in the city's North End. In 1919 they arrested Katsutaro Uyeto along with Josie Wheeler, a White housekeeper at the Villa House. Agents said Wheeler was reportedly selling whiskey at fifty cents per drink, and an officer seized two quarts as evidence. Under Oregon's prohibition law, in force in 1916 before national prohibition, a place where liquor was sold was considered a "common nuisance." If a manager allowed any part of the building to be used in an activity found to be a "a common nuisance," that manager would be "deemed guilty of assisting in the maintaining of such nuisance" and subject to fines. The court released both Katsutaro and Wheeler on $250 bail and apparently neither was convicted. In many similar cases the accused forfeited bail for a dismissal of charges.[110] The arrest made Villa House a place for agents of various surveillance groups to watch closely and often. Katsutaro left Portland for a visit to Japan and stayed with family in Hiroshima until his return in September, perhaps as a way to deflect attention from his arrest at Villa House. The Uyetos listed Mitsuyo ("M. Uyeto") as manager of Villa House in the *Portland City Directory* for 1920, and she conducted the family business in Katsutaro's absence.[111]

The Emergency Squad was not the only agency to have Issei business license holders under surveillance. The members of the Portland City Council and Portland police used the annual issuance and renewal of licenses for residents to operate businesses such as hotels and rooming houses, pool halls, and, in this prohibition era, "soft drink" parlors, to control who could engage in commerce and pursue a livelihood. In the postwar years agents targeted the North End, and Nihonmachi within it, in this scrutiny. The granting of licenses meant unannounced city inspections conducted by police officers that expanded official and undercover surveillance over workplaces and the people working in them. Because the Uyetos lived in their rooming house, as did many other Japanese Portlanders who resided with their families in rooms above or behind their restaurants or laundries, city licenses and inspections extended local surveillance over private lives. By 1921 the *Oregon Journal* reported, the

200 / CHAPTER 7

city Bureau of Licenses headed by Joseph S. Hutchinson was issuing some three hundred licenses per day. Licensing placed residents and workers under the direct and frequent scrutiny of Portland police who would keep a "proper check" on goings-on, both public and private. When the council decided to require licenses for cigar stands that year, the *Oregon Journal* noted that the license fee of one dollar was "a mere incidental, the real purpose being to give the police department direct supervision of the cigar stands in the North End district, many of which have been simply cloaks for bootleggers."[112]

By 1921 rooming house and hotel managers, with other Japanese American license holders in Portland, were also under surveillance by the Federal Bureau of Investigation. Special agent and former Multnomah sheriff Tom Word provided a six-page report listing the names and addresses of all Japanese American residents who had a city license of any kind. This included 73 soft drink, restaurant, grocery, and confectionery establishments and 102 hotel and rooming house licenses. Market gardeners and other producers who had stalls at the Yamhill Public Market, a thriving hub of daily trade spanning six blocks of food-related businesses, also had to have a license to conduct business, and Agent Word counted sixty-three Japanese American licensees there. The report only listed Japanese Portlanders, not the hundreds of other license holders, singling out Issei for specific surveillance.[113]

Portland officials targeted Japanese Americans specifically even though the licensing policy gave the city council the power to revoke licenses only on the grounds of "health, morals, or sanitation" as a legacy of the wartime anti–venereal disease campaign.[114] In March 1921, when T. Akamura applied to the council for a rooming house license in Japantown, patrol officer Fred Short reported that "it was practically impossible for police officers to obtain information from Japanese." Mayor George Baker suggested that given this information and reports from "previous hearings where Japanese rooming house operators were concerned[,] it would be a good policy for the council to grant no additional licenses to Japanese in Portland." The council adopted the policy, noting it was especially important because police officers "could obtain no co-operation from the Japanese when they sought information."[115] The clear implication was that licensing, and the ability to make a living the license conveyed, depended on a quid pro quo agreement for managers to cooperate with the city's surveillance projects and provide police with information about lodgers and family members without a search warrant or other tools of due process. But the ban against all Japanese Portlanders meant that the council was denying civil liberties to a particular class of residents, the Fourteenth Amendment protections for all people, resident or citizen, for due process and against unreasonable search and seizure and self-incrimination.

Japanese Portlanders turned to their community organization, the Japanese Association of Oregon, to protest and strategize. Association secretary Iwao Oyama wrote a letter to Mayor Baker with a "vigorous" objection to the ban and a request for the city council to lift it. Baker's initial verbal response to reporters' questions was firm: "We will not recede from our position. This council has had too much trouble with Jap hotel keepers in the past, and we intend to grant no more hotel or lodging house licenses to these people." Some in the Japanese Association began discussing a legal challenge. Baker's subsequent written response to Oyama shifted to more formal legal distinctions with language likely drafted with the assistance of Frank Grant, city attorney. "The action of the council, in cases of refusal to grant licenses or revocations of hotel licenses," Baker noted, "will be based upon the morality of the persons operating the hotels, or upon the fitness of the persons to operate the hotels." A reporter for the *Oregonian* quoted Baker as stating: "the council had no intention of refusing licenses to Japanese merely because they were Japanese." But "he made it plain in his letter that licenses for the operation of lodging houses and hotels would not be issued to Japanese or anybody else to continue hotels or lodging houses of questionable repute."[116] The mayor's new careful language represented a policy that could protect the city from legal action but one that council members could still exercise against Japanese Portlanders in practice.

Over the next several months, wary of legal challenges, Baker and city council members denied or revoked some licenses for Japanese American applicants but approved a select few, enough to demonstrate that there was not a total ban specifically on Japanese Oregonians. At the council meeting on March 16, council members revoked Y. O. Mikagawa's license for a hotel on 108 ½ Fourth Street but granted one for T. Okamura for the Australia Hotel on First and Hall. As the *Oregon Journal* put it, Okamura "discovered that he could speak very good English even in the presence of a policeman," implying that Okamura had agreed to cooperate with police inspections and surveillance.[117] When T. Saguchi applied for a hotel license at the council meeting on March 31, the *Oregon Journal* reported that he spoke "very broken English, and members of the council felt he was hardly capable of properly conducting a hotel because of this disability." But when they noticed the button Saguchi was wearing indicating he had contributed to the community chest fund drive and found out he had contributed twenty-five dollars to the cause, members agreed to give him thirty days to keep his license and find "a purchaser who can speak good English." But in "connection with the discussion of this case," council members "reopened" the matter of the "advisability of continuing to grant hotel licenses to Japanese." Officer Short was again on hand. The problem, he said, was that "the Japanese hotel and rooming house proprietors affect not to be able to understand or speak English" when the police wanted information, creating "serious" limitations in "securing required information as to violation of law."[118] Speaking without fluency in English or refusing to speak to help surveillance agents were both strikes against hotel managers in Nihonmachi.

The Uyetos entered this ongoing debate about licensing when Katsutaro applied for a renewal of the license for Villa House on May 4, 1921, council members denied it, and he attended the next council meeting on May 11 to appeal the decision.[119] Prominent Portland attorney John H. Stevenson, a former reporter for the *Portland Telegram* and former deputy district attorney who would soon be appointed to the Multnomah County Circuit Court, represented the Uyetos. Stevenson had advocated successfully for the creation of Portland's short-lived public defender office in 1914, and it is possible that he was providing pro bono support.[120] Six police officers testified at the appeal hearing and reported that "Uyeto's wife was one of the persons who had refused to give information." She "was 'sassy' to patrolmen when they questioned her." "Sassy" was a loaded and coded word. It meant speaking with impudence, disrespect, audacity, a lack of modesty, including a lack of gendered propriety. Police officers described Mitsuyo Uyeto as an Issei woman who had not only refused to give information to the police, but in her interactions with them was actively defiant, insubordinate, immodest. That Uyeto resisted by choosing to speak on her terms, and not when the police wanted her voice to support their surveillance efforts at Villa House, compounded their angry response.[121] Given the historic association of Nihonmachi and the North

End with "disorderly" women, the accusation against Uyeto for "sassing" carried the stigma of prostitution.

City councilors decided not to revoke the license for Villa House but to allow the Uyetos to continue under probation provided Mitsuyo not "sass" any police officer in the future.[122] Without additional specifics, it's interesting to consider why the council did not just revoke the Uyetos' license completely as they had done for other Japanese hotel managers. Perhaps council members were enjoining Katsutaro to control his wife Mitsuyo, a woman they considered acting and speaking out of her place. Perhaps Katsutaro and Mitsuyo signaled they were willing to cooperate with police and other agents moving forward. Or perhaps city councilors were wary of the legal challenges that the Oregon Japanese Association held at the ready if a hotel license were denied in the Uyetos' case. Perhaps attorney Stevenson had clout. In any case we can certainly consider the situation as a challenge to Mitsuyo Uyeto's ability as a resident to speak and act freely in addition to her freedom from unlawful search and seizure and to defend her privacy and the privacy of her family and lodgers.

The May 11 Portland City Council meeting engendered a discussion among members about the problem of hotel keepers' lack of cooperation with police. After resolving the Uyetos' case, council members engaged in a "serious discussion . . . likely to result in an extensive revocation of licenses." Commissioner C. A. Bigelow suggested "the police department be required to make a list of all persons holding hotel or rooming house licenses who cannot speak English fluently or who cannot read English and that hereafter they be eliminated from the license holders." The *Oregon Journal* reporter, from whom we have these details, did not note any specific references to Japanese Americans in Portland. The council appeared to discuss noncooperators and those who did not speak English in general, not a specifically "Japanese" problem, even though Mitsuyo Uyeto was the catalyst for the discussion.[123] When we place this in the context of the Oregon Japanese Association's challenge to the targeting of Japanese Americans and their hotel licenses and the need for the city council to walk a fine legal line, we may have a good part of the story. And it appears this was precisely the point. By broadening the complaint, the council was looking for a way to control licenses for the Uyetos and others without the legal challenges that might result from singling out a single class of residents such as Japanese American Portlanders. In the face of

204 / CHAPTER 7

these deliberations and with a conditional probationary license, Mitsuyo and Katsutaro Uyeto chose to resist Portland police and city council discrimination by leaving Oregon soon thereafter.[124]

Over the next months, City Attorney Grant, responding to an antiradical, anti-"foreigner" call from American Legion members, tried to draft a city ordinance that would prevent all noncitizens from being employed in public works jobs. Council members continued to deny hotel licenses because of nationality and language.[125] In September 1921, when the council denied his license to sell soft drinks because he was a Greek citizen, George B. Goritzan appealed the decision. When the council denied the license on appeal, Goritzan hired an attorney to petition for a restraining order preventing the council from revoking his license.[126] Circuit court judge Robert G. Morrow issued the restraining order, citing health, morals, and sanitation as the only grounds for revoking the license in the ordinance.[127] Grant continued to try to find a strategy for the council to enact a legal ban on noncitizens for city licenses and public works jobs, but council members did not find a way to pass such ordinances.[128]

Grant and his anti-Japanese supporters had a Plan B: statewide "anti-alien" legislation; and they had the means to accomplish it when Multnomah County voters sent "an almost solid [Ku Klux] Klan delegation" to the 1923 legislative session.[129] After the November 1922 election, Grant teamed up with Portland Republican Thomas H. Hurlburt, who won his seat to represent Multnomah County's 18th District in the Oregon House, to craft "anti-alien" license and employment bills for the upcoming legislative session. Hurlburt had Klan support and "went to the legislature as the representative of anti-Catholic and anti-alien prejudice."[130] Hurlburt was also "a considerable property owner in Portland." He "operated a large lodging hotel in Portland, and made money at it," placing him in direct economic competition with other hotel and lodging house license holders.[131] Despite this obvious conflict of interest, Hurlburt introduced two House bills banning licensing for noncitizens in the 1923 legislative session and one of them, HB 205, "Prohibiting issuance of licenses to aliens in certain instances," prevailed and passed.[132] When Hurlburt introduced HB 205, he told legislators it had been "drawn up at the request of the fraternal and patriotic associations of Portland by the city attorney [Grant]."[133] Under the bill's provisions, no city, town, or county could issue licenses to noncitizens to operate a soft drink establishment, a pawn brokerage, a pool or billiard hall, a card-playing or dance hall business. Noncitizens who had licenses for "a hotel, lodging house, rooming house or apartment house," a fruit stand, or a meat market were required to "keep displayed, in full view, on a card sign, [their] nationality and the nationality of [their] help." Violation of these provisions was a misdemeanor offense carrying up to six months in jail and a $500 fine, or both.[134]

Even though HB 205 referred to noncitizens generally, the Uyetos and other Japanese American Portlanders who held and sought hotel and rooming house licenses were never far from the mind of Hurlburt, the man who had "operated a large lodging hotel in Portland and made money at it." As he introduced the bill, Hurlburt insisted: "Portland needs such a bill to protect itself against foreigners. I might say there are 322 Japanese places of business in Portland, and a great many are hotels." Some were "ostensibly operated by the white employees but" were "really owned and operated by Japanese. In many cases these places are immoral and are operated for that purpose. We need such a law to be able to get action."[135] One representative asked whether the bill was "against the Japanese or against all nationalities," so clearly did Hurlburt target Japanese Americans in his presentation.[136] Another striking feature of the legislative discussion of HB 205 was the open acknowledgment of the questionable constitutionality of the measure and the willingness of many legislators to support it despite the boundaries of law and ethics it crossed. Representative William F. Woodward (R-Multnomah), a member of the Klan who had been a member of the Central Library board who pressured M. Louise Hunt to resign, had called for the library to burn "Pro German" books on July 4, 1918. A founding member of the Oregon Social Hygiene Association and chair of the Oregon Council of National Defense during the war, Woodward spoke in favor of the measure. "This law is stringent, but it is badly needed. Possibly it is unfair, and possibly it is unjust, but it will tend to eliminate a very vicious class of people who are working against, directly against, our young men and women."[137] Representative George A. Lovejoy (D-Multnomah) stated: "I don't really like the bill, and I don't consider it along the lines of our constitution." But "we must have some drastic law to enable us to regulate and control a vicious business," he said, and urged colleagues to pass it.[138]

The members of the Portland City Council and City Attorney Grant continued to use their expansive surveillance tools in combination with the

FIGURE 24 Mrs. S. Kojima with her child of Independence, Oregon, August 1916. s#0126G068, Cronise Collection, Oregon Historical Society Research Library, Portland.

new statewide legislation to harass and exclude Japanese American hotel managers. Matsumi Kojima's license case provides an example. Kojima and her husband, Shigeki, relocated from the hop fields of Independence to a farm in Troutdale by 1917 and then to work in a fruit business in Portland by 1920 as their family grew. Daughter Tatsuka Vivian, born in Independence, and two sons were part of the family by 1922.

Kojima established herself as the manager the Fremont Hotel rooming house on First Street in Nihonmachi.[139] In 1923 the city council announced plans to revoke her license, claiming that Kojima had permitted "improper conduct" at the small hotel. Kojima fought back. With attorney John Stevenson, who had represented the Uyetos two years before, and her family at her side, Kojima attended the May 13, 1923, hearing prepared to have her hotel license reinstated. According to an *Oregonian* reporter, Stevenson "took offense at the manner in which City Attorney Grant was conducting the hearing and stalked from the council chamber without waiting for his case to be called." The council revoked Kojima's license but agreed to a rehearing, which led to her reinstatement.[140]

But by the end of 1923, police added another surveillance strategy to scrutinize hotels and rooming houses in Portland, drawing on Oregon's 1893 expansion of miscegenation law preventing marriages across ethnic and racial lines that included "Mongolians" and the practice of counting Japanese Americans in that "racial" category.[141] In December 1923 police chief Leon Jenkins after "discoveries regarding the association of young white women with Chinese" men, ordered the vice squad to "conduct a relentless campaign" against "keepers of hotels who allow persons of different races to congregate in their places." Oregon had "'state laws that forbid the intermarriage of persons of different races,'" Jenkins noted. Based on state miscegenation law, he instructed vice police to "'take steps that will break up these associations'" and to "'see to it that the keeper of any hotel who allows such conduct is not only arrested but that steps will be taken to revoke the place's license as well.'"[142] The city's multiple surveillance projects were indeed relentless, and Kojima decided to leave the hotel business, and Oregon, with her family after 1925. When D. K. Noda applied to take over the license for the Fremont Hotel that May, the record showed the police had raided the establishment thirteen times.[143]

Ironically, because City Attorney Grant, Representative Hurlburt, and others in their coalition had broadened the license bans to noncitizens in general rather than targeting Japanese Americans specifically to avoid legal challenges, the state's 1923 "anti-alien" licensing ban did not stand judicial scrutiny in Oregon. In 1924 noncitizen soft-drink vendors who had been denied licenses by the Portland City Council based on an ordinance passed after the statewide licensing law filed a class action suit, *George v. City of Portland*. None of the plaintiffs was Japanese American. Grant represented Portland and the case went to the Oregon Supreme Court, whose members declared the law unconstitutional in 1925. Chief Justice George H. Burnett delivered the majority opinion striking down the state law and the Portland ordinance based on it, citing violations of the due process and equal protection clauses of the Fourteenth Amendment. Significantly, Justice Burnett gave equal weight to the Oregon Constitution, Article I, Section 31 that embedded Whiteness into the Oregon legal system: "White foreigners who are, or may hereafter become, residents of this

208 / CHAPTER 7

State shall enjoy the same rights in respect to the possession, enjoyment, and descent of property as native born citizens." Burnett concluded: "It is plain that in respect to persons proposing to engage in an otherwise lawful occupation, a distinction based solely on whether the applicant is or is not an alien, is not permitted in this state." But non-White "foreigners" such as Japanese Americans had no such constitutional protection.[144]

Federal, state, and community scrutiny and discrimination against Issei women and their families in Oregon in the 1910s and 1920s was a part of the growth of the surveillance state and race-based exclusionary policies in Oregon and the nation. The identification of Japanese Americans in Oregon and the nation as internal enemies continued in the years that followed, leading to the mass incarceration of an entire group of residents and citizens during World War II. In the 1920s many White policymakers situated Issei mothers at the heart of the "Japanese Problem" in the state and nation and proclaimed their reproductive and productive work as fundamentally "alien" and dangerous to an American way of life, even though that work was the sanctioned work of the nation for White women to be constructive citizens. Policymakers' "solutions" included exclusion, discrimination, calls for revising the citizenship clause of the Fourteenth Amendment, legislation prohibiting Issei from owning land, attempts to limit business licenses, and Owens-Adair's call for sterilization of all Japanese American women.

When city authorities called out Mitsuyo Uyeto for "sassing" police officers and refusing to provide private information about her residents, and when Mitsumi Kojima contested the label of "improper conduct" for her Fremont Hotel, their cases became part of a larger movement to restrict Japanese Oregonian businesses by using hotel licensing ordinances originally crafted in the anti-prostitution and anti–venereal disease campaign of the war years. Their experiences demonstrate the extent to which Portland authorities used warrantless surveillance to police the private lives of residents of Nihonmachi. Among the significant number of Japanese Oregonian hotel and rooming house managers, including many women as managers and partners, the anti-Japanese licensing movement, which expanded statewide in 1923, was the urban equivalent of the "anti-alien" land ownership restriction campaigns of the early twentieth century and a parallel to Oregon's 1923 Alien Land Act.

The Uyetos and the Kojimas left Oregon, and perhaps the nation, after the relentless police and city council actions to raid and surveil their Portland rooming houses in the name of that licensing policy. Adam Goodman urges us to understand and name their actions as self-deportation, part of the nation's long history of exclusion, removal, and deportation. The Portland and Oregon licensing laws that coerced the Uyetos and Kojimas to leave are part of the history of state and community "fear campaigns, vigilante violence, and other measures," including economic ones, undertaken to coerce people to leave their homes and businesses and communities.[145] Issei women resisted these ideas and actions by attending to reproductive health and childbirth recording and sustaining by families and communities in paid and unpaid labor. And when Mitsuyo Uyeto refused to cooperate with Portland police in their unwarranted surveillance of the Villa Hotel, and when Mutsumi Kojima hired lawyer John Stevenson to help her retain her license for the Fremont Hotel, they participated in resistance and called for civil liberties protections.

The vital resistance work of Issei women within their circumstances and possibilities constitutes an important chapter in the antidiscrimination and social justice history of this period. It is also part of the long movement for civil liberties protections against the anti-Japanese policies and actions that led to the creation of American concentration camps for Japanese American residents and citizens during the World War II and the postwar movements for redress and apology that continue today.

Conclusion

Before, during, and after World War I the quest to identify, restrict, and punish internal enemy others, combined with eugenic thinking and policies to identify the "unfit," severely curtailed civil liberties for many people in Oregon and the nation. At this same time most Oregon women had gained the right to vote, and many were building additional rights as women citizens. Many White women embraced eugenic and nativist policies that restricted the rights and liberties of other people in the state. It is necessary to consider these processes in tandem to build a history that accounts for achievements and regressions and exclusions in rights and liberties, a history that analyzes the precarious nature of victories in the struggle for full human rights, a history that includes both fierce advocacy for liberties and stern imposition of restrictions, and a history that assists the work of building, repair, and reconciliation in the present and future.

People whose stories are detailed in this book engaged in resistance to practices restricting citizenship, violations of civil liberties, and policies of exclusion that labeled them unfit internal enemies. Women who refused the Food Pledge, women's war service registration, or participation in Liberty Loan and War Stamp drives did so under powerful pressure to comply, and their resistance helped maintain a citizenship of dissent. This included Food Pledge resisters, war registration resisters, and M. Louise Hunt and Anna Mary Weston, who encountered the registration drives at their workplaces at Portland's Central Library and the Pullman railroad yards at Portland's North Bank Station. Women required to register as noncitizen enemies engaged in vocal protest and subversion of the registration forms, including creating their own representations in the required photographs.

Ruth Brown and other inmates at The Cedars filed writs of habeas corpus to maintain their liberty in the face of anti–venereal disease campaigns based on a gendered double standard of incarceration without due process. Teddy Gloss fought back against a medical examination that was the legacy of those same campaigns when convicted of breaking a window, and hunger-struck when committed to the State Industrial School for Girls. Winnie Springer sued physicians and administrators of the Oregon State Hospital for violating rights to due process and cruel and unusual punishment; following her release, she worked to establish organized challenges to those practices in advocacy. Louise Burbank and her advocates exercised some agency in the negotiations to accept deportation to avoid state-imposed sterilization at the Oregon State Hospital. Issei women made birthing choices and insisted on the birth registration of their children and labored for their families and communities on their own terms. Mitsuyo Uyeto chose when and if to speak to police who wanted her to surveil the residents of the Villa House Hotel she managed with her husband. Matsumi Kojima joined Uyeto in challenging the restrictive licensing policies in Portland and Oregon that targeted Japanese residents. These examples demonstrate the importance and power of everyday acts of resistance alongside other organized challenges to restrictions and exclusions and comprise an important chapter in the long history of the movement for equal citizenship and civil liberties in Oregon and the nation. Affirming resistance and making it visible is not a critique of people who were unable to resist, or whose resistance was private and personal or otherwise not part of the historical record. Their lives and struggles move through these pages in less tangible but still powerful ways.

The impact of Oregon First boosterism during these years was consequential. The perceived need to maintain star-state status meant that local and state officials and volunteer leaders placed incredible pressure on residents to conform to the latest Oregon First project, encouraging relentless adherence to the cause and the ruthless policing of others. Oregon First boosterism magnified the already powerful wartime and postwar imperatives to identify and punish an array of dangerous internal enemies across the nation. And because leadership in radical eugenic policy was one of Oregon's star "accomplishments," eugenic thinking intensified the hunt for internal enemy others. These included people considered disabled or insane; all women who might be sex workers, infected with syphilis or gonorrhea, or sexually active outside of heterosexual marriage; gender-nonconforming residents; and ethnic others including specific campaigns against Japanese Oregonians, in addition to radicals and dissenters. Patriotic loyalty fused with competitive and economic boosterism

212 / CONCLUSION

in the wartime emergency and the "New Patriotism" in the "extended emergency" of the postwar period and fostered new registration projects, nativist and restrictive legislation, and the growth of White supremacy and the Ku Klux Klan in the state. Oregon First boosterism mandated unquestioning loyalty to the means and the ends of these "crises" and promoted a systematic lack of critical thinking, what Charles Rothwell called "the stupor of patriotism and intense nationalism." This history provides a vital cautionary tale for our own time and beyond.

Enfranchised women in Oregon used their voting power after 1912 to exercise citizenship rights and impact their communities based on their status and identities. Black women and Catholic Religious Sisters organized voter registration drives to address exclusionary and racist discriminatory practices and legislation. Many White, elite, and middle-class women helped to enact laws to support teachers and other wage-earning women, and to expand rights such as jury service, but also lobbied actively for eugenic sterilization laws that declared disabled and gender-nonconforming people, sex workers, and others to be unfit citizens subject to state-coerced sterilization. Federal and local policymakers made the unquestioned and absolute support of the various registrations and pledge drives the only sanctioned practice of female citizenship during the war and after. Many women leaders in Oregon, some women of color, and some women in immigrant communities embraced this work as a way to claim a more complete citizenship for themselves and their communities. But for some women organizers, participation became such an important way to engage in the sanctioned work of the nation, they did not accord other women residents and citizens the rights of citizenship and civil liberties. Drawing on ideas about patriotic womanhood and the productive work of the nation, they curtailed and violated other women's citizenship rights in an attempt to build their own.

The surveillance, policing, and regulating of bodies during the war and its aftermath, combined with the parallel policies inspired by eugenic thinking, targeted women, gender-nonconforming people, and residents of color in ways that are painfully familiar today. The ability to control one's body and to have safety in one's person are core civil liberties and human rights. Eugenic thinkers built "sexual perversion" into sterilization bills and statutes that named internal enemies and reached beyond institutions to threaten all residents after 1919. Canvassers in the last stages of

CONCLUSION / 213

the wartime Food Pledge placed special scrutiny on unmarried people in Portland, sweeps that threatened to expose same-sex relationships in the name of patriotic scrutiny. Noncitizen enemy registration and surveillance sent Riedl to an internment camp and eventual deportation because of "sex perversion."

Anti–venereal disease and eugenic policies and practices meant the scrutiny of bodies and particular targeting of Black women and other women of color in Portland, the genital exam to which gender-non-conforming Teddy Gloss reacted in self-defense, and the deportation of Leonor Brunicardi as an "unfit" Mexican American immigrant. Winnie Springer's actions to consider a nonbinary body and to avoid an opera-tion her physician brother-in-law advocated were part of an unfolding family drama that led to her commitment to the Oregon State Hospital. Leaders and community members who embraced the hunt for internal enemy others politicized reproduction for Issei mothers of US citizen children and for women considered "feebleminded" or "insane." They criminalized people engaging in nonsanctioned sex, including all women who might be infected with or suspected of carrying syphilis or gonorrhea. Oregon authorities put a durable hold-for-health policy in place during the anti–venereal disease campaigns in The Cedars era with multiple double standards and violations of due process for women. The practice continued through the early 1970s in Portland. Press coverage during a 1970 challenge to the policy revealed that women "designated as VD sus-pects—including all prostitutes" often stayed most of a week without bail at the Portland city jail's Emergency Hospital because they had to have three culture smear tests on successive days for gonorrhea in addition to the blood test for syphilis given to everyone. If women refused the test, they could be jailed indefinitely until they agreed, echoing Margaret Mathew's April 1918 letter to Portland's mayor George Baker in 1918 about her four-week-and-counting health hold.[1]

Local, state, and federal authorities also used deportation during these years to punish people identified as internal enemy others. Adam Good-man's framework of formal, voluntary, and self-deportation and the com-parative lens used in this book help us gather seemingly disparate cases together to trace the use of deportation as a tool in the broad context of policies of exclusion in Oregon and the nation. These cases include the calls for the deportation of librarian M. Louise Hunt to Germany for exercising her citizenship of dissent during wartime, Riedl's "voluntary" return to Germany after incarceration as an "enemy alien," the attempt by Oregon State Hospital officials to deport Margarita Ojeda Wilcox who was born in Mexico but married to a US citizen, and the negotiations in which Canadian-born Louise Burbank and her advocates engaged with state hospital and immigration authorities between deportation and forced state sterilization. The cases also include Leonor Brunicardi's deportation during the anti–venereal disease campaign. Portland and Oregon policymakers expanded hotel and rooming house licensing laws originally crafted for the wartime anti-prostitution and anti–venereal disease campaigns to use against Japanese American managers in Portland. Mitsuyo Uyeto and Matsumi Kojima and their families left Oregon because of discriminatory treatment and relentless surveillance of their Portland rooming houses in acts of coerced self-deportation. Uyeto and Kojima's stories link coerced self-deportation via Portland and Oregon's hotel licensing laws to the broad history of systematic discrimination by gender, race, ethnicity, and class embedded in policies about housing, including practices of real estate redlining for mortgage and business loans and restrictive covenants. These vital cases all underscore the importance of understanding the long history of deportation as well as the local histories of that deportation. By Goodman's 2020 count, the United States has deported fifty-seven million people since 1882.[2] Deportation, like other tools of exclusion, has cost Oregon and the nation in incalculable ways by removing members of the community whose future contributions to the community cannot be measured.

Eugenic thinking in Oregon and the nation and the tenacity of Oregon's early eugenics advocates lived on in the post-1923 eugenics movement in the state.[3] Oregon's 1923 "model" eugenics law addressed some civil liberties concerns about due process and class legislation but reached to all residents. By 1929, Oregon legislators added the State Industrial School for Girls as one of the state institutions with the duty to report people for eugenic sterilization. And Oregon voters adopted a Marriage Examination Law for all applicants in 1938 during a second national wave of state marriage examination laws including blood tests for both partners for syphilis as part of the "broader federal effort to combat syphilis as a public health issue."[4] Oregon's marriage law contributed to Owens-Adair's ultimate eugenic goal of policing all state residents for ability and disability.

CONCLUSION / *215*

The state's 1938 "Act Requiring Marriage License Applicants Medically Examined, Physically and Mentally" required a blood test and medical exam but also required a physician to report people who failed because of "feeble-mindedness, insanity" or other "mental or physical" conditions to a committee appointed by the State Board of Eugenics. That committee could refuse permission to marry.

The 1938 law did not refer to the next step of state-ordered sterilization explicitly, but because of Oregon's capacious 1923 sterilization law, that same committee could recommend sterilization for either or both of the applicants to the state health officer. The Oregon legislature referred the law to voters in November 1938, and the measure passed with an astonishing 81 percent of votes cast.[5] By 1954, Oregon was alone among the forty-two other states with marriage examination laws to include reporting to a eugenic board.[6] The federal government had the goal of making marriage, in Deborah Doroshow's description, "a life cycle checkpoint through which all Americans would pass, separating the diseased from the pure" by monitoring sexually transmitted infections.[7] Oregon's law separated the "fit" from the "unfit" in eugenic terms, with the power to sterilize people the state considered "unfit." Oregon legislators repealed the marriage law in 1981, in step with other states because of high costs to administer the policy and few infections revealed with testing.[8] Peggy Pascoe showed us that Oregon's miscegenation laws, not repealed until 1951, defined marriage as being about property, propriety, and Whiteness.[9] Understanding Oregon's eugenics movement and its eugenic marriage laws help us to extend that framework to include ability along with Whiteness, property, and propriety. The forced and coerced sterilizations of Indigenous women and other women of color, poor women, disabled women, and other people into our own day call on us to connect the early twentieth-century developments covered in this book with the continuing violations of human rights and genocides related to eugenic thinking that have been and are part of the lives of so many in Oregon, the nation, and the world.

Winnie Springer's legal action against the Oregon State Hospital for violations of her civil liberties, which culminated in the Oregon Supreme Court's overturning of her civil suit in *Springer v. Steiner* (1919) and Ruth Brown's 1921 habeas corpus suit against incarceration at The Cedars were significant developments in the movement to claim and safeguard civil liberties for people committed to institutions in Oregon and the nation. Some fifty-five years later in 1974, Linda Gheer, a resident of Fairview Training Center, the former Oregon State Institution for the Feeble-Minded, helped to organize People First, an organization by and for people with disabilities. The People First conference at Otter Crest that year, with five hundred attending, is considered to be the "beginning of the self-advocacy movement in the United States."[10]

Oregon's two foremost eugenic activists, lobbyist Bethenia Owens-Adair and advocate and practitioner Lewis Frank Griffith, of the Oregon State Hospital, were proponents of a radical vision of the state sterilization of the "unfit" that reached all Oregonians. Their work and the active advocacy of others, including many thousands of White women voters, meant that Oregon was one of the most radical eugenic states by the time the 1919 law and its 1923 successor put this vision into practice. All people suspected of being "unfit" were reportable to the State Board of Health for sterilization. As eugenics advocates worked to enact legislation that made Oregon one of the most significant eugenic states in the twentieth century, opponents of state-mandated sterilization voted in opposition and engaged in referendum projects. But with the success of Oregon's sterilization legislation, by 1923 it fell to individuals and their advocates to resist, as the case of Louise Burbank and the OSH demonstrates. Sterilization was official Oregon state policy until 1983, when legislators abolished the state eugenics board, by then called the Board of Social Protection. On December 2, 2002, Oregon governor John Kitzhaber, a former emergency room physician, issued an apology on behalf of the people of the state for Oregon's forced sterilization of more than twenty-six hundred people; he declared December 10 to be Human Rights Day in the state, coinciding with the United Nations Human Rights Day to commemorate the day the UN Assembly ratified the Universal Declaration of Human Rights in 1948.[11]

Many dedicated activists, curators, archivists, historians, editors, teachers, and others in Oregon and the nation are engaged in the vital ongoing work of education, repair, and reconciliation in our communities to address the destructive historical processes of exclusion, restriction, deportation, ableism, White supremacy, and the hatred and violence engendered by the hunt for and vilification of "internal enemy others." They are putting Oregon's and the nation's diverse history into the landscape, in exhibits, in journal articles and monographs, in digital collections, and into lesson plans, classrooms, and documentary films. Reconciliation and empowerment projects address the history of lynching and other acts of race-based violence including past and present incarceration, and violence against queer people and people with disabilities in Oregon and the nation. Actions to build inclusive communities challenge the policies of hatred and violence based on some people's continuing quest to identify and punish "internal enemy others."

Activists are redefining the concept of the civic work of the nation to be the labor of educating people about the injustices of the past, promoting healing and reconciliation, and affirming a citizenship of mutual rights and duties to each other based on shared membership and respect in the community. If we believe that the long history of struggles for human rights must ultimately result in a just community, then our diverse histories of discrimination and resistance help us to hold up the mirror of the past to our own present. If we believe that until all human rights and liberties are protected, no human rights and liberties are safe, understanding our complicated history, sharing it with others, and taking action for our present and future is indeed consequential action for social justice.

Notes

ABBREVIATIONS

BIA	Bureau of Indian Affairs
GPO	United States Government Printing Office, Washington, DC
NARA	National Archives and Records Administration, College Park, Maryland
NARA Seattle	National Archives, Seattle
OHQ	*Oregon Historical Quarterly*
OHS	Oregon Historical Society Research Library Portland, Oregon
OSA	Oregon State Archives, Salem, Oregon
OSBH	Oregon State Board of Health
SPO	Oregon State Printing Office, Salem
WCTU	Woman's Christian Temperance Union
YWCA	Young Women's Christian Association

PREFACE

1   Chaudhuri, Katz, and Perry, *Contesting Archives*, xv.

2   Richards and Burch, "Documents, Ethics, and the Disability Historian."

3   Oregon Revised Statutes (ORS) 192.398, "Medical records," accessed November 19, 2023, https://oregon.public.law/statutes/ors_192.398; and US Department of Health and Human Services, "Health Information of Deceased Individuals," accessed November 19, 2023, https://www.hhs .gov/hipaa/for-professionals/privacy/guidance/health-information-of -deceased-individuals/index.html.

INTRODUCTION

1   "State of the Union Address, President Woodrow Wilson, December 7, 1915," Project Gutenberg, accessed November 19, 2023, https://www .gutenberg.org/files/5034/5034-h/5034-h.htm#dec1915.

2   L. F. Griffith, "The Prevention of Insanity," *Medical Sentinel* 23, no. 8 (August 1915): 2351–2357.

3   Jensen, "'Neither Head nor Tail to the Campaign'"; and Jensen, "Revolutions in the Machinery."

4   Carlisle, "Summary of the Oregon State Survey," 16, 20.

5   Wilson, *Eugenic Mind Project*.

6   Carey, *On the Margins of Citizenship*, 7, 1, 213.

7   Gardner, *Qualities of a Citizen*, 50–86.

8   Canaday, *Straight State*, 23.

9   Kerber, *No Constitutional Right*, xx–xxi.

10   VanBurkleo, *Gender Remade*, 299, 253.

11   Lister, *Citizenship*, 15; and Jensen, "'Women's Positive Patriotic Duty to Participate.'"

12   Geller, *Nations and Nationalism*, 7; and Marshall, *Class, Citizenship, and Social Development*.

13   Kessler-Harris, *In Pursuit of Equity*.

14   Nielsen, "Incompetent and Insane."

15   Dumenil, *Second Line of Defense*, 155–203.

16   Shenk, *Work or Fight*; and Hunter, *To 'Joy My Freedom*, 227–232.

17   Kerber, *No Constitutional Right*, xxii–xxiii, 50–55, 51, emphasis in original; and Gardner, *Qualities of a Citizen*, 87–99, 99.

18   Glenn, *Unequal Freedom*, 56–92, 89.

19   *Oregon Laws* 95 (1911), 138–139.

20   Bristow, *Making Men Moral*; Kline, *Building a Better Race*, 44–47; Clement, *Love for Sale*, 119; and Shah, "'Against Their Own Weakness,'" 468.

21   Goodman, *Deportation Machine*.

22   Gardner, *Qualities of a Citizen*, 87–99; Ngai, *Impossible Subjects*; Baynton, "Disability and the Justification of Inequality in American History"; and Howard L. Bevis, "The Deportation of Aliens," *University of Pennsylvania Law Review and American Law Register* 68, no. 2 (January 1920): 97–119.

23   Marshall, *Class, Citizenship, and Social Development*; Kessler-Harris, *In Pursuit of Equity*; Dawley, *Changing the World*; Jensen, "Revolutions in the Machinery"; and Dilg, "'For Working Women in Oregon.'"

24   Steinson, *American Women's Activism in World War I*; and Kennedy, *Disloyal Mothers and Scurrilous Citizens*.

25 Murphy, *World War I and the Origin of Civil Liberties*, 15, 177; and Capozzolla, *Uncle Sam Wants You*, 19 and passim.

26 Wheeler, *How Sex Became a Civil Liberty*.

27 Higgonet et al., *Behind the Lines*, 6, 4.

28 Parenti, *Soft Cage*; Hier and Greenberg, eds., *Surveillance Studies Reader*; and Murphy, *World War I and the Oregon of Civil Liberties*, 178.

29 Pascoe, *What Comes Naturally*, 77–80, 77; Smith, "Oregon's Civil War," 169; and Millner, "Blacks in Oregon."

30 *Oregon Laws*, An Act to Amend Laws Relating to Marriages (1893), 41; Lord's *Oregon Laws* (1910). vol. 1, chapter 3, 2163–2165, 945; and Pascoe, *What Comes Naturally*, 87–91. Pascoe quoted "Law Will Block Mesalliance Here," *Oregonian*, March 26, 1909, 1, 3.

31 Platt and Cray, "'Out of Order,'" 81.

32 Lewis, "Four Deaths," 414–437.

33 Jensen, "'Neither Head nor Tail to the Campaign.'"

34 Article II on Suffrage and Elections, in Carey, *Oregon Constitution*, 404.

35 Oregon Secretary of State, *Voter Pamphlet Proposed Amendments and Measures General Election 1914* (Salem: SPO, 1914), 3–5; Oregon Secretary of State, *Initiative, Referendum, and Recall Ballot Results*, accessed November 19, 2023, https://sos.oregon.gov/blue-book/Pages/state/elections/history-introduction.aspx; and Hayduk, *Democracy for All*, 1–40, 15, 4.

36 *Oregon Laws* 126 (1923), 183–186; and Anderson, *One Person, No Vote*.

37 Reid, "Multilayered Loyalties."

38 Bredbenner, *Nationality of Her Own*.

39 Johnson, *"They Are All Red Out Here"*; Van Nuys, *Americanizing the West*; Molina, "In a Race All Their Own"; Ogden, "Ghadar, Historical Silences, and Nations of Belonging"; Ngai, *Impossible Subjects*; and Lee, *America for Americans*.

40 Daniels, *Guarding the Golden Door*; Lee, *Making of Asian America*; and Azuma, "Oregon's Issei."

41 "From 1904–1920," *Oshu Nippo*, July 4, 1924, 37.

42 "Table 1. Population of Oregon," US Bureau of the Census, *Fourteenth Census of the United States, State Compendium, Oregon* (Washington, DC: GPO, 1925), 22.

43 *The Official Catholic Directory 1924* (New York: P. J. Kennedy and Sons, 1924), 155, 245; Ogden, "Ghadar, Historical Silences, and Nations of Belonging," 166–169; and Eisenberg, "Jews in Oregon."

44 "Election Laws Made More Simple," *Sunday Oregonian*, January 11, 1914, Section 2, 7; "Election Laws Up for Vast Changes," *Oregonian*, February 5, 1913, 2; and Lord's *Oregon Laws*, vol. 2, chapter 10, 3447, 1365.

45 "Registration Law Termed Invalid," *Oregonian*, November 26, 1913, 7; "Confusion Feared in State Election," *Sunday Oregonian*, December 14, 1913, Section 1, 8; "Permanent Registration Bill Passed," *Oregon Journal*, February 2, 1915, 4; "Repeal of Registration Act," *Biennial Report and Opinions of the Attorney General of the State of Oregon to the Twenty-Eighth Legislative Assembly 1915* (Salem, OR: SPO, 1914), 257; and "Portland Voters Slow to Register," *Oregon Journal*, January 31, 1916, 5.

46 Cancelled Voter Registration Cards, 1908–2010, Multnomah County Election Records database, Multnomah County Archives, Portland, Oregon. With thanks to Terry Baxter, Multnomah county archivist.

47 "Table 13. Age for Portland" in *Thirteenth Census of the United States Taken in the Year 1910, with Supplement for Oregon* (Washington, DC: GPO, 1913), 592. "Colored Folk Join Republican Force," *Oregonian*, October 14, 1914, 14; "Women Voters Taking Active Interest," *Oregonian*, October 16, 1914, 7; and "Republican Club Is Busy," *Oregonian*, February 2, 1915, 18.

48 "Colored Women's Republican Club." *Oregon Journal*, September 23, 1916, 3.

49 "Women's Power Felt at Capitol," *Oregonian*, February 10, 1913, 1; and Women's Legislative Council of Oregon, "Women Jurors: Official Argument Affirmative," *Oregon Voter*, April 2, 1921, 22–26. Oregon women were in step with California women, who established a legislative council in 1912 following their 1911 suffrage ballot victory, and Washington State women, who formed their council in 1918. See Gullett, *Becoming Citizens*, 201–205; and "Gen. Greene Will Speak to Legislative Council," *Tacoma Times*, April 10, 1918, 8. For the National Women's Joint Congressional Committee (WJCC) formed in November 1920, see Wilson, *Women's Joint Committee and the Politics of Maternalism*.

50 "Women to Consider Proposed Measures," *Oregon Journal*, December 24, 1916, 9; and "The Women's Legislative Council," *Oregonian*, January 3, 1917, 10.

51 Alma Splidsboel sued the Oregon Women's Klan for back wages and won, and named leaders. "Suit to Collect Wages from Klan Women is Begun," *Oregon Journal*, May 19, 1924, 8. Voter Registration Cards for Mae E. Gifford (May 10, 1913), Kristine R. Belt (April 7, 1913), Nellie Hurd (April 12, 1913), and Minnie M. Schonberg (April 18, 1922), Multnomah County Archives. Vora S. Sowers, Medford, Bound Volume, Official Register of Electors 1914, Jackson County, 663, 51/7/2, 20/5A 35, OSA, Salem.

52 Abrams, *Cross Purposes*; Saalfeld, *Forces of Prejudice*; and Gordon, *Second Coming of the KKK*, 149–156.

53 Abrams, *Cross Purposes*, 125–126; "Catholics Request School Injunction," *Oregonian*, August 23, 1923, 3. Correspondence, Provincial Superior Alphonsus Mary Daly to Oregon Sisters, March 31, 1921, Oregon Province Records, Archives of the Sisters of the Holy Names of Jesus and Mary, U.S.–Ontario Province, Lake Oswego, Oregon. For her help with these records, I am most grateful to Sarah Cantor, director of Heritage Center and archivist, Sisters of the Holy Names of Jesus and Mary, U.S.-Ontario Province, Lake Oswego, Oregon.

54 April 21, 1921, *Chronicles*, Convent of the Holy Names, Marylhurst; May 19, 1922, and November 7, 1922, *Chronicles*, St. Paul's Academy, St. Paul; November 7, 1922, *Chronicles*, Sacred Heart Academy, Salem; November 7, 1922, *Chronicles*, St. Mary's Academy, The Dalles; *Chronicles*, St. Mary's Academy, Jacksonville; and Archives of the Sisters of the Holy Names of Jesus and Mary, U.S.–Ontario Province, Lake Oswego, Oregon.

55 Butler, *Across God's Frontiers*, 288.

56 Abrams, *Cross Purposes*, 51.

57 Rothwell, "Ku Klux Klan in the State of Oregon," 113.

58 William F. Ogburn, "Oregon, An Experimental Station in Government," *Welfare: The Journal of Municipal and Social Progress* (April 1914): 10–11, 14–15, copy at Pacific Northwest Special Collections, University of Washington Libraries, Seattle; Oregon Secretary of State, *Initiative, Referendum and Recall Introduction, Oregon Blue Book*; and Southwell, "Political Parties and Elections," 39–43.

59 Dilg, "'For Working Women in Oregon'"; Woloch, *Muller v. Oregon*; and Miriam Theresa (Caroline Gleason), *Legislation for Women in Oregon*.

60 Ogburn, "Oregon," 10.

61 See chapter 5.

62 Rothwell, "Ku Klux Klan in Oregon," 111–112.

63 "Oregon's Patriotic Record," *Oregon Statesman*, April 24, 1918, 4; Oregon Secretary of State, "Oregon and the World War," *Oregon Blue Book and Official Directory* (Salem: SPO, 1921): 13–14; and "Oregon First Due to George A. White," *Oregonian*, July 29, 1917, 17.

64 Dr. W. A. Pettit, "Oregon Sets Pace in Hygienic Work of United States" *Sunday Oregonian*, January 19, 1919, Section 5, 8; and "Clean Manhood," *Oregon Journal*, December 17, 1918, 10.

65 US Public Health Service, "Relative Standing of 444 Cities in Respect to Measures in Force February 1, 1920, for Combating Venereal Diseases," 1–8; and "Keep It in First Place," *Oregonian*, October 30, 1920, 4.

66 Carey, *History of Oregon*, 876; Wheat, *Story of the American Legion*; and Rothwell, "Ku Klux Klan in Oregon," 113.

67 See chapter 1.

68 Joan M. Jensen, *Price of Vigilance*; Capozzola, *Uncle Sam Wants You*; and Fronc, *New York Undercover*.

69 Anderson, *American Census*; Pearson, *Birth Certificate*; Nock, *Costs of Privacy*; and Parenti, *Soft Cage*.

70 Pfaelzer, *Driven Out*; Parenti, *Soft Cage*, 50–51, 61–76; and Robertson, *Passport in America*.

71 Hyman, *To Try Men's Souls*, vii.

72 McGirr, *War on Alcohol*.

73 Canaday, *Straight State*, 1–90, 56–57.

CHAPTER 1 / EUGENICS AND INTERNAL ENEMY OTHERS

1 For eugenic thinking, see Wilson, *Eugenic Mind Project*; and see Rafter, *Creating Born Criminals*, 144.

2 For national trends, see Largent, *Breeding Contempt*; Stern, *Eugenic Nation*; Kline, *Building a Better Race;* Ordover, *American Eugenics*; and Lira, *Laboratory of Deficiency*. Also see Schoen, *Choice & Coercion*.

3 Largent, "'Greatest Curse of the Race'"; Stern, *Eugenic Nation*, 23; and Ward, "Bethenia Angelina Owens-Adair," 147–194.

4 Owens-Adair, *Human Sterilization*, 55, 95–99; Boag, *Same-Sex Affairs*, 206–216; and Largent, "'Greatest Curse of the Race.'"

5 "Sterilization Bill Is Killed," *Oregonian*, February 20, 1907, 5; "Will Force the Bill," *Yakima Herald*, February 20, 1907, 8; "Bill Is Introduced," *Yakima Herald*, March 6, 1907, 8; and Owens-Adair, *Human Sterilization*, 95.

6 "Chamberlain Sterilizes the Dr. Owens Adair Bill," *Morning Astorian*, February 26, 1909, 1; "Sterilization Bill Killed," *Oregonian*, January 27, 1911, 7; and Owens-Adair, *Human Sterilization*, 55–65.

7 "Sterilization Bill Killed"; Largent, "'Greatest Curse of the Race,'" 195–200; and Owens-Adair, *Human Sterilization*, 65–76.

8 Oregon Secretary of State, *Oregon Voter Pamphlet Special Election 1913 Measures* (Salem: SPO, 1913), 13–14; *Oregon Laws* 279 (1917), 518–521; "Some of Referendum Petitions Will Not Meet Requirements," *Oregon Journal*, May 20, 1917, 13; Boag, *Same-Sex Affairs*, 206–216; and Lola Baldwin quoted in "Mrs. Edmunds Writes of Referendum Laws," *Ashland Tidings*, October 30, 1913, 1, 8. Other states had similar patterns of expansion. Kline, *Building a Better Race*, 50–51; and Ordover, *American Eugenics*, 78–82.

9 *Oregon Laws* 279 (1917), 518–521.

10 "Farrell Sterilization Bill Killed," *Oregonian*, February 20, 1917, 4.

11 *Oregon Laws* 264 (1919), Section 87, 415–416. Harry H. Laughlin, "The Present Status of Eugenical Sterilization in the United States," reprint from *Eugenics in Race and State*, vol. 2, 1923, digital copy in Eugenics in Oregon Collection, State Library of Oregon, accessed November 25, 2023, https://digital.osl.state.or.us/islandora/object/osl%3A99503.

12 Largent, "'Greatest Curse of the Race,'" 200; and Laughlin, *Eugenic Sterilization in the United States*, 271–289, 318–321.

13 "Health Bills Are Prepared," *Oregon Statesman*, December 20, 1922, 7; "Sterilization Bill To Be Reported Favorably," *Oregon Statesman*, January 25, 1923, 9; and *Oregon Laws* 194 (1923), 280–284.

14 "The New Eugenics Law of Oregon," *Eugenical News* 10, no. 3 (March 1924): 25–28.

15 Lombardo, *Three Generations, No Imbeciles*; and Largent, *Breeding Contempt*, 71–73. The eight states were Delaware, Idaho, Iowa, Michigan, North Carolina, Oregon, South Dakota, and Vermont. Popenoe, "Sterilization as a Social Measure."

16 Lombardo, "Child's Right To Be Well Born," 212; Largent, *Breeding Contempt*, 65; Hall, *Medical Certification for Marriage*; US Public Health Service, *Premarital Health Examination Legislation*; Grossberg, "Guarding the Altar"; and Pascoe, *What Comes Naturally*, 138–140.

17 "Governor Hands Down 8 Vetoes," *Oregonian*, February 24, 1909, 1, 7; *Oregon Laws* 187 (1913), 350; and Owens-Adair, *Eugenic Marriage Law*, 5.

18 "Medical Certificate Retained by House," *Oregon Journal*, January 27, 1915, 3; "Medical Certificates Still Necessary," *Oregon Journal*, May 19, 1917, 8; "House Kills Marriage Bill," *Oregonian*, February 20, 1919, 6; and "Wiping Out a Gretna Green," editorial, *Oregonian*, February 19, 1921, 8.

19 "Examine Both Sexes," *Oregon Voter*, February 5, 1921, 39–41.

20 "Sterilization Bill," *Oregon Voter*, March 5, 1921, 24–25, 32; Oregon Secretary of State, *Proposed Constitutional Amendments and Measures at the Special Election June 7, 1921* (Salem: SPO, 1921), 13–15; and Oregon Secretary of State, *Initiative, Referendum, and Recall Ballot Results*, *Oregon Blue Book*.

21 Lombardo, "Child's Right To Be Well Born," 212; "New Marriage Law Proposed," *Albany Evening Herald*, December 20, 1922, 4; and "Bill on Marriage Examination Is Killed in Senate," *Oregon Journal*, February 20, 1923, 2.

22 Oregon voters approved a marriage examination law in 1938. Oregon Secretary of State, *Initiative, Referendum, and Recall Ballot Results*.

23 "Program for State Meeting of Women's Federation," *Ashland Tidings*, October 18, 1915, 4; "Confronting Social Questions Discussed by Federa-

tion Head," *Oregon Statesman*, October 28, 1915, 3; "Address: President, Mrs. Sarah A. Evans" in *Oregon Federation of Women's Clubs Year Book 1915–1916* (Portland: Oregon Federation of Women's Clubs, 1916), 10–17; "Clubwomen Open Session at Seaside," *Oregonian*, October 10, 1916, 6; "Women Approve Bills," *Oregonian*, January 25, 1917, 5; "Women's Activities: The Latest Message to the Clubwomen of Oregon," *Sunday Oregonian*, April 3, 1921, Section 3, 10; and "Clubwomen Back Social Welfare Bills," *Oregon Sunday Journal*, January 21, 1923, Section 4, 5. California women lobbied for the Pacific Colony, the state's institution for the "feebleminded," through their Women's Legislative Council. Lira, *Laboratory of Deficiency*, 49–51.

24 Myers, *Municipal Mother*, 91–107.

25 Millie Trumbull to Bethenia Owens-Adair, October 22, 1922, reprinted in Owens-Adair, *Human Sterilization*, 345–346; Owens-Adair, *Human Sterilization*, 73; Millie Trumbull to Mr. Walter Pierce, n.d. [1917], 2 pp., Box 1, Folder Correspondence June–December 1917, Walter M. Pierce Papers 1888 to 1969, Coll 068, University of Oregon Special Collections and University Archives, Knight Library, Eugene, Oregon. Dilg, "Millie R. Trumbull (1866–1940)."

26 Cornelia Marvin to Bethenia Owens-Adair, February 7, 1922, reprinted in Owens-Adair, *Souvenir*, 57; Gunselman, "'Wheedling, Wangling, and Walloping' for Progress," 376–378; and "Oregon Started Reading When State Library Came," *Salem Capital Journal*, August 1, 1955, 6. Pierce served as Oregon governor from 1923 through 1927.

27 "People Urged to Stand for a White Nation," *Oregon Statesman*, March 19, 1921, 1–2; Mrs. Isaac Lee Patterson, "Patriotism in Peace," quoted in Owens-Adair, *Human Sterilization*, 128–130; and "Ex Governor's Widow Hears Last Summons," *Oregon Journal*, March 21, 1938, 4.

28 Carey, *On the Margins of Citizenship*, 74.

29 Linda Gordon notes the odd use of a Catholic heroine in an anti-Catholic movement, but both Gordon and Wendy Thorson urge us to consider that Oregon Klanswomen viewed Joan of Arc as a symbol of female power. Gordon, *Second Coming of the KKK*, 128; and Thorson, "Oregon Klanswomen of the 1920s," 41–42. Thorson reprints a LOTIE Joan of Arc poster, 46–47. The links to World War I imagery and militarism are my interpretations.

30 Creel, *Complete Report of the Chairman of the Committee on Public Information 1917: 1918: 1919*, 214; "All Praise Due Yank Soldiers in Russia," *Daily Capital Journal*, May 24, 1919, 1, 3; and Dever, *Masks Off!*, frontispiece.

226 / NOTES TO PAGES 28–29

31 For additional perspective on Klanswomen in the 1920s, see Blee, *Women of the Klan;* and MacLean, *Behind the Mask of Chivalry.*

32 Mark Largent noted a likely Klan connection, including similar platforms and Governor Pierce's support. Largent, "Greatest Curse of the Race,'" 202.

33 "Examine Both Sexes," 41; and Bethenia Owens-Adair, "The Crime Wave," letter to editor, *Oregon Journal,* December 28, 1922, 8.

34 Millie Trumbull to Bethenia Owens-Adair, October 25, 1922, reprinted in Owens-Adair, *Human Sterilization,* 345–346; and Owens-Adair, *Eugenic Marriage Law,* 12.

35 Patterson, "Patriotism in Peace"; and "People Urged to Stand for a White Nation."

36 "Doctor Suggests Sterilization of Japanese Women," *Oregon Journal,* January 9, 1921, 6.

37 "Report of the Committee on Resolutions," Annual Session of Southern Oregon District Federation of Women's Clubs Ashland, Oregon, May 3, 1924, 63, bound volume, First District Federation Women's Clubs of Oregon, Minutes 1913–1933, Book I, Box 5, Oregon Federation of Women's Clubs Records, Box 174, Special Collections, Knight Library, University of Oregon.

38 "America Must Clean House," *Western American,* May 24, 1923, 5.

39 "Recent Mental Hygiene Surveys," *Mental Hygiene Bulletin* 1, no. 1 (January 1923): 3; and Trent, *Inventing the Feeble Mind,* 129–193.

40 "Oregon," *American Journal of Public Health* 10, no. 12 (December 1920), 1011–1012; and "First Movement in Mental Hygiene Is Under Way in State," *Oregon Journal,* November 21, 1920, 21.

41 For more on California, see California State Board of Charities and Corrections, *Surveys in Mental Deviation in Prisons, Public Schools, and Orphanages* (Sacramento: California State Printing Office, 1918); and Kline, *Building a Better Race,* 42–44.

42 Carlisle, "Physician as a Factor in a Statewide Cooperative Program"; Senate Joint Resolution 19, *Oregon Laws* (1919), 834; and Senate Joint Resolution 28, *Oregon Laws* (1919), 838.

43 Carlisle, "Summary of the Oregon State Survey," 1–40, 4.

44 "The Oregon Survey of Mental Defect, Delinquency and Dependency," *American Journal of Psychiatry* 1, no. 4 (April 1922): 689–691; and Carlisle, "Physician as a Factor in a Statewide Cooperative Program."

45 Henry Waldo Coe, editorial, "A State Survey," *Medical Sentinel* 28, no. 12 (December 1920): 579.

46 Carlisle, "Summary of the Oregon State Survey," 39 (emphasis in original); and Carlisle, "Physician as a Factor in a Statewide Cooperative Program."

47 Carlisle, ed., *Preliminary Statistical Report of the Oregon State Survey*, 2. See "Survey First in World," *Eugene Morning Register*, January 21, 1921, 8.

48 Carlisle, ed., *Preliminary Statistical Report of the Oregon State Survey*, 67.

49 Laughlin, *Second International Exhibition of Eugenics*, 29.

50 For example, see "65,423 in Oregon Are Incompetent," *Oregonian*, July 10, 1922, 9.

51 Owens-Adair, *Human Sterilization*, 109–113; and Owens-Adair, *Eugenic Marriage Law*, 3–4, 5 (emphasis in original).

52 Millie R. Trumbull, "The Mentally Defective Child in Industry," in Carlisle, ed., *Preliminary Statistical Report of the Oregon State Survey*, 11–14, 14.

53 For general histories of these processes, see Starr, *Social Transformation of American Medicine*; and Leavitt, *Brought to Bed*.

54 Stern, *Eugenic Nation*; Schoen, *Choice & Coercion*; Theobald, *Reproduction on the Reservation*; Lawrence, "Indian Health Service and the Sterilization of Native American Women," 400–419; Ralstin-Lewis, "Continuing Struggle against Genocide," 71–95; and Ladd-Taylor, *Fixing the Poor*.

55 Anderson appears as a midwife in the 1918 database of birth certificates; see "Local Briefs: Mrs. Addie Anderson," *The Advocate*, February 12, 1927, 4. Thompson was the "recognized midwife" among Siletz people; in Allottee 456, Industrial Survey Siletz 1925, Box 1, GRS 70: Agency and Tribal Council Records, 1876–1951 (previous boxes 162–168), Records of the Grand Ronde Siletz Indian Agency, RG 75, BIA, NARA Seattle.

56 Hancock, "Health and Well-being," 166–197; and Theobald, *Reproduction on the Reservation*, 44–70, 62.

57 Theobald, *Reproduction on the Reservation*, 95.

58 Yellowtail became an antisterilization activist. See Theobald, *Reproduction on the Reservation*, passim and 86, 89.

59 "Medical Department, US Indian Service," *Polk's Medical Register and Directory of the United States and Canada* (New York: R. L. Polk, 1917), 75–77.

60 Virgil M. Pinkley, "Physician's Semiannual Report, Siletz Agency, Siletz, Oregon, for the Six Months Ending December 31, 1916"; and Virgil M. Pinkley, "Physician's Semiannual Report, Siletz Agency, Siletz, Oregon, for the Six Months Ending June 30, 1917," Folder 1916–1917, Physician's Semiannual Report, Box 1, GRS 49, Records of the Grand Ronde Siletz Indian Agency, RG 75, BIA, NARA Seattle; and "Dr. Virgil Pinkley Called by Death," *Los Angeles Mirror*, February 13, 1957, 4.

61 Britten, *American Indians in World War I*, 153.

62 US Department of the Interior, *Forty-Ninth Annual Report Board of Indian Commissioners*, 87.

63 A. A. Soule to Fred A. Baker, March 29, 1924, and Fred A. Baker to Dr. A. A. Soule, April 9, 1924, File 109, Physicians & Reports 1917–1924, Box 27, Series KL 009: Numerical Correspondence, Records of the Klamath Indian Agency, RG 75, BIA, NARA Seattle; and "Indian Hospital to Rise," *Klamath Falls Evening Herald*, April 18, 1925, 1. For more on Soule and also the hospital, see Hancock, "Health and Well-being," 171–173.

64 Cahill, *Federal Fathers & Mothers*, 244–246.

65 Circular No. 1774, 1922 Industrial Survey, Charles E. Burke to Superintendents, March 23, 1922, Folder Industrial Program (Siletz), 1922, Box 10, GRS Series 2: Decimal Files, 1897–1955, Records of the Grand Ronde Siletz Indian Agency, RG 75, BIA, NARA Seattle.

66 Industrial Program, (Siletz), 1922; Folder Industrial Survey 1925 Grand Ronde Reservation, Box 10, GRS Series 2, Decimal Files, 1897–1955, Records of the Grand Ronde Siletz Indian Agency; Box 1, UM 63 Industrial Survey Reports, 1925, Records of the Umatilla Indian Agency; Box 1 and 2, KL 119 Home Industrial Survey Reports, 1927, Records of the Klamath Indian Agency, RG 75, BIA, NARA Seattle. Grand Ronde quote, Allottee 127, Grand Ronde Industrial Survey.

CHAPTER 2 / PATRIOTIC WOMANHOOD AND INTERNAL ENEMIES

1 Steinson, *American Women's Activism in World War I*; Kennedy, *Disloyal Mothers and Scurrilous Citizens*; Capozzola, *Uncle Sam Wants You*, 98–103; and Dumenil, *Second Line of Defense*, 58–104. Some material in this chapter is part of Jensen, "'Women's Positive Patriotic Duty to Participate.'" Thank you to OHQ editor Eliza Canty-Jones and managing editor Erin Brasell for their helpful suggestions and support.

2 See Finnegan, *Selling Suffrage*.

3 Blair, *Woman's Committee*; Brownell, "Women's Committees of the First World War"; Breen, *Uncle Sam at Home*; and Dumenil, *Second Line of Defense*, 60–69.

4 Kennedy, *Over Here*, 144–190; Keene, *Doughboys, the Great War, and the Remaking of America*; Keith, *Rich Man's War, Poor Man's Fight*; and Capozzola, *Uncle Sam Wants You*.

5 Brownell, "Women's Committees of the First World War," 69.

6 Jensen, *Mobilizing Minerva*, 77–97.

7 Brownell, "Women's Committees of the First World War," 71; Breen,

Uncle Sam at Home, 123–124. "Women's Clubs—Mrs. Charles H. Castner," *Oregonian*, September 12, 1917, 12; and "Women Asked to Register for War Help," *Rogue River Courier*, September 2, 1917, 1.

8 Examples are "Saturday Day Set for Registration of Women of Country," *Salem Capital Journal*, September 10, 1917, 5; and "Women Register Saturday," *East Oregonian*, September 12, 1917, 8.

9 "Women Meet to Plan for Saving," *Oregonian*, August 23, 1917, 18; "Defense Women Meet," *Sunday Oregonian*, September 2, 1917, Section 1, 12; and "Patriotic Women to Register Today," *Oregonian*, September 15, 1917, 6. The official census population for Portland was 207,214 in 1910 and 258, 288 in 1920 (https://www.portlandoregon.gov/archives/article/284517). Castner to James A. B. Scherer, September 15, 1917, Woman's Committee of Council of National Defense, Oregon Committee, in Dr. James A. B. Scherer, "Confidential Report on Oregon," Box 783 14-D1 Confidential Reports on State Council of Defense, RG 62, Council of National Defense, Committee on Women's Defense Work, NARA; and Woman's Committee of the Council of National Defense, *Organization Charts, May 1917–1918* (Washington, DC: GPO, 1918), 11.

10 "Women Respond in Numbers Offering Services to Country," *Oregon Journal*, September 16, 1917, 9.

11 "Portland Women Willing to Work," *Sunday Oregonian*, September 16, 1917, Section 1, 10. For more on Cannady, see Mangun, *Force for Change*.

12 "10,000 Women Are Registering Today," *Portland Evening Telegram*, September 15, 1917, 1. The *Portland City Directory* estimated a total city population of 286,753 for the year 1917. *PCD* (1917), 12.

13 "Patriotic Women To Register Today," *Oregonian*, September 15, 1917, 6.

14 "Women Will Register at the Public Library," *Springfield News*, September 13, 1917, 1; "War Registry for Women On," *Bend Daily Bulletin*, September 15, 1917, 1; and "Better Register Now Save Trouble Later," *Corvallis Gazette-Times*, September 20, 1917, 1.

15 "Ten Million Men to Register Today," *Oregonian*, June 4, 1917, 4; "Registering of Oregon Women to Take Place on Saturday," *Oregon Journal*, September 14, 1917, 2; and "10,000 Women Are Registering Today."

16 "Cards Show Detail of Women's Work," *Sunday Oregonian*, September 9, 1917, Section 1, 19; and "Registration Card, Woman's Committee Council of National Defense," *Oregonian*, September 15, 1917, 6.

17 "Returns Show Only 15 Per Ct. of Women Registered Saturday," *Oregon Journal*, September 18, 1917, 2.

18 "Response Small on Registration Day," *Bend Daily Bulletin*, September 17, 1917, 1.

19 "Registration Was Light," *East Oregonian*, September 17, 1917, 8; and Department of Commerce and Labor, Bureau of the Census, *Thirteenth Census of the United States Taken in the Year 1910 with Supplement for Oregon*, 600.

20 "Registration Not What Was Expected," *Salem Capital Journal*, September 17, 1917, 5.

21 "Only Fourteen Signed," *Coos Bay Times*, September 18, 1917, 8; and "Registration Cut by Rumor," *Oregonian*, September 20, 1917, 12.

22 "Society: Of Special Interest This Week," *Eugene Guard*, September 22, 1917, 6; and "Women Generally Are Anxious to Sign Cards," *Eugene Morning Register*, September 21, 1917, 3.

23 "Woman's Committee of the Council of National Defense," *Ashland Tidings*, October 1, 1917, 4.

24 Levi Pennington, Case 8000–82671, Old German Files 1909–1921, Investigative Reports of the Federal Bureau of Investigation, 1908–1922, M1085, NARA. An informant reported him to the Department of Justice for investigation.

25 Levi Pennington, "Miscellany," 1, Box 6, Folder 10, "Writings by Pennington (1 of 4)," Levi Pennington Papers, George Fox University Archives, Newberg, Oregon.

26 "The Insidious Nature of Pro-German Activities," *Sunday Oregonian*, November 25, 1917, Section 3, 8.

27 Just 5,482 of 198,114 of Oregon women over sixteen years of age in the state registered; nationwide there were 1,173,000 registrants, with just eighteen state Woman's Committees reporting registration figures by May 1918. Woman's Committee of the Council of National Defense, *Organization Charts, May 1917–1918*, 11.

28 Blair, *Woman's Committee*, 68; Brownell, "Women's Committees of the First World War," 72; and "Table 5: Population Age 21 Years and Over" in Department of Commerce, Bureau of the Census, *Thirteenth Census of the United States Taken in the Year 1910*, vol. 3, Population, 18.

29 Blair, *Woman's Committee*, 57; US Council of National Defense, Section on Cooperation with States, Bulletin 56, September 8, 1917, Folder: Pledge Card Campaign Washington, Box 47, 138A-A1 General Correspondence July–December 1917 M-P, State Food Administrator for Oregon, General Correspondence 1917–1919, RG 4 Records of the United States Food Administration (USFA), NARA Seattle; USFA, *Organizer's Manual*, 7.

30 Congress debated and passed the Lever Food and Fuel Control Bill, and President Wilson signed it into law on August 10, 1917. Hoover led the

Belgian relief effort before taking the leadership of the new USFA and directed the program throughout the war. Mullendore, *History of the United States Food Administration 1917–1919*; Veit, *Modern Food, Moral Food*, 58–76; and Eighmey, *Food Will Win the War*, 16–26.

31 Mullendore, *History of the Food Administration 1917–1919*, 55–56. Castner was the chair of the Oregon Women's Committee of the CND and president of the Oregon Federation of Women's Clubs. Kemp was active in the state Woman's Christian Temperance Union. "W.B. Ayer Named State Food Agent," *Oregonian*, August 17, 1917, 7; and "Pledge Card Campaign Executive Committee," Folder: "Directories," Box 45 138A-A1 General Correspondence July–December 1917 D–H, RG 4, USFA Records.

32 USFA, *Organizer's Manual*, 5–7, 13–16.

33 "Uncle Sam Has 'A Bone to Pick' with Every Housewife This Week," *Oregonian*, October 29, 1917, 1.

34 "Women Start Terrific Drive to Save Food All over State," *Portland Evening Telegram*, October 29, 1917, 1, 2. The district captains were real estate developers, contractors, managers, lawyers, professors, religious leaders, former legislators, Portland city auditor George R. Funk, Multnomah County sheriff Thomas M. Hurlburt, Multnomah County superintendent of schools William C. Alderson, and Multnomah County commissioner A. A. Muck. "Directions to Volunteers: Hoover Food Conservation Drive," *Oregonian*, October 23, 1917, 8, correlated with *PCD* (1918).

35 "Pledge Drive Is Tremendous State Success," *Portland Evening Telegram*, October 30, 1917, 1, 2.

36 "Wanted—Women Volunteers," *Oregonian*, October 23, 1917, 1; and "Directions to Volunteers Hoover Food Conservation Drive," *Oregonian*, October 23, 1917, 8.

37 "Schools Are Enlisted," *Oregonian*, October 12, 1917, 15; and "Home Pledges in Portland Run Over," *Oregonian*, November 16, 1917, 8.

38 "County Chairmen," Folder: Directories, Box 45 138A-A1 General Correspondence July–December 1917, D–H, RG 4, USFA Records; and "Will Use Schools in Food Campaign," *East Oregonian*, October 18, 1917, 1.

39 "Final School Drive Outlined by Supt.," *Ashland Tidings*, October 22, 1917, 7.

40 Telegram Ayer to USFA, Matscheck, Washington DC, November 3, 1917, and Telegram, Ayer to Matscheck, USFA, Washington, DC, November 3, 1917, Folder: Pledge Card Campaign Washington, Box 47 138A-A1 General Correspondence July–December 1917, M–P, RG 4, USFA Records.

41 "Women Near Unit in Signing Pledge," *Portland Evening Telegram*, Oc-

tober 31, 1917, 2; and "Food Pledges Are in Popular Favor," *Oregonian*, October 31, 1917, 13. For O'Hara, see Dilg, "'For Working Women in Oregon.'"

42   "Liberty Loan and Food Campaigns in Oregon Are United," *Eugene Guard*, October 13, 1917, 1, 9.

43   "Pastors to Aid Food Pledge Week," *Oregon Journal*, October 27, 1917, 14.

44   "Cooperative Workers Designated to Represent Various Organizations in Food Conservation Work for Your State," [n.d.] Folder: Miscellaneous, Box 47 138A-A1 General Correspondence July–December 1917 M–P, RG 4, USFA Records; "Negro Women Help Conserve Food," *Sunday Oregonian*, November 18 1917, Section 3,10; Regular Meeting of the Portland Branch of the National Council of Jewish Women, October 3, 1917, 73; Regular board meeting October 31, 1917, 76–77, both in Item 4: Book of Minutes, 1915–1920, Bound Volume, Series 10: National Council of Jewish Women Minutes, Rosters, Ledgers, 1896–1985, Oregon Jewish Museum and Center for Holocaust Education, Portland, Oregon.

45   "Hosts of Labor Join Food Drive,"12. For campaigns outside of Oregon, see Veit, *Modern Food, Moral Food*; and Eighmey, *Food Will Win the War*.

46   "Put Cards in Windows—Save Trouble," *Corvallis Gazette-Times*, October 30, 1917, 1.

47   "Eugene Housewives To Be Canvassed Today," *Eugene Morning Register*, October 30, 1917, 8.

48   "Progress of Pledge Campaign Continues," *Baker Herald*, November 1, 1917, 1, 8.

49   "Put Cards in Windows—Save Trouble."

50   An example is "Victory Is Now in Sight for Marion County," *Oregon Statesman*, November 2, 1917, 8.

51   Liljeqvist as quoted in "Pledge Drive Is Tremendous State Success," *Portland Evening Telegram*, October 30, 1917, 1, 2.

52   Espionage Act of 1917 (chapter 30, tit. I § 3, 40 Stat. 217, 219).

53   Helquist, "Resistance, Dissent, and Punishment in WWI Oregon," 256–259; and Helquist, WWI Sedition in Oregon Project.

54   The Portland and Multnomah County "Record of Home Managers Not Seen or Declining to Sign" sheets are listed by precinct number in two folders. "Report of Family Pledge Card Campaign, Multnomah County, Oregon and Record of Home Managers Not Seen or Declining to Sign," Folders 4740-855-1 and 4740-855-2, Box 11, RG 118, Records of US Attorneys Western Judicial District of Oregon, Portland, Oregon, Civil and Criminal Significant Case Files, 1899–1925, NARA Seattle. There were 1,905 names listed, 4 percent of Portland's 43,740 pledges. Canvassers did

not note the gender for 879 of the 1,905 respondents, but the comments section suggests that the large majority of them were women. Hereafter I refer to specific cases by precinct number of the sheet and folder number.

55 Precinct 250, Folder 4740-855-2.

56 Written comments about the 102 refusers labeled directly as men suggests that canvassers used the name of the male head of household on their lists but were still often speaking to women at the doors. "Record of Food Pledge Decliners" and "Hoover Pledges in Portland Run Over," *Oregonian*, November 16, 1917, 8.

57 District 1, Subdistrict C, Precinct 13, Folder 4740-855-1; and *PCD* 1921, 1052.

58 Kite and her husband had been arrested in Portland in July 1913, along with Marie Equi and Jean Bennett, during free speech protests stemming from a cannery strike. Precinct 319, Folder 4740-855-2; and *PCD* 1917, 649; Arthur Quantock Kite World War I Draft Registration Card, Oregon, Multnomah, Roll 1852140, Draft Board 3; 1910 Census, Precinct 36, Sheet 8A; "Officers, Defied, Charge Agitators," *Oregonian*, July 18, 1913, 1, 5; and "Court Warning Out," *Oregonian* July 19, 1913, 8. For an overview of the strike and arrests, see Helquist, *Marie Equi*, 116–121.

59 Precinct 85E, Folder 4740-855-1; and *PCD* 1918, 978.

60 Precinct 257 1/2, Folder 4740-855-2; and *PCD* 1918, 1091.

61 Precinct 282, Folder 4740-855-2; and *PCD* 1918, 272.

62 District 1, Subdistrict C, Precinct 32, Folder 4740-855-1. For more on the Weinhard family, see Edmunson-Morton, "Maybe You've Heard of Her Husband?," 128–157.

63 Precinct 148, Folder 4740-855-1.

64 District 1, Subdistrict C, Precinct 12, Folder 4740-855-1.

65 Precinct 10 Record and Precinct 11, Folder 4740-855-1.

66 Precinct 149½, Folder 4740-855-1.

67 Precinct 101H, Folder 4740-855-1.

68 District 1, Subdistrict C, Precinct 15, Folder 4740-855-1. "Anthony Neppach," in Carey, *History of Oregon*, vol. 2, 142–143.

69 Precinct 256, Folder 4740-855-2; Mrs. Bergren, "Pledge Cards for Federal Food Administration," RG 118, Records of US Attorneys Western Judicial District of Oregon, Portland, Oregon Civil and Criminal Significant Case Files, 1899–1925, NARA Seattle; and *PCD* 1918, 171, 1243.

70 "Food Slackers Will Have Another Week in Which to Comply," *Oregon Journal*, November 5, 1917, 12; and "Pledge Campaign Now Centers on Spinsters," *Baker Herald*, November 9, 1917, 1.

71 "Food Slackers Will Have Another Week"; and "Mary Pickford's Daily

Talk-The Hallroom Girl's Life Is Lonely," *Long Beach Press*, December 5, 1917, 12.

72 "Police Raid More Disorderly Houses," *Oregon Journal*, November 6, 1917, 6; and "Women, Re-Arrested, Are Again Released," *Oregon Journal*, November 7, 1917, 3.

73 "Are Local Families Slacking?" *East Oregonian*, November 15, 1917, 3.

74 "98 Percent Join the Big Food Drive," *La Grande Evening Observer*, November 6, 1917, 1.

75 "A Spotted Report," *Oregon City Courier*, November 15, 1917, 4.

76 W. S. U'Ren, "Would Deport Kaiserists," letter to editor, *Oregon Journal*, November 10, 1917, 8. For U'Ren's progressive career, see Johnston, *Radical Middle Class*, 127–137.

77 Funk was captain for Precincts 184–197 and 200, Folder 4740-855-2.

78 Precinct 190, Precinct 193, Folder 4740-855-2.

79 "Vigilantes Are Formed," *Oregonian*, January 26, 1918, 7; "Vigilantes Plan Crusade," *Oregonian*, February 7, 1918, 13; and "Citizens Invited to Join Vigilantes," *Oregon Journal*, March 3, 1918, 12.

80 "Dance Will Mark War on Sedition," *Portland Evening Telegram*, April 16, 1918, 2; "Vigilantes to Hold Dance," *Oregonian*, April 16, 1918, 11; "Vigilantes to Give Ball," *Oregonian*, April 17, 1918, 6; and War Veterans at Dance," *Oregonian*, April 18, 1918, 5.

81 "Vigilantes Smear Paint over Sign," *Oregon Journal*, April 18, 1918, 1; "Publisher Heeds Warning Statement," *Oregon Journal*, April 19, 1918, 1; "Teutonic Signs Removed," *Oregonian*, April 20, 1918, 14; and "Vigilantes as an Organization Firm in Upholding Laws," *Oregon Journal*, April 21, 1918, 14.

82 Chafee Jr., "Freedom of Speech in War Time," 935–936. Sedition Act of 1918, *United States Statutes at Large*, vol. 40, *April 1917–March 1919* (Washington, DC: GPO, 1919), 553–554. For more on the Espionage and Sedition Acts and the reach of the campaigns against dissent, see Work, *Darkest before Dawn;* Thomas, *Unsafe for Democracy*; Capozzola, *Uncle Sam Wants You*, 144–172; and Helquist, "Resistance, Dissent, and Punishment in WWI Oregon" and WWI Sedition in Oregon Project.

83 Kennedy, *Over Here*, 193–106, 106, 105; St. Clair, *Story of the Liberty Loans*; US Department of the Treasury, *United States Government War-Savings Stamps*; and "Uncle Sam to Hold Bargain Sale of Money," *Oregon Journal*, November 14, 1917, 3.

84 The First Liberty Loan was by Federal Reserve district. Specific state figures for the other four are available. Oregon's totals were: Second Liberty Loan, October 1917, $25 million; Third, April 1918, $28.3 million;

NOTES TO PAGES 54–57 / 235

Fourth, September–October 1918, \$38.3 million; and the Fifth "Victory" loan drive, April 1919, \$28.4 million. St. Clair, *Story of the Liberty Loans*. Oregon figures are on 52, 62, 79, 94. See 103–104 for the Woman's Committee.

85   Report of State Chairman [Sarah A. Evans], "Oregon," in US Department of the Treasury, *Report of National Woman's Liberty Loan Committee for the Victory Loan Campaign*, 70–71; US Department of the Treasury, *Report of National Woman's Liberty Loan Committee for the Third Liberty Loan Campaign*, 3, 9; "Women's Patriotic Service: Portland Will Be Represented," *Sunday Oregonian*, July 14, 1918, Section 3, 12; James K. Lynch to Edward Cookingham, March 15, 1918, Scrapbook 1, p. 6, Edward Cookingham Papers, 1900–1948, MSS 2658, OHS. For more on the origins of and women's activism in the club movement, see Blair, *Clubwoman as Feminist*; and Haarsager, *Organized Womanhood*.

86   Thomas W. Ross, "About a Few Community Chest Solicitors," *Medico* 1, no. 12 (April 1921): 2–3.

87   "Reproduction of Third Liberty Loan Questionnaire," *Oregonian*, March 8, 1918, 6; "Women Volunteers Wanted to Work on Questionaires [sic]," *Oregon Statesman*, March 26, 1918, 6; and "Liberty Loan Organization Is Complete," *Grants Pass Daily Courier*, March 31, 1918, 1, 5.

88   R. E. Lee Steiner, "United States Third Liberty Loan Campaign, Instructions for Workers," Folder 1, Box 9, World War I Publications and Ephemera, Oregon State Defense Council Records, 87A-42 2/20/2/7, Oregon State Archives, Salem, Oregon. "How Returns Are Noted," *Bend Bulletin*, April 6, 1918, 3.

89   "Partial List of Liberty Bond Subscribers," *Hood River Glacier*, April 25, 1918, 8; "Liberty Bond Subscriptions," *Seaside Signal*, October 18, 1917, 6; and "Banks Asked to Send Mail Tribune Lists of Patriots," *Medford Mail Tribune*, October 27, 1917, 1.

90   "Eugene Patriots Wax Enthusiastic," *Sunday Oregonian*, April 21, 1918, Section 3, 10.

91   "Liberty Temple Built in One Day," *Oregonian*, March 11, 1918, 1; and "Women's Patriotic Service: This Will Be the Week," *Sunday Oregonian*, April 7, 1918, Section 3, 12.

92   "Tillamook Celebrates with Parade," *Oregon Journal*, April 21, 1918, 12; and "Liberty Temple Finished," *Bend Bulletin*, November 1, 1918, 1.

93   Telegram from William Gibbs McAdoo to Edward Cookingham, April 13, 1918, Edward Cookingham Papers, 1900–1948, MSS 2658, OHS; "Jubilant City to Celebrate Bond Victory," *Portland Evening Telegram*, April 11, 1918, 1, 2; "Oregon Is First to Boost Loan Over," *Oregonian*, April 13, 1918,

14; and "Oregon's Patriotic Record," *Oregon Statesman*, April 24, 1918, 4.

94   "Bond for Every 3D Person, Plan," *Oregon Journal*, August 28, 1918, 1; "Big Parade to End in Rally at Local Park," *Oregon Statesman*, September 15, 1918, 1, 2; "Slackers and Shirkers of the Fourth Loan To Be Hunted Down in the City Campaign," *Oregon Journal*, September 22, 1918, 2; and "Multnomah Guard Companies Called for Special Liberty Loan Service," *Oregonian*, September 23, 1918, 1.

95   Britten, *American Indians in World War I*, 132–136.

96   See the many letters and estimates for the negotiations about assessments and Report of Liberty Loan Taken by Indians and Employees [May 1918], J. M. Johnson to Charles J. Ferguson, May 6, 1918; Report of Liberty Loan Taken by Indians and Employees [May 1918]; File 10, Folder 1: Liberty Bonds and Loans and War Matters, 1918, Box 4, Series KL 009: Numerical Correspondence, Records of the Klamath Indian Agency, RG 75, BIA, NARA Seattle.

97   "Dallas Women Buy Liberty Bond," *Sunday Oregonian*, June 10, 1917, Section 1, 8; "Women Sell $12,650 Liberty Loan Bonds," *St. Helens Mist*, April 12, 1918, 1; Minutes of the Oregon Central Woman's Christian Temperance Union (WCTU), April 10, 1918, 47, and September 25 1918, 75, Folder 1 Central Union Minute Book 1917–1922, Box 7, MSS 2535, WCTU of Oregon Records, 1881–1990, OHS. Minutes of the Regular Meeting of the Portland Woman's Club September 27, 1918, 78, and April 25, 1919, 113, Bound Volume "Club, 1917–1923," Folder 10, Box 1, Portland Woman's Club (Or.) Records, 1895–1995, MSS 1084, OHS. Minutes of the Portland American Association of University Women Portland (AAUW) Board, March 2, 1918 [volume not paginated] Folder 6, AAUW Portland Board Minutes 1915–1923, Box 1, MSS 2964, AAUW Branch Records, 1881–1992, OHS. Minutes of Derthick Club, April 5, 1918, 70, Book 2, October 1912–November 1915, Derthick Club Records, Accession 28505, OHS.

98   "Employes [sic] of the Hotel Multnomah," *Sunday Oregonian*, October 28, 1917, Section 2, 7; "Woolen Mills Employes [sic] Buy Bonds," *Oregonian*, September 18, 1918, 4; and "Grade Teachers' Association Shows Steady Growth," *Sunday Oregonian*, December 30, 1917, Section 3, 8.

99   Report of State Chairman [Sarah A. Evans], "Oregon," 70.

100   "Response of Loyal Women Entitles State to Tribute," *Sunday Oregonian*, December 30, 1917, Section 3, 8; and "Woman Suffragists Have Good Loan Record," *Sunday Oregonian*, October 27, 1918, Section 3, 7.

101   "Women To Do Part," *Oregonian*, April 3, 1918, 13; "Women's Patriotic Service: To Be Ready To Work for the Fourth Liberty Loan," *Sunday*

Oregonian, April 28, 1918, Section 3, 10; "Women's Patriotic Service: In Anticipation of the Day," *Sunday Oregonian*, September 29, 1918, Section 3, 11; and Report of State Chairman [Sarah A. Evans], "Oregon," 70–71.

102 "Women's Patriotic Service: This Will Be the Week," *Sunday Oregonian*, April 7, 1918, Section 3, 12.

103 "To Be Ready To Work for the Fourth Liberty Loan" and "Women To Do Part."

104 "Women To Do Part"; "Foreigners Help Out in Big Loan Drive," *Sunday Oregonian*, September 29, 1918, Section 3, 11; and "Society: Woman's Committee for Work among Foreign Speaking People," *Oregonian*, September 21, 1918, 10.

105 "Women's Patriotic Service: To Be Ready To Work."

106 Dumenil, *Second Line of Defense*, 84–94.

107 "Colored Women's Patriotic Drive Association," *Sunday Oregonian*, April 7, 1918, Section 3, 12.

108 "Loyal Thousands Aid Red Cross," *Sunday Oregonian*, August 4, 1918, Section 1, 12; "Colored Boys Are Cheered by Throng," *Oregonian*, August 3, 1918, 18; and Vella Winner, "Colored Women Served Own Draftees," *Oregon Journal*, August 3, 1918, 3.

109 Weisensee, "Portland Rose Festival"; and "Local Labor Hosts March in Pageant," *Oregonian*, September 3, 1918, 1, 6.

110 "Goggles, Girl Debaters New Factor at Franklin," *Sunday Oregonian*, April 23, 1916, Section 5, 10; and *PCD* 1920, 294.

111 "Panorama of Nations Is Cheered by Crowds," *Oregon Journal*, July 4, 1918, 11; and "All Nations March in Vast Portland Pageant," *Oregon Journal*, July 4, 1918, 1. The 1920 census counted 53 Armenians in Oregon and 235 in Washington State. Craver, "On the Boundary of White," 47.

112 "Allied Women to Parade State Fair," *Oregonian*, September 23, 1918, 8; "Women Assist in Presenting Picture Play," *Oregon Sunday Journal*, November 17, 1918, Section 2, 8; and "Women's Patriotic Service: "Crashing Through to Berlin," *Oregonian*, October 13, 1918, 8.

113 "Luncheon to Open Big Relief Drive," *Oregonian*, February 3, 1918, 18; and "Portland Residents Recall Turk Crimes," *Oregonian*, March 6, 1919, 12. For an overview, see Balakian, *Burning Tigris*.

114 Trouillot, *Silencing the Past*, 121.

115 "Armenian Fight Begun in Court," *Oregonian*, May 9, 1924, 1, 2, 2; and Craver, "On the Boundary of White," 46. *U.S. v. Tatos Osgihan Cartozian*, US District Court, District of Oregon, Portland, May 8–9, 1924. For a thoughtful interpretation of the representation of citizenship in images, see Gürsel, "Classifying the Cartozians," 349–380.

116   Judy Yung identifies this same nurturing in the actions of Chinese American YWCA women in San Francisco during this period. See Yung, *Unbound Feet*, 96.

117   Wong, *Sweet Cakes, Long Journey*, 175–181; *PCD* 1923, 1151; and "Minister Pleads for Toil," *Oregonian*, June 12, 1920, 10.

118   "Chinese Entertainment Is Excellent and Profitable," *Oregonian*, March 19, 1921, 7; and "Chinese Tots Who Are Selling Life Saving Stamps for Relief Fund," *Sunday Oregonian*, March 13, 1921, Section 4, 6.

119   YWCA Board Meeting Minutes October 24, 1919, 62; October 27, 1919, 68; November 12, 1919, 72; Box 9A, Bound Volume Board Minutes October 22, 1918–January 22, 1924, and Pearl Moy Membership Record, 66, Box 4, Folder 5, Bound Volume, Memberships 1920–1921, Young Women's Christian Association (YWCA) of Portland Records, Special Collections & Archives, Lewis and Clark College; and "Women's Activities: Y.W.C.A. Will Hold Special Americanization Services," *Oregonian*, February 17, 1922, 12.

120   "Chinese Student Life Is Found Full of Interest and Delight," *Sunday Oregonian*, April 23, 1922, Section 5, 1.

CHAPTER 3 / TROUBLE AT WORK

1   I am indebted to the historians who have previously explored M. Louise Hunt's Portland case. Bartholomae, "Conscientious Objector"; Kingsbury, "'To Shine in Use'"; Wiegand, "Oregon's Public Libraries during the First World War"; and Hummel, *"Making the Library Be Alive."* For a more detailed discussion of my interpretation of Hunt and her case, see Jensen, "'Immoral' and 'Disloyal' Woman.'" With thanks to the *Peace & Change* editors and reviewers.

2   "Mr. Woodward Is Lauded for Stand," *Oregonian*, April 17, 1918, 9; and "Library Workers Give Their Oath to Support Flag," *Oregon Journal*, April 17, 1918, 3, 2.

3   "Librarian with Big Pay Will Not Purchase Bonds," *Portland Evening Telegram*, April 12, 1918, 1, 2.

4   "Librarian with Big Pay Will Not Purchase Bonds."

5   Minutes Board of Directors of the Library Association of Portland, April 12 and 15, 1918, Bound Volume, Library Association Minutes, November 1913–September 1927, 127–129, 131–132; Administrative Board Room Collection, Multnomah County Public Library Isom Building, Portland, Oregon; "Librarian with Big Pay Will Not Purchase Bonds"; "Citizens Rise in Protest on Board's Action," *Portland Evening Telegram*, April 13,

1918, 1, 2; "Regarding Miss Hunt," *Portland News*, April 13, 1918, 1; and "Library Board Allows Pacifist to Resign Post," *Portland Evening Telegram*, April 15, 1918, 1, 2.

6   Montague reported the death threats in his written statement in "Mr. Woodward Is Lauded for Stand."

7   Mumford, "Patriotism and Its Consequences," 406–407. Joan Jensen quotes Mumford in *Price of Vigilance*, 78.

8   "Librarian with Big Pay," 2; and "Miss Louise Hunt Is Cleared by Board," *Oregonian*, April 13, 1918, 8.

9   Jensen, "'Women's Positive Patriotic Duty to Participate'"; and "The Portland Incident," *Eugene Guard*, April 17, 1918, 4.

10   "Just a Girl," *Oregon Journal*, April 13, 1918, 6.

11   For women informants and spies portrayed in "intimate traffic with the enemy," see Proctor, *Female Intelligence*.

12   "Library Board Will Take Up Hunt Case Again," *Oregon Journal*, April 14, 1918, 4; "Women's Federation Meeting Is the Most Important Yet Held," *Oregon Journal*, April 14, 1918, 22; "Discharge of Miss Hunt Is Demanded," *Oregonian*, April 14, 1918, 1, 12; "Citizens Rise in Protest," 2; and "Miss Mary Isom Also Charged with Disloyalty," *Portland Evening Telegram*, April 15, 1918, 1." Bartholomae quotes from "Library Board Will Take Up Hunt Case Again," and Wiegand quotes from Bartholomae on the women's club vote. Bartholomae, "Conscientious Objector," 232; and Wiegand, "Oregon's Public Libraries during the First World War," 54.

13   "Citizens Rise in Protest," 2; and "Discharge of Miss Hunt Is Demanded," 1, 12.

14   Spencer as quoted in "Citizens Rise in Protest," 1, 2.

15   "Library Assistant Named," *Oregonian*, October 23, 1910, 8; Bartholomae, "Conscientious Objector." Hummel, *"Making the Library Be Alive"*; and Kingsbury, "'To Shine in Use.'"

16   Jim Carmin, "Central Library (Multnomah County Library)."

17   See Assistant Librarian Reports, January 1912–October 1922, Administration 027L697ral, 1912–1922, Administrative Board Room Collection, Multnomah County Public Library, Isom Building, Portland, Oregon.

18   Assistant Librarian Report, May 1912, 1.

19   See Jensen, "'Immoral' and 'Disloyal' Woman," for more on Hunt's community and peace activities prior to her refusal to purchase a bond. The phrase "prewar heyday" is from Dawley, *Changing the World*, 3.

20   Kessler-Harris, *In Pursuit of Equity*.

21   Nelly Fox to Cornelia Marvin, April 22, 1918, Folder 55 Portland 1918,

Box 54, Local Library Correspondence, P; Oregon State Library Records, 89A-35 4/13/10/6, OSA.

22 Louise Hunt to Bernard Van Horn, March 5, 1959, Library Association of Portland; and Hummel, *"Making the Library Be Alive,"* 16–19.

23 "In the Matter of Oaths of Allegiance for Employees of Multnomah County," April 15, 1918, 312, Multnomah County Board of County Commissioners Minutes, Bound Volume 9, December 5, 1917–May 13, 1918, Multnomah County Archives; "County Employe [sic] Must Take Oath," *Portland News*, April 15, 1918, 2; and "County to Hunt Slackers," *Oregonian*, April 17, 1918, 11.

24 "Library Staff to Show Allegiance," *Oregon Journal*, April 16, 1918, 1.

25 "In the Matter of Oaths of Allegiance for Employees of Multnomah County."

26 "Miss Hunt Is Not a Good Citizen," *Portland News*, April 16, 1918, 1; and "Miss Hunt, Portland's Pacifist Assistant Librarian," *Corvallis Gazette Times*, April 16, 1918, 2.

27 Withycombe as quoted in "Dismiss Her Says Governor," *Oregonian*, April 15, 1918, 1.

28 Ross, *World War I and the American Constitution*, 288.

29 "A Lady by the Name of Louise Hunt," *Hillsboro Argus*, April 18, 1918, 2.

30 Mrs. W. C. Kantner, letter to editor, "Offer Is Made To Start Fund," *Oregonian*, April 15, 1918, 6.

31 See Jensen, "'Immoral' and 'Disloyal' Woman."

32 "Woman Arrested on Charge of Sedition," *Oregon Journal*, June 29, 1918, 2; and "Federal Grand Jury Returns Indictments Covering 19 Offenses," *Oregon Journal*, June 30, 1918, 14.

33 Lena is a pseudonym as her records are not yet housed at the Oregon State Archives. See preface.

34 Greenwald, *Women, War and Work*, 87–138, quotes and data 92–93. See also US Railroad Administration, *Number of Women Employed and Character of Their Employment*.

35 Oregon Bureau of Labor Statistics, *Eighth Biennial Report of the Bureau of Labor Statistics*, 31.

36 US Railroad Administration, *Number of Women Employed and Character of Their Employment*, 36, 27.

37 "War-Savings Drive To Start Tuesday," *Sunday Oregonian*, June 23, 1918, Section 1, 22; "Telegraphers Get W.S.S. Pledges," *Oregon Journal*, June 27, 1918, 1; and "W.S.S. Salesgirls Have Thrilling Experiences, and They Get the Money," *Oregon Sunday Journal*, June 30, 1918, Section 1, 12.

38 Muhammad, "Separate and Unsanitary," 89–92.

39 Greenwald, *Women, War and Work*, 25–26.

40 Taylor, *In Search of the Racial Frontier*, 194; McLagan, *Peculiar Paradise*, 116–117; and Toll, "Black Families and Migration to a Multiracial Society," 45–46.

41 1920 Census for Sadie Baker, Oregon, Multnomah Portland District 0004, Sheet 9B; 1920 Census for Louisa Waddy, Oregon, Multnomah Portland District 0159, Sheet 15B; 1909 *PCD* William Waddy Pullman Porter 1371; Oregon, US, State Deaths, 1864–1968 for William James Waddy, Multnomah 1919, 2440.

42 1920 Census for Lucile Simalton Oregon Multnomah Portland District 0004, Sheet 29B; 1920 Census for Alice Edmondson Oregon Multnomah Portland District 0004, Sheet 7A; 1920 Census for Belle Gallagher Oregon Multnomah Portland District 0114, Sheet 10B; 1920 Census for Lena Rogers Oregon Multnomah Portland District 0004, Sheet 30A; 1920 Census for J. Elizabeth Smith Oregon Multnomah Portland District 0060, Sheet 10A; and 1920 Census for Louise Rhoades Oregon Multnomah Portland District 0161, Sheet 2A.

43 Muhammad, "Separate and Unsanitary," 9.

44 "Railroad Employs Women as Cleaners," *Oregon Journal*, May 27, 1917, 10.

45 Greenwald, *Women, War and Work*, 87–92; Muhammad, "Separate and Unsanitary"; and "New Passenger Rate Is in Effect Monday," *Oregon Journal*, June 9, 1918, 14.

46 "War Has Expanded Work of People's Institute Greatly," *Oregon Sunday Journal*, December 22, 1918, Section 2, 2; "Women's Clubs: The Martha Washington," *Oregonian* August 9, 1917, 12; and Dilg, "Uncovering 'The Real Work' of the Portland YWCA, 1900–1923."

47 Ordinance 15220—"An ordinance creating a free employment bureau in the City of Portland and providing for the maintenance of the same," February 28, 1906, City Auditor—City Recorder—Council Ordinances AF/53290, PARC; and "Free Employment Bureau," *Oregonian*, March 31, 1906, 10.

48 *Oregon Laws* 128 (1915), 134–139.

49 "Uncle Sam Is the World's Greatest Labor Employer," *Oregon Sunday Journal*, June 9, 1918, Section 2, 1; "Situations Female: Public Employment Bureau" and "Situations Male: Public Employment Bureau," *Oregon Journal*, January 27, 1918, 23; and "Wide Field Opening for Women Workers as Result of War," *Oregon Journal*, June 5, 1918, 9.

50 Oregon Industrial Welfare Commission, *Third Biennial Report*, 28. For the commission, see Dilg, "'For Working Women in Oregon.'"

51 "Interest Shown in Women's Welfare," *Oregon Journal*, May 28, 1918, 7.

52 "Pullman Order Is Blow to Officers," *Sunday Oregonian*, August 18, 1918, Section 1, 16.

53 "Sheriff Is Blameless," *Sunday Oregonian*, September 29, 1918, Section 1, 6; and "Officers Free to Act," *Oregonian*, September 30, 1918, 1.

54 "S.O.S. Call Sounds for W.S.S.," *Oregon Journal*, June 27, 1918, 1; and "No Respite until Quotas Attained," *Oregonian*, June 28, 1918, 11.

55 Ironically, four women canvassers had been fired when they joined the Telegraphers' Union. "Telegraphers Get W.S.S. Pledges" and "W.S.S. Salesgirls Have Thrilling Experiences."

56 C. H. Grisim, "In Re Mrs. Anna M. Weston, Disloyal," Case Number 8000-229103, 1–2, Roll 641, M1085 Old German Files 1909–1921, Investigative Reports of the Bureau of Investigation 1908–1922, NARA; and *United States of America v. Anna M. Weston*, in the District Court of the United States for the District of Oregon, Judgement Roll 7857, Register No. 8078, Filed December 14, 1918, NARA Seattle.

57 "Woman Pullman Car Worker Is Acquitted," *Portland Evening Telegram*, October 22, 1918, 10.

58 Mary Murphy, Yard Force Employment Record, and Madeline Hoffert, Yard Force Employment Record, Box 331, Pullman Company Records, Employee and Labor Relations Department: Case Pullman 06/02/03, Subgroup 02: Personnel Administration Department Records, Series 03: Employee Service Records, Oregon Portland Yard Force A-Z, Special Collections, Newberry Library, Chicago, Illinois. With thanks to Ginger Frere of Information Diggers. 1940 Census for Madeline Hoffert, Oregon Multnomah Portland 37–139, Sheet 63A; and "Madeline Hoffert Obituary," *Oregon Journal*, April 15, 1956, 8.

59 David Robinson served as Portland's city-funded public defender from 1915 through 1917, until the city council followed Mayor George Baker's request to abolish the office. Robinson reported that the police had resumed the practice of the holds after the abolition of the public defender office. Thomas A. Larremore, "Portland and Legal Aid," *Oregon Law Review* 1, no. 2 (June 1921) 8n29; "Council Abolishes the Public Defender," *Oregon Journal*, July 13, 1917, 4; and Leeson, *Rose City Justice*, 81–83.

60 "Woman Arrested on Charge of Sedition," *Oregon Journal*, June 29, 1918, 2; and "Federal Grand Jury Returns Indictments Covering 19 Offenses," *Oregon Journal*, June 30, 1918, 14.

61 Oregon Secretary of State, *State of Oregon Blue Book and Official Directory 1919–1920* (Salem, OR: SPO, 1917), 130–131; "John C. Veatch Is Recommended To Be Assistant Attorney," *Oregon Journal*, February 20, 1918,

2; and "News of the Profession: Fred H. Drake," *Law Notes*, November 1918, 155.

62   Thomas Larremore outlined the situation in his 1921 study "Portland and Legal Aid," 8–13.

63   "Sanity of Woman Is under Investigation," *Oregon Journal*, July 3, 1918, 3.

64   *United States v. Anna M. Weston.*

65   She appeared "in her proper person" at the indictment, meaning alone and representing herself. October 5, 1918, indictment, *United States v. Anna M. Weston.* It appears that Weston was able to make her bond and bail.

66   See "Andrew Hansen," in Colmer and Wood, eds., *History of the Bench and Bar of Oregon*, 147; and "Town Topics: To Discuss Capital Punishment," *Oregon Journal*, November 17, 1923, 5. Hansen represented Harry W. Stone of Monmouth in his action against the local draft board in *Stone v. Christensen*, 1940, https://casetext.com/case/stone-v-christensen. See "Andrew Hansen Obituary," *Oregon Journal*, September 12, 1945, 11.

67   *United States v. Anna M. Weston.*

68   "Woman Pullman Car Worker Is Acquitted." My thanks to Layne Sawyer, who shared her knowledge of OSA commitment records with me and the fact that if there was no commitment, there would be no record of the proceedings.

69   Helquist's WWI Sedition in Oregon Project locates Weston, Blachly, and Equi and three other women for whom accusations did not lead to arrest. Elsie Osborne, of Prineville, and Mrs. M. A. Thomas, of Brooklyn, New York, were members of the International Bible Students Association (Jehovah's Witnesses) and were held and questioned in early March 1918 in Portland, where they were distributing literature that affirmed conscientious objection to participating in the conflict. Assistant US attorney Robert Rankin released them both without charge "pending further examination of the teachings of the association." See "Bible Student Women Arrested," *Oregon Journal*, March 2, 1918, 1; and "Women Apprehended on Sedition Charges," *Oregon Journal*, March 3, 1918, 4. For the broad context for the group, see Knox, "'Greater Danger Than a Division of the German Army.'" Kate Kidwell was apprehended for political and union activity, and for distributing literature defending Marie Equi. It appears she was not put on trial. "Couple May Escape," *Sunday Oregonian*, July 21, 1918, Section 1, 17.

70   "Alleged Disloyal Citizens Examined," *Klamath Falls Evening Herald*, May 7, 1918, 1; "Mrs. Blachley [*sic*] Demands Full Investigation," *Klam-*

ath Falls Evening Herald, May 15, 1918, 1; and "Woman Denies Sedition," *Oregonian*, May 15, 1918, 3.

71 "Woman Rouses Ire of Klamath People," *Oregon Sunday Journal*, May 12, 1918, Section 1, 1; "Criticised Woman and Man Depart," *Klamath Falls Evening Herald*, May 13, 1918, 1; and "Woman Held Pro-Hun," *Oregonian*, May 14, 1918, 12.

72 "Grand Jury Must Act," *Oregonian*, May 16, 1918, 5; and "Mrs. Blachly Now Released from Custody," *Klamath Falls Evening Herald*, May 18, 1918, 1.

73 Anna and her husband returned to their home and work in Klamath Falls, where raw, angry emotions in the community remained. The county judge, district attorney, Home Defense League members, and many of their neighbors sent a petition to federal officials requesting attorney general Thomas Gregory intervene in her case to charge her, but it appears there was no action. "Copies of an Appeal," *Oregon Journal*, June 18, 1918, 8.

74 Helquist, *Marie Equi*; Kennedy, *Disloyal Mothers and Scurrilous Citizens*, 97–100; Mayer, *Beyond the Rebel Girl*, 141–156; and Krieger, "Queen of the Bolsheviks," 55–73.

75 Helquist, *Marie Equi*, 162.

76 Helquist, *Marie Equi*, 119–120.

77 Anna's younger brother was committed to the Oregon State Hospital in 1908. Commitment Record 474465, Washington County Commitment Records, vol. 2, 19, OSA.

78 Certificate of Examining Physician, Oregon State Hospital, Female Patient File #2057 (2020–1117), Oregon State Institution for the Feeble Minded 2020–1117, Records, Redacted Copy, Oregon Health Authority, Salem, Oregon; Commitment Case Record # 474642, December 26, 1918, vol. 3, 37, Commitment Records, Washington County, OSA. My appreciation to Layne Sawyer for her help with and insights about these files.

79 Female Patient File #2057. It is significant that doctors discharged Lena after her sterilization rather than paroled her. Discharge was permanent, parole required a smooth year out of the institution before permanent discharge.

80 Female Patient File #2057. Estate Case 2514, Record 519894, Washington County, Oregon, OSA; "News Items," *Beaverton Times*, March 18, 1921, 1; Oregon, US, State Deaths, 1864–1968 Washington-Yamhill 1926 Certificate 142; Oregon, US, State Deaths, 1864–1968 Baker-Coos 1966, Certificate 003090. Later notes in Lena's file have a diagnosis of "congenital cerebral maldevelopment" with "mental deficiency," or a developmental

disability. The file indicates Lena was paroled to her sister Anna in 1925 but does not have a readmit date.

81 Henry Waldo Coe, "State Sterilization," *Medical Sentinel* 21, no. 5 (May 1913): 905–908; and Siegler, "Morningside Hospital." Coe wrote the editorial in May 1913, after the Oregon legislature passed a sterilization bill but before the citizen-led referendum that defeated the law in November 1913. For the national context, see Trent, *Inventing the Feeble Mind*.

82 Clinical History, June 7, 1951, Female Patient File #2057.

83 Plaintiff Complaint, *Weston, D. J. v. Weston, Anna M.*, 1914, Circuit Court Case File 12863, Box 23, Circuit Court Criminal—Civil—Domestic, 12746–12870, Clackamas County, 97B-24, 2/25/10/1, OSA (hereafter Weston Divorce Record).

84 Weston Divorce Record; *1914 Los Angeles City Directory*, Robert A. Campbell, 255 Harvard Blvd., 686; "Robert Alexander Campbell, M.D.," in George H. Kress, *A History of the Medical Profession in Southern California*, 2nd ed. (Los Angeles: Times-Mirror Press, 1910), 117; Robert A. Campbell, "Sterility," *Pacific Coast Journal of Homeopathy* 8, no. 2 (February 1900): 29–31; and Robert A. Campbell, "Genito-Urinary Conditions," *Pacific Coast Journal of Homeopathy* 33, no. 11 (November 1922): 354–358.

85 Physicians sometimes removed organs infected with gonorrhea as a treatment effort. See Rockafellar, "Making the World Safe for the Soldiers of Democracy," 34.

86 1920 Census for Anna M. Weston, Oregon, Multnomah Portland District 0081, Sheet 5A; Durkin Washington, US, Marriage Records, 1854–2013 for John Durkin and Mary Weston Clarke, Marriage Certificates 1923 May–August, Certificate 448; John and Mary Durkin Surety Bond, June 26, 1925, File 2057; 1930 Census for Anna M. Durkin, Oregon, Multnomah Portland (Districts 1–219) District 0190, Sheet 6B; and 1932 Cohen Washington, Marriage Records, 1854–2013, for Anna M. Durkin and David G. Cohen, Clark Marriage Certificates 1932 January–April, Certificate B 2762. Anna Mary was listed as a widow on her death certificate, but David Cohen was living in Portland and listed as divorced in 1940; Anna Mary Cohen Certificate of Death, Multnomah, Oregon, December 13, 1938, Certificate 334; and 1940 US Federal Census for David G. Cohen, Oregon, Multnomah Portland 37–58, Sheet 3A.

87 Anna Mary Cohen, December 7, 1938, #12252, Resident Admissions Register, vol. 6, 1937–1954, 156, Multnomah County, Poor Farm Records, Multnomah Archives Digital Collections; Anna Mary Cohen Death Certificate; and Nesbit, "Multnomah County Poor Farm (Edgefield)." The former poor farm is now McMenamin's Edgefield Resort.

CHAPTER 4 / "ALIEN" ENEMIES

1 Proctor, *Civilians in a World at War: 1914–1918*, 203–238; Stibbe, "Enemy Aliens and Internment"; Capozzola, *Uncle Sam Wants You*, 173–190; and Nagler, "Victims of the Home Front," 191–215. US Department of Justice, *Annual Report of the Attorney General of the United States for the Year 1918*, 24–37.

2 Bredbenner, *Nationality of Her Own*.

3 I created a database from the Oregon files contained in MSS 1540, US Department of Justice, World War I Alien Registration Forms [Oregon], OHS (hereafter WWI AR). My sincere thanks to Scott Daniels at OHS for helping me with this important collection. Part of this research appeared in Jensen, "From Citizens to Enemy Aliens." Thank you to *OHQ* editor Eliza Canty-Jones and managing editor Erin Brasell for their helpful suggestions and support.

4 "Claws of Teuton Women Clipped," *Oregonian*, April 21, 1918, 1.

5 "Women Enemy Aliens Must Register Like the Men," *St. Johns Review*, November 29, 1918, 2. The reference comes from Rudyard Kipling's 1911 poem "The Female of the Species."

6 "It Is a Matter of Congratulation," *Oregonian*, April 20, 1918, 10.

7 "Table 1. Color, Nativity, and Parentage" in Bureau of Commerce and Labor, Bureau of the Census, *Thirteenth Census of the United States Taken in the Year 1910, Abstract of the Census, Supplement for Oregon*, 587.

8 "Proclamation No. 1364, April 6, 1917, Declaring the Existence of a State of War with the German Empire and Setting Forth Regulations Prescribing Conduct Toward Alien Enemies by the President of the United States of America," *Papers Relating to the Foreign Relations of the United States*, 1918, Supplement 2, The World War, Office of the Historian, US Department of State, https://history.state.gov/historicaldocuments /frus1918Supp02/d158. See *Oregon Laws*, Constitutional Amendment, Amending Section 2 of Article II (1915), 11; "Full Citizenship Required to Vote," *Oregon Journal*, April 24, 1918, 14; and US Department of Labor, Bureau of Naturalization, *Naturalization Laws and Regulations*, 10. Congress relaxed some of these restrictions in May 1918 legislation. *Report Attorney General 1918*, 37–38.

9 "Proclamation No. 1364, April 6, 1917."

10 "All Germans Must Give Up Weapons," *Eugene Guard*, April 18, 1917, 6; "Notice," *Klamath Falls Evening Herald*, April 23, 1917, 4; and "Unnaturalized Foreigners Are Given Warning," *Corvallis Gazette-Times*, April 21, 1917, 1.

11 "Proclamation No. 1364, April 6, 1917"; and *Report Attorney General 1918*, 31–32.

12 Oregon Secretary of State, *State of Oregon Blue Book and Official Directory 1917–1918* (Salem, OR: SPO, 1918), 114.

13 "Germans Must Avoid Vicinity of Armory Is Rule of Future," *Eugene Guard*, June 5, 1917, 5; "Enemy Aliens To Be Affected by Ruling," *Oregon Journal*, May 27, 1917, 10; and "Notice to Alien Enemies," *Hood River Glacier*, June 7, 1917, 2.

14 "Aliens Must Have Permit or Stay Out," *Ashland Tidings*, June 7, 1917, 1; and "Warning Issued by Dist. Attorney," *Roseburg News Review*, June 5, 1917, 1.

15 "Proclamation No. 1408, November 16, 1917, Setting Forth Additional Regulations Prescribing Conduct Toward Alien Enemies by the President of the United States of America," *Papers Relating to the Foreign Relations of the United States*, 1918, Supplement 2, The World War, Office of the Historian, US Department of State, https://history.state.gov/historical documents/frus1918Supp02/d178; *Report Attorney General 1918*, 32–34; "Barred Zones," *Oregon Journal*, January 17, 1918, 10; and "Aliens Must Use Cars on All Bridges," *Oregon Journal*, December 5, 1917, 1.

16 "Map of Half Mile Radius about the Armory," *Oregonian*, May 27, 1918, 14; and "Enemy Aliens Make Rush for Permits," *Oregon Journal*, May 28, 1917, 1.

17 "Enemy Aliens' Use of Streets Is Restricted," *Oregon Journal*, May 26, 1917, 1; "Enemy Aliens To Be Affected by Ruling," 10; "Germans by Score Ask for Permits," *Oregonian* May 29, 1917, 8; and "Marshal Lists Aides for Service in State," *Oregon Journal*, June 6, 1917, 4. John Schurman, Work Permit, Willamette Heritage Center Collections 2016.101.0003.001, Willamette Heritage Center, Salem, Oregon. Thank you to Kylie Pine for sharing this important resource with me.

18 See "Green Card Must Be Shown," *Roseburg News Review*, June 5, 1917, 1.

19 "Eight To Be Interned," *Oregonian*, December 25, 1917, 18; "Federal Net Is Set," *Oregonian*, November 23, 1917, 14; and "100 Germans Lose Jobs in Portland," *Oregonian*, November 29, 1917, 12.

20 Attorney General Thomas W. Gregory gave the figure as "more than 260,000" in *Report of Attorney General 1918*, 30; Nagler's research yielded 254,138. For an overview of Oregon men registrants, see Maureen Mc-Nassar, "A General Look at German 'Enemy Alien' Registration Records Collected from Feb. 3–15, 1918, During WWI," History 415 term project (Portland State University), Winter 1980. McNassar examined only the male files. Copy with Finding Aid for MSS 1540 WWI AR Forms. Boxes

1–3 contain male registration forms, and Boxes 4–5 female registration forms; Nagler, "Victims of the Home Front," 206–214; Stibbe, "Enemy Aliens and Internment"; and *Report Attorney General 1918*, 678–729, reprinted all of the forms, permits, registration blanks, and card.

21 Hodges, "'Enemy Aliens' and 'Silk Stocking Girls,'" 431–458.

22 Clarence Reames, US Attorney for Oregon, to Oregon Attorney General George Brown, April 6, 1917, 2; Reames to Brown, April 4, 1917; Copies of Reames to District Attorneys, April 3, 1917; Folder 14: April 1917, Box 20, Attorney General Correspondence, Accession 89A-001, Department of Justice Files, OSA, Salem, OR (hereafter AG Corr, OSA); and "An Act Defining Vagrancy and Prescribing Punishment Therefor," *Oregon Laws* 95 (1911), 138–139.

23 "Government Is Ready to Suppress Disloyal Utterances and Acts," *Oregon Journal*, April 7, 1917, 7. For secret service, see George Brown to Walter Evans April 10, 1917, Folder 14: April 1917, Box 20, AG Corr, OSA. For additional deputies, see H. H. De Armond to George Brown, April 9, 1917, Folder 12: April 1917, Box 20 AG Corr, OSA.

24 "Parker Is Enrolled: Rose City Captain and Other Officers Get Certificates," *Sunday Oregonian*, January 13, 1918, Section 2, 14.

25 "Vigilantes Are Formed," *Oregonian*, January 26, 1918, 7; and "Vigilantes To Give Ball," *Oregonian*, April 17, 1918, 6.

26 "Must Have Permit," *Oregon Journal*, January 3, 1918, 9.

27 "Regulation of the Conduct of Alien Enemies" and "Exhibit 30, Section 5: Existence of War—Austro Hungarian Empire," *Report Attorney General 1918*, 28, 682–684; and Stergar, "Nationalities (Austria-Hungary)."

28 "German Women To Be Interned," *Oregonian*, January 10, 1918, 4.

29 *Report of Attorney General 1918*, 30.

30 Database from Box 4 and 5, Female Files, WWI AR.

31 "Registration of Women on Today," *Oregonian*, June 17, 1918, 5.

32 "German Alien Women to Register ToDay," *Ashland Tidings*, June 17, 1918, 1.

33 "German Women Warned They Must Obey Alien Rules," *Oregon Journal*, May 1, 1918, 9. Bert Haney was confirmed in March 1918 after US Attorney General Gregory tapped Clarence Reames for special war work in the Pacific Northwest. "Haney Assumes Office," *Oregonian*, March 19, 1918, 11.

34 Stibbe, "Enemy Aliens and Internment." No women from Oregon appear to have been interned.

35 "Article II: Definitions To Be Observed in the Interpretation, Construction, and Enforcements of These Regulations," Exhibit 30, Section 9:

Registration of German Alien Females, *Report Attorney General 1918*, 703–705.

36   See "Alien Enemy Women under Restriction," *Ashland Tidings*, April 22, 1918, 5; "Rules Sent to Police Chief," *Oregon Statesman*, June 5, 1918, 8; and "Woman Belongs to Her Husband's Own Country," *Eugene Morning Register*, June 5, 1918, 6.

37   "Rules Given for Registration of German Women," *Oregon Journal*, June 16, 1918, 6.

38   WWI AR; and *Report Attorney General 1918*, 29–31, 702–720.

39   Yawman & Erbe Manufacturing Co., *Criminal Identification by Y and E Bertillon and Finger Print Systems* (Rochester, NY: Yawman & Erbe Manufacturing Co., 1913); and Robertson, *Passport in America*, 72–75, 241–244. The Astoria Public Library's *Wanted and Reward Letters and Posters Scrapbook*, volume 1913–1917, has many examples. My thanks to Jane Tucker for assistance with this source.

40   *Report of the Attorney General 1918*, 713; WWI AR; "Only Half of Alien Women Registered Up to Present Time," *Oregon Journal*, June 23, 1918, 14; "About 900 German Women Register in Past 9-Day Period," *Oregon Journal*, June 27, 1918, 5; and "German Women Must Get Cards Saturday," *Oregon Journal*, July 11, 1918, 11.

41   For examples, see "65 Women Register," *Oregon Journal*, June 18, 1918, 9; "Registering Women of Alien Nationality," *Salem Capital Journal*, June 18, 1918, 7; "Four Cards Not Called For," *East Oregonian*, July 10, 1918, 6; and "Martha Shafer and Mamie Jaquet," *East Oregonian*, June 22, 1918, 5.

42   "Alien Registrations Confidential," in *Spy Glass: A Bulletin of News and Better Methods Issued by the American Protective League*, August 10, 1918, 2.

43   "Only Half of Alien Women Registered Up to Present Time," *Oregon Journal*, June 23, 1918, 14.

44   "Three Alien Women Registered to Date," *Roseburg Evening News*, June 21, 1918, 1.

45   "Registration of Alien Women Starts in Salem," *Oregon Statesman*, June 18, 1918, 1.

46   "Local and Personal: Only Four German Alien Women," *Medford Mail Tribune*, June 21, 1918, 2.

47   "Alien Women Registered," *Bend Bulletin*, June 21, 1918, 1.

48   "Only Half of Alien Women Registered."

49   "124 German Women Have Registered," *Portland Evening Telegram*, June 19, 1918, 4.

50   Harms as quoted in "Women Must Sign," *Portland News*, June 20, 1918, 7.

51 "Alien Women Are Registering Today," *Oregon Journal*, June 17, 1918, 1.

52 "Women Register at Station; All Are Loyal to U.S.," *Portland News*, June 18, 1918, 7.

53 "65 Women Register," *Oregonian*, June 18, 1918, 9.

54 "124 German Women Have Registered."

55 "Women Register at Station," 7.

56 "Only 145 Women Apply to Register, 29 Complete the Task," *Oregon Journal*, June 18, 1918, 2.

57 "300 German Alien Women Are Listed," *Oregonian*, June 20, 1918, 6.

58 "Women Register at Station."

59 "300 German Alien Women Are Listed."

60 Leo Harms to W. F. Johnson, July 19, 1918, "Ordinances—Women and Children," Baker Mayor Subject Files, A2000-003, PARC.

61 "Women Register at Station."

62 "Soldier's Mother Is Listed as Enemy," *Portland Evening Telegram*, June 17, 1918, 1.

63 Olive Siegenfuhr File, Marie Tuerck File, and Maggie Kiss File, in WWI AR.

64 *PCD* 1918, 1583–1584; *Astoria and Clatsop County Directory*, 1918, 350; *The Dalles City Directory*, 1917, 281; and *Salem City Directory*, 1917, 404.

65 For an overview, see Beil, *Good Pictures*. Soldiers, nurses, and other war workers used cameras to document their World War I journeys. See Higgonet, "X-Ray Vision: Women Photograph War"; and McKenzie, "Picturing War."

66 See, for example, "There's No Trouble about a Kodak," *Klamath Falls Evening Herald*, June 20, 1918, 2.

67 "Instructions on How to Register Given to Women," *Oregon Journal*, June 16, 1918, 6; and "Alien Women Are Registering Today."

68 Meta Koehring File, WWI AR; and "Husbands Not Naturalized," *Oregon Statesman*, June 23, 1918, 4.

69 Anna Bertha Neureither File, WWI AR; and 1920 Census for Anna Neureit[h]er, Oregon, Douglas Roseburg District 0161.

70 Mathilde Schafer and Pauline Elsbeth Schafer File, WWI AR; 1920 Census for Mathilda Schafer, Oregon, Josephine, Kerby, District 0213.

71 Eugenie Kromminga File, WWI AR.

72 "Permitted to Wear Hat in Posing for Photos," *Washington [DC] Times*, June 20, 1918, 4; and "Alien Women Will Number 600 to 700," *Oregonian*, June 16, 1918, 18. Gregory did not discuss the issue in his *Annual Report* for 1918.

73 Database from Box 4 and 5, Female Files, WWI AR.

NOTES TO PAGES 97–102 / 251

74 "Portland War Widows Are Sisters in Sorrow Despite Color of Flag,"
Sunday Oregonian, November 1, 1914, Magazine Section 6; Case Number
73327, *Grace Reimers v. Paul Reimers*, September 10, 1918, Multnomah
County Court Records, Multnomah County Courthouse, Portland, Or-
egon; Grace Reimers File, WWI AR.; *PCD*, 1918 1045; and "German
Women Must Also Have Permits," *Oregon Journal*, September 19, 1918, 8.

75 Hattie Allie Dahrens File, WWI AR; "Funeral Is Today for Mrs. Burbank,"
Oregon Statesman, December 28, 1933, 2; and "Orlando Burbank Passes
at Pedee," *Salem Capital Journal*, December 4, 1929, 9.

76 The peeled, dried bark, also known as chittim, was a traditional laxative
native to the Pacific Northwest, used for centuries by Indigenous Ka-
lapuyans and other Native people, and adopted by settler-colonial residents. Hattie Allie Dahrens File, WWI AR; and Walls, "Lady Loggers and
Gyppo Wives."

77 Hattie Allie Dahrens File, WWI AR; Adolph Herman Dahrens WWI
AR; US World War I Draft Registration Cards, 1917–1918, for Adolph
Dahrens, Oregon, Clackamas County Draft Card D.

78 Hattie Allie Dahrens File, WWI AR.

79 1920 Selected US Naturalization Records, Original Documents, 1790–
1974 for Adolph Dahrens, Oregon District Court (Rolls 14–59, 14–59)
1911–1941 (Roll 18) Petition and Record, 1919, #998–1050.

80 Thomas Riedl File, WWI AR; Thomas Riedl Draft Registration, June 5,
1917, San Francisco Roll 1543845, Board 1; "Ten Register as 'Alien Enemies,'" *Oregon City Courier*, February 7, 1918, 1; "Alien Enemy Act Calls
59 in Co.," *Oregon City Courier*, February 14, 1918, 1; and *Oregon Blue
Book and Official Directory, 1919–1920*, 175. The press often misspelled
Riedl's name as Reidl or other variations.

81 "Wilhelm Agent Arrested Here," *Oregon City Courier*, April 18, 1918, 1;
"Interned Probable Fate of Hun Suspect," *Oregon City Enterprise*, April
19, 1918, 1; "The Electric Hotel and Annex Oregon City's Leading Hos-
telry," *Oregon City Courier*, February 12, 1914, 16; and "Spy Suspect Held:
Young German Believed to Be Female Impersonator," *Oregonian*, April
16, 1918, 4.

82 "Interned Probable Fate of Hun Suspect."

83 Helquist, *Marie Equi;* and Hodges, "At War over the Espionage Act in
Portland."

84 Peter Boag argues persuasively that newspaper editors, doctors, medical
experts, and other creators of popular and scientific culture obscured the
reality of the gender fluidity in the American West in the nineteenth and
early twentieth centuries by focusing on "cross-dressing" and thereby

erasing more complex gender identities. Boag, *Re-Dressing America's Frontier Past.* "Wilhelm Agent Arrested"; "Interned Probable Fate of Hun Suspect"; and "Spy Suspect Held."

85   US Attorney for Oregon Bert Haney to Attorney General Thomas Watt Gregory, April 22, 1918, Volume: "Letters March 14, 1918 to July 24, 1918," Box 7: "Correspondence Sent, Letterpress Books: 1914–1921," RG 118, Records of US Attorney's Office for The District of Oregon, Portland, Oregon, 1870–1954, NARA Seattle.

86   Haney to Gregory, April 22, 1918, 2–3.

87   "Three Germans Interned," *Oregonian*, May 11, 1918, 16.

88   "Additional List of Civilian Alien Enemies Desiring Repatriation," 2, Case Number 185211, Old German Files, 1909–1921, Investigative Case Files of the Bureau of Investigation, M1085, NARA.

89   Woodrow Wilson, Presidents, Presidential and Secretaries Travel Abroad, Office of the Historian, US Department of State, https://history.state.gov /departmenthistory/travels/president/wilson-woodrow. A. Mitchell Palmer reprinted the proclamation in his 1919 report. "A Proclamation Abrogating, Annulling, and Rescinding Certain Regulations Prescribing the Conduct of Alien Enemies by the President of the United States of America," in US Department of Justice, *Annual Report of the Attorney General of the United States for the Year 1919*, 651. For Oregon, see "War Restrictions on Alien Enemies Are Now Removed," *Oregon Journal*, December 24, 1918, 12; and "Germans to Regain Freedom of Action," *Oregonian*, December 24, 1918, 6.

90   Ngai, *Impossible Subjects*, 87, 169–201; Lee, *Making of Asian America*, 183–219; Daniels, *Prisoners without Trial*; and Tamura, *Hood River Issei*.

91   Canaday, *Straight State*, 19–90.

92   Goodman, *Deportation Machine*.

CHAPTER 5 / HELD FOR HEALTH

1   Kline, *Building a Better Race*, 44–47; Clement, *Love for Sale*, 119; and Shah "Against Their Own Weakness,'" 468.

2   Gloria Myers and Adam Hodges have analyzed parts of this history. See Myers, *Municipal Mother*; and Hodges, *World War I and Urban Order.*

3   Report for December 1918, Seventh District, Lola G. Baldwin, Supervisor, Folder 5, Government Reports, World War I 1915–18, War Department, Commission on Training Camp Activities, Section on Women and Girls, Section 7, Lola Greene Baldwin Papers, Coll 388, OHS.

4   Shah, "'Against Their Own Weakness": 458–482; Rockafellar, "Making

the World Safe for the Soldiers of Democracy"; Brandt, *No Magic Bullet*, 52–121; Bristow, *Making Men Moral*; Parascandola, *Sex, Sin, and Science*; Stern, *Trials of Nina McCall*; Keire, *For Business & Pleasure*, 89–113; Clement, *Love for Sale*, 114–143; and Fairchild, Bayer, and Colgrove, *Searching Eyes*.

5   Strange, *Toronto's Girl Problem*, 127; D'Emilio and Freedman, *Intimate Matters*, 194–201; Odem, *Delinquent Daughters*; Peiss, *Cheap Amusements*; Alexander, *"Girl Problem"*; Kline, *Building a Better Race*, 32–60; Bristow, *Making Men Moral*, 91–136; and Myers, *Municipal Mother*. For an earlier period of policing women, see Wood, *Freedom of the Streets*.

6   William T. Foster, "State-Wide Education in Social Hygiene," *Social Hygiene* 2, no. 3 (July 1916): 309–239.

7   Connelly, *Response to Prostitution in the Progressive Era*, 91–113, 196n2; Portland Vice Commission, *Report of the Portland Vice Commission to the Mayor and City Council of the City of Portland, Oregon* (Portland, OR: Portland Vice Commission, 1913), accessed November 23, 2023, https://iiif.lib.harvard.edu/manifests/view/drs:3580398$1i. MacColl, *Shaping of a City*, 402–412; Rockafellar, "Making the World Safe for the Soldiers of Democracy," 132–137; Myers, *Municipal Mother*, 91–107; and Boag, *Same Sex Affairs*, 185–193. Toronto had a 1913–1914 Social Survey. Strange, *Toronto's Girl Problem*, 105–115.

8   *Portland Vice Commission Report*, 133–135.

9   *Portland Vice Commission Report*, 136; and Boag, *Same Sex Affairs*, passim and 199.

10 "Mrs. Edmunds Writes of Referendum Laws," *Ashland Tidings*, October 30, 1913, 1, 8, quoting Lola Baldwin. See similar world war references in Canaday, *Straight State*, 60–62.

11 "Mashers Must Go," *Oregonian*, July 9, 1913, 12.

12 Mayor H. Russell Albee, Statement on Dress Ban, Albee Mayor Subject Files, A2000-003, PARC; and "Mayor Puts 'Lid' on X-Ray Gowns," *Oregonian*, August 20, 1913, 1.

13 "Report of Committee on Detention Home for Women," July 19, 1913, Rushlight Mayor Subject Files, Detention Home, AF/64760, PARC.

14 Keire, *For Business & Pleasure*, 69–88, 70.

15 Shah, "Against Their Own Weakness,'" 481, 459.

16 Report of Sub-Committee on School Cooperation October 9, 1913; Minutes Executive Committee October 31, 1913; Box 6, Minutes, Old Volume 5, Minutes of Meetings of the OSHS September 1, 1913, to October 9, 1914; and Report of Executive Committee, February 28, 1913, Box 6, Min-

utes, Old Volume 4, Minutes OSHS, November 1, 1912, to September 5, 1913, OSHS Records, OHS.

17 Box 7, Minutes, Old Volume 6, Minutes of Meetings of Executive Committee OSHS, April 14, 1916–November 9, 1917, front matter and *passim*, OSHS Records, OHS. "City News in Brief: Millie R. Trumbull Appointed on Vice Commission," *Oregonian*, June 6, 1912, 9; *Portland Vice Commission Report*, 79, 122, 216; "Report of Committee on Detention Home for Women"; and "Detention Home Is Recommended for Offenders," *Oregon Sunday Journal*, July 20, 1913, Section 1, 8.

18 "Clubs Well Represented," *Oregonian*, March 9, 1919, 21; and "Women's Activities," *Oregonian*, February 3, 1921, 10.

19 For national trends, see Odem, *Delinquent Daughters*, 118–119; Kelly Butte Report Week ending May 3, 1918, Box 7, Bound Volume 8, Old Volume 7, Minutes, November 16, 1917–October 25, 1918, OSHS Records, OHS.

20 Minutes of Meeting February 7, 1920, 31, Box 75, Folder 5, Bound Volume, Child Welfare Commission Minutes, 1919–1921, Accession 88A-63, Public Welfare Commission Records, OSA, Salem, Oregon; and Jensen, "Lizzie Weeks (1879–1976)"; and "Colored Women's Council Will Meet," *Sunday Oregonian*, March 24, 1918, Section 3, 12.

21 Bristow, *Making Men Moral*, 91–136; Brandt, *No Magic Bullet*, 88; and Rockafellar, "Making the War Safe for the Soldiers of Democracy," 186–260.

22 "66 Women Taken in Cleanup Raid," *Portland Evening Telegram*, November 5, 1917, 2; "27 More Arrests Are Made in Underworld," *Portland Evening Telegram*, November 6, 1917, 2; "Police Raid More Disorderly Houses," *Oregon Journal*, November 6, 1917, 7; and "Interne at City Emergency Hospital Leads Woeful Life," *Sunday Oregonian*, March 10, 1918, Section 3, 5.

23 "Sudden Clean-Up on Army Complaint Hint," *Oregon Journal*, November 5, 1917, 14.

24 "Social Condition Problem to City," *Portland Evening Telegram*, November 9, 1917, 18; Minutes Executive Committee, October 25, 1917, Old Volume 6, Minutes Executive Committee November 16, 1917; November 23, 1917; January 4, 1918; Bound Volume 8, Minutes, November 16, 1917–October 25, 1918, Old Volume, all in Box 7, OSHS Records, OHS; "Women Are To Be Put in Quarantine," *Portland Evening Telegram*, November 17, 1917, 20; and "$10,075 Is Provided for Women's Camp," *Oregonian*, November 20, 1917, 13.

25 "War on Vice a Patriotic Duty," *Oregonian*, December 17, 1917, 6.

26 "Time's Terrible Tale," *Cayton's Weekly*, November 17, 1917, 1.

27 Ordinance 33510, November 23, 1917, Office of City Auditor, 3700, Council, 3750, Ordinance Duplicate, Reel 628, August 22, 1917–March 26, 1919, PARC; "Isolation Act Law," *Oregonian*, November 24, 1917, 16; and "Venereal Disease Legislation: A Compilation of Laws and Regulations Showing the Trend of Modern Legislation for the Control of Venereal Diseases," *Public Health Reports* 33, no. 3 (January 18, 1918): 55–84. Rockafellar, "Making the War Safe for the Soldiers of Democracy," compares West Coast states.

28 Ordinance 33649, January 2, 1918, Office of City Auditor, 3700, Council, 3750, Ordinance Duplicate, Reel 628, August 22, 1917–March 26, 1919, PARC.

29 May 21, 1917, 92; October 18, 1917, 226; November 19, 1917, 244; March 4, 1918, 303; March 13, 1918, 313; April 2, 1918, 332; January 21, 1918, 273–274, City of Astoria, Oregon, Council Minutes, Volume 4: February 1917–January 1919, Astoria Public Library Collection, Astoria, Oregon.

30 H. H. Moore, "Four Million Dollars for the Fight against Venereal Diseases," *Social Hygiene* 5, no. 1 (January 1919): 15–26, 15; Dr. W. A. Pettit, "Oregon Sets Pace in Hygienic Work of United States," *Sunday Oregonian*, January 19, 1919, Section 5, 8; Rockafellar, "Making the War Safe for the Soldiers of Democracy," 272, 275–294; and Bristow, *Making Men Moral*, 129 and passim. For OSHS lobbying, see Executive Committee Minutes for January–June 1918, OSHS Records, OHS.

31 Rockafellar, "Making the War Safe for the Soldiers of Democracy," 226–227.

32 Connelly, *Response to Prostitution in the Progressive Era*, 24, 163–164n30; Rosen, *Lost Sisterhood*, 50–51; *Oregon Laws* 274 (1913): 519–522; Bascom Johnson, "The Injunction and Abatement Law," *Social Hygiene* 1, no. 2 (March 1915): 231–256; George Cosson, "Why an Injunction and Abatement Law?" *American City* 16, no. 1 (January 1917): 44–45; "'Tin Plate' Bill Passes Council; Vote Is 9 to 5," *Oregon Journal*, October 23, 1912, 10; "Tin Plate Bill Passes Council," *Oregonian*, October 24, 1912, 11; Myers, *Municipal Mother*, 105; MacColl, *Shaping of a City*, 411–412; and Boag, *Same-Sex Affairs*, 191.

33 "Tin Plate Ordinance in Portland," *The Survey*, February 8, 1913, 658; and "Items of Civic and Municipal Progress: Tin Plate Ordinance in Portland," *American City* 8, no. 3 (March 1913): 319.

34 "Sections of Hotel Ordinance Voided," *Oregonian*, March 6, 1914, 15; "Three Sections of Bonding Ordinance Are Declared Void," *Oregon Journal*, March 6, 1914, 11; "Conference Is Postponed," *Oregon Journal*, March 14, 1914, 12; and "Ordinance Held Unfair," *Oregonian*, March 17, 1914, 13.

35 David Robinson to H. H. Moore, December 31, 1917, 3, Folder Oregon Legislation, Box 313 Legislative Files, RG 90, Records of the Public Health Service, 1912–1968, 90.3.5. Venereal Disease Division, NARA. "Hotel Aid Enlisted," *Oregonian*, December 27, 1917, 4. In Portland's commission form of government Mayor George Baker was also in charge of the Department of Public Safety, under which this application was housed.

36 Typewritten comments signed "G.E.W." appended to "Application for License to Conduct Hotel, Rooming-House, or Lodging House City of Portland, Oregon, Department of Public Safety," Folder Oregon Legislation, RG 90.3.5, Venereal Disease Division, NARA. Underlining in original (represented in italics here). In pencil on the application is the note: "From H. H. Moore."

37 Robinson, ed., *Venereal Disease Ordinances*, 15, with ordinance reprinted 16–18.

38 Brandt, *No Magic Bullet*, 88–90.

39 "Another Call for Emergency," *Oregon Statesman*, April 4, 1918, 4; "State Aid in Fight on Disease Asked," *Oregon Journal*, April 3, 1918, 2; "Emergency Fund of $15,000 Given to Purify State," *Oregon Journal*, April 9, 1918, 11; and "State Asked to Combat Social Evil."

40 "Oregon Soldiers Lead All in Health," *Salem Capital Journal*, December 2, 1918, 1; "Fit to Fight and Fit to Work," *Sunday Oregonian*, December 15, 1918, Section 3, 6; and "Men of Oregon in Army Declared Cleanest by Surgeon General Blue," *Oregon Journal*, December 15, 1918, 1, 10.

41 *Oregon Laws* 264 (1919), 407–408, 437.

42 September 7, 1918, Bound Volume 1918, Police Investigative Report Books 8090-08, PARC; and "Social Condition Problem to City," *Portland Evening Telegram*, November 9, 1917, 18.

43 H. F. McInturff, "Law Enforcement in Its Relation to Public Health," *Medical Sentinel* 28, no. 2 (February 1920): 69–71.

44 Baldwin Semi Monthly Text Report, April 1, [1918], and Report May 8, 1918, Folder 5, Government Reports, Baldwin Papers, OHS; and August 21, 1918, Bound Volume, Police Investigative Report Books 8090–08, PARC.

45 "War Emergency Squad Formed by Local Police," *Oregon Journal*, January 13, 1918, 13; "Captain Circle Is Head of Inspectors," *Oregon Journal*, February 1, 1918, 2; "Moral Rise Noted," *Oregonian*, February 4, 1918, 4; and Myers, *Municipal Mother*, 132.

46 Database from the Portland Police Investigative Report Books November 1917–December 1919, Boxes 15–17, 8090-08, PARC. The books do not represent all police investigations or Women's Protective Bureau cases.

NOTES TO PAGES 121–123 / 257

47 "County Will Hire Men to Break Rock at the Kelly Butte Quarry," *Oregon Journal*, July 5, 1916, 2; "Needy Men Will Be Given Employment by the City This Week," *Oregon Journal*, February 13, 1916, 7; and "Rock Piles Opened for I.W.W. Hordes," *Oregonian*, December 30, 1916, 14.

48 "Twelve Escape in Jail Delivery at Kelly Butte," *Oregon Journal*, March 27, 1916, 1; and "Kelly Butte To Be in Care of Sheriff," *Oregonian*, March 29, 1916, 7.

49 "In the Matter of Providing Shelter, Sustenance, and Medicine for Women Infected with Venereal Diseases," November 19, 1917, Detention Home Kelly Butte, Baker Mayor Subject Files, AF/5682, 12/6/1917, PARC; "Kelly Butte Haven," *Sunday Oregonian*, November 18, 1917, Section 1, 20; "Kelly Butte Will House Women for Medical Attention," *Oregon Journal*, November 18, 1917, 6; and "Women at Butte," *Portland News*, November 19, 1917, 3.

50 "Home for Women Will Be Rushed," *Oregonian*, December 31, 1917, 9.

51 Today the Poor Farm building and grounds are the site of McMenamin's Edgefield Hotel and Brewery. Nesbit, "Multnomah County Poor Farm (Edgefield)."

52 "Detention Home Is Named," *Oregonian*, April 8, 1918, 4.

53 "Home for Women Rushed"; "New Home Too Small," *Sunday Oregonian*, June 2, 1918, Section 1, 21; "Army Plan Considered," *Oregonian*, June 6, 1918, 18; and "More Room Is Necessary," *Oregonian*, June 14, 1918, 11.

54 "Home Being Outfitted"; "New Detention Home for Women Is a Step in Solving Problem," *Oregon Journal*, August 11, 1918, 7; and "Cedars Now Open," *Sunday Oregonian*, August 11, 1918, Section 1, 12.

55 Detention Hospital Report for "The Cedars," July–December 1918, Folder 235.4.1, Box 90, Venereal Disease Division, NARA.

56 Minutes OSHS Executive Committee, October 4 and 11, 1918, OSHS Records, OHS; and "Health Held Paramount," *Oregonian*, November 19, 1918, 10.

57 A. C. Seeley to Surgeon General Rupert Blue, December 3, 1918, Folder 235.8, Box 90, Venereal Disease Division, NARA; and "Two Nurses Succumb to Influenza While Caring for Patients," *Oregon Journal*, December 21, 1918, 3.

58 No information about what happened is in the file or in other records. Margaret Mathews to Mayor Baker, April 14, 1918, Detention Home— Prisoners, Baker Mayor Subject Files, AF/6306 A2000-003, PARC.

59 "To Establish a Court at Night," *Oregon Journal*, December 5, 1918, 1.

60 "October Fines $1456.50," *Oregonian*, November 6, 1918, 11; "House Raided by Police," *Oregonian*, March 25, 1918, 7; "Six Taken into Custody,"

Oregonian, September 23, 1918, 12; and "Whiskey Factory Found," *Oregonian*, October 22, 1918, 2.

61 Ordinance 33986, "An Ordinance on Public Health and Sanitation," April 10, 1918, Auditor City Recorder, AD 13864, PARC; and "Ordinance No. 939," *Medford Mail Tribune*, July 19, 1918, 5.

62 Oregon Industrial Welfare Commission, *Fourth Biennial Report*, 19.

63 It's not clear from the documents whether authorities detained McKie at the jail or at The Cedars as she prepared and posted her bond. Detention Home, McKie, Baker Mayor Subject Files, November 12, 1918, AF/9922 A2000-003, PARC.

64 "Hotels under License," *Oregonian*, January 3, 1918, 9; "Interned Women Escape," *Oregonian*, October 12, 1918, 9; Elizabeth Rogers to N. F. Johnson, Chief of Police and Mayor George Baker, December 1, 1918, Detention Home—Prisoners, December 31, 1918, Baker Mayor Subject Files, AF/6306 A2000-003, PARC; and Report January 13–20, 1919, Folder 5, Government Reports, Baldwin Papers, OHS.

65 May Peterson in "Woman's Release Sought," *Oregonian*, November 16, 1918, 11; Minnie Brooks and Jessie Smith in "Two Women Yet Held," *Oregonian*, November 22, 1917, 11; Louise Troutville in "Liberty Issue at Stake," *Oregonian*, April 13, 1918, 9; Kate Stewart in "Cedars Inmate Asks Release," *Oregonian*, November 24, 1918, 14; Mary Main in "Health Held Paramount" and Detention Home, Mary Main Petition, November 18, 1918, Baker Mayor Subject Files, AF/9921, A2000-003, PARC; and Ruth Brown in "Writ Lost by Negress," *Oregonian*, April 16, 1921, 7.

66 Baldwin Weekly Report February 10–17, 1919, and February 17–24, 1919, Folder 5, Government Reports, Baldwin Papers, OHS.

67 "War Practice to Stop," *Oregonian*, July 23, 1919, 11; Blue to Baker, August 28, 1919; Baker to Blue, September 9, 1919, Folder 235.7.1, Section 235.7 Law Enforcement, Box 90, 90.3.5 Venereal Disease Division, NARA; "Launch Movement for Eradication of Social Diseases in Women," *Oregon Journal*, September 10, 1919, 8; and "Better Health Is Aim," *Oregonian*, September 10, 1919, 6.

68 Lola Baldwin to C. C. Pierce, September 17, 1919, Folder 235.8.1, Section 235.8 Misc., Box 90, Venereal Disease Division, NARA; "Launch Movement for Eradication"; and "Better Health Is Aim."

69 Portland Police Investigative Report Books, 8090-08, PARC.

70 September 5, 1919, Bound Volume 1919; November 12, 1920, Bound Volume 1920–1921, Police Investigative Report Books 8090-08, PARC.

71 It appears that the name Ruth Brown was an alias. *PCD* (1921), 1037.

72 "In the matter of the Petition of Ruth Brown for Writ of Habeas Corpus,"

Rendered April 15, 1921, Filed May 11, 1921, Judgment #84069, Reel 00-1146, Multnomah County Circuit Court Files, Multnomah County Courthouse, Portland, Oregon.

73 "Lou Wagner, Police Court Lawyer, Dies," *Oregon Journal*, March 5, 1953, 11.

74 "Release of Ruth Brown from Cedars Is Sought," *Oregon Journal*, April 10, 1921, 3; "Woman's Release Demanded," *Sunday Oregonian*, April 10, 1921, Section 1, 2; "Cedars Case Is Fought," *Oregonian*, April 12, 1921, 4; and "Lawyers Deny Case Was Taken before Judge for Reason, *Portland Evening Telegram*, April 12, 1921, 3.

75 "Petition of Ruth Brown for Writ of Habeas Corpus"; "Lawyers Deny Case Was Taken before Judge for Reason"; "Girl Is Sent Back to Cedars by Judge," *Oregon Journal*, April 14, 1921, 2; "Returns to Cedars When Liberty Denied," *Portland News*, April 14, 1921, 11; and "Writ Lost by Negress."

76 "Oregon Women in the 1920 Census Born in Mexico," Oregon Women's History Consortium, accessed November 23, 2023, https://www.oregon womenshistory.org/oregon-women-in-the-1920-census-born-in-mexico/.

77 Leonor Zambrano Marriage Record, April 24, 1920, Cameron Texas, Document 19200104, Texas County Marriage Records 1837–2015; Leonor Z. Brunicardi Border Crossing from Mexico to the US, November 22, 1920; "Deportation Is Asked," *Oregonian*, November 28, 1922, 2; "Latin Beauties Clash," *Oregonian*, December 6, 1922, 4; and "Vice Ring Story Closed," *Oregonian*, April 8, 1923, 21.

78 "Vice Ring Story Closed." For the Mann Act, see D'Emilio and Freedman, *Intimate Matters*, 202–203.

79 "More Aliens on Carpet," *Oregonian*, November 14, 1922, 9; "11 Undesirables Will Be Deported," *Oregonian*, January 23, 1923, 10; and "Latin Beauties Clash."

80 "Women Rivals in Love Battle in Courthouse," *Oregon Journal*, December 6, 1922, 6.

81 Beltrán, *Latina/o Stars in U.S. Eyes*, 17–22.

82 Erickson, "'In the Interest of the Moral Life of Our City'"; and Fronc, *Monitoring the Movies*.

83 "Latin Beauties Clash"; "Vice Ring Story Closed"; and Gardner, *Qualities of a Citizen*, 50–86.

84 Goodman, *Deportation Machine*; Balderrama, *Decade of Betrayal*; and Ngai, *Impossible Subjects*.

85 "'Teddy's All Right,' Friends Declare," *Oregonian*, November 11, 1924, 8; and "Aurora Cowgirl Again Free Has Yearnings for Movies," *Oregon Sunday Journal*, April 8, 1923, Section 1, 13.

86 "Amazon, 15, Craves Life of a Buckaroo," *Sunday Oregonian*, April 8, 1923, Section 1, 14.

87 Frank Gloss, letter to editor, *Aurora Observer*, February 15, 1923, 1; "Aurora Cowgirl Again Free"; "Amazon Craves Life of a Buckaroo"; "'Teddy's All Right'"; "Mother Wants Teddy's Release," *Salem Daily Capital Journal*, February 2, 1923, 1; "Teddy Gloss in Salem," *Oregonian*, February 2, 1923, 6; "Hunger Strike Ended," *Oregonian*, February 5, 1923, 2; and "Pretty Girl Robber 15 Arrives in Salem Strapped to Deputies," *Salem Capital Journal*, February 1, 1923, 1.

88 "Teddy Gloss in Salem'"; "Hunger Strike Ended"; and "Aurora Cowgirl Again Free."

89 Frank Gloss letter to editor; "Mother Wants Teddy's Release"; "Mrs. Gloss Threatens Suit," *Oregonian*, February 2, 1923, 6; "Control Board Paroles 'Teddy,'" *Oregonian*, April 7, 1923, 15; "Amazon Craves Life of a Buckaroo"; and "Aurora Cowgirl Again Free."

90 "City Jail 'Health Hold' Explained by Medic," *Oregon Journal*, January 9, 1970, 4; "'Health Hold' on Prostitutes Challenged," *Oregon Journal*, January 9, 1970, 5; "Portland City Jail 'Closed,'" *Oregon Journal*, June 3, 1972, 5; and "Clean Up Park Blocks, Hotelmen Demand," *Oregon Journal*, September 2, 1972, 1. A year and a half later, Gloss was arrested for riding the railroad without paying in San Diego, presenting as male, and refusing to provide their identity. As Sarah, Gloss married and divorced twice, lived in Clackamas County managing horses until their death in 1983. "Local Girl Is Held in Male Togs," *Oregon Journal*, November 10, 1924, 1; "'Teddy's All Right'"; Oregon, US, State Divorces, 1925–1968, July 7, 1927, and #35662, July 13, 1944; 1940 Census, Barlow Precinct Sheet 6A, Clackamas County, Oregon; and Sarah Gloss Death Record, Certificate 83-14489, Oregon, US, Death Index, 1898–2008.

91 This first group included those for whom both beginning and end dates of incarceration were listed. Detention Homes List of Detainees, AF/9904 A2000-003 Baker Mayor Subject Files, December 31, 1918, PARC; and Dietzler, *Detention Houses and Reformatories*, 33. Kelly Butte/The Cedars was not among the detention homes studied. It's likely that many women used aliases, and it has proved difficult to link any of the inmates listed with other vital records with any certainty.

92 Detention Homes List of Detainees, "Buster Taylor to Leave," *Rogue River Courier*, August 30, 1918, 4.

93 1920 census for The Cedars, Oregon, Multnomah, Troutdale District 0199, Sheets 4B and 5A.

94 Andrew C. Smith, "Report Concerning The Cedars, September 23, 1920,"

Regular Quarterly Meeting of the OSBH, September 23, 1920, 145–146, Vol. 2., Oregon State Board of Health Minutes, 1903–1960, Health Division, 96A/019, OSA.

95 "Bend Officials Here for Inspection of Public Institutions," *Oregon Journal*, December 14, 1920, 3.

96 Murphy's case notes are scattered across Box 7, Bound Volume 8, Old Volume 7, Minutes, November 16, 1917–October 25, 1918; Box 8 Minutes, Old Volume 8, Box 8 Minutes, Old Volume 9, of the OSHS Records, OHS. Hodges surveyed the first year's group of 104 women in *World War I and Urban Order*, 120–121. Stern mentioned several cases in *Trials of Nina McCall*. For New York examples, see Alexander, *"Girl Problem,"* 123–149; and for Toronto, Strange, *Toronto's Girl Problem*, 139–143.

97 Report of the War Work Council, February 21, 1918, Box 7, Bound Volume 8, Old Volume 7, OSHS Records, OHS.

98 Henry Waldo Coe, "Here's to Miss Murphy," *Medical Sentinel* 27, no. 12 (December 1919): 1186–1187; "Local Brevities: Miss Anna Murphy," *Shoshone [Idaho] Journal*, June 24, 1904, 8; "Studies Problems of Working Girl," *Oregon Sunday Journal*, August 3, 1913, Section 1, 7; "Miss Anna Murphy," *Oregonian*, December 31, 1912, 10; Chicago School of Civics & Philanthropy, *Year Book 1912–1913 Bulletin 15*, 16; and Chicago School of Civics and Philanthropy, *Alumni Register 1903–1913, Bulletin 17*, 42.

99 "League Secures Miss Anna Murphy," *Oregonian*, June 2, 1913, 7; "Big Sisterhood Has a Successful Year," *Oregon Sunday Journal*, April 12, 1914, Section 5, 5; Fred Lockley, "What Charities of the City Are Doing," *Oregon Sunday Journal*, January 3, 1915, Pictorial Supplement Section, 5; and "What Catholic Women of Portland Are Doing," *Oregon Sunday Journal*, June 13, 1909, Magazine Section, 4.

100 Gleason (later Sister Miriam Teresa of the Sisters of the Holy Names) was also active in the Catholic Women's League and a student at the Chicago School of Civics & Philanthropy two years before Murphy attended. See Dilg, "'For Working Women in Oregon'"; Freedman, *Maternal Justice*; Eisenberg, *Embracing a Western Identity*, 91–124, for Lowenberg and Neighborhood House; and for Prichard, see Piasecki, "Portland Free Dispensary." Van Waters and Murphy are pictured together in "Two Women Who Are Identified with Social Service Work in Portland," *Oregon Sunday Journal*, April 12, 1914, Section 5, 5.

101 Coe, "Here's to Miss Murphy," 1186.

102 Case 118, June 6, 1919. All of the following are in OSHS Records, OHS.

103 Cases 3, 5, 22, 73, 124, 131.

104 Case 64.

105 Case 93.

106 Cases 132 and B.G.

107 Case 37; and "Colored Women's Council Will Meet," *Sunday Oregonian*, March 24, 1918, Section 3, 12.

108 Case 40; Case 70; and Case A.F.

109 Odem, *Delinquent Daughters*, 118–119; Michel, *Children's Interests/Mother's Rights*, 35–39; "Mrs. Weeks Goes East," *The Advocate*, May 30, 1925, 1; and Jensen, "Lizzie Weeks (1879–1976)."

110 Oregon was not among the twenty-eight states studied. US Interdepartmental Social Hygiene Board, *Manual for the Various Agents*, 78. An appendix on p. 95 reprinted a blank report form used by field agents in the study listed "illegitimate children" and "illegitimate pregnancies" but no data was presented from this category in the study. Dietzler, *Detention Houses and Reformatories*, 34.

111 "Baby Boarding Houses," *Oregon Journal*, July 26, 1920, 6; and Michel, *Children's Interests/Mothers Rights*, 50–90.

112 MacKie Divorce Record 34849, Case 5547 Mackie Ralph W. v. Margaret Divorce Benton County 1916, OSA (divorce record has variant spellings of McKie); "Accused of Non-support," *Oregon Journal*, August 13, 1915, 2; "Two Marriages to Same Man Fail," *Oregonian*, October 23, 1919, 15; and "Mrs, McKie's Condition Serious," *Oregonian*, April 7, 1920, 11.

113 Case 1. Case 11 is one example among many of court parole.

114 Case 66, November 15, 1918.

115 Andrew C. Smith, "Report Concerning The Cedars, September 23, 1920," Regular Quarterly Meeting of the OSBH, September 23, 1920, 145–146, Vol. 2. Board of Health Minutes, OSA; *Oregon Laws* 264 (1919), 408; Health Parole Resolutions Adopted at Special Meeting of the OSBH, May 10, 1921, 185–187; and Regular Quarterly Meeting OSBH August 30, 1920, 136; Vol. 2, Board of Health Minutes, OSA.

116 Case 113a, 204a, and 205a.

117 Health Parole Resolutions; *Oregon Laws* 264 (1919), 437.

118 "Woman Wanted by Health Board Is Found in Albany," *Albany Democrat Herald*, November 16, 1921, 1; and "Liquor Gives Way to Fair Prisoner in Albany Jail Cell," *Oregon Journal*, November 17, 1921, 8.

119 Seeley to Blue, December 3, 1918. Both Rockafellar and Hodges quote Seeley's report, but this interpretation is my own.

120 "Work and Fun on City's Farm Is Health Restorer," *Sunday Oregonian*, May 16, 1920, Magazine Section, 1; Earl C. Brownlee, "'Sunshine Annie,'" *Oregon Sunday Journal*, August 22, 1920, Magazine Section, 3, 7;

NOTES TO PAGES 139–144 / *263*

Hodges, *World War I and Urban Order*, 121–122; and Malacrida, *Special Hell*, 147.

121 Connelly, *Response to Prostitution in the Progressive Era*, 41–44; Kline, *Building a Better Race*, 44–47; and Trent, *Inventing the Feeble Mind*.

122 "Confronting Social Questions Discussed by Federation Head," *Oregon Statesman*, October 28, 1915, 3.

123 George A. Thacher et al., "Final Report of Committee on Detention Home for Women," July 19, 1913, Detention Home, Rushlight Mayor Subject Files, AF/64760, PARC; and Thacher, "Detention Homes Are Recommended," *Sunday Oregonian*, July 20, 1913, Section 1, 14.

124 George A. Thacher, "Feeble-Mindedness and Crime in Oregon," *Journal of Delinquency* 2, no. 4 (July 1917): 211–224. Thacher, *Why Some Men Kill; or, Murder Mysteries Revealed* (Portland, OR: Press of Pacific Coast Rescue and Protective Society, 1919); "Fewer Defectives Object of Social Workers' Meet," *Oregon Sunday Journal*, June 8, 1919, 10; and "Geo. A. Thacher Taken by Death," *Oregon Journal*, October 29, 1919, 1.

125 Millie R. Trumbull, "On the Border-Line," *Welfare: The Journal of Municipal and Social Progress* (April 1914): 14–15, copy at Pacific Northwest Special Collections, University of Washington Libraries, Seattle.

126 For other case studies, see Alexander, *"Girl Problem,"* 80–92; and Strange, *Toronto's Girl Problem*, 113–115.

127 Minutes Executive Committee, OSHS, February 7, 1919, and June 7, 1918, Box 8 Minutes (old vol. 8), OSHS Records, OHS; "Samuel Kohs Dies on Coast; Active in Jewish Social Work," *New York Times*, February 1, 1984, Section B, 10; "Women's Clubs: Dr. Emma Wickstrom," *Oregonian*, June 29, 1917, 12; and "Dr. Emma Maki Wickstrom," *Medical Sentinel* 28, no. 2 (February 1920), 91; and OSHS Records, passim, OHS.

128 Lira, *Laboratory of Deficiency*, 45.

129 Report of the War Work Council February 21, 1918, Box 7, Bound Volume 8, Old Volume 7, OSHS Records, OHS.

130 Cases 1, 66, 178, 189, 97. 94, 123, 47, 15, 169, 130, 21, and 37; and "Discoverer of Ptomaine Germs Explains Origin," *Oregon Sunday Journal*, December 19, 1920, Section 3, 3.

131 US Department of the Interior, *Forty-Ninth Annual Report Board of Indian Commissioners*, 11; Fred A. Baker to Superintendent, Oregon Industrial School for Girls, May 2, 1923, R. B. Goodin to Baker, May 9, 1923, Fred A. Baker telegram to US District Attorney, Oregon, October 26, 1923, File Punishments and Fines, Box 39, Series KL 009: Numerical Correspondence, Records of the Klamath Indian Agency, RG 75, BIA, NARA Seattle.

132 Harwood Hall to L. Vivian Zinn, Mary 23, 1923, Folder Miscellaneous Correspondence 1923, Box 3, CH 04: Correspondence of the Superintendent, 1909–1932, Records of the Chemawa Indian School, RG 75, BIA, NARA Seattle.

133 Quoted in "Women Are Sentenced," *Oregonian*, May 23, 1922, 13.

134 "Cedars Is Tax Waste, Say Critics," *Oregon Journal*, January 23, 1923, 1, 2; "The Cedars," *Oregon Journal*, January 23, 1923, 8; and "Cedars Jobs Medium for Patronage," *Oregon Journal*, January 24, 1923, 1.

135 "Test the Cedars," *Oregon Sunday Journal*, January 28, 1923, Section 2, 2.

136 "Funds Denied Cedars Home," *Oregon Journal*, February 14, 1923, 1; and Stricker, Oregon State Health Officer, to City and County Authorities, March 17, 1923, Sheriff Harley Slusher Correspondence, Clatsop County Historical Society Archives, Astoria, Oregon.

137 1924 Correspondence between Chalcraft and Pacific Coast Rescue and Protective Society officials, Folder 1924 W. G. MacLaren et al., Box 3, Records of the Grand Ronde Siletz Indian Agency, RG 75, BIA, NARA Seattle.

138 "Mental Survey at Industrial School Is Made," *Oregon Sunday Journal*, May 16, 1920, Section 3, 2; and *Oregon Laws* 348 (1929), 397–398. George Painter first identified this shift. See George Painter, "Oregon Sodomy Law," Gay and Lesbian Archives of the Pacific Northwest, notes 84, 85, accessed November 24, 2023, https://www.glapn.org/6070sodomy law.html.

CHAPTER 6 / "INSANE" OR "UNFIT"

1 Article II on Suffrage and Elections, in Carey, *Oregon Constitution*, 404. This was not changed until 1980 with Ballot Measure 2; see "Fix Archaic Portion of State Constitution," *Oregonian*, October 10, 1980, Section B, 10.

2 *Oregon Laws* 78 (1913), 119–133; "Pendleton Asylum Is Now Completed," *Oregon Statesman*, January 1, 1913, 23; "The Care of the Insane," in Larsell, *Doctor in Oregon*, 544–567; "Legislature Receives Governor West's Message," *Oregonian*, January 14, 1913, 5 and full text at Governor Oswald D. West Administration, OSA, accessed November 24, 2023, http://records.sos.state.or.us/ORSOSWebDrawer/Recordhtml/6777846.

3 *Oregon Laws* 104 (1913), 177–178. The Oregon State Hospital Memorial in Salem, adjacent to the Oregon State Hospital and the Oregon State Hospital Museum of Mental Health, commemorates people whose remains were unclaimed and connects families and community with this vital part

of Oregon history. See the many resources at Oregon State Hospital Memorial, accessed November 24, 2023, https://www.oregon.gov/oha/OSH/Pages/Memorial.aspx.

4   *Oregon Laws* 342 (1913), 679–688.

5   "The Care of the Insane," in Larsell, *Doctor in Oregon*; and Goeres-Gardiner, *Inside Oregon State Hospital*.

6   Goeres-Gardiner placed well-researched charts in the appendix and reports on overall population trends throughout *Inside Oregon State Hospital*.

7   See the *Biennial Reports of the Oregon State Board of Control: First*, 47; *Second*, 77; *Third*, 61, 63; *Fourth*, 55, 57; and *Fifth*, 69, 72.

8   Patient File 2251, Box 32, Female Patient Medical Case Files 2200–2260, Oregon State Hospital Female Patient Files 2017A-027, OSA, Salem.

9   Burch, *Committed*.

10   *Oregon Laws* 78 (1913), Section 10, 124.

11   Carey, *On the Margins of Citizenship*, 68; Malacrida, *Special Hell*; Nielsen, "Incompetent and Insane"; Nielsen, *Money, Marriage, and Madness*; Braslow, *Mental Ills and Bodily Cures*; and Trent, *Inventing the Feeble Mind*.

12   *Second Biennial Report Oregon State Board of Control*, women's work, 68; population totals, 66; and laundry, 106.

13   Matron's Reports of Sewing Room for *Biennial Reports of the Oregon State Board of Control: First*, 83; *Second*, 106; *Third*, 85; *Fourth*, 83; and *Fifth*, 92.

14   Largent, "'Greatest Curse of the Race,'" 204, 200–201. A systematic study is beyond the scope of this project but calls for additional research.

15   *Fifth Biennial Report Board of Control*, 61.

16   Largent, "'Greatest Curse of the Race'"; Largent, *Breeding Contempt*; and "Care of the Insane," in Larsell, *Doctor in Oregon*.

17   "Long Illness Is Ended for Dr. Griffith," *Oregon Statesman*, June 15, 1930, 1, 2; "Register of Vanderbilt University 1889–1900" and "Announcement 1890–1891," Vanderbilt University, Nashville, Tennessee, 1890, 68, 69; "Graduated Last Night," *Oregon Statesman*, February 27, 1890, 4; "Returns to Salem," *Salem Capital Journal*, March 6, 1891, 3; and "Social Events," *Daily Capital Journal*, June 3, 1897, 4.

18   "University Notes," *Oregon Statesman*, January 4, 1899, 5; "Fifty-Eighth Year Book of the Willamette University, Salem, Oregon for the Year 1901–1902 with Announcement and Curricula for 1902–1903," Salem, Oregon, 1902, 8; "Medical College," *Weekly Oregon Statesman*, September 6, 1904, 2; "Willamette Medical College," *Salem Capital Journal*, November 28, 1907, 10; and "The Medical College," *Oregon Statesman*, January 1, 1910, 18.

19 "The University of Oregon School of Medicine Catalogue 1921–1922," *University of Oregon Bulletin* 19, no. 8 (October 1922), 31, 34; "The University of Oregon School of Medicine Catalogue 1929–1930," *University of Oregon Bulletin* 27, no. 3 (March 1930), 7, 32; and Larsell, *Doctor in Oregon*, 397, 203.

20 "City News: Was Adjudged Insane" and "Committed to Asylum," *Oregon Statesman*, February 25, 1914, 5.

21 See the introduction for this legislative history.

22 "Oregon State Medical Association Reported Editorially," *Medical Sentinel* 21, no. 10 (October 1913): 1200; "Report of Friday Morning Session, Oregon State Medical Association, September 10, 1913," *Medical Sentinel* 21, no. 10 (October 1913): 1208–1210; "Diagnosis of Insanity," *Medical Sentinel* 21, no. 10 (October 1913): 1173–1175; and William House, "Recoverability of the Insane," *Northwest Medicine* 6, no. 5 (May 1914): 121–125.

23 "Lane County Medical Society," *Medical Sentinel* 21, no. 4 (April 1913): 880–881; "Causes of Insanity," *Oregon Statesman*, November 29, 1914, 13–14; Griffith, "Prevention of Insanity"; "Defective Ones Are Heavy Burden on Civilization," *Oregon Statesman*, May 16, 1915, 19; and "Danger Shown," *Oregon Statesman*, January 18, 1914, 1.

24 Griffith, "Prevention of Insanity."

25 Griffith, "Prevention of Insanity," 2352–2353, 2355; and "Defective Ones Are Heavy Burden on Civilization."

26 Patient File 2251.

27 For context, see Gardner, *Qualities of a Citizen*, 87–99; Ngai, *Impossible Subjects*; Goodman, *Deportation Machine*, 24–28; Baynton, "Disability and the Justification of Inequality in American History"; and "Immigration Bill Recently Passed Is to Increase Powers," *Oregon Journal*, February 19, 1917, 14.

28 *Oregon Laws* 71 (1917), 92–93.

29 Stern, *Eugenic Nation*, 86–92, 87; and Kline, *Building a Better Race*, 58–59.

30 Goodman, *Deportation Machine*, 24.

31 *Board of Control Biennial Reports: First*, 36–37; *Second*, 66; *Third*, 58; *Fourth*, 46; and *Fifth*, 61.

32 "Continued Notes: December 4, 1919," Patient File 2251.

33 "Bonham Inspects Salem Institutions," *Oregon Journal*, March 21, 1921, 2; "Aliens Are Being Weeded Out of the State Institutions," *Oregon Journal*, September 21, 1921, 5; and Goodman, *Deportation Machine*, 28.

34 L. F. Griffith to R. P. Bonham, Patient File 2251.

35 "Continued Notes," Patient File 2251.

NOTES TO PAGES 155–159 / *267*

36 "Responsibility Permit," Patient File 2251.

37 R. B. Bonham to F. L. Griffith, January 17, 1920, Patient File 2251.

38 W.R.W. to Superintendent, Oregon State Hospital, January 19, 1921, Patient File 2251.

39 "Engineer Dies in Car Plunge Near Summit," *San Bernardino County Sun*, October 1, 1926, 13; and "Natural Death Jury Verdict," *Las Vegas Age*, September 4, 1928, 1.

40 "William Gordon Holford," in *Architects of Oregon: A Biographical Dictionary of Architects Deceased—19th and 20th Centuries*, edited by Richard Ellison Ritz, 190–191 (Portland, OR: Lair Hill, 2002); 1920 US Federal Census for William G. Holford Oregon Multnomah Portland District 0103; and 1925 *PCD*, 304.

41 Commitment Record, Patient File 3305, Box 47, Female Patient Medical Case Files 3271-3344, Oregon State Hospital Female Patient Files, 2017A-027, OSA, Salem.

42 "H. Francis Dyruff, 'Great Men of Brooklyn Who Made History: Dr. George Ryerson Fowler,'" *Sunday Brooklyn* [New York] *Times Union*, August 9, 1936, 12, 1, 7A; and Florence Fowler Holford, "Praises Article," letter to editor, *Brooklyn* [New York] *Times Union*, August 31, 1936, 3.

43 Commitment Record and Continued Notes, November 1, 1924, Holford to Steiner November 9, 1924; Holford to Steiner, n.d.; Griffith to Holford, November 14, 1924; Holford to Steiner December 13, 1924; Griffith to Holford, December 15, 1924; and Holford to Steiner, July 6, 1925, Patient File 3305.

44 Griffith to Holcomb, November 14, 1924; Looney to Holcomb, January 14, 1925; and Looney to Ena Wiley, July 18, 1925, Patient File 3305.

45 Report of the Superintendent of the Oregon State Hospital in the Matter of Louise Burbank, Patient File 3305.

46 Stricker to Steiner, March 17, 1925, Patient File 3305.

47 Lafferty to Dear Sir, August 24, 1925; and Looney to Lafferty, August 26, 1925.

48 "Junius V. Ohmart," in Carey, *History of Oregon*, vol. 3, 620; and "Ohmart Disagrees with Ruling of City's Attorney," *Oregon Sunday Journal*, October 10, 1920, 12.

49 Ohmart to Steiner, September 1, 1925, Patient File 3305; and *Oregon Laws* 194 (1923), 280–284.

50 Steiner to Ohmart, September 2, 1925; Steiner to Bonham, September 2, 1925; and Louise Burbank signed sterilization consent form, September 2, 1925—all in Patient File 3305.

51 Alberta passed sterilization legislation in 1928, British Columbia in 1933. McLaren, *Our Own Master Race*, 89–106.

52 Griffith to Ohmart, September 17, 1925, Patient File 3305.

53 Romacly and Lafferty to Steiner, September 21, 1925; Griffith to Romacly, September 23, 1925; Ohmart to Steiner, September 28, 1925; Griffith to Ohmart, September 29, 1925; Griffith to Bonham, September 29, 1925, Patient File 3305.

54 Louise Burbank intake property inventory, November 1, 1924, with Louise Burbank signature upon receipt; W. F. Smith, Acting District Director, Portland Office, Immigration Bureau to Steiner, October 3, 1925; and Bonham to Steiner, October 16, 1925, Patient File 3305.

55 Goodman, *Deportation Machine*, 26–34.

56 Swensen, "Pilgrims at the Golden Gate," 229–263, 234.

57 Goodman, *Deportation Machine*, 27.

58 Burbank had a listing in the *Portland City Directories* for these years with her employment as a maid for W. C. Holford. *PCD* 1927, 354; *PCD* 1929, 385; and *PCD* 1930, 324.

59 Winnie Springer searched for understanding about a nonbinary body but identified as female throughout life. Given this, I use female pronouns to refer to Winnie in this book. I hope that in so doing, I am being respectful of Winnie's experiences and memory.

60 "Graveside Services Due Winnie Pierson," *Corvallis Gazette-Times*, May 22, 1952, 8; "Ballots for Women Song," *Salem Capital Journal*, June 29, 1912, 5; "Woman Suffrage Amendment League Organized," *Monmouth Herald*, August 9, 1912, 1; Winnie Springer, "The Ballots of Men," *Corvallis Gazette-Times*, August 6, 1912, 4; Springer, "The Women Should Have Equal Suffrage," *Corvallis Gazette-Times*, August 7, 1912, 2; and Springer, "Men Haters," *Corvallis Gazette-Times*, August 9, 1912, 4.

61 Winnie Springer testimony, 5; *Springer v. Steiner* (1919) Case File, Oregon Supreme Court, Case Files, 78A-23, 4/2/5/3, Oregon Supreme Court Records, OSA. And see *Springer v Steiner et al.*, 91 Or. Feb 1919, 100–114; and "Court Is Asked to Annul Proceedings in Case of Insanity," *Oregon Journal*, January 4, 1917, 2.

62 Deposition of Perry Joseph Green, May 2, 1917, *Springer v. Steiner* Case File.

63 *Springer v. Steiner Case File*; and Winnie Springer to Ellen Hull, ca. March 1915, Patient File 1427, Box 19, Female Patient Medical Case Files 1370-1439, Oregon State Hospital Female Patient Files. 2017A-027, OSA, Salem.

64 "In the Matter of the Examination and Commitment of Mrs. Winnie Springer, An Insane Person," December 14, 1916, *Springer v. Steiner* Case File, Intake and Discharge materials, Patient File 1427.

65 Winnie Springer to George M. Brown, November 10, 1915; Brown to

Springer, November 22, 1915, Box 17, Folder 19, November 1915, Attorney General Correspondence, Accession 89A-001, Department of Justice Files OSA; and Griffith/Springer Correspondence, November 1915–December 1916, Patient File 1427.

66 "In the Matter of the Examination and Commitment of Mrs. Winnie Springer, An Insane Person," December 14, 1916, *Springer v. Steiner* Case File. Dr. Sanford Whiting was out of the state and was not served. Springer's father William Hull was named but never served. *Springer v. Steiner* 91 Or. Feb 1919, 100–114; "Court Is Asked to Annul Proceedings"; "Record To Be Expunged," *Oregonian*, January 5, 1917, 3; "Woman Sues Father and Others Because She Went to Asylum," *Oregon Journal*, May 9, 1917, 6; and "Woman Sent to Asylum Gets $2500," *Sunday Oregonian*, May 13, 1917, Section 1, 10. A partial transcript of the May 1917 verdict is included in *Springer v. Steiner* Case File.

67 "Woman Sues Father and Others."

68 "Judgment for Defendants," *Oregon Statesman*, December 16, 1917, 5. "Grant Corby," in Colmer and Wood, eds., *History of the Bench and Bar of Oregon*, 114; and Springer Testimony, 35, *Springer v. Steiner* Case File.

69 *Springer v. Steiner* Case File.

70 Springer testimony, 3–10, *Springer v. Steiner* Case File. A copy of the entire complaint in *Springer v. Steiner et al.* is in Patient File 1471 for the formal charges of violation of Springer's due process rights.

71 Springer testimony, 11–18, *Springer v. Steiner* Case File.

72 Springer testimony, 81–90, *Springer v. Steiner* Case File.

73 Springer testimony, 24, *Springer v. Steiner* Case File.

74 Springer testimony, 31–33, *Springer v. Steiner* Case File. Einolf, *America in the Philippines*; Regali, *Torture and Democracy*; and Paul Kramer, "The Water Cure: Debating Torture and Counterinsurgency—a Century Ago," *New Yorker*, February 25, 2008, https://www.newyorker.com /magazine/2008/02/25/the-water-cure.

75 Springer testimony, 26–29, *Springer v. Steiner* Case File.

76 "In the Matter of the Examination and Commitment of Mrs. Winnie Springer"; and "Court Is Asked to Annul Proceedings."

77 *Oregon Laws* 37 (1913), 69–71; and "Teachers Present Statement of Bill," *Oregon Journal*, January 19, 1913, 4.

78 R. B. Goodin, Secretary, Oregon State Board of Control, to George M. Brown, January 9, 1917. This letter was misfiled in Box 17, Folder 28, January 1916, AG Correspondence, OSA.

79 Thad Vreeland to F. L. Griffith, May 14, 1917, Box 20, Folder 20, May 1917, AG Correspondence, OSA.

80 R. E. Lee Steiner to George Brown, May 15, 1917, Box 20, Folder 20, May 1917, AG Correspondence, OSA.

81 *Springer v. Steiner,* 91 Or. Feb 1919, 100–114, 114.

82 Springer testimony, 3; WS [Winnie Springer] to C[lare] G, Springer, March 5 and 6, 1915, *Springer v. Steiner* Case File, Ellen Reasoner Hull to Dr., January 13, 1915, Patient File 1427.

83 WS [Winnie Springer] to R. E. Lee Steiner, March 15, 1915, Patient File 1427.

84 WS [Winnie Springer] to Ellen Reasoner Hull, n.d., Patient File 1427.

85 In a March 1915 letter to Steiner, Marvin wrote that C. G. Springer had contacted her with accusations that the library books she had checked out to his wife had resulted in her commitment. She felt these were books that were safe but was worried and wanted to send alternative books to Springer while she was at OSH. Cornelia Marvin to R. E. Lee Steiner, March 13, 1915, Patient File 1427; and Perry Joseph Green Deposition, 3, *Springer v. Steiner* Case File.

86 Springer testimony, 5, *Springer v. Steiner* Case File.

87 Springer testimony, 4–7, *Springer v. Steiner* Case File. Griffith provided the detail of Springer's detour in a letter to Dr. Curtis Holcomb; Griffith to Holcomb, February 1, 1917, *Springer v. Steiner* Case File, as did Dr. Howard in his testimony, 50, *Springer v. Steiner* Case File.

88 Lipin, *Eleanor Baldwin and the Women's Point of View.*

89 Green Deposition, *Springer v. Steiner* Case File; "1000 Members Coming," *Oregonian,* June 24, 1913, 11; "Religious Meet Opens," *Oregonian,* June 25, 1914, 4; "New Thought Entertainment," *Oregonian,* October 27, 1914, 11; "Dr Perry Joseph Green," *Sunday Oregonian,* January 3, 1915, Section 5, 8; and "Reasons for Opposing New Law," *Oregonian,* October 23, 1913, 10.

90 Green Deposition 3, *Springer v. Steiner* Case File.

91 Green Deposition 3, 7, *Springer v. Steiner* Case File; and "William Hull, Farmer of Bellfountian, Dies Thursday at Albany," *Corvallis Gazette-Times,* December 10, 1920, 1.

92 E[mil]. W[ashington], Howard testimony, 46–51, *Springer v. Steiner* Case File.

93 Eleanor Hull to WS [Winnie Springer] May 13, 1915, note in pencil "Filed May 18, 1915. Not delivered to patient," Patient File 1427.

94 Howard testimony, 55–58, *Springer v. Steiner* Case File.

95 Elizabeth Rogers testimony, 112–113, *Springer v. Steiner* Case File.

96 Boag, *Same-Sex Affairs,* 1–2, 101–105, 167. For the national context, see Chauncey, *Gay New York,* 155–158 and *passim.*

97 The files say nothing about Winnie presenting as male at the Y when requesting a room. The "Clothing Sheet" admission to OSH lists women's clothing. Patient File 1427.

98 Griffith to Holcomb, February 1, 1917, *Springer v. Steiner* Case File. Dr. Prince Wolverton Byrd to C. G. Springer, April 27, 1915, Patient File 1427. Oregon Supreme Court Chief Justice Thomas A. McBride felt "the filthy and profane letters written by her when in the asylum" were grounds for insanity. *Springer v. Steiner*, 91 Or. Feb 1919, 105–106.

99 WS [Winnie Springer] to Steiner, March 15, 1915, *Springer v. Steiner* Case File (emphasis in original).

100 Question List, *Springer v. Steiner* Case File.

101 Letter fragment WS [Winnie Springer] to Ellen R. Hull, ca. March 1915, *Springer v. Steiner* Case File (emphasis in original).

102 Helquist, *Marie Equi*, 198–199, 279n25; Boag, *Re-Dressing America's Frontier Past*, 82, 209n69; and Sueyoshi, *Queer Compulsions*.

103 March 1, 1916, C[lare]. G. S[pringer]. to Griffith; March 2, 1916, Griffith to C[lare]. G. Springer, Patient File 1427.

104 "Teacher Aids Prisoner," *Oregonian*, November 27, 1920, 9; and "Slayer Delays Plea," *Oregonian*, December 4, 1920, 10.

105 "Wife Convenience, Charge," *Oregonian*, May 1, 1919, 22; and "Mrs. Winifred Springer, Secretary State Society for Mental Hygiene," *Sunday Oregonian*, March 30, 1919, Section 5, 9.

106 "Mental Hygiene Is Topic," *Oregonian*, June 28, 1919, 11; and "Social Conference Outlines Reforms," *Sunday Oregonian*, June 29, 1919, Section 1, 16.

107 "William Hull Farmer of Bellfountian Dies Thursday at Albany," 1; "Woman's Parole Revoked: Going to State Hospital," *Oregon Journal*, December 16, 1920, 18; and "Mrs. Springer Committed," *East Oregonian*, December 18, 1920, 3. Winnie's mother, Ellen R. Hull, her advocate while at OSH, had died in 1918. "Mrs. Amelia Reasoner Was Well Known," *Oregon Journal*, July 25, 1918, 13. Patient Population Register 1913–1933, 96, 98, 88A-66, Eastern Oregon State Hospital Records, 88A-66, OSA

108 *Arizona Educational Directory* 1924–1925, 71, and *Arizona Educational Directory* 1925–1926, 78 (full text for these directories is at HathiTrust Digital Library, www.hathitrust.org); T. H. Stice, Medical Director and Superintendent, Napa State Hospital to Medical Superintendent Oregon State Hospital, September 10, 1932; Patient File 1427; "F. E. Woitke Obituary," *Los Angeles Times*, July 9, 1943, 16; Superintendent Patton State Hospital to Superintendent Oregon State Hospital, April 12, 1949, Patient File 1427; and "Graveside Services Due Winnie Pierson."

CHAPTER 7 / JAPANESE OREGONIAN WOMEN'S RESISTANCE

1   Lee, *Making of Asian America*, 124, 109–136. See also Lee, *America for Americans*, 183–219; Daniels, *Politics of Prejudice*; and Molina, *Fit To Be Citizens?*.

2   Smith, *Japanese American Midwives*, 38.

3   Lee, *Making of Asian America*, 132–133; and Barkan, *From All Points*, 217–218.

4   Azuma, "Oregon's Issei," 336–339. Oregon's Alien Land Act was repealed in *Kenji Namba v. McCourt* in 1949. 185 Ore. 579, 204 P. 2d. 569. Robinson, "Kenji Namba vs. McCourt," *Densho Encyclopedia;* and Villazor, "Rediscovering *Oyama v. California*.

5   Rosenbloom, "Policing the Borders of Birthright Citizenship," 311–330, 321.

6   Senate Joint Memorial No. 1, *Oregon Laws* (1920), 116.

7   "Westerners Unite to Curb Japanese," *New York Times*, April 21, 1921, 15; and "McNary, Sinnott Put on Committee," *Oregon Journal*, April 22, 1921, 1. Rosenbloom, "Policing the Borders of Birthright Citizenship," 318, quotes the *New York Times* article.

8   Ngai, *Impossible Subjects*, 21–55; and Nagae "Asian Women."

9   *Fourteenth Census of the United States, 1920, State Compendium, Oregon* (Washington, DC: GPO, 1925), 25.

10 Johnson, "Anti-Japanese Legislation in Oregon," 180.

11 Tamura, *Hood River Issei*, 48–49; Azuma, "Oregon's Issei," 332; Gardner, *Qualities of a Citizen*, 17; and Nakamura, "Picture Brides."

12 "An Act Creating the Bureau of Labor Statistics and Inspector of Workshops and Factories," *Oregon Laws* (1903), 205–209, 206–207.

13 See *Biennial Report of the Bureau of Labor Statistics and Inspector of Factories and Workshops of the State of Oregon* for these years.

14 "Foreign Nations Represented in Oregon," Oregon Secretary of State, *Blue Book and Official Directory, 1921–1922* (Salem: SPO, 1921), 162–163.

15 *PCD* 1918, 648. For a general discussion, see Ichioka, *The Issei*, 156–164.

16 Katagiri, "Oshu Nippo"; and "*Oshu Nippo* Project," Japanese American Museum of Oregon. The original pages are digitized, and the translations transcribed and posted on the site. *Oshu Nippo* materials cited here may be found at https://jamo.org/collections/oshu-nippo-translation-project/, accessed November 24, 2024.

17 "The Conditions of the Japanese within the Jurisdiction of the Japanese Consulate in Portland," *Oshu Nippo*, New Year's Special Edition, January 1, 1918, 3.

18 "Immigration Board in S. F.," *Oregon Statesman*, July 8, 1920, 1.

19 "Japanese Births Show Material Gain in Oregon," *Oregon Journal*, August 5, 1920, 3; "2815 Acres Owned by 3493 Japanese," *Oregonian*, August 5, 1920, 1, 3; and "Japanese Invite Thorough Inquiry, Declares Raker," *Oregon Journal*, August 7, 1920, 2.

20 W. H. Hudson, "Japanese Situation, General," October 4, 1921, 1–9; and Tom M. Word, "Japanese Residents of Hood River Valley, October 7, 1921," 1–4; File 1766-Z-403 DJ, Japanese Americans in Oregon cities, Box 562, RG 165, Military Intelligence Division, Correspondence 1917–1941, Entry NM-84 65, NARA.

21 Yasui, "Nikkei in Oregon," 238; Tamura, *Hood River Issei*, 91–92; Kessler, *Stubborn Twig*, 73–74; Stearns, "Settlement of the Japanese in Oregon," 263–64; and "Frank Davey Dies," *Oregon Statesman*, February 18, 1937, 1, 2.

22 Yasui, "Nikkei in Oregon," 238.

23 Davey, *Report on the Japanese Situation*, 3–4.

24 Davey, *Report on the Japanese Situation*, 5.

25 Davey, *Report on the Japanese Situation*, 8, 9.

26 Davey, *Report on the Japanese Situation*, 14, 6.

27 Molina, *Fit To Be Citizens?* 55–57.

28 "Oregon State Japanese Population and Statistics Table (Survey of June 1919)," *Oshu Nippo*, January 1, 1920, 17; and *Portland Vice Commission Report*, 46.

29 Oharazeki, *Japanese Prostitutes in the North American West*. See also Nakamura, "Issei Women and Work."

30 Teruko Takeshi, "New Year's Letter from America," *Oshu Nippo*, January 1, 1922, 16.

31 I compiled a database of Japanese American Women Barbers from the 1920 and 1930 Federal Census. For women barbers in Hawai'i, see Nakamura, "Issei Women and Work."

32 Julie A. Willett argues that the stigma of prostitution was one of the reasons for the development of a separate women's beauty shop culture. See Willett, *Permanent Waves*, 45–48.

33 "$175 in Silks Sold for $70 Traps Thief," *Sunday Oregonian*, October 24, 1920, Section 1, 11.

34 *Portland Vice Commission Report*, 8, 32–33, 34–35, 45, 61, 65, and 67.

35 "Mental Examination for Marriage To Be Proposed at Session," *Oregon Statesman*, January 8, 1921, 1; and "Doctor Suggests Sterilization of Japanese Women," *Oregon Journal*, January 9, 1921, 6.

36 "If Thy Right Hand Offend Thee, Cut It Off," *Oregon Statesman*, February

2, 1921, 4; and "Open Forum," *Capital Journal*, February 3, 1921, 4.

37 Owens-Adair, *Human Sterilization*, 218.

38 Ichioka, *The Issei*, 168.

39 Iwao Oyama, "Resisting the Anti-Japanese Movement and Solemn Actions for Our Compatriots," *Oshu Nippo*, January 1, 1922, 10.

40 Masuo Yasui, "Request to Japanese Ladies," ca. 1920, in Yasui Brothers Company Records, MSS, OHS, quoted in Eiichiro Azuma, "The Struggle Against Exclusion," chapter 5 in *In This Great Land of Freedom: The Japanese Pioneers of Oregon*, 1993, Japanese American National Museum.

41 Susan Smith makes this important general point in *Japanese American Midwives*, 38, 102. The following discussion builds on Smith's assertion by analyzing specific birthing choices as part of what she termed the "special meaning" of birth certificates for Issei women and their families.

42 Tamura, *Hood River Issei*, 113; and Smith, *Japanese American Midwives*, 99–100.

43 Pearson, *Birth Certificate*; Robertson, *Passport in America*, 102–109; S. Shapiro, "Development of Birth Registration and Birth Statistics in the United States," *Population Studies* 4, no. 1 (June 1950): 86–111; and Wilbur, *Federal Registration Service of the United States*.

44 "The Need of Accurate Vital Statistics," *Northwest Medicine*, June 6, 1914, 181; Edith Knight Holmes, "Registration of Births and Deaths Gains Attention of Clubwomen," *Sunday Oregonian*, January 17, 1915, Section 3, 10; "Births and Deaths To Be Registered," *Salem Capital Journal*, September 2, 1915, 6; "An Act to Establish a State Board of Health," *Oregon Laws* (1903), 82–86; and *Oregon Laws* 268 (1915), 376–388. Oregon qualified as part of the census-related national death registration area in 1918 and the national birth registration area in 1919, making state figures reportable to the federal government. See Shapiro, "Development of Birth Registration," 94; and *Biennial Reports of the State Board of Health: Seventh*, 3–5; *Eighth*, 3–5; and *Ninth*, 7. See Pearson, *Birth Certificate*, 54–58, for model law context.

45 I created a Birth Certificate Database by consulting all the Oregon birth certificate records for major counties in which Japanese Oregonians might have lived in 1917 and 1918. Records available at the OSA and Ancestry.com.

46 Larsell, *Doctor in Oregon*, 302; "Brief Local Matters: Articles of Incorporation," *Hood River Glacier*, November 23, 1905, 7; "Hood River Will Have New Hospital," *Hood River Glacier*, November 30, 1905, 7; and "Writes about New Hospital," *Hood River Glacier*, February 15, 1906, 6. Announcements about births at the Cottage Hospital appear with regu-

larity. See, for example, "Brief Local Mention: Born," *Hood River Glacier*, November 8, 1917, 7. Howard Dumble was one of the incorporators.

47 Tamura, *Hood River Issei*, 103.

48 Smith, *Japanese American Midwives*, 78.

49 Birth Certificate Database; and Tamura, *Hood River Issei*, 102.

50 "Dr. and Mrs. Dumble Hold Anniversary," *Hood River Glacier*, October 11, 1923, 2; and "Dumble Wins in the City Election," *Hood River Glacier*, November 12, 1914, 1.

51 Birth Certificate Database.

52 "Hood River, Oregon," *American Medical Directory 1918*, 6th ed. (Chicago: American Medical Association, 1918), 1322.

53 Tamura, *Hood River Issei*, 103.

54 Dr. Homer Yasui, interview II with Margaret Barton Ross, Portland, Oregon, October 10, 2003, Segment 9, Oregon Nikkei Endowment Collection, Densho Digital Archive, Densho ID: denshovh-yhomer-02, accessed November 24, 2023, https://ddr.densho.org/media/ddr-one-7/ddr-one-7 -27-transcript-3744bcdf97.htm. Kessler, *Stubborn Twig*, 94.

55 Birth Certificate Database; and "Yamahiro Heads Truckers' Agency," *Hood River Glacier*, February 7, 1918, 6.

56 Birth Certificate Database. Yamaguchi and Uchida had few births during this period, and so they both may have offered the two options to women in other years of their practices.

57 Rin Miura, interview with Michiko Kornhauser, February 11, 2003, Densho Digital Archive Japanese American Museum of Oregon, Densho ID: denshovh-mrin-01-0012, accessed November 24, 2023, https://ddr .densho.org/interviews/ddr-one-7-5-11/?tableft=segments.

58 Smith, *Japanese American Midwives*, passim, 78–80, 80.

59 *American Medical Directory 1918*, 1324–1328; and Birth Certificate Database.

60 Birth Certificate Database; *American Medical Directory 1918*, 1328; 1920 US Federal Census for Charles Zeebuyth, Oregon, Multnomah, Portland District 0092, Sheet 4A; and "The Portland Sanitarium," *PCD* 1918, 1394. The Portland Sanitarium was a Seventh-Day Adventist general hospital.

61 Birth Certificate Database; *American Medical Directory 1918*, 1325; "Dr. Ralph S. Fisher Is Army Captain," *Oregon Journal*, October 26, 1918, 5; US, World War I Draft Registration Cards, 1917–1918 for Ralph Stephen Fisher, Oregon, Portland City 02 Draft Card F. Fisher left for service with the Army Medical Corps in October 1918 and so he may have attended more Issei women's births in years when in full-time residence.

62 See "Memorable Manitobans: Jessie Margaret McGavin (1866–1952),"

Manitoba Historical Society, accessed November 24, 2023, https://www.mhs.mb.ca/docs/people/mcgavin_jm.shtml; and "Death Claims Dr. McGavin," *Oregonian*, March 2, 1952, 29. For a previous book project I investigated Multnomah County death records for the 1907–1909 period. During this time McGavin signed twenty-three death certificates and ten of those were Chinese or Japanese Americans. And of those ten, eight were infants or children under two years of age. Death Certificates, Multnomah County, Boxes 5–8, 10–11, Accession 91A-7, Health Division, Portland Death Records, OSA, Salem, Oregon. McGavin attended the 1912 birth of Portland aviator Hazel Ying Lee. Trish Hackett Nicola, "Hazel Ying Lee: Portland Female Aviator," Chinese Exclusion Act Case Files Blog, accessed November 24, 2023, https://chineseexclusionfiles.com/2018/03/26/hazel-ying-lee-portland-female-aviator/.

63   University of Oregon, *University of Oregon Medical School, Portland, Oregon, Catalogue of the Thirty-Second Session, 1918–1919* (Eugene: University of Oregon Press, 1919), 8, 9.

64   "Health Office Plans to Clean Up City," *Oregonian*, November 6, 1918, 16; and T. R. Ratcliff, Patient Ledger and Public Auditorium Report, December 20, 1918, and January 31, 1919, Container B/1030—Baker Mayor Subject Files—Inc—Inv, AF/6679, 0205-01 1918, A2000-003, 8/41 04-07-68, PARC.

65   Birth Certificates 1–2434 and 2–134, Portland, Multnomah County, 1918.

66   "Young Japanese Midwife Wants Position with Lady Physician," *Oregonian*, January 8, 1917, 15.

67   Birth Certificate 1-1116, Portland, Multnomah County, 1918.

68   Birth Certificate 2-30, Portland, Multnomah County, 1918.

69   Birth Certificate Database for the information that follows.

70   Hughes, the long-serving mayor of Gresham, became a founding director of Oregon Anti-Japanese, Inc. in 1944, a group opposed to Japanese Oregonians returning to the state after wartime incarceration. He reportedly refused to deliver an Issei baby after Pearl Harbor. Robin Franzen, "Gresham Buries Monument Project for a Former Mayor," *Oregonian*, March 17, 2006, Section D, 1, 4.

71   Birth Certificates 55 and 65, Multnomah County, 1917; "'Medicos' Graduate," *Oregonian*, June 9, 1916, 16; and 1920 Census for Tokugi Hirata California, Los Angeles, Los Angeles Assembly District 63, District 0186, Sheet 8B.

72   Birth Certificate 199, Polk County, 1917; and Birth Certificate 363, 364, Clatsop County, 1917.

73   Birth Certificate 166, Deschutes County, 1918.

74 Birth Certificates 30, 42, Lake County, 1917

75 Ichioka, *The Issei*, 168–169; and Nakano, *Japanese American Women*, 43–44.

76 Tei Endow quoted in Tamura, *Hood River Issei*, 106–107, 275.

77 Tamura, *Hood River Issei*, 102–105.

78 Nakamura, "Issei Women and Work," 120, 145.

79 For overviews, see Azuma, "Oregon's Issei," 321–332; and Yasui, "Nikkei in Oregon," 233–234.

80 Miyoshi Noyori, interview with Linda Tamura, May 28, 29, 30, 31, 1986, in Dee, Oregon, and Sacramento, California, translation Mamoru Noji, quote from Tape 2/7 Side A, May 28, 1986, SR 0980, OHS. Tamura quotes part of her interview with Noyori on this topic in *Hood River Issei*, 83–84, and with Nishimoto, 99–100.

81 Kazuo Ito, *Issei: A History of Japanese Immigrants in North America*, translated by Shinichiro Nakamura and Jean S. Girard (Seattle, WA: Japanese Community Service, 1973), 499, quoted in Iwatsuki and Tamura, "Making of an American," 513.

82 1920 Census for Sowa Uchimada, Oregon, Benton Kings Valley, District 0011 2, Sheets 2A and 2B.

83 Yada, "Yada Family," 96–99; "Japanese Concern Will Handle Oregon Products," *Oregon Statesman*, November 8, 1919, 2; and "Officers Are Elected by Japanese Celery Growers," *Oregon Statesman*, February 17, 1924, 3.

84 1920 Census, Oregon, Josephine, Slate Creek District, 0208, Sheet 9A.

85 1920 Census, Oregon, Deschutes, Bend, District 0031, Sheet 5A; and Sanborn Fire Insurance Map, Bend, Oregon, February 1920, Image 7, Library of Congress, Washington, DC, accessed November 24, 2023, http://hdl .loc.gov/loc.gmd/g4294bm.g4294bm_g073281920.

86 1920 Census for Sumino Fujii, Oregon, Benton Bellfountain District 0003, Sheet 3A.

87 Henry Sakamoto, "Japantown, Portland (Nihonmachi)"; and Toll, "Permanent Settlement," 19–43.

88 George Azumano, interview with Stephan Gilchrist, September 20, 2004, Segment 2, Oregon Nikkei Endowment Collection, Densho Digital Archive, accessed November 24, 2023, https://ddr.densho.org/media/ddr -one-7/ddr-one-7-32-transcript-d9d1264842.htm; 1920 Census for Satsuki Azumano, Oregon, Multnomah, Portland District 0026, Sheet 1B; and Hatsutaro and Satsuki Azumano, Oregon Bureau of Labor, *Census: Japanese Population in Oregon*, 8.

89 1920 Census for Suzu and Tagae Yamada, Oregon, Multnomah, Portland District 0005 Sheet 10B; 1930 Census for Suzu and Kho T. Yamada, Ore-

gon, Multnomah, Portland (Districts 1–219) District 0011, Sheet 9B; 1925 *PCD*, 1690; and 1930 *PCD*, 1786.

90 Birth Certificate 2–1270, Multnomah 1918; and 1920 Census for Suge Teshima, Oregon, Multnomah, Portland District 0028, Sheet 1A.

91 1920 Census for Tomo Kiyohiro, Oregon, Multnomah, Portland District 0028, Sheet 2A; Tomo and Junichi Kiyohiro and children Masaaki, Yukio, Kimiyo, Hiroshi, in Oregon Bureau of Labor, *Census: Japanese Population in Oregon*, 34. Tomo gave birth to Kimiyo in Japan in 1924; and 1930 Census for Tomo Kiyohiro, Oregon, Multnomah, Portland (Districts 1–219) District 0039, Sheet 15B. Kiyohiro was a barber for all of her life. See "Tomo Kiyohiro Obituary," *Spokane Chronicle*, July 19, 1977, 18.

92 Natsu Sato, Midwife, 1918 *PCD*, 1099; and 1920 Census for Natsu Sato, Oregon, Multnomah, Portland District 0130, Sheet 10B.

93 1930 Census, Oregon, Marion, Salem District 0057, Sheet 8A.

94 "Japanese Hand Laundry Salem, Oregon c. 1918–1919," print from Trover Negative from State Library of Oregon, Willamette Heritage Center Collections X2011.003.0072. My appreciation to Kylie Pine for her assistance with this image.

95 I compared a Cronise studio image of the Nakamuras with the laundry photograph. See "T Nakamura and Family of Salem, Oregon, January 14, 1917," #0144G011, Cronise Collection, OHS; and 1920 Census for Toya Nakamura, Oregon, Marion, Riverview District 0340, Sheet 7B.

96 I made another comparison with a Cronise photograph of the Mitomas. "J Mitomo [sic] and Family of Independence, Oregon, December 4, 1917," # 0142G026, Cronise Collection, OHS; and Birth Certificates 1–1710, Multnomah 1913, 12 Marion-Umatilla 1917, Polk, Independence.

97 Birth Certificates 47 and 48, Marion-Umatilla 1916.

98 For a discussion of these patterns in Seattle, see Yanagisako, *Transforming the Past*, 41–51. Smith, in *Japanese American Midwives*, has case studies that reflect these patterns.

99 1921 Washington, US, Arriving and Departing Passenger and Crew Lists, 1882–1965, for Kikuno and Kichisaburo Hirabayashi M1383 Arriving Seattle, 1890–1957, 058; and *PCD* 1923, 824, 1857.

100 *PCD* 1926, 717, 773; and Kichisaburo and Kikuno Hirabayashi, in Oregon Bureau of Labor, *Census: Japanese Population in Oregon*, 18.

101 "Japantown in the Center: Panama Hotel, Kisaburo Hirabayashi, Owner," *Oshu Nippo*, Hotel Special, August 15, 1925, 7. Translators used Kisaburo for Kichisaburo.

102 *PCD* 1928, 791.

103 Members of the Japanese School Board and Japanese Association down-

played the vandalism as not worthy of an "international incident." See "Youthful Vandals Destroy Property," *Oregonian*, August 30, 1927, 1; "Accused of Vandalism," *Oregonian*, August 31, 1927, 11; "Damage to School Laid to Bad Boys," *Oregonian*, September 1, 1927, 6; and "Query on School Fails," *Oregonian*, September 9, 1927, 7.

104 *Oregon Laws* 163 (1923), 232–233; and Johnson, "Anti-Japanese Legislation in Oregon," 200.

105 1920 Census for Mitsuyo and Katsutaro Uyeto, Oregon, Multnomah, Portland, District 0006; Washington, Marriage Records, 1854–2013, for K. Uyeto and Mitsu Suginato, Pierce, Marriages, 1914 September–December; US, World War I Draft Registration Cards, 1917–1918, for Katsutaro Uyeto, Oregon, Portland City, 01 Draft Card U.

106 Azuma, "Oregon's Issei," 315–367, 319; Sakamoto, "Japantown"; and 1920 Census for Uyeto.

107 "South Portland," *Oshu Nippo*, January 1, 1918, 27.

108 Senichi Tomihiro, "The General Economy and Compatriot Business Now and in the Future," *Oshu Nippo*, January 1, 1922, 8.

109 See "Morals Squad Hit," *Oregonian*, July 14, 1916, 20, for an example of entrapment.

110 "Liquor Seizures Heavy," *Oregonian*, December 31, 1919, 9; "Prohibition Violators Arrested," *Oregon Journal*, March 3, 1919, 16; and *Oregon Laws* 141 (1915), Section 19, 130.

111 Katsutaro listed his nephew on his September 1919 arrival form for Seattle. Washington, Passenger and Crew Lists, 1882–1965, for Katsutaro Uyeto M1383 Arriving Seattle, 1890–1957 042; and *PCD* 1920, 1455. They listed Katsutaro ("K. Uyeto") for 1921.

112 "Activities of Portland's City Hall," *Oregon Sunday Journal*, January 9, 1921, Section 2, 6; "Commissioners and Mayor in Clash on Policies for Police," *Oregon Journal*, January 22, 1921, 5; and "License System Will Be Extended to Cigar Stands," *Oregon Journal*, July 29, 1921, 3.

113 Agent T. M. Word, "List of Japanese That Pay City Licenses, Portland, Oregon," November 12, 1921, 6, File 1766-Z-403, Folder 1766-Z-400 to 1766-Z-410, Box 562, RG 165 Military Intelligence Division, Correspondence 1917–1941 Entry NM-84 65, NARA; and Engeman, "Portland Public Market."

114 "Revocation Is Blocked," *Oregonian*, October 15, 1921, 14.

115 "Council Bars Japanese," *Oregonian*, March 3, 1921, 10.

116 "Japanese Hotel Keepers Are Barred from Portland," *Eugene Guard*, March 9, 1921, 7; and "Japanese Make Protest," *Oregonian*, March 9, 1921, 4. For more on the Japanese Association, see Azuma, "Oregon's Issei," 334–335.

117 "Veteran Pool Hall Man Is Deprived of License," *Oregon Journal*, March 17, 1921, 3. The *Oregon Journal* was often critical of the city police force.

118 "Japanese Wears Button; His Hotel License Extended," *Oregon Journal*, April 1, 1921, 8.

119 "City Hall Briefs," *Oregon Journal*, May 4, 1921, 3.

120 Minutes of Portland City Council Meeting May 11, 1921, Volume 70, May 4, 1921–October 3, 1921, 57, Microfilm Copy, PARC. For Stevenson, see Leeson, *Rose City Justice*, 81–82, and "John H. Stevenson," in Colmer and Wood, eds., *History of the Bench and Bar of Oregon*, 229.

121 "Woman Is Accused of 'Sassing' Police; Put on Probation," *Oregon Journal*, May 12, 1921, 3.

122 "Woman Is Accused of 'Sassing' Police."

123 "Woman Is Accused of 'Sassing' Police."

124 There are no additional English-language records for the Uyetos. It appears that the couple returned to Japan.

125 "Legion Asks That City Plans Specify Work by Americans," *Oregon Journal*, March 25, 1921, 7; "Alien Labor Plan Hit," *Oregonian*, March 26, 1921, 11; "American Labor Preferred," *Oregon Journal*, March 26, 1921, 2; "Measure Would Bar Foreigners from City Work," *Oregon Journal*, April 5, 1921, 6; "New Ordinance Easier on Alien Labor for City," *Oregon Journal*, April 22, 1921, 3; and "Aliens Are Denied License Privilege," *Oregon Journal*, July 7, 1921, 1.

126 "Seek to Enjoin City Officials in License Case," *Oregon Journal*, September 24, 1921, 3; and "Man Appeals to Court for Soft Drink License," *Oregon Journal*, September 22, 1921, 18.

127 "Council Puzzles Over Alien's Revoked License," *Oregon Journal*, October 15, 1921, 11; and "Revocation Is Blocked."

128 "Report of the City Attorney," in *Mayor's Message and Annual Reports for the Fiscal Year Ending November 30, 1921* (Portland: City of Portland, 1922), 32; "May Deny Aliens Work," *Oregon Journal*, May 24, 1922, 2; "Bar Aliens Is Demand," *Oregonian*, June 8, 1922, 7; and "To Ask Council to Confine Licenses to American Citizens," *Oregon Journal*, June 8, 1922, 9.

129 Jackson, *Ku Klux Klan in the City*, 207; and Saalfeld, *Forces of Prejudice*, 37–40.

130 "Representatives 18th District: Thos. H. Hurlburt," *Oregon Voter*, May 17, 1924, 27; and "Thos. H. Hurlburt," *Oregon Voter*, April 26, 1924, 15–18. Sydney Teiser, lawyer for George Goritzan, had been Hurlburt's opponent in the June primary. "Semi-Official Ballot Returns Filed," *Oregon Journal*, June 7, 1922, 2.

131 "Thos. H. Hurlburt," *Oregon Voter*, December 30, 1922, 89–90; "Sargent

Building Is Leased at $120,000," *Oregon Sunday Journal,* June 19, 1921, Section 3, 1; and *PCD* 1920, 719.

132   HB 154, *Journals of the Senate and the House of the Thirty-Second Legislative Assembly Regular Session* (Salem, OR: SPO, 1923).

133   "Swatting the Aliens," *Oregon Voter,* February 17, 1923, 10–11; and "To Ask Council to Confine Licenses to American Citizens," *Oregon Journal,* June 8, 1922, 9. For patriotic societies, see Gordon, *Second Coming of the KKK,* 141.

134   *Oregon Laws* 163 (1923), 232–233.

135   "Swatting the Aliens"; Johnson discusses Hurlburt in "Anti-Japanese Legislation in Oregon," 200. Azuma notes the law in "Oregon's Issei," 339.

136   "Swatting the Aliens." During the debate on HB 34, the successful anti-Japanese land act, Hurlburt again discussed the "322 Japanese-operated businesses." See "Ousting the Japanese," *Oregon Voter,* January 27, 1923, 37–39, 38.

137   "Swatting the Aliens." For Woodward, see Jackson, *Ku Klux Klan in the City,* 207; and Saalfeld, *Forces of Prejudice,* 38; "Pro-German Books Will Be Interned," *Oregonian,* June 13, 1918, 4; "H. L. Corbett Resigns," *Oregonian,* August 9, 1918, 7; and "Civic Leader Long Active in Portland," *Oregon Journal,* October 7, 1940, 5.

138   "Swatting the Aliens." George Lovejoy was previously married to physician and activist Esther Pohl Lovejoy. They divorced in 1920. See Jensen, *Oregon's Doctor to the World.*

139   Birth Certificates, Marion-Umatilla 1917, State #110 for Troutdale farm; and *PCD* 1920, 813, for fruit vendor. Agent Word had her on his 1921 "List of Japanese that Pay City Licenses," 4.

140   *PCD* 1923, "Mrs. M. Kojima, Fremont Hotel," 953; "Bunch of Licenses Killed by Council," *Oregonian,* June 1, 1923, 4; "City News in Brief: Council Defers Action," *Oregonian,* June 21, 1923, 9; and *PCD* 1924, "Mrs. M. Kojima, Fremont Hotel," 985.

141   See introduction and also Peggy Pascoe's discussion of the 1909 case of Helen Emery and Gunjiro Aoki in Pascoe, *What Comes Naturally,* 87–91.

142   Jenkins as quoted in "Hotels Clean Up by Police Ordered," *Oregonian,* December 4, 1923, 15.

143   *PCD* 1925, "Mrs. M. Kojima, Fremont Hotel," 931; and "Hotel License Opposed," *Oregonian,* May 12, 1925, 9.

144   *George v. City of Portland* (1925), 114 Or. 418, 235 P. 681; "Aliens Want Licenses," *Oregonian,* February 3, 1924, 13. Article 1, Section 31 of the Oregon Constitution was repealed by H.J.R. 16, 1969 adopted by voters May 26, 1970. *Oregon Blue Book,* Current Oregon Constitution with Index, p.

7, accessed November 24, 2023, https://sos.oregon.gov/blue-book /Documents/oregon-constitution.pdf.

145 Goodman, *Deportation Machine*, 14–20, 208–209, 208.

CONCLUSION

1 "'Health Hold' on Prostitutes Challenged," *Oregon Journal*, January 9, 1970, 5; and "City Jail 'Health Hold' Explained by Medic," *Oregon Journal*, January 9, 1970, 4.

2 Goodman, *Deportation Machine*.

3 Largent uses the term "tenacity" for Oregon policymakers in *Breeding Contempt*, 65–66.

4 Doroshow, "Wassermann before Wedding Bells," 145; and Brandt, *No Magic Bullet*, 174–176.

5 "Bill Requiring Marriage License Applicants Medically Examined, Physically and Mentally," in Oregon Secretary of State, *Oregon Voter Pamphlet General Election 1938* (Salem: SPO, 1938), 12–15. "These Are the Laws Which the People Passed," *Oregon Sunday Journal*, November 13, 1938, Section 3, 6; and Oregon Secretary of State, *Initiative, Referendum, and Recall Ballot Results*.

6 US Public Health Service, *Premarital Health Examination Legislation*, 80–82.

7 Doroshow, "Wassermann before Wedding Bells," 142.

8 "House Kills Prenuptial Medical Tests," *Oregon Journal*, May 22, 1981, 5; "VD Test Not Required to Wed," *Corvallis Gazette-Times*, June 3, 1981, 15; and Brandt, *No Magic Bullet*, 213.

9 Pascoe, *What Comes Naturally*.

10 Horton, "People First: In the Shadow of Fairview" and the OPB documentary *In the Shadow of Fairview*.

11 John A. Kitzhaber, "Proclamation of Human Rights Day, and Apology for Oregon's Forced Sterilization of Institutionalized Patients," December 2, 2002, State of Oregon Library, https://digital.osl.state.or.us/islandora /object/osl%3A99742; and Human Rights Day, United Nations, accessed November 24, 2023, https://www.ohchr.org/en/about-us/human-rights -day.

Bibliography

ARCHIVAL AND MANUSCRIPT COLLECTIONS

Administrative Board Room Collection. Multnomah County Public Library Isom Building, Portland, Oregon.

Albee Mayor Subject Files. Accession A2000-003. PARC, Portland, Oregon.

Attorney General Correspondence. Accession 89A-001. Department of Justice Files. OSA, Salem, Oregon.

Baker Mayor Subject Files. Accession A2000-003. PARC, Portland, Oregon.

Cancelled Voter Registration Cards, 1908–2010. Multnomah County Election Records. Multnomah County Archives, Portland, Oregon.

City Auditor City Recorder. Council Ordinances. AF/53290. PARC, Portland, Oregon.

City Auditor City Recorder. Council Minutes, 1917–1921. Microfilm Copy. PARC, Portland, Oregon.

City of Astoria, Oregon. Council Minutes, Volume 4: February 1917–January 1919. Astoria Public Library Collection, Astoria, Oregon.

Council of National Defense, Committee on Women's Defense Work. RG. 62. NARA, College Park, Maryland.

Court of Domestic Relations, 1919–1921. Board of County Commissioners, Chair's Office Archival Records, Departmental Files 1913–1970. Multnomah County Archives, Portland, Oregon.

Derthick Club Records. Accession 28505. OHS, Portland, Oregon.

Eastern Oregon State Hospital Records. 88A-66. OSA, Salem, Oregon.

Edward Cookingham Papers, 1900–1948. MSS 2658. OHS, Portland, Oregon.

Japanese Americans in Oregon Cities. File 1766-Z-403. Entry NM-84 65DJ.

Military Intelligence Division, Correspondence 1917–1941. RG 165. NARA, College Park, Maryland.

Japanese American Museum of Oregon. Densho Digital Archive. https://ddr.densho.org/.

Levi Pennington Papers. George Fox University Archives, Newberg, Oregon.

Lola Greene Baldwin Papers. Collection 388. OHS, Portland, Oregon.

Multnomah County Board of County Commissioners Minutes. Multnomah County Archives. Portland, Oregon.

Multnomah County Circuit Court Files. Multnomah County Courthouse, Portland, Oregon.

Multnomah County Court Records. Multnomah County Courthouse, Portland, Oregon.

Multnomah County Poor Farm Records. Multnomah County Archives, Portland, Oregon.

National Council of Jewish Women Minutes, Rosters, Ledgers, 1896–1985. Oregon Jewish Museum and Center for Holocaust Education, Portland, Oregon.

Old German Files 1909–1921. Investigative Reports of the Bureau of Investigation 1908–1922. M1085. NARA, College Park, Maryland.

Oregon Federation of Women's Clubs Records, Box 174. University of Oregon Special Collections and University Archives, Knight Library, Eugene, Oregon.

Oregon Historical Society Research Library, Portland, Oregon.

Oregon Nikkei Endowment Collection. Densho Digital Archive. https://ddr.densho.org/.

Oregon Social Hygiene Society Records. MSS 1541. OHS, Portland, Oregon.

Oregon State Americanization Department Records 1926–1935. Department of Education. Superintendent of Public Instruction. 04/08/06/05. OSA, Salem, Oregon.

Oregon State Board of Health Minutes, 1903–1960. Health Division. 96A/019. OSA, Salem, Oregon.

Oregon State Defense Council Records. 87A-42 2/20/2/7. OSA, Salem, Oregon.

Oregon State Hospital Female Patient Files. 2017A-027. OSA, Salem, Oregon.

Oregon State Institution for the Feeble-Minded Records. Oregon Health Authority, Salem, Oregon.

Oregon State Library Records. 89A-35 4/13/10/6. OSA, Salem, Oregon.

Oregon Supreme Court Records. OSA, Salem, Oregon.

Police Investigative Report Books. 8090–08. PARC, Portland, Oregon.

Portland Woman's Club (Or.) Records, 1895–1995. MSS 1084. OHS, Portland, Oregon.

Public Welfare Commission Records. Accession 88A-63. OSA, Salem, Oregon.

Pullman Company Records. Pullman 06/02/03, Subgroup 02: Personnel Administration Department Records. Special Collections, Newberry Library, Chicago, Illinois.

Records of the Chemawa Indian School. BIA. RG 75. NARA Seattle.

Records of the Division of Venereal Diseases. Records of the Public Health Service, 1912–1968. RG 90. NARA, College Park, Maryland.

Records of the Grand Ronde Siletz Indian Agency. BIA. RG 75. NARA Seattle.

Records of the Klamath Indian Agency. BIA. RG 75. NARA Seattle.

Records of the Umatilla Indian Agency. BIA. RG 75. NARA Seattle.

Records of the United States Food Administration (USFA). RG 4. NARA Seattle.

Records of US Attorney's Office for the District of Oregon. Portland, Oregon, 1870–1954. RG 118. NARA Seattle.

Records of US Attorneys Western Judicial District of Oregon. Portland, Oregon. Civil and Criminal Significant Case Files, 1899–1925. RG 118. NARA Seattle.

Reuben H. Sawyer Papers. Collection 488. OHS, Portland, Oregon.

Rushlight Mayor Subject Files. AF/64760. PARC, Portland, Oregon.

Sheriff Harley Slusher Correspondence. Clatsop County Historical Society Archives. Astoria, Oregon.

Special Collections. State of Oregon Library, Salem, Oregon.

Walter M. Pierce Papers 1888 to 1969. Collection 068. University of Oregon Special Collections and University Archives, Knight Library, Eugene, Oregon.

Wanted and Reward Letters and Posters Scrapbook, Volume 1913–1917. Astoria, Oregon Public Library.

Washington County Commitment Records. OSA, Salem, Oregon.

Willamette Heritage Center Collections. Willamette Heritage Center, Salem, Oregon.

Woman's Christian Temperance Union of Oregon Records, 1881–1990. MSS 22535. OHS, Portland, Oregon.

World War I Alien Registration Forms [Oregon] (WWI AR). United States Department of Justice. MSS 1540. OHS, Portland, Oregon.

Young Women's Christian Association (YWCA) of Portland Records. Special Collections and Archives, Lewis and Clark College, Portland, Oregon.

GOVERNMENT DOCUMENTS AND REPORTS

Blair, Emily Newell. *The Woman's Committee: United States Council of National Defense: An Interpretive Report.* Washington, DC: GPO, 1920.

Creel, George. *Complete Report of the Chairman of the Committee on Public Information 1917: 1918: 1919.* Washington, DC: GPO, 1920.

Davey, Frank. *Report on the Japanese Situation in Oregon: Investigated for Governor Ben W. Olcott August 1920.* Salem: SPO, 1920.

Mayor's Message and Annual Reports for the Fiscal Year Ending November 30, 1921. Portland: City of Portland, 1922.

Oregon Blue Book and Official Directory

Oregon Bureau of Labor. *Census: Japanese Population in Oregon, October 1, 1928.* Salem, SPO, 1929.

Oregon Bureau of Labor Statistics. *Biennial Report of the Bureau of Labor Statistics and Inspector of Factories and Workshops of the State of Oregon.* Salem: SPO, 1914–1924.

Oregon Industrial Welfare Commission. *Third Biennial Report of the Industrial Welfare Commission of the State of Oregon.* Salem: SPO, 1919.

Oregon Industrial Welfare Commission. *Fourth Biennial Report of the Industrial Welfare Commission of the State of Oregon.* Salem: SPO, 1921.

Oregon State Board of Control. *Biennial Report of the Oregon State Board of Control.* Salem: SPO: 1914–1922.

Oregon State Board of Health. *Biennial Report of the State Board of Health.* Salem: SPO, 1916–1920.

United States Food Administration (USFA). *Organizer's Manual, National Family Pledge Card Campaign.* Washington, DC: USFA, 1917.

United States Department of Justice. *Annual Report of the Attorney General of the United States for the Year 1918.* Washington, DC: GPO, 1918.

—— . *Annual Report of the Attorney General of the United States for the Year 1919.* Washington, DC: GPO, 1919.

United States Department of Labor, Bureau of Naturalization. *Naturalization Laws and Regulations.* Washington, DC: GPO, 1920.

United States Department of the Interior. *Forty-Ninth Annual Report Board of Indian Commissioners.* Washington, DC: GPO, 1918.

United States Department of the Treasury. *Report of National Woman's Liberty Loan Committee for the Third Liberty Loan Campaign.* Washington, DC: GPO, 1918.

—— . *Report of National Woman's Liberty Loan Committee for the Victory Loan Campaign.* Washington, DC: GPO, 1920.

—— . *United States Government War-Savings Stamps: What They Are and Why You Should Buy Them.* Washington, DC: GPO, 1917.

United States Interdepartmental Social Hygiene Board. *Manual for the Various Agents of the United States Interdepartmental Social Hygiene Board.* Washington, DC: GPO, 1920.

United States Public Health Service. *Premarital Health Examination Legislation.* Washington, DC: GPO, 1954.

—— . "Relative Standing of 444 Cities in Respect to Measures in Force February 1, 1920, for Combating Venereal Diseases." *Venereal Disease Bulletin No. 57*. Washington, DC: GPO, 1920.

United States Railroad Administration. *Number of Women Employed and Character of Their Employment*. Washington, DC: GPO, 1919.

Wilbur, Cressy L. *The Federal Registration Service of the United States: Its Development, Problems, and Defects*. Washington, DC: GPO, 1916.

Woman's Committee of the Council of National Defense. *Organization Charts, May 1917–1918*. Washington, DC: GPO, 1918.

NEWSPAPERS AND HISTORICAL PERIODICALS

The Advocate
Albany Daily Democrat
Albany Democrat Herald
Albany Evening Herald
American City
American Journal of Public Health
Ashland Tidings
Aurora Observer
Baker Herald
Beaverton Times
Bend Bulletin
Brooklyn Times Union (New York)
Capital Journal (Salem)
Cayton's Weekly
Coos Bay Times
Corvallis Gazette-Times
East Oregonian (Pendleton)
Eugene Guard
Eugene Morning Register
Eugenical News
Grants Pass Daily Courier
Hillsboro Argus
Hood River Glacier
Journal of Delinquency
Klamath Falls Evening Herald
La Grande Evening Observer
Las Vegas Age
Library Journal
Long Beach Press (California)
Medford Mail Tribune

Medical Sentinel
Medico
Mental Hygiene Bulletin
Monmouth Herald
Morning Astorian
New York Times
Northwest Medicine
Oregon City Courier
Oregon City Enterprise
Oregon Clubwoman
Oregon Federation of Women's Clubs Year Book
Oregon Journal
Oregon Sunday Journal
Oregon Statesman (Salem)
Oregon Teachers Monthly
Oregon Voter: Magazine of Citizenship for Busy Men and Women
Oregonian
Oshu Nippo (*Oregon Daily News*)
Pacific Coast Journal of Homeopathy
Portland Evening Telegram
Portland News
Public Health Reports
Rogue River Courier
Roseburg News Review
Salem Capital Journal
San Bernardino County Sun
Seaside Signal
Social Hygiene

BIBLIOGRAPHY / *289*

Springfield News

Spy Glass: A Bulletin of News and
Better Methods Issued by the American Protective League

St. Helens Mist

Survey

Washington (DC) Times

Welfare: The Journal of Municipal
and Social Progress

Western America (Astoria and
Portland)

Yakima Herald (Washington)

ADDITIONAL PRIMARY SOURCES

Carey, Charles Henry. *History of Oregon*. 3 volumes. Portland, OR: Pioneer Historical Publishing Company, 1922.

———. *The Oregon Constitution*. Salem, OR: SPO, 1926.

Carlisle, Chester L. "The Physician as a Factor in a Statewide Cooperative Program for Prophylaxis of Sociological Disorders." *Journal of the American
Medical Association* 75 (November 13, 1920): 1364–1366.

———. "A Summary of the Oregon State Survey of Mental Defect, Delinquency,
and Dependency Conducted in 1920 by the University of Oregon." *University of Oregon Extension Monitor* 9, nos. 4 and 5 (April and May 1921): 1–40.

———, ed. *Preliminary Statistical Report of the Oregon State Survey of Mental
Defect, Delinquency, and Dependency* published as *Public Health Bulletin
No. 112*. December 1921.Washington, DC: GPO, 1922.

Chafee, Zechariah, Jr. "Freedom of Speech in War Time." *Harvard Law Review*
32, no. 8 (June 1919): 932–973.

Colmer, Montagu, and Charles Erskine Scott Wood, eds. *History of the Bench
and Bar of Oregon*. Portland, OR: Historical Publishing Company, 1910.

Dever, Lem A. *Masks Off! Confessions of an Imperial Klansman*. 2nd ed. Vancouver, WA: Lem Dever, 1925.

Dietzler, Mary Macey. *Detention Houses and Reformatories as Protective Social
Agencies in the Campaign of the United States Government against Venereal
Diseases*. Washington, DC: GPO, 1922.

Goddard, Henry H. *The Kallikak Family: A Study in the Heredity of Feeblemindedness*. New York: Macmillan, 1912.

Hall, Fred S. *Medical Certification for Marriage*. New York: Russell Sage Foundation, 1925.

Helquist, Michael. WWI Sedition in Oregon Project. https://www.michael
helquist.com/wwi-sedition-in-oregon.html.

Larremore, Thomas A. "Portland and Legal Aid." *Oregon Law Review* 1, no. 2
(June 1921): 1–25.

Laughlin, Harry H. *Eugenic Sterilization in the United States*. Chicago: Psycho-
pathic Laboratory of the Municipal Court of Chicago, 1922.

———. *The Second International Exhibition of Eugenics*. Baltimore, MD: Williams & Wilkins, 1923.

Mumford, Lewis. "Patriotism and Its Consequences." *The Dial* (April 19, 1919): 406–407.

Oregon Federation of Women's Clubs. *Oregon Federation of Women's Clubs Year Book 1915–1916*. Portland: Oregon Federation of Women's Clubs, 1916.

Owens-Adair, Bethenia. *The Eugenic Marriage Law and Human Sterilization: The Situation in Oregon*. Salem, OR: B. A. Owens-Adair, 1922.

———. *Human Sterilization: It's [sic] Social and Legislative Aspects*. B. A. Owens-Adair, 1922.

———. *A Souvenir: Dr. Owens-Adair to Her Friends, Christmas, 1922*. Salem, OR: Statesman Publishing, 1922.

Popenoe, Paul. "Sterilization as a Social Measure." *Journal of Psycho-Asthenics* 41 (June 1936): 60–65.

Portland Vice Commission. *Report of the Portland Vice Commission to the Mayor and City Council of the City of Portland, Oregon*. Portland, OR: Portland Vice Commission, 1913.

Robinson, David, ed. *Venereal Disease Ordinances: Compilation of Suggested and Adjudicated Ordinances Which Have Proved Successful in Combating Venereal Diseases*. Washington, DC: GPO, 1919.

St. Clair, Labert. *The Story of the Liberty Loans*. Washington, DC: James William Bryan Press, 1919.

Wheat, George Seay. *The Story of the American Legion*. New York: G. P. Putnam's Sons, 1919.

Yada, Tats. "The Yada Family." In *The Pioneers of Lake Labish*. Edited by Duane Bibby, 96–99. Brooks, OR: The Sons of Labish, 2000.

SECONDARY SOURCES

Abrams, Paula. *Cross Purposes:* Pierce v. Society of Sisters *and the Struggle over Compulsory Public Education*. Ann Arbor: University of Michigan Press, 2009.

Alexander, Ruth M. *The "Girl Problem": Female Sexual Delinquency in New York, 1900–1930*. Ithaca, NY: Cornell University Press, 1995.

Anderson, Carol. *One Person, No Vote: How Voter Suppression Is Destroying Our Democracy*. New York: Bloomsbury, 2019.

Anderson, Margo J. *The American Census: A Social History*. 2nd edition. New Haven, CT: Yale University Press, 2015.

Azuma, Eiichiro. "A History of Oregon's Issei, 1880–1952." *OHQ* 94, no. 4 (Winter 1993–1994): 315–367.

Balakian, Peter. *The Burning Tigris: The American Genocide and America's Response*. New York: HarperCollins, 2003.

Balderrama, Francisco E. *Decade of Betrayal: Mexican Repatriation in the 1930s*. Revised edition. Albuquerque: University of New Mexico Press, 2006.

Barkan, Robert. *From All Points: America's Immigrant West, 1870s–1952*. Bloomington: Indiana University Press, 2007.

Bartholomae, Annette. "A Conscientious Objector: Oregon, 1918." *OHQ* 71, no. 3 (September 1970): 213–245.

Baynton, Douglas C. "Disability and the Justification of Inequality in American History." In *The New Disability History: American Perspectives*. Edited by Paul K. Longmore and Lauri Umansky, 33–82. New York: New York University Press, 2001.

Beil, Kim. *Good Pictures: A History of Popular Photography*. Stanford, CA: Stanford University Press, 2020.

Beltrán, Mary C. *Latina/o Stars in U.S. Eyes*. Urbana: University of Illinois Press, 2009.

Blair, Karen. *The Clubwoman as Feminist: True Womanhood Redefined, 1868–1914*. New York: Holmes & Meier, 1980.

Blee, Kathleen. *Women of the Klan: Racism and Gender in the 1920s*. Berkeley: University of California Press, 1991.

Boag, Peter. *Re-Dressing America's Frontier Past*. Berkeley: University of California Press, 2011.

———. *Same-Sex Affairs: Constructing and Controlling Homosexuality in the Pacific Northwest*. Berkeley: University of California Press, 2003.

Brandt, Allen. *No Magic Bullet: A Social History of Venereal Disease in the United States since 1880*. Expanded edition. New York: Oxford University Press, 1987.

Braslow, Joel. *Mental Ills and Bodily Cures: Psychiatric Treatment in the First Half of the Twentieth Century*. Berkeley: University of California Press, 1997.

Bredbenner, Candice Lewis. *A Nationality of Her Own: Women, Marriage, and the Law of Citizenship*. Berkeley: University of California Press, 1998.

Breen, William J. *Uncle Sam at Home: Civilian Mobilization, Wartime Federalism, and the Council of National Defense, 1917–1919*. Westport, CT: Greenwood Press, 1984.

Bristow, Nancy K. *Making Men Moral: Social Engineering during the Great War*. New York: New York University Press, 1996.

Britten, Thomas A. *American Indians in World War I: At Home and War*. Albuquerque: University of New Mexico Press, 1997.

Brownell, Penelope. "The Women's Committees of the First World War: Women in Government, 1917–1919." PhD dissertation, Brown University, 2002.

Burch, Susan. *Committed: Remembering Native Kinship in and beyond Institutions*. Chapel Hill: University of North Carolina Press, 2021.

Butler, Anne M. *Across God's Frontiers: Catholic Sisters in the American West, 1850–1920*. Chapel Hill: University of North Carolina Press, 2012.

Cahill, Cathleen D. *Federal Fathers & Mothers: A Social History of the United States Indian Service, 1869–1933*. Chapel Hill: University of North Carolina Press, 2011.

Canaday, Margot. *The Straight State: Sexuality and Citizenship in Twentieth Century America*. Princeton, NJ: Princeton University Press, 2009.

Capozzola, Christopher. *Uncle Sam Wants You: World War I and the Making of the Modern American Citizen*. New York: Oxford University Press, 2008.

Carey, Allison C. *On the Margins of Citizenship: Intellectual Disability and Civil Rights in the Twentieth Century*. Philadelphia, PA: Temple University Press, 2009.

Carmin, Jim. "Central Library (Multnomah County Library)," *Oregon Encyclopedia*.

Chaudhuri, Nupur, Sherry J. Katz, and Mary Elizabeth Perry, eds. *Contesting Archives: Finding Women in the Sources*. Urbana: University of Illinois Press, 2010.

Chauncey, George. *Gay New York: Gender, Urban Culture, and the Making of the Gay Male World, 1890–1940*. New York: Basic Books, 1994.

Clement, Elizabeth Alice. *Love for Sale: Courting, Treating, and Prostitution in New York City, 1900–1945*. Chapel Hill: University of North Carolina Press, 2006.

Connelly, Mark Thomas. *The Response to Prostitution in the Progressive Era*. Chapel Hill: University of North Carolina Press, 1980.

Craver, Earlene. "On the Boundary of White: The *Cartozian* Naturalization Case and the Armenians, 1923–1925." *Journal of American Ethnic History* 28, no. 2 (Winter 2009): 30–56.

D'Emilio, John, and Estelle B. Freedman. *Intimate Matters: A History of Sexuality in America* 3rd edition. Chicago: University of Chicago Press, 2012.

Daniels, Roger. *Guarding the Golden Door: American Immigration Policy and Immigrants since 1882*. New York: Hill and Wang, 2004.

——— . *The Politics of Prejudice: The Anti-Japanese Movement in California and the Struggle for Japanese Exclusion*. Berkeley: University of California Press, 1962.

——— . *Prisoners without Trial: Japanese Americans in World War II*. New York: Hill and Wang, 1993.

Dawley, Alan. *Changing the World: American Progressives in War and Revolution*. Princeton, NJ: Princeton University Press, 2003.

Dilg, Janice. "'For Working Women in Oregon': Caroline Gleason/Sister Miriam Theresa and Oregon's Minimum Wage Law." *OHQ* 110, no. 1 (Spring 2009): 96–129.

——. "Millie R. Trumbull (1866–1940)." *Oregon Encyclopedia.*

——. "Uncovering 'The Real Work' of the Portland YWCA, 1900–1923." *Journal of Women's History* 15, no. 3 (Autumn 2003): 175–182.

Doroshow, Deborah B. "Wassermann before Wedding Bells: Premarital Examination Laws in the United States, 1937–1950." *Social History of Medicine* 34, no. 1 (February 2021): 141–169.

Dumenil, Lynn. *The Second Line of Defense: American Women and World War I.* Chapel Hill: University of North Carolina Press, 2017.

Edmunson-Morton, Tiah. "Maybe You've Heard of Her Husband? Finding Louise Weinhard." *OHQ* 122, no. 2 (Summer 2001): 128–157.

Eighmey, Rae Katherine. *Food Will Win the War: Minnesota Crops, Cooks, and Conservation during World War I.* St. Paul: Minnesota Historical Society Press, 2010.

Einolf, Christopher J. *America in the Philippines, 1899–1902: The First Torture Scandal.* New York: Palgrave Macmillan, 2014.

Eisenberg, Ellen. *Embracing a Western Identity: Jewish Oregonians, 1849–1950.* Corvallis: Oregon State University Press, 2015.

——. "Jews in Oregon." *Oregon Encyclopedia.*

Engeman, Richard. "Portland Public Market." *Oregon Encyclopedia.*

Erickson, Mary P. "'In the Interest of the Moral Life of Our City': The Beginning of Motion Picture Censorship in Portland, Oregon." *Film History* 22, no. 2 (2010): 148–169.

Fairchild, Amy L., Ronald Bayer, and James Colgrove. *Searching Eyes: Privacy, the State, and Disease Surveillance in America.* Berkeley: University of California Press, 2007.

Finnegan, Margaret. *Selling Suffrage: Consumer Culture and Votes for Women.* New York: Columbia University Press, 1999.

Freedman, Estelle B. *Maternal Justice: Miriam Van Waters and the Female Reform Tradition.* Chicago: University of Chicago Press, 1996.

Fronc, Jennifer. *Monitoring the Movies: The Fight over Film Censorship in Early Twentieth-Century Urban America.* Austin: University of Texas Press, 2017.

——. *New York Undercover: Private Surveillance in the Progressive Era.* Chicago: University of Chicago Press, 2009.

Gardner, Martha. *The Qualities of a Citizen: Women, Immigration, and Citizenship, 1870–1965.* Princeton, NJ: Princeton University Press, 2005.

Geller, Ernest. *Nations and Nationalism.* Ithaca, NY: Cornell University Press, 1983.

Glenn, Evelyn Nakano. *Unequal Freedom: How Race and Gender Shaped American Citizenship and Labor*. Cambridge, MA: Harvard University Press, 2002.

Goeres-Gardiner, Diane L. *Inside Oregon State Hospital: A History of Tragedy and Triumph*. Charleston, SC: The History Press, 2013.

Goodman Adam. *The Deportation Machine: America's Long History of Expelling Immigrants*. Princeton, NJ: Princeton University Press, 2020.

Gordon, Linda. *The Second Coming of the KKK: The Ku Klux Klan of the 1920s and the American Political Tradition*. New York: Livermore, 2017.

Gould, Stephen Jay. *The Mismeasure of Man*. New York: W. W. Norton, 1981.

Greenwald, Maureen Weiner. *Women, War and Work: The Impact of World War I on Women Workers in the United States*. Ithaca, NY: Cornell University Press, 1980.

Grossberg, Michael. "Guarding the Altar: Physiological Restrictions and the Rise of State Intervention in Matrimony." *American Journal of Legal History* 26, no. 3 (July 1982): 197–226.

Gullett, Gail. *Becoming Citizens: The Emergence and Development of the California Women's Movement, 1880–1911*. Urbana: University of Illinois Press, 2000.

Gunselman, Cheryl. "'Wheedling, Wangling, and Walloping' for Progress: The Public Service Career of Cornelia Marvin Pierce." *OHQ* 110, no. 3 (Fall 2009): 362–389.

Gürsel, Zeynep Devrim. "Classifying the Cartozians: Rethinking the Politics of Visibility Alongside Ottoman Subjecthood and American Citizenship" *Photographies* 15, no. 3 (2022): 349–380.

Haarsager, Sandra. *Organized Womanhood: Cultural Politics in the Pacific Northwest, 1840–1920*. Norman: University of Oklahoma Press, 1997.

Hancock, Christin. "Health and Well-being: Federal Indian Policy, Klamath Women, and Childbirth." *OHQ* 117, no. 2 (Summer 2016): 166–197.

Hayduk, Ronald. *Democracy for All: Restoring Immigrant Voting Rights in the United States*. New York: Routledge, 2006.

Helquist, Michael. "'Lewd, Obscene, and Indecent': The 1916 Portland Edition of *Family Limitation*." *OHQ* 117, no. 2 (Summer 2016): 274–287.

——— . *Marie Equi: Radical Politics and Outlaw Passions*. Corvallis: Oregon State University Press, 2015.

——— . "Resistance, Dissent, and Punishment in WWI Oregon." *OHQ* 118, no. 2 (Summer 2017): 256–259.

Hier, Sean P., and Joshua Greenberg, eds. *The Surveillance Studies Reader*. New York: Open University Press, 2007.

Higgonet, Margaret R. "X-Ray Vision: Women Photograph War." *Miranda* 2 (2010). http://journals.openedition.org/miranda/1085.

Higgonet, Margaret Randolph, Jane Jenson, Sonya Michel, and Margaret Collins Weitz, eds. *Behind the Lines: Gender and the Two World Wars*. New Haven, CT: Yale University Press, 1987.

Hodges, Adam J. "At War over the Espionage Act in Portland: Dueling Perspectives from Kathleen O'Brennan and Agent William Bryon." *OHQ* 108, no. 3 (Fall 2007): 474–496.

———. "'Enemy Aliens' and 'Silk Stocking Girls': The Class Politics of Internment in the Drive for Urban Order during World War I." *Journal of the Gilded Age and Progressive Era* 6, no. 4 (October 2007): 431–458.

———. *World War I and Urban Order: the Local Class Politics of National Mobilization*. New York: Palgrave MacMillan, 2016.

Horton, Kami. "In the Shadow of Fairview." *Oregon Public Broadcasting*. November 16, 2020. https://www.opb.org/article/2020/11/16/oregon-history -in-the-shadow-of-fairview-documentary/.

———. "People First: In the Shadow of Fairview." *Oregon Public Broadcasting*. July 19, 2020. https://www.opb.org/news/series/move-to-include/people -first-in-the-shadow-of-fairview/.

Hummel, Penny. *"Making the Library Be Alive": Portland's Librarian, Mary Frances Isom*. Portland, OR: Multnomah County Library, 2009. https:// multcolib.org/sites/default/files/mcl-his_isom.pdf.

Hunter, Tera W. *To 'Joy My Freedom: Southern Black Women's Lives and Labors after the Civil War*. Cambridge, MA: Harvard University Press, 1997.

Hyman, Harold. *To Try Men's Souls: Loyalty Tests in American History*. Berkeley: University of California Press, 1960.

Ichioka, Yuji. *The Issei: The World of the First Generation Japanese Immigrants, 1885–1924*. New York: Free Press, 1988.

Imai, Shiho. "*Ozawa v. United States*." Densho Encyclopedia. http://encyclopedia.densho.org.

Iwatsuki, Shizue, and Linda Tamura, "The Making of an American." *OHQ* 103, no. 4 (Winter 2002): 510–529.

Jackson, Kenneth T. *The Ku Klux Klan in the City: 1915–1930*. Chicago: John Dee, 1992.

Jensen, Kimberly. "An 'Immoral' and 'Disloyal' Woman in 'Such a Responsible Place': M. Louise Hunt's Refusal to Purchase a Liberty Bond, Civil Liberties, and Female Citizenship in the First World War." *Peace & Change* 44, no. 2 (April 2019): 139–168.

———. "From Citizens to Enemy Aliens: Oregon Women, Marriage, and the

Surveillance State during the First World War." *OHQ* 114, no. 4 (Winter 2014): 427–442.

———. "Lizzie Weeks (1879–1976)." *Oregon Encyclopedia.*

———. *Mobilizing Minerva: American Women in the First World War.* Urbana: University of Illinois Press, 2008.

———. "'Neither Head nor Tail to the Campaign': Esther Pohl Lovejoy and the Oregon Woman Suffrage Victory of 1912." *OHQ* 108, no. 3 (Fall 2007): 350–383.

———. *Oregon's Doctor to the World: Esther Pohl Lovejoy and a Life in Activism.* Seattle: University of Washington Press, 2012.

———. "Revolutions in the Machinery: Oregon Women and Citizenship in Sesquicentennial Perspective." *OHQ* 110, no. 3 (Fall 2009): 336–361.

———. "'Women's Positive Patriotic Duty to Participate': The Practice of Female Citizenship in Oregon and the Expanding Surveillance State during the First World War and Its Aftermath." *OHQ* 118, no. 2 (Summer 2017): 198–233.

Johnson, Daniel P. "Anti-Japanese Legislation in Oregon, 1917–1923." *OHQ* 97, no. 2 (Summer 1996): 176–210.

Johnson, Jeffrey A. *"They Are All Red Out Here": Socialist Politics in the Pacific Northwest, 1895–1925.* Norman: University of Oklahoma Press, 2008.

Johnston, Robert D. *The Radical Middle Class: Populist Democracy and the Question of Capitalism in Progressive Era Portland, Oregon.* Princeton, NJ: Princeton University Press, 2003.

Katagiri, George. "Oshu Nippo." *Oregon Encyclopedia.*

Keene, Jennifer D. *Doughboys, the Great War, and the Remaking of America.* Baltimore, MD: Johns Hopkins University Press, 2001.

Keire, Mara L. *For Business & Pleasure: Red-Light Districts and the Regulation of Vice in the United States.* Baltimore, MD: Johns Hopkins University Press, 2010.

Keith, Jeanette. *Rich Man's War, Poor Man's Fight: Race, Class, and Power in the Rural South during the First World War.* Chapel Hill: University of North Carolina Press, 2004.

Kennedy, David M. *Over Here: The First World War and American Society.* New York: Oxford University Press, 1980.

Kennedy, Kathleen. *Disloyal Mothers and Scurrilous Citizens: Women and Subversion during World War I.* Bloomington: Indiana University Press, 1999.

Kerber, Linda K. *No Constitutional Right to Be Ladies: Women and the Obligations of Citizenship.* New York: Hill and Wang, 1998.

Kessler, Lauren. *Stubborn Twig: Three Generations in the Life of a Japanese American Family.* New York: Random House, 1993.

Kessler-Harris, Alice. *In Pursuit of Equity: Women, Men, and the Quest for Economic Citizenship in 20th-Century America.* New York: Oxford, 2001.

Kingsbury, M. E. "'To Shine in Use': The Library and War Service of Oregon's Pioneer Librarian, Mary Frances Isom." *Journal of Library History* 10, no. 1 (January 1975): 22–34.

Kline, Wendy. *Building a Better Race: Gender, Sexuality, and Eugenics from the Turn of the Century to the Baby Boom.* Berkeley: University of California Press, 2001.

Knox, Zoe. "'A Greater Danger Than a Division of the German Army': Bible Students and Opposition to War in World War I America." *Peace & Change* 44, no. 2 (April 2019): 207–243.

Krieger, Nancy. "Queen of the Bolsheviks: The Hidden History of Dr. Marie Equi." *Radical America* 17, no. 4 (1983): 55–73.

Ladd-Taylor, Molly. *Fixing the Poor: Eugenic Sterilization and Child Welfare in the Twentieth Century.* Baltimore, MD: Johns Hopkins University Press, 2017.

Largent, Mark A. *Breeding Contempt: The History of Coerced Sterilization in the United States.* New Brunswick, NJ: Rutgers University Press, 2008.

——— . "'The Greatest Curse of the Race': Eugenic Sterilization in Oregon 1909– 1983." *OHQ*, 103, no. 2 (Summer, 2002): 188–209.

Larsell, Olof. *The Doctor in Oregon: A Medical History.* Portland: Binfords & Mort for the Oregon Historical Society, 1947.

Lawrence, Jane. "The Indian Health Service and the Sterilization of Native American Women." *American Indian Quarterly* 24, no. 3 (Summer 2000): 400–419.

Leavitt, Judith Walzer. *Brought to Bed: Childbearing in America, 1750–1950.* New York: Oxford University Press, 1986.

Lee, Erika. *America for Americans: A History of Xenophobia in the United States.* New York: Basic Books, 2019.

——— . *The Making of Asian America: A History.* New York: Simon and Schuster, 2015.

Leeson, Fred. *Rose City Justice: A Legal History of Portland, Oregon.* Portland: Oregon Historical Society Press, 1998.

Lewis, David G. "Four Deaths: The Near Destruction of Western Oregon Tribes and Native Lifeways, Removal to the Reservation, and Erasure from History." *OHQ* 115, no. 3 (Fall 2014): 414–437.

Lipin, Lawrence M. *Eleanor Baldwin and the Women's Point of View.* Corvallis: Oregon State University Press, 2017.

Lira, Natalie. *Laboratory of Deficiency: Sterilization and Confinement in California, 1900–1950s.* Oakland: University of California Press, 2022.

Lister, Ruth. *Citizenship: Feminist Perspectives*. New York: New York University Press, 2003.

Lombardo, Paul A. "A Child's Right To Be Well Born: Venereal Disease and the Eugenic Marriage Laws, 1913–1935." *Perspectives in Biology and Medicine* 60, no. 2 (Spring 2017): 211–232.

———. *Three Generations, No Imbeciles: Eugenics, The Supreme Court, and Buck v. Bell*. Updated edition. Baltimore, MD: Johns Hopkins University Press, 2022.

MacColl, E. Kimbark. *The Shaping of a City: Business and Politics in Portland, Oregon 1885–1915*. Portland, OR: Georgian Press, 1976.

MacLean, Nancy. *Behind the Mask of Chivalry: The Making of the Second Ku Klux Klan*. New York: Oxford University Press, 1994.

Malacrida, Claudia. *A Special Hell: Institutional Life in Alberta's Eugenic Years*. Toronto: University of Toronto Press, 2015.

Mangun, Kimberley. *A Force for Change: Beatrice Morrow Cannady and the Struggle for Civil Rights in Oregon, 1912–1936*. Corvallis: Oregon State University Press, 2010.

Marshall, T. H. *Class, Citizenship, and Social Development*. Garden City, NY: Doubleday, 1964.

Mayer, Heather. *Beyond the Rebel Girl: Women and the Industrial Workers of the World in the Pacific Northwest, 1905–1924*. Corvallis: Oregon State University Press, 2018.

McGirr, Lisa. *The War on Alcohol: Prohibition and the Rise of the American State*. New York: W. W. Norton, 2016.

McKenzie, Andrea. "Picturing War: Canadian Nurses' First World War Photography." *Journal of War & Culture Studies* 11, no. 4 (October 2018) 318–334.

McLagan, Elizabeth. *A Peculiar Paradise: A History of Blacks in Oregon, 1788–1940*. Portland, OR: Georgian Press, 1980.

McLaren, Angus. *Our Own Master Race: Eugenics in Canada, 1885–1945*. Oxford University Press Canada, 1990. Toronto: University of Toronto Press, 2014.

Michel, Sonya. *Children's Interests/Mother's Rights: The Shaping of America's Child Care Policy*. New Haven, CT: Yale University Press, 1999.

Millner, Darrell. "Blacks in Oregon." *Oregon Encyclopedia*.

Miriam Theresa, Sister (Caroline Gleason). *Legislation for Women in Oregon*. Washington, DC: Catholic University of America, 1924.

Molina, Natalia. *Fit To Be Citizens? Public Health and Race in Los Angeles, 1879–1939*. Berkeley: University of California Press, 2006.

———. "'In a Race All Their Own': The Quest to Make Mexicans Ineligible for U.S. Citizenship." *Pacific Historical Review* 79, no. 2 (May 2010): 167–201.

Muhammad, Robin Dearmon. "Separate and Unsanitary: African American Railroad Car Cleaners and the Women's Service Section, 1918–1920." *Journal of Women's History* 23, no. 2 (Summer 2011): 87–111.

Murphy, Paul L. *World War I and the Origin of Civil Liberties in the United States*. New York: W. W. Norton, 1979.

Mullendore, William Clinton. *History of the United States Food Administration 1917–1919*. Stanford, CA: Stanford University Press, 1941.

Myers, Gloria E. *A Municipal Mother: Portland's Lola Greene Baldwin, America's First Policewoman*. Corvallis: Oregon State University Press, 1995.

Nagae, Peggy. "Asian Women: Immigration and Citizenship in Oregon." *OHQ* 113, no. 3 (Fall 2012): 334–359.

Nagler, Jörg. "Victims of the Home Front: Enemy Aliens in the United States during the First World War." In *Minorities in Wartime: National and Racial Groupings in Europe, North America and Australia during the Two World Wars*. Edited by Panikos Panayi, 191–215. Providence, RI: Berg Publishers, 1993.

Nakamura, Kelli Y. "Issei Women and Work: Washerwomen, Prostitutes, Midwives and Barbers." *Hawaiian Journal of History* 49 (2015): 119–148.

———. "Picture Brides." *Densho Encyclopedia*. http://encyclopedia.densho.org.

Nakano, Mei T. *Japanese American Women: Three Generations 1890–1990*. Berkeley, CA: Mina Press Publishers. San Francisco: National Japanese American Historical Society, 1990.

Nesbit, Sharon. "Multnomah County Poor Farm (Edgefield)." *Oregon Encyclopedia*.

Ngai, Mae M. *Impossible Subjects: Illegal Aliens and the Making of Modern America*. Princeton, NJ: Princeton University Press, 2004.

Nielsen, Kim E. "Incompetent and Insane: Labor, Ability, and Citizenship in Nineteenth- and Early Twentieth-century United States." *Rethinking History* 23, no. 2 (2019): 175–188.

———. *Money, Marriage, and Madness: The Life of Anna Ott*. Urbana: University of Illinois Press, 2020.

Nock, Steven L. *The Costs of Privacy: Surveillance and Reputation in America*. New York: De Gruyter, 1993.

Odem, Mary E. *Delinquent Daughters: Protecting and Policing Adolescent Female Sexuality in the United States, 1885–1920*. Chapel Hill: University of North Carolina Press, 1995.

Ogden, Johanna. "Ghadar, Historical Silences, and Nations of Belonging: Early 1900s Punjabis of the Columbia River." *OHQ* 113 no. 2 (Summer 2012): 164–197.

Oharazeki, Kasuhiro. *Japanese Prostitutes in the North American West, 1887–1920*. Seattle: University of Washington Press, 2016.

Ordover, Nancy. *American Eugenics: Race, Queer Anatomy, and the Science of Nationalism*. Minneapolis: University of Minnesota Press, 2003.

Parascandola, John. *Sex, Sin, and Science: A History of Syphilis in America*. Westport, CT: Praeger, 2008.

Parenti, Christian. *The Soft Cage: Surveillance in America from Slave Passes to the War on Terror*. New York: Basic Books, 2003.

Pascoe, Peggy. *What Comes Naturally: Miscegenation Law and the Making of Race in America*. New York: Oxford University Press, 2008.

Pearson, Susan J. *The Birth Certificate: An American History*. Chapel Hill: University of North Carolina Press, 2021.

Peiss, Kathy. *Cheap Amusements: Working Women and Leisure in Turn-of-the-Century New York*. Philadelphia, PA: Temple University Press, 1986.

Pfaelzer, Jean. *Driven Out: The Forgotten War against Chinese Americans*. Berkeley: University of California Press, 2008.

Piasecki, Sara. "Portland Free Dispensary." *Oregon Encyclopedia*.

Platt, Amy E., and Laura Cray. "'Out of Order': Pasting Together the Slavery Debate in the Oregon Constitution." *OHQ* 120, no. 1 (Spring 2019): 74–101.

Proctor, Tammy M. *Civilians in a World at War, 1914–1918*. New York: New York University Press, 2010.

———. *Female Intelligence: Women and Espionage in the First World War*. New York: New York University Press, 2003.

Rafter, Nicole Hahn. *Creating Born Criminals*. Urbana: University of Illinois Press, 1997.

Ralstin-Lewis, D. Marie. "The Continuing Struggle against Genocide: Indigenous Women's Reproductive Rights." *Wicazo Sa Review* 20, no. 1 (Spring 2005): 71–95.

Regali, Darius. *Torture and Democracy*. Princeton, NJ: Princeton University Press, 2007.

Reid, Kay. "Multilayered Loyalties: Oregon Indian Women as Citizens of the Land, Their Tribal Nations, and the United States," *OHQ* 113, no. 3 (Fall 2012): 392–407.

Richards, Penny, and Susan Burch, "Documents, Ethics, and the Disability Historian." In *The Oxford Handbook of Disability History*. Edited by Michael Rembis, Catherine Kudlick, and Kim E. Nielsen, 161–174. New York: Oxford University Press, 2018.

Robertson, Craig. *The Passport in America: The History of a Document*. New York: Oxford University Press, 2010.

Robinson, Greg. "Kenji Namba vs. McCourt." *Densho Encyclopedia*. http://encyclopedia.densho.org.

Rockafellar, Nancy Moore. "Making the World Safe for the Soldiers of Democracy: Patriotism, Public Health and Venereal Disease Control on the West Coast, 1910–1919." PhD dissertation, University of Washington, 1990.

Rosen, Ruth. *The Lost Sisterhood: Prostitution in America, 1900–1918*. Baltimore, MD: Johns Hopkins University Press, 1989.

Rosenbloom, Rachel E. "Policing the Borders of Birthright Citizenship: Some Thoughts on the New (and Old) Restrictionism." *Washburn Law Journal* 51, no. 2 (2012): 311–330.

Ross, William G. *World War I and the American Constitution*. New York: Cambridge University Press, 2017.

Rothwell, Charles Easton. "The Ku Klux Klan in the State of Oregon." BA thesis, Reed College, 1924.

Saalfeld, Lawrence J. *Forces of Prejudice: The Ku Klux Klan in Oregon, 1920–1925*. Portland, OR: Archdiocesan Historical Commission and University of Portland, 1984.

Shenk, Gerald E. *Work or Fight! Race, Gender, and the Draft in World War I*. New York: Palgrave MacMillan, 2005.

Schoen, Johanna. *Choice & Coercion: Birth Control, Sterilization, and Abortion in Public Health and Welfare*. Chapel Hill: University of North Carolina Press, 2005.

Shah, Courtney Q. "'Against Their Own Weakness': Policing Sexuality and Women in San Antonio, Texas, during World War I." *Journal of the History of Sexuality* 19, no. 3 (September 2010): 458–482.

Siegler, Aurora. "Morningside Hospital." *Oregon Encyclopedia*.

Smith, Stacey L. "Oregon's Civil War: The Troubled Legacy of Emancipation in the Pacific Northwest." *OHQ* 115, no. 2 (Summer 2014): 154–173.

Smith, Susan L. *Japanese American Midwives: Culture, Community and Health Politics, 1880–1950*. Urbana: University of Illinois Press, 2005.

Southwell, Priscilla L. "Political Parties and Elections." In *Governing Oregon: Continuity and Change*. Edited by Richard A. Clucas, Mark Henkels, Priscilla L. Southwell, and Edward P. Weber, 38–43. Corvallis: Oregon State University Press, 2018.

Starr, Paul. *The Social Transformation of American Medicine*. New York: Basic Books, 1982.

Stearns, Marjorie R. "The Settlement of the Japanese in Oregon." *OHQ* 39, no. 3 (September 1938): 262–269.

Steinson, Barbara J. *American Women's Activism in World War I*. New York: Garland, 1982.

Stergar, Rok. "Nationalities (Austria-Hungary)." *1914–1918 Online: International Encyclopedia of the First World War.*

Stern, Alexandra Minna. *Eugenic Nation: Faults & Frontiers of Better Breeding in Modern America.* Berkeley: University of California Press, 2005.

Stern, Scott W. *The Trials of Nina McCall: Sex, Surveillance, and the Decades-Long Government Plan to Imprison "Promiscuous Women."* Boston, MA: Beacon Press, 2018.

Stibbe, Matthew. "Enemy Aliens and Internment." *1914–1918 Online: International Encyclopedia of the First World War.*

Strange, Carolyn. *Toronto's Girl Problem: The Perils and Pleasures of the City, 1880–1930.* Toronto, Ontario: University of Toronto Press, 1995.

Sueyoshi, Amy Hariko. *Queer Compulsions: Race, Nation, and Sexuality in the Affairs of Yone Noguchi.* Honolulu: University of Hawai'i Press, 2012.

Swensen, Rolf. "Pilgrims at the Golden Gate: Christian Scientists on the Pacific Coast, 1880–1915." *Pacific Historical Review* 72, no. 2 (May 2003): 229–263.

Tamura, Linda. *The Hood River Issei: An Oral History of Japanese Settlers in Oregon's Hood River Valley.* Urbana: University of Illinois Press, 1993.

Taylor, Quintard. *In Search of the Racial Frontier: African Americans in the American West.* New York: Norton, 1998.

Theobald, Brianna. *Reproduction on the Reservation: Pregnancy, Childbirth, and Colonialism in the Long Twentieth Century.* Chapel Hill: University of North Carolina Press, 2019.

Thomas, William H., Jr. *Unsafe for Democracy: World War I and the U.S. Justice Department's Covert Campaign to Suppress Dissent.* Madison: University of Wisconsin Press, 2008.

Thorson, Wendy P. Reilly. "Oregon Klanswomen of the 1920s: A Study of Tribalism, Gender, and Women's Power." MA thesis, Oregon State University, 1997.

Toll, William. "Black Families and Migration to a Multiracial Society: Portland, Oregon, 1900–1924." *Journal of American Ethnic History* 17, no. 3 (Spring 1998): 38–70.

———. "Permanent Settlement: Japanese Families in Portland in 1920." *Western Historical Quarterly* 28 (Spring 1997): 19–43.

Trent, James W. *Inventing the Feeble Mind: A History of Disability in the United States* 2nd edition. New York: Oxford University Press, 2017.

Trouillot, Michel. *Silencing the Past: Power and the Production of History.* Boston: Beacon Press, 1995.

VanBurkleo, Sandra F. *Gender Remade: Citizenship, Suffrage, and Public Power in the New Northwest.* New York: Cambridge University Press, 2015.

Van Nuys, Frank. *Americanizing the West: Race, Immigrants, and Citizenship, 1890–1930.* Lawrence: University Press of Kansas, 2002.

Veit, Helen Zoe. *Modern Food, Moral Food: Self-Control, Science, and the Rise of Modern American Eating in the Early Twentieth Century*. Chapel Hill: University of North Carolina Press, 2013.

Villazor, Rose Cuison. "Rediscovering *Oyama v. California*: At the Intersection of Race, Property, and Citizenship." *Washington University Law Review* 87, no. 5 (2010): 979–1042.

Walls, Robert E. "Lady Loggers and Gyppo Wives: Women and Northwest Logging." *OHQ* 103, no. 3 (Fall 2002): 362–382.

Ward, Jean M. "Bethenia Angelina Owens-Adair." In *Eminent Astorians*. Edited by Karen Kirtley, 147–194. Salem: East Oregonian Publishing Company, 2010.

Weisensee, Erika. "Portland Rose Festival." *Oregon Encyclopedia*.

Wheeler, Leigh Ann. *How Sex Became a Civil Liberty*. New York: Oxford University Press, 2013.

Wiegand, Wayne A. "Oregon's Public Libraries during the First World War." *OHQ* 90, no. 1 (Spring 1989): 39–63.

Willett, Julie A. *Permanent Waves: The Making on the American Beauty Shop*. New York: New York University Press, 2000.

Wilson, Jan Doolittle. *The Women's Joint Committee and the Politics of Maternalism, 1920–30*. Urbana: University of Illinois Press, 2007.

Wilson, Robert A. *The Eugenic Mind Project*. Cambridge, MA: MIT Press, 2017.

Woloch, Nancy. *Muller v. Oregon: A Brief History with Documents*. Boston: Bedford Books of St. Martin's Press, 1996.

Wong, Marie Rose. *Sweet Cakes, Long Journey: The Chinatowns of Portland, Oregon*. Seattle: University of Washington Press, 2004.

Wood, Sharon. *The Freedom of the Streets: Work, Citizenship, and Sexuality in a Gilded Age City*. Chapel Hill: University of North Carolina Press, 2005.

Work, Clemens P. *Darkest before Dawn: Sedition and Free Speech in the American West*. Albuquerque: University of New Mexico Press, 2005.

Yanagisako, Sylvia Junko. *Transforming the Past: Tradition and Kinship among Japanese Americans*. Stanford, CA: Stanford University Press, 1985.

Yasui, Barbara. "The Nikkei in Oregon, 1834–1940." *OHQ* 76, no. 3 (September 1975): 225–257.

Yung, Judy. *Unbound Feet: A Social History of Chinese Women in San Francisco*. Berkeley: University of California Press, 1995.

Index

Page numbers in *italics* refer to illustrations.

Abe, Toyoji, 183

ability, 1, 20, 82–84, 216. *See also* disability and disabled people; "feeblemindedness"

ableism, 1, 37, 217

abortion, 38, 85, 140

Albany, OR, 143

Albee, H. Russell, 112–13

alcohol, illicit, 76–77, 128, 199–200

Alexander, George F., 94, 104, 108

alias, 34, 123, 143, 259n71

"alien" enemies, 16, 17, 20, 88; Austro-Hungarian citizens, 92–93; barred zones, 90–91; identity booklet, 91, 94, 96; men's registration, 89–93, 105; permits, 90–91, 94, 103, 108; photographs, 95–96, 100–104; registration forms, 91, 95–96; restrictions on, 90–91, 105, 108; women's registration, 93–104, *98, 99*; women's resistance, 100–104, 109; and World War II, 108. *See also* Riedl; surveillance; surveillance products

Alien Land Act (Oregon, 1923), 10, 13, 180, 183, 198

Alien Registration Act (US, 1940), 108

alternative healing, 167, 168–69, 173–74. *See also* Christian Science; New Thought

American Association of University Women, 61

American Civil Liberties Union, 72

American Fund for the French Wounded, 62

American Legion, 16, 205

"American Plan," 110–11, 113. *See also* anti–venereal disease campaigns

Ames, Everett, 49

Anderson, Addie, 37

anti–venereal disease campaigns, 14–15, 18, 110–23, 214, 215. *See also* Cedars, The; Commission on Training Camp Activities; Oregon Social Hygiene Society; Portland Vice Commission; sexually transmitted infections; sex workers

Armenian Oregonians, 61–63

Armistice (November 1918), 46, 63, 108, 126

armories, 90

Ashland, OR, 44

Associated Charities, 138, 145–46
Astoria, OR, 100, 111, 118–19, 149, 183
Aurora, OR, 135
Austro-Hungarian Empire, 92–93
Ayer, Winslow B., 47, 51, 66
Azumano, Satsuki, 194–95

Baird, Alvin, 191
Baker, George, 16, 66, 80, 121, 127, 129–30, 201–2, 214
Baker, Sadie, 74
Baker City, OR, 51
Baldwin, Eleanor, 173
Baldwin, Lola Greene, 24, 27–28, 110, 123, 114, 129–30
Ballard, Charles, 192
bank clerks, 161–66
barbers and barbershops, 170, 185, 195, 199
Bean, Robert S., 80
Belgium, 67
Belt, Kristine, 12
Bend, OR, 43, 44, 59, 97, 137, 149, 192, 194
Benton County, OR, 166, 172, 194
Bernstein, Salome Solis-Cohen, 50
Bertillon identification system, 17, 95
Big Sisterhood, 138, 139
birth certificates, 16, 22, 179, 186–92
birthright citizenship, 22, 179, 180, 184, 186–92
Blachly, Anna, 81–82
Black Oregonians: 1920 population, 10; exclusions and restrictions, 7–8; railroad work, 73–74; soldiers, 62
Black women in Oregon: arrests among, 116, 136; at The Cedars, 140; held for health, 128, 131; mug shots, 123; at Oregon State Hospital, 152; organizations, 50, 61,

114, 140; as railroad car cleaners, 73–74; Rosebud Study Group, 62; voter registration and voting activism, 8, 10–12, 213; World War I home front, 61–62. *See also* Anderson; Brown, Ruth; Gray; Weeks
Blue, Rupert, 122, 127, 129–30
boarding house managers, 139, 185, 195, 197–209
boarding schools, Indian, 40; Chemawa, 21, 147
bodies: power over, 111, 174; surveillance of, 17, 20, 110–13, 127–28, 136, 213–14. *See also* gender-non-conforming people; Gloss; Riedl; Springer, Winnie Hull
Bondurant, Margaret, 27
Bonham, Ralph P., 158–60, 163
book burning, 206
Bright Jim, Annie, 60
Brown, George M., 92, 168, 171–72
Brown, Ruth, 21, 131–33, *133*, 149, 211, 216
Brunicardi, Anselmo, 133–34
Brunicardi, Leonor Zambrano, 5, 21, 132–34, 214, 215
Bryon, William, 45, 66, 78, 79, 81
Buck v. Bell (1927), 26
Buland, Bertha, 27
Bunting v. Oregon (1917), 14
Burbank, Louise, 5, 21, 160–66, *162*, 178, 212, 215, 217
Bureau of Immigration (US), 17, 18, 158–60, 163–66
Bureau of Indian Affairs (US), 17, 19; health care and sterilization, 37–39; industrial surveys, 17, 39–40; Liberty Loan Drives and, 59–60; "wayward girls" and eugenics, 21, 147, 148

Bureau of Investigation (US), 17, 45, 66, 78–79, 123, 183, 201

Burnett, George H., 208–9

business licensing, 13, 205–6, 208–9. *See also* hotel licensing

Bynon, Allan, 133–34

Cable Act (US, 1922), 9

Callahan, Ida, 27

Campbell, Robert A., 85

Camp Lewis, WA, 62, 115

Canada, 160–66

Cannaday, Beatrice, 43

Carlisle, Chester L., 2, 33–36

Cartozian, Hazel, 61–63

Castner, Therese, 42–43, 45, 47

Catholic Oregonians, 10, 13–14, 102, 137–38, 213

Catholic Religious Sisters, 13–14, *102*, 213

Catholic Women's League, 137–38, 145–46

Cedars, The, 15, 21, 110, 123, *125*; 1923 closure of, 147–48; admittance card, 17, 132, *133*; Brown and, 131–33, 211, 216; Brunicardi and, 132–34; conditions at, 124–27; demographics of inmates, *126*, 136–37, 139–41; escapes from, 129, 136, 139, 148; eugenic thinking and, 144–47; mothers incarcerated at, 140–41; overcrowding, 126–27; productive labor and, 142–44; women of color at, 140; work placement, 139. *See also* anti–venereal disease campaigns; health parole; Oregon Social Hygiene Society

censorship, 123, 134, 152, 170, 171

Central Labor Council, Portland, 77

Chalcraft, Edwin, 148

Chamberlain, George, 24, 26, 70, 119

Chamberlain-Kahn Act (US, 1918), 119

Chemawa Indian Boarding School, 21, 147

childbirth, 22, 36–39, 179, 186–92

childcare, 140–41, 192–94

child custody, 141

Chinese Exclusion, 16

Chinese Oregonians, 16, 132, 180–81, 191; 1920 population, 10; Chinese Student Association, 64; and Food Pledge, 53; marriage restrictions, 7–8, 208; naturalization restrictions, 9; at Oregon State Hospital, 152; as "unfit," 19, 35–36; voting, 7–9. *See also* Moy

Chinese Student Association, 64

Christian nationalism, 28

Christian Science, 25, 162–63, 165–66, 167

citizenship: birthright, 22, 179, 180, 184, 186–92; definitions of, 2–7; of dissent, 2, 17, 19, 42, 52, 211; economic, 3–4, 6, 69, 168, 170–71; and eugenics, 164–66; "fit," 2; "inadequate," 2, 34; Nisei and, 21, 79, 180, 184, 186–92; obligations of, 3, 4, 18; practice of, 3, 5; productive, 2, 3–4, 40; workplace and, 66–71, 72–79. *See also* "alien" enemies; birth certificates; Cable Act; Expatriation Act; "first papers"; *Halladjian*; Indian Citizenship Act; loyalty; naturalization; *Ozawa*; slackers; Thind; voting; woman suffrage in Oregon

Citizenship and Voting Amendment (Oregon, 1914), 9, 90

City Council, Portland, 120–21, 200–205

INDEX / *307*

Civilian Committee to Combat Venereal Disease (US), 119

civil liberties, 1–2, 6, 55–56, 211; violations at The Cedars, 127–36, 144–47, 216; violations at Oregon State Hospital, 150–78, 216; Anna Mary Weston and, 80. *See also* cruel and unusual punishment; due process; false imprisonment; Fourteenth Amendment; habeas corpus; health parole; "held for health"; "held for investigation"; loyalty oaths; restraint; search warrant; surveillance; surveillance products; torture

Clackamas County, OR, 103, 135

Clark, John, 112

class legislation, 25–26

Clatsop County, OR, 118–19, 183, 192

Clayton, Horace R., 116–17

Cleeton, T. J., 167, 170

Coe, Henry Waldo, 33, 83–84, 138–39

Colby, Clara, 173

collateral scrutiny. *See* surveillance

Colored Women's Council (Portland), 50, 114, 140

Colored Women's Protective Association, 114

Colored Women's Republican Club, 11

Columbia Park Hospital and Training Center, 83

Commission on Training Camp Activities (CTCA), 115–17, 119, 123

commitment (institutional), 3, 72–73, 151, 158, 160, 178, 216. *See also* Cedars, The; Eastern Oregon State Hospital; Oregon State Hospital; Oregon State Institution for the Feeble-Minded; Weston, Anna Mary

Compulsory Education Bill (Oregon, 1922), 13–14

compulsory military service. *See* military draft for men

compulsory national service. *See* World War I: women's "draft"

Congressional Union for Woman Suffrage, 68–69

Conlee, Lucinda (Mrs. Reuben A.), 78

conservation of food. *See* Food Pledge

Cookingham, Edward, 57

Corbett, Gretchen Hoyt, 114

Corby, Grant, 168

Corvallis, OR, 43

Council of Jewish Women, Portland Branch, 27, 50, 61, 138

Council of National Defense (US), 119; Oregon Women's Committee of, 42–43, 45–46

Court of Domestic Relations, 146

cremation, 151

"cross-dressing," 106–9

cruel and unusual punishment, 152, 168, 170, 212

Dahrens, Hattie Burbank, 103–4

Dallas [OR] Woman's Club, 61

Dalles, The, OR, 83, 100

Daughters of the American Revolution (DAR), Oregon chapter, 28

Davey, Frank, 183–84

Day, Marie K., 78

Deich, Richard, 148

Department of Justice (US, DOJ), 78, 79, 91, 96, 108. *See also* Bureau of Investigation

deportation, 5, 9, 54, 109, 150, 152, 178, 209–10, 214–15; Brunicardi and, 21, 132–34; Burbank and, 160, 163–65; Hunt and, 70–71; Kojima

308 / INDEX

and, 208, 209–10; Riedl and, 20, 109; Uyeto and, 204–5, 209–10; Margarita Wilcox and, 157–58

Derthick Music Club, 61

developmentally disabled people, 82–83, 151, 156, 212. *See also* disability and disabled people; eugenics; "feeblemindedness"; intellectually disabled people

Dever, Lem, 29

disability and disabled people, 18, 35, 73, 144, 203, 212, 215–16. *See also* developmentally disabled people; "feeblemindedness"; intellectually disabled people

dissent. *See* citizenship: of dissent; resistance

Domestic Relations, Court of, 146

domestic workers, 75–76, 86, 128, 139, 141, 160, 166

double standard, gendered: in anti-venereal disease campaigns, 111, 117–18, 128–29, 131–32, 147–48, 211, 214; and citizenship, 109

draft. *See* military draft for men; selective service; World War I: women's "draft"

Drake, Fred H., 79–80

dress ban, 112–13

dressmakers, 81, 82

due process, 6, 17, 91, 108; and The Cedars, 131–32, 142–44; and Oregon State Hospital, 160–61; and Portland hotel licensing, 120–21, 200–202; Springer and, 167, 168–69, 178, 212

Dumble, Howard L., 188

Dunbar, Sadie Orr, 43

Duniway, Abigail Scott, 173

Dutro, Edgar O., 188

Eastern Oregon State Hospital, 24, 151, 177

Eastport, ID, 165

Edmundson, Alice, 74

education, 192–93, 197–98. *See also* teachers

employment bureaus, 75–76, 145

Endow, Tei, 188, 192–93

enemies. *See* "alien" enemies; internal enemies

epilepsy, 24, 151

Equi, Marie, 81–82, 106

espionage, 106–7

Espionage Act (US, 1917), 6, 19, 51, 55–56, 64, 65, 69, 81

ethnic profiling, 92

Eugene, OR, 51, 59, 67

eugenics in Oregon, 19; 1921 court ruling, 25; 1983 end of, 217; bills and laws, 23–25, 35–36, 82–83, 163, 168, 174; The Cedars and, 144–47; coerced sterilization beyond institutions, 24–27, 35–36, 154–56, 215–16; Indigenous Oregonians and, 36–40; Oregon apology for, 217; Oregon State Hospital and, 21, 150, 160–66; Oregon State Industrial School for Girls and, 148, 215; postwar, 31–32; premarital health examination legislation, 25–27, 35–36, 185, 215–26; settler colonialism and, 155–56. *See also* "feeblemindedness"; Griffith; Oregon Social Hygiene Society; Oregon State Board of Eugenics; Oregon State Board of Health; Oregon State Institution for the Feeble-Minded; Oregon State Survey of Mental Defect; Owens-Adair; White club-women: eugenics support

INDEX / *309*

eugenic surveillance, 2, 18, 31, 35, 78–79, 109, 212, 215–16
eugenic thinking, 2, 28, 30, 36, 83, 110, 211–12, 213–14, 215–17; The Cedars and, 144–47; at Oregon State Hospital, 150. *See also* social hygiene; Oregon Social Hygiene Society
Evans, Sarah A., 27, 57, 61, 97, *98*, 144–45
exclusion, 1, 4, 9–10, 211–17; federal legislation, 9; hotel licensing and, 198–209; in Oregon Constitution, 7–8; voting, 7. *See also* "alien" enemies; Alien Land Act; Black; Chinese; deportation; Hawai'ian; Immigration Act; immigration restriction; Japanese; Latinx; nativism; South Asian; White supremacy
Expatriation Act (US, 1907), 9, 20, 52, 88, 94, 104, 159

Fairview Training Center, 83–84, 217. *See also* Oregon State Institution for the Feeble-Minded
false imprisonment, 169–70. *See also* habeas corpus; "held for health"; "held for investigation"
family economy, 22, 192–98
farm work, 102, 139, 144, 153, 183–84, 188, 189–94, 197
Farrell, Robert, 25
FBI (Federal Bureau of Investigation). *See* Bureau of Investigation
"feeblemindedness," 16, 21; The Cedars and, 144–47; citizenship and, 2; "hygienic marriage" and, 215–16; Indigenous women and, 147; Oregon eugenics and, 24, 32–36,

79, 155–56, 214; sex workers and, 144–47. *See also* developmentally disabled people; disability and disabled people; intellectually disabled people; Oregon State Institution for the Feeble-Minded; Weston, Anna Mary
Felts, Aristina, 114
"female impersonator," 106
film (motion pictures), 134, 135
fingerprinting, 17, 95
Finley, Anna Ries, 192
"first papers" and naturalization process, 70, 89–90, 103
Fisher, Ralph S., 190–91
Fitzgerald, J. J., 131–32
Food Pledge, 15, 17, 19, 46–56, *47*, *48*
Fort Douglas, UT, 91, 106, 107–8
Fort Oglethorpe, GA, 91
Fort Stevens, OR, 118–19
Foster, William T., 112
Fourteenth Amendment (US), 22, 25, 180, 202, 208. *See also* citizenship; due process
Frazer Home, 138
Free Dispensary, 138
freedom of speech, 52, 81–82, 90, 106, 204. *See also* Espionage Act; Hunt; sedition; Sedition Act; Weston, Anna Mary
Fruit and Flower Mission, 141
Fujii, Kino, 194
Fujii, Sumino, 194
Funk, George R., 54–55

Gallagher, Belle, 74
Gatens, William, 132
gender identity, 1, 104–8, 175–77, 178
gender-nonconforming people, 2, 18, 20, 21, 139, 150, 172, 212; anti–ve-

nereal disease campaigns and, 112; eugenics law and, 24, 36; Food Pledge surveillance of, 53–54. *See also* Gloss; homophobia; intersex; nonbinary people; nonsanctioned sexual activity; Portland Vice Scandal; Riedl; same-sex intimacy; "sexual perversion"; Springer, Winnie; Taylor

gender presentation, 1, 3, 17, 105–8, 134–36, 175

genocide, 8, 216

"Gentlemen's Agreement" (US and Japan, 1907), 181, 199

George v. City of Portland (1924), 208

German Oregonians, 53, 55; noncitizen registration, 88–109. *See also* "alien enemies"

Gheer, Linda, 217

Gifford, Mae, 12

Gilbert, J. Allen, 177

Gleason, Caroline, 138

Gloss, Teddy, 18, 21, 132–34, 148, 211–12, 214

gonorrhea, 38, 111, 117, 128, 212, 214. *See also* sexually transmitted infections (STIs)

Goritzan, George B., 205

Grand Ronde Agency, 39, 40

Grant, Frank, 202, 205

Grants Pass, OR, 59, 194

Gray, Katherine, 50, 61, 62

Greek Oregonians, 205

Green, Perry Joseph, 167, 169, 173–74

Gregory, Thomas, 55–56, 93, 102, 107, 108

Gresham, OR, 183–84

Griffith, Lewis Frank, 1, 178; authority at Oregon State Hospital, 156; background, 154–55; and Burbank,

160–66; eugenics views, 155–56; and Springer, 168–70, 171–72, 175–77; and Margarita Wilcox, 156–60

Grisim, Charles R., 78, 79

habeas corpus, 21, 129, 131–32, 149, 211, 216, 259n65

Hall, Harwood, 147

Halladjian case (1909), 63

Haney, Bert, 66, 94, 106–7, 108

Hansen, Andrew, 80

Harms, Leo, 97, *98*

Hart, Milla Wessinger, 53

Hawai'ian Native people, 7–8, 128

Hayashi, Koyo, 192

health care: on reservations, 37, 39, 40. *See also* alternative healing; Indian Health Service; Japanese Oregonians: prejudice against, in health care; physicians; reproductive health care

health parole, 21, 110, 123, 142–44, 148

Hedges, Gilbert, 106

"held for health," 20, 110, 127–28, 129–31, 134, 136, 148, 214

"held for investigation," 79, 127

heterosexual intimacy, 2, 54, 111, 112, 118

Hirabayashi, Kikuno, 197–98

Hirata, Tokuji, 192

Hoffert, Madeline, 78, 79

Holcomb, Curtis, 167–68, 169, 171–72

Holford, Florence, 160–61, 165–66

Holford, William, 160, 166

Holman, Rufus, 66–67, 69–70

homophobia, 24

Hood River, OR, 90, 183–84, 186, 188–89, 193

Hoover, Herbert, 46, 47, 52

INDEX / *311*

hotel and rooming house operators, 185, 195, 197–98, 198–209
Hotel Association, 120–21
hotel licensing, 17, 18, 80, 118–23, 125, 179–80, 198–209, 215
House, William, 160
House Committee on Immigration and Naturalization (US), 182
House of the Good Shepherd, 148
Howard, Emil Washington, 167–68, 169, 173–75
Howard, Tena, 167, 169, 173–75, 178
Hughes, Herbert H., 192, 277n70
Hull, Eleanor (Ellen), 170, 174, 176
Hull, William, 167, 169, 174–75, 177
Hull, Willie, 172, 178
Hull House, 137–38
Hume, Wilson T., 168, 170, 171
hunger strike, 135, 212
Hunt, M. Louise, 5, 17, 20, 65, 66–72, 71, 86, 214–15
Hurd, Nellie, 12
Hurlburt, Thomas (sheriff), 77
Hurlburt, Thomas H. (legislator), 205–6
"hygienic marriage," 26–27, 35, 185

identification: Bertillon system, 17, 95; and The Cedars, 17, 132, *133*, 137. *See also* photographic identification
"imbecility," 82. *See also* "feeblemindedness"
immigrants, 215; and Food Pledge, 49–50, 53; and Liberty Loan Drives, 61–64; at Oregon State Hospital, 152, 156–60, 160–66; and Portland Central Library, 68; railroad work and, 73. *See also* "alien" enemies; deportation; exclusion;

second language matters; *and specific ethnicities and nationalities*
Immigration Act (US, 1917), 157–58, 159
Immigration Act (US, 1924), 32, 181
immigration restriction, 9–10, 31–32, 157–58, 180, 193
incarceration, 108, 110, 113, 210. *See also* Cedars, The; internment; jail; Kelly Butte
incommunicado, 79, 131
Independence, OR, 196–97
Indian Citizenship (Snyder) Act (1924), 9, 40
Indian Health Service, 38. *See also* health care: on reservations
Indigenous Oregonians: 1920 population, 10; eugenics and, 19, 36–40, 216; industrial surveys, 17, 39–40; marriage restrictions, 7–8; mental testing and, 147; at Oregon State Hospital, 152; voting, 9; "wayward girls," 21, 147, 148. *See also* Bright Jim; Bureau of Indian Affairs; Chemawa; Grand Ronde; Klamath; Siletz; Umatilla; Warm Springs
Industrial Workers of the World (IWW), 9, 81, 91, 124
influenza, 127, 140, 191
Inglis, George, 192
inmate labor, 143–44, 152–53, 167
insanity: Marie Equi and, 82; Oregon eugenics and, 24, 32–36, 212, 214; Oregon State Hospital, 151, 160, 164; Winnie Springer and, 168–69
intellectually disabled people, 35, 82–83, 144–45, 151. *See also* developmentally disabled people; disability and disabled people; "feeblemindedness"

312 / INDEX

intelligence testing, 146. *See also* mental testing

Intercollegiate Socialist Society, 69

Interdepartmental Social Hygiene Board (US), 119–20, 141

internal enemies, 1, 5, 15–16, 18, 212–13, 218; eugenics and, 23, 32–36; Hunt as, 67–72; Issei women as, 21–22, 179–86; Riedl as, 107; sex workers as, 143–44; wartime registrations and, 41, 46, 56, 64, 211; Anna Mary Weston as, 85; women with STIs as, 110. *See also* Food Pledge; Liberty Loan Drives; slackers

internment, 54, 89, 91, 94, 97, 106, 116

interpreters, 61, 73, 97–98

intersex, 176. *See also* gender-nonconforming people

IQ testing, 146. *See also* mental testing

Isom, Mary Frances, 68, 69, 173

Issei (first generation). *See* Japanese Oregonians

Italian Oregonians, 53, 73

Ito, Sui, 192

Iwatsuki, Shizue, 193

Jackson County, OR, 49, 136

jail, 91, 124–25, 127. *See also* Multnomah County jail

Japanese Association of Oregon, 182, 183, 202, 204

Japanese consulate, 182, 187

Japanese Hand Laundry (Salem), 195–97, *195, 196*

Japanese Oregon Growers' Exchange, 194

Japanese Oregonians, 181–82; 1920 population, 10; in Bend, 194; in Benton County, 193, 194; business

and hotel licensing, 1, 13, 17, 18, 22, 179–80, 198–209; exclusion, 10; and Food Pledge, 53; in Grants Pass, 194; in Hood River, 188–89, 193; as hotel and rooming house managers, 185, 195, 197–209; in Independence, 196–97; as internal enemies, 21–22, 180–86; Issei midwives, 37, 189–92; Issei women barbers, 185, 195; Issei women's labor and family economy, 192–98, 209; Issei women's resistance, 179–80, 186–92; in Labish Meadows, 194; marriage restrictions, 8, 208; in Multnomah County, 183–84, 192; naturalization and voting restrictions, 9; Nisei citizenship, 21, 79, 180, 184, 186–92; Nisei education, 192–93, 197–98; "picture brides," 180, 183; prejudice against, in health care, 188, 190–91, 277n70; in Salem, 195–97; sterilization of Issei women proposed, 31, 179, 185; surveillance of, 21, 181–82, 190, 199–210; as "unfit," 19, 35–36; and World War II incarceration, 108, 210. *See also* Alien Land Act; Kojima; *Oshu Nippo; Ozawa;* Uyeto

"Japanese Problem," 179, 183–86

Japanese School (Portland), 197–98

Japantown (Nihonmachi), 179–80, 184–85, 189–90, 194–95, 197–208

Jenkins, Leon, 208

Jewish Oregonians, 10, 43. *See also* Council of Jewish Women, Portland Branch

Joan of Arc, 29

Johnson, Hiram, 181

Johnson, N. F., 123, 129

INDEX / *313*

Justice Department. *See* Department of Justice

Kahn, Julius, 119
Kariya, Riki, 189, 191
Kavanaugh, John, 132
Kelly Butte, 116, 124–26, 136
Kemp, Jennie, 47
Kinney, Mary Strong, 26
Kiss, Maggie, 100
Kite, Geraldine, 52
Kitzhaber, John, 217
Kiyohiro, Tomo, 195
Klamath County, OR, 39, 60
Klamath Falls, OR, 81
Klamath Falls Home Defense League, 81
Klamath Tribes, 37, 39, 40, 60, 147
Klanswomen (KKK), 12–13, 28–30, *29, 32*
Koehring, Meta, 101
Kohs, Samuel C., 146, 177
Kojima, Matsumi, 5, 22, 179, 198, 206–8, *207,* 209–10, 215
Kromminga, Eugenie, *101,* 102
Ku Klux Klan, 1, 10, 12–13, 16, 28–30, 205, 206, 213

Labish Meadows, Oregon, 194
labor: inmate, 143–44, 152–53, 167; Issei women's, and family economy, 192–98, 209. *See also* Central Labor Council; Oregon Bureau of Labor and Industry; productive labor
Labor Day, 62
Lafferty, Lilian, 161–66
La Grande, OR, 54
Lakeview, OR, 192
Lane, Franklin, 60

Lane County, OR, 51
language barriers. *See* second language matters
Latina identity, 134
Latin lovers, 134
Latinx Oregonians, 8, 10, 132–34, 156–60, 214. *See also* Wilcox, Margarita
Latourette, E. C., 106
Laughlin, Harry H., 25
laundry workers, 61, 62, 86, 195–97
Lena (A. M. Weston's sister), 73, 82–83, 241n33
lesbians, 53–54, 81–82, 112. *See also* Equi; gender-nonconforming people; same-sex intimacy; "sexual perversion"
Liberty Loan Drives, 15, 19, 20, 56–64, *58,* 65–71
Liberty Temple, 59, 68
librarians, 66–72
licensing. *See* business licensing; hotel licensing
Liljeqvist, Lawrence A., 51
logging, 103, 194
Looney, Walter W., 161–62
Lovejoy, George A., 206
Lowenberg, Ida, 138
loyalty, 5, 15, 41–42; oaths, 17, 69–70, 90. *See also* Food Pledge; Liberty Loan Drives; "100% Americanism"; War Savings Stamps; wartime service registration; Weston, Anna Mary; World War I

Mallory, Lucy Rose, 173
Manion, Florence, 192
Mann Act (US, 1910), 133
marriage: arranged, 181; heterosexual, 2, 118, 212; "hygienic," 26–27, 35, 185; "picture brides," 180, 183. *See*

also Cable Act; Expatriation Act; miscegenation

"mashers," 112–13

mass media, 50–51

Marvin, Cornelia (Mrs. Walter Pierce), 28, 69, 173

Mathews, Margaret, 127, 214

McAdoo, Eleanor Wilson, 57

McAdoo, William, 56

McCarran-Walter Act (US, 1952), 180

McCourt, John, 116

McGavin, Jessie, 191, 192

McInturff, Herman F., 123

McKie, Margaret, 128–29, 141

McNary, Charles, 181

Medford, OR, 44, 57, 59, 96–97

mental hygiene, 32, 177

"mental incapacity," 65, 72

mental testing, 34, 146–47, 148

Metschan, Julia (Mrs. Lewis Frank Griffith), 154

Mexican Oregonians, 8, 10, 132–34, 156–60, 214. *See also* Brunicardi, Leonor; Wilcox, Margarita

Mexican Revolution, 1, 133, 156–57

midwives, 22, 37, 187, 189–92. *See also* Sato, Natsu; Thompson, Agnes

military draft for men, 44, 45, 91, 96, 105. *See also* selective service

military draft for women. *See* World War I: women's "draft"

Military Intelligence Branch, US Army, 17, 81, 123, 183

Mill City, OR, 167, 172

minimum wage, 6, 14, 75–76

Mirayasu, Tora, 189

miscegenation laws (marriage restrictions), 7–8, 208, 216

Mitoma, Hisa, 197

Mitoma, Koshizu Susie, 197

Miura, Rin, 190

"Mongolians," 8, 208

Monmouth Normal School, 167

Montague, Richard W., 66

Moore, Harry, 119–21

morality, 111, 113, 201, 202

Morrow, Robert G., 120, 121, 205

motion pictures, 134, 135

Moy, Pearl, 63–64

Moy Back Hin, 63

Muller v. Oregon (1908), 14

Multnomah County, OR, 65–71, 124–26, 192

Multnomah County Bar Association, 80

Multnomah County Hospital, 139, 140

Multnomah County jail, 167, 169–70

Multnomah County Poor Farm, 86, 125

Multnomah Home Guard, 17, 59

Murphy, Anna (railroad car cleaner), 78

Murphy, Anna E. (social worker with The Cedars), 114, 137–43, *138*, 145–46, 148

Murphy, Mary, 78, 79

Myrick, Maud, 127

Nakamura, Shiyo, 196

Nakamura, Towa, 197

Napa State Psychiatric Hospital (California), 177

National Council of Jewish Women. *See* Council of Jewish Women, Portland Branch

national security, STIs and sex workers as threats to, 4, 110, 144, 147

national service. *See* military draft for men; World War I: women's "draft"

National Woman's Liberty Loan Committee (NWLLC), 57

nativism, 1, 28, 31, 89, 133, 150, 158, 179, 211

naturalization, 69–70

Near East Relief, 63

Neighborhood House, 138

Neosalvarsan (syphilis treatment), 111

Neureither, Anna Bertha, 101–2

"New Patriotism," 30–31, 213

New Thought, 167, 168–69, 173–74

Nihonmachi. *See* Japantown (Nihonmachi)

Ninomiya, Kariki, 192

Nisei (second generation). *See* Japanese Oregonians

Nishimoto, Hatsumi, 193

nonbinary people, 2, 166, 175–77, 212, 214

noncitizens, 9, 17–18, 90, 180, 205–9. *See also* "alien" enemies

nonsanctioned sexual activity, 20, 111–12, 118, 149, 212, 214. *See also* anti–venereal disease campaigns; Cedars, The

North Bank Railroad Station, 20, 65, 72–74, 76–79, 86, 211

North Bend, OR, 45

North End (Portland), 115, 184–85, 200, 203–4

Noyori, Miyoshi, 193

nuisance: arrest for, 128; houses of prostitution as, 120; liquor sales locations as, 200

nurses, 127, 139

O'Hara, Edwin V., 50

Ohmart, Junius, 162–66

Olcott, Ben, 183

"100% Americanism," 18, 30, 62

Ordinance 33510, Suppression of Venereal Diseases (Portland), 117–18

Ordinance 33649, Regulation of Hotels, Rooming Houses, and Lodging Houses (Portland), 118, 120–22

Oregon Bureau of Labor and Industry (BOLI), 35, 181–82

Oregon City, OR, 44, 54, 105–7, 135

Oregon Congress of Mothers, 12

Oregon Consumers' League, 12

Oregon Equal Suffrage Alliance, 61

Oregon Federation of Colored Women's Clubs, 50, 61

Oregon Federation of (White) Women's Clubs, 12, 27, 42, 57, 144–45. *See also* White clubwomen

Oregon First: anti–venereal disease campaigns and, 20, 116, 119–25; boosterism, 14–16, 212–13; eugenics and, 25; Liberty Loan Drives and, 59, 64, 68

Oregon Humane Society, 135

Oregon Marriage Examination Law (1938), 215–16. *See also* "hygienic marriage"

Oregon Peace League, 69

Oregon Social Hygiene Society (OSHS), 15, 16; and anti–venereal disease campaigns, 112, 116, 119; and The Cedars, 126–27, 137–44, 146–47, 148; eugenics and, 155; "feeblemindedness" and, 146–47; undercover agents of, 123

Oregon Social Workers Association, 68

Oregon State Board of Control, 135, 151, 171–72

Oregon State Board of Eugenics, 24, 25, 83, 153–54, 159, 161–66, 216, 217

Oregon State Board of Health, 16, 24, 122–23, 137, 142, 148, 187

Oregon State Board of Social Protection, 217

316 / INDEX

Oregon State Hospital: demographics, 152; deportation, 17, 150, 152, 156–60; eugenics and, 24, 155–56; inmate labor, 152–53, 167; Lena and, 82–83; medical and surgical procedures, 152–53; overcrowding, 150–51, 153; resistance at, 157–60, 161–66; voting rights loss for inmates, 8, 150, 170–71. *See also* Burbank; Eastern Oregon State Hospital; Griffith; restraint; Springer, Winnie; *Springer v. Steiner*; Wilcox, Margarita

Oregon State Industrial School for Girls, 135, 147, 148, 212, 215

Oregon State Industrial Welfare Commission, 28, 75–76

Oregon State Institution for the Feeble-Minded, 8, 24, 83, 85–86, 217

Oregon State Normal School, Monmouth, 167

Oregon State Survey of Mental Defect, Delinquency, and Dependency, 2, 16, 18, 19, 32–36; Chinese and Japanese Oregonians as "unfit" in, 19, 35–36; "feeblemindedness" in, 2, 16. *See also* eugenic surveillance

Oregon State Women's Press Club, 27

"Oregon System" of government reforms, 10–12, 14

Oregon Voter Literacy Amendment (1924), 9

Oregon Women's Committee of the Council of National Defense, 42–43, 45–46

Oregon Women's Legislative Council, 12, 27, 28

Oshu Nippo (*Oregon Daily News*), 10, 182, 183, 197

Ottoman Empire, 92. *See also* Armenian Oregonians

ovariectomy, 153–54

Owens-Adair, Bethenia, 23–28, 31, 35–36, 154–56, 185, 215–16

Oyama, Iwao, 182, 186, 202

Ozawa v. United States (1922), 9–10, 180, 181

Pacific Coast Rescue and Protective Society, 148

Parent Teacher Association, 12

parole, 9, 21, 83–86, 114, 135, 137–40, 142, 156, 161. *See also* health parole

passport requirement, 16–17

Patriotic Drive Association, 62

"'patriotic' inquisition," 20, 67, 71

patriotic scrutiny, 213–14

patriotic womanhood, 6, 19, 41–42, 67, 213

Patterson, Mary Woodworth (Mrs. Isaac Lee Patterson), 28, 31

Patton State Hospital (California), 178

Pease, George N., 160

Pendleton, OR, 54, 135, 151

Pendleton Round-up, 135

Pennington, Levi, 45

People First, 217

People's Institute, 75, 138

permanent voter registration, 10–12

Pettit, Joseph, 191

Philomath College, 167, 168

photographic identification, 16–17, 91, 95–96, 109, 123, 165

physicians: and birth certificates, 187; and eugenics, 21, 36–40, 83–84, 155–56; Indigenous Oregonians and, 19, 36–40; institutional commitment, 151, 155

—men, 38–39, 85, 160–62, 177, 188,

INDEX / *317*

190–92, 195, 217. *See also* Blue; Carlisle; Coe; Griffith; Holcomb; Howard, Emil Washington; Seeley; Steiner; Whiting
—women, 114, 119, 146, 191–92; and OSHS, 113–14; and wartime registration, 42. *See also* Equi; Owens-Adair
"picture brides," 180, 183
Pierce, Cornelia. *See* Marvin
Pierce, Walter, 25, 28, 135
Pinkley, Virgil M., 38–39
police: and "alien" enemy registration, 91, 93; "cleanup raids," 54, 115–16, 123, 133, 136; "held for investigation" by, 79; "morals" squad, 199–200; War Emergency Squad, 123, 127–28, 199–200. *See also* hotel licensing; Women's Protective Bureau
Polk County, OR, 103, 192
Portland, OR: "alien" enemy women's registration in, 94, 97–98, 100; as "cleanest city" 16; dress ban, 112–13; "firsts," 112; Food Pledge in, 49–54; jail, 136; Liberty Loan Drives in, 65–71; Liberty Temple in, 59; mashers in, 112; police headquarters, 78; "Portlandizing" women, 116–17; Rose Festival, 62; War Service Stamp Drive in, 77; wartime service registration in, 43–44. *See also* Japantown (Nihonmachi); North End; Ordinance 33510; Ordinance 33649; Union Station; Women's Protective Bureau
Portland Central Labor Council, 77
Portland Central Library, 20, 65–71, 211
Portland City Council, 120–21, 200–205

Portland Court of Domestic Relations, 146
Portland Emergency Hospital, 115–16, 214
Portland Grade Teachers' Association, 61
Portland Hotel Association, 120–21
Portland Mental Hygiene Society, 177
Portland Vice Commission (1912–1913), 15, 112–13, 116, 120, 145, 185
Portland Vice Scandal (1912–1913), 24, 112, 175
Portland Vigilantes, 17, 55, 59, 92
Portland Woman's Club, 27, 61
Portland Women's Union, 75
Portland Woolen Mills, 61
postal employees and surveillance, 17, 96, 104, 123
post office and "alien" enemy registration, 91, 93
post-traumatic stress, 157
Prichard, Valentine, 138
Prime, Walter O., 131
productive labor, 82–86, 142–44, 152–53, 159, 179, 183–84
profiling, racial or ethnic, 92
"pro-German" characterization, 51, 53, 55, 78, 206
prohibition, 12, 17, 76–77, 123, 199–200, 201
prostitution, 110, 112, 115–18, 120–21, 136, 184, 204. *See also* anti-venereal disease campaigns; "held for health"; police: "cleanup raids"; Portland Vice Commission; sex workers
public charges (government dependents), 24, 25, 157–58, 163–66
public defenders, 80, 119, 203, 243n59
public health. *See* anti-venereal dis-

ease campaigns; quarantine; US Public Health Service; vaccination

Pullman Company, 20, 74, 75, 78, 86, 211

Pullman railroad cars, 74–75. *See also* railroad car cleaners

quarantine, 113, 116, 117, 122, 125, 149, 191

queerness, 175, 176–77. *See also* gender-nonconforming people; same-sex intimacy; "sexual perversion"

racial profiling, 92

racism, 1, 37, 92, 114, 133, 190. *See also* deportation; exclusion; nativism; White supremacy; *and specific racial and ethnic groups*

railroad car cleaners, 72–79, 82

railroads, 17, 194

Randall, Martha, 130–31, 148

Rankin, Robert, 81

rape, 67

Reames, Clarence, 92

recession, economic, 198–99

Red Cross, 62

redlining, 215

Red Scare, 9

registration for women, World War I. *See* "alien" enemy registration; Food Pledge; Liberty Loan Drives; wartime service registration for women

Reimers, Grace, 103

religion. *See* Catholic Oregonians; Christian nationalism; Christian Science; Jewish Oregonians; New Thought; Woman's Christian Temperance Union

religious attire, 13, 102

repatriation, 108. *See also* deportation

Report of the Japanese Situation in

Oregon (1920), 183–84

reproductive health care, 22, 179, 186–92. *See also* abortion; childbirth; midwives

resistance, 19, 212–13; to "alien" enemy registration, 100–104, 109; at The Cedars, 129, 139; to Food Pledge, 46, 51–56, 211; hunger strike, 135, 212; Issei women and, 179–80, 186–92, 192–98, 203–4; to Liberty Bond Drives, 65–71, 211; at Oregon State Hospital, 157–60, 161–66, 212; to wartime service registration, 42–46. *See also* Burbank; Gloss; Hunt; Kojima; Springer, Winnie; Uyeto, Mitsuyo; Weston, Anna Mary; Wilcox, Margarita

restraint (physical), 135, 152, 153, 161, 167, 170, 177

Reynolds, Tige, *48*, 49

Rhodes, Louise, 74

Riedl, 5, 18, 20, 89, 104–8, *105*, 109, 215

Robinson, David, 79, 116, 119–22

Robison, Charles W., 78

Rogers, Elizabeth, 129, 169, 174

Rogers, Lena, 74

Romacly, Marguerite, 161–66

rooming houses, 17, 185. *See also* hotel and rooming house operators; hotel licensing

Roseburg, OR, 96

Rose Festival, 62

Rossman, George, 114

Salem, OR, 42–43, 44–45, 100, 111; "alien" enemy women's registration in, 96; Japanese community in, 195–97; Liberty Loan Drives, 59; Oregon State Hospital, 151–52

INDEX / *319*

salpingectomy, 153–54

same-sex intimacy, 53–54, 81, 111, 112, 175, 214

Sandy, OR, 83, 103–4

San Francisco, 76–77

Sasaki, Ko, 189, 192

"sassy" (term), 203–4, 209

Sato, Natsu, 189, 191, 195

Schum, John, 97

search warrant, 77, 200, 202, 209

Sears, Irma Metz, 61

Seattle, WA, 115, 116–17

Second International Congress of Eugenics (1922), 34

second language matters, 8, 49–50, 61, 97–98, 186, 189, 202–3, 204

Secret Service, 17, 92

sedition, 6, 55–56

Sedition Act (US, 1918), 6, 19, 64, 65, 69, 244n69; Equi and, 81–82; Food Pledge resistance and, 55–56; Anna Mary Weston and, 72, 75, 78–81

Seeley, A. C., 127, 143–44

selective service, 105, 107, 115

settler colonialism, 155

sexually transmitted infections (STIs), 4, 15–16, 85; exposure of others to, as crime, 117, 119, 122; posting bond for, 117–18, 128–29, 131–32; reporting, 111, 147; testing for, 111, 116, 127, 159, 216; and World War I, 110–23. *See also* anti–venereal disease campaigns; gonorrhea; syphilis

"sexual perversion," 3, 20, 24, 33, 53–54, 107, 109, 112, 213–14

sex workers, 4, 24, 34; aliases, 34, 123, 212, 214; in Astoria, 118–19; Black women as, 131; as developmentally disabled, 144–47; "cleanup raids" against, 54, 115–16, 123, 133, 136; Food Pledge surveillance of, 54; Hunt case and, 67; as internal enemies, 143–44; Japanese women as, 184–85, 203–4; in Portland's North End, 184–85; "reasonably suspected" of STIs, 117, 122, 127; useful employment, 143–44; World War I campaigns against, 110, 113, 115–17, 120–22. *See also* anti–venereal disease campaigns; prostitution

Shafer, Mathilde, 102

Shafer, Pauline, 102

Sherwood, OR, 103–4

Shiraishi, Natsu, 192

Siletz Indian Reservation and Siletz Tribal Members, 37, 38–39, 40, 148

Simalton, Lucile, 74

Sinnott, Nicholas J., 181

Sister Mary Stanislaus (Victoria Schindler), *102*

slackers and slacking, 4–5, 41; Food Pledge and, 46, 49, 54, 55, 59; Liberty Bonds and, 72; Anna Mary Weston and, 85

Smith, J. Elizabeth, 74

social hygiene, 14–16, 20–21, 110. *See also* anti–venereal disease campaigns; Oregon Social Hygiene Society

socialism and socialists, 68–69, 81, 91, 106

social workers, 137–39. *See also* Murphy, Anna E.

soldiers, 62, 67, 115, 122, 123, 143–44. *See also* military draft for men; selective service

Soule, A. A., 39

320 / INDEX

South Asian Oregonians, 10, 152

Sowers, Vora, 12

Spanish-American-Philippine War, 170

Springer, Clare G., 167, 172–73, 177

Springer, Winnie Hull, 18, 21, 166–78, *169*, 212, 216

Springer v. Steiner (1919), 21, 150, 166, 168–72, 216

Stanley, Emma K. Griffin, 50, 114, 140

statelessness, 70. *See also* citizenship

Steiner, Robert E. Lee, 154, 160–61, 162–64, 168, 171–72. See also *Springer v. Steiner* (1919)

sterilization (state-coerced): "consent" for, 161–64; "feeblemindedness" and, 144–47; and Indigenous Oregonians, 36–40; legislation, 24–32; Lena and, 83; opposition to, 24–27, 161–66; Oregon State Hospital, 150, 152, 153–54, 161–66; Oregon State Industrial School for Girls, 148; radical, 154–56, 161, 213. *See also* Griffith; Owens-Adair

Stevenson, John H., 203–4, 207–8

St. Helens [OR] Woman's Club, 61

straitjacket, 135, 153, 170

Stricker, Frederick, 148

St. Vincent's Hospital (Portland), 160, 191

suicide attempt, 140, 141

surveillance, 6–7, 16–18; "alien" enemies and, 90–93, 94–96, 105–8, 108–9; of bodies, 20, 112–13, 123; of Chinese Oregonians, 181–82; collateral scrutiny, 18, 65, 123, 127–28; eugenics and, 32–36, 144–48, 150; Food Pledge and, 52–56; hotels and rooming houses, 117–19; of Indigenous people, 39–40; of Japanese Oregonians, 18, 21, 181–82, 199–210; Liberty Loan Drives and, 57–59; at North Bank Station, 74–78; at Oregon State Hospital, 150; at Portland Central Library, 65–71; private, 17, 123; prohibition and, 17, 76–77, 123; wartime service registration and, 41. *See also* Military Intelligence Division; Multnomah Home Guard; Oregon Social Hygiene Society; Portland Vigilantes; War Emergency Squad

surveillance products, 16–17; "alien" enemy identity booklet, 16–17, 91, 94, 96, 108, 109; "alien" enemy permits, 91, 94, 108; "alien" enemy registration forms, 91, 95–96, 109; The Cedars admittance card, 17, 132, *133*; Food Pledge cards, 17, 46; health parole card, 143; loyalty oaths, 17, 69–70, 90; Oregon State Survey of Mental Defect data card, 33–34; photographs, 91, 95–96, 123, 165, 178; voter registration cards, 10–11; "Wanted" posters, 95; wartime service registration card for women, 17, 44

Sutton, Laura, 78

Swett, Julia, 61

syphilis, 111, 116, 117, 154, 155–56, 159, 212, 214. *See also* anti-venereal disease campaigns; sexually transmitted infections (STIs)

Takagi, Ichi, 195

Takehara, Ito, 194

Takeichi, Kiyono, 194

Tanimoto, Yoshino, 192

Taylor, Buster, 136

Tazwell, George, 160

teachers, 12, 49–50, 170–71, 197–98; Grade Teachers' Association, 61; tenure for, 12, 171. *See also* education

telephone and telegraph operators, 62

Teshima, Suge, 195

Thacher, George A., 145

The Cedars. *See* Cedars, The

Thind, Bhagat Singh, 10

Thomas, Burt, 81

Thomas, Louise, 140

Thompson, Agnes, 37, 39

Thompson, Sylvia, 27

Thrane, Marcus, 188

Thrift Stamps, 65, 72, 77–78. *See also* War Savings Stamps

Tilden, Viola G., 53

Tillamook, OR, 59

Tin Plate Law (Portland), 120

torture, 170

Towne, Elizabeth, 173

travel restrictions, 90–91, 105

Troutdale, OR, 124–25, 136–37

Trumbull, Millie, 28, 31, 36, 114, 145–46, 173

Tsukamoto, Kiku, 195

Tsukamoto, Ume, 196

typesetters, 197

Uchida, Kimi, 189

Uchimada, Sowa, 194

Umatilla County, OR, 44, 167

Umatilla Indian Reservation and Umatilla Tribal Members, 38, 40

"unassimilable aliens," 180, 184

Uncle Sam, *48*, 49, *71*

"unfit," 1, 213, 216

Union County, OR, 54

Union Station (Portland), 72, 77

Universal Declaration of Human Rights (UN, 1948), 217

University of Oregon Medical Department, 154–55

unreasonable search and seizure, 77, 200, 202, 204, 209

Urakami, Takako, 189, 192

U'Ren, William S., 54, 55

US Army Military Intelligence, 17, 81, 123, 183

US Department of Justice. *See* Department of Justice

US Department of War, 119

US Employment Service, 75–76

US Food Administration (USFA), 46–56, *47*

US Public Health Service, 15–16, 17–18, 119, 123; Division of Venereal Diseases, 119, 121, 126, 130

US Railroad Administration, 75

US Treasury Department: William McAdoo, 56; NWLLC, 57; Secret Service, 17

US v. Tatos Osgihan Cartozian (1924), 63

Uyesugi, Take, 192

Uyeto, Katsutaro, 198, 200, 203–5, 206, 209–10

Uyeto, Mitsuyo, 5, 22, 179, 198–200, 203–5, 206, 209–10, 215

vaccination, 162, 165

vagrancy, 4–5, 128, 131

Vagrancy Act (Oregon, 1911), 4, 18, 92, 115

Vancouver Barracks (Washington), 91, 107, 115, 116, 125

Van Waters, Miriam, 138

Veatch, John C., 79–80

venereal disease. *See* anti–venereal disease campaigns; sexually transmitted infections

Vernon, Nellie, 119

vice, 110. *See also* Portland Vice Commission; Portland Vice Scandal

vigilantism, 16, 17, 81. *See also* Portland Vigilantes

violence, 55, 81, 92, 112–13, 157, 172, 186, 197–98, 218

voter registration, 10–14, 213

voter suppression, 10–12

voting: Black women's activism, 8; institutionalized people and, 8, 150, 170–71; Klanswomen and, 12–13; noncitizens and, 9, 90; Oregon exclusions, 7; Oregon Voter Literacy Amendment (1924), 9; Oregon women, 10–14, 211, 213; White clubwomen and, 12–13, 213. *See also* woman suffrage in Oregon

Vreeland, Thad, 171

Waddy, Louisa, 74

wage-earning women, 6, 14, 65, 97, 118, 139, 142; and Christian Science, 165–66; Issei, 185, 193. *See also specific jobs*

Wagner, Lou, 131–32

waitresses, 62, 139

Wallbrook, John, 97

"Wanted" posters, 95

ward of the state. *See* public charge

Warm Springs Indian Reservation and Warm Springs Tribal Members, 38

War Savings Stamps (WSS), 19, 56, 58, 65, 77–79

Wartime Emergency Squad (WES), 123, 127–28, 199–200

wartime service registration for women, 19, 42–46

Wassermann blood test, 111, 159

Waverly Baby Home, 139, 140, 141

Weeks, Lizzie Koontz, 11–12, *12*, 114–15

West, Oswald, 24, 26, 151

Western Congressional Delegation on the Japanese Question, 181

Weston, Anna Mary, 10, 20, 65, 72–87

Weston, David, 84–85

White clubwomen, 12–13, 19; actions against Hunt, 66, 67–68; eugenics support, 21, 27–31, 156, 213; and OSHS, 113–14

"White foreigners" in Oregon Constitution, 8, 208

White privilege, 150, 211

Whiteside, Sarah, 114

White supremacy, 2, 28, 31–32, 213. *See also* exclusion; nativism; racism; settler colonialism

Whiting, Sanford, 167–68, 169, 172

Wickstrom, Emma Maki, 146

Wilcox, Margarita Ojeda, 5, 9, 21, 152, 156–60, 157, 178, 215

Wilcox, Walter, 156–60

Willamette University Medical College, 154–55

Wilson, Woodrow, 1, 54, 72, 78, 108

Wilson Administration, 89–91, 92–93, 107, 108. *See also* Food Pledge; Liberty Loan Drives

Wise, Jonah, 126–27, 177

Withycombe, James, 66, 77

woman suffrage in Oregon: 1912 ballot measure, 8, 211; Springer and, 167; voter registration and voting, 10–14, 41; voting exclusion, 7, 8–9. *See also* Congressional Union for Woman Suffrage; Oregon Equal Suffrage Alliance; voting

Woman's Christian Temperance Union, 12, 61

Woman's Committee of the Council of National Defense (CND), 47; Oregon, 42–43, 45–46
women physicians. *See* physicians—women
Women's Political Study League of Portland, 27
Women's Protective Bureau, Portland Police Department, 24, 75–76, 123, 127–28
Woodward, William F., 66–67, 206
Woolen Mills, 61
Word, Tom, 201
work of the nation, 3, 5, 40, 213; ability and, 83; Food Pledge and, 50, 57, 60–64; Liberty Loans and, 56, 60–61; Thrift Stamps and, 72; Anna Mary Weston and Lena, 82–84. *See also* citizenship: productive; productive labor
"work or fight" imperative, 4
World War I, 1, 6; Armistice, 63; gender relations, 6–7; loyalty, 5, 6, 15, 212–13; wage work during, 4; women's "draft," 42–46. *See also* "alien" enemies; Food Pledge; Liberty Loan Drives; military draft; soldiers; War Savings Stamps; wartime service registration for women

"X-ray gown," 113

Yada, Hatsuno Fukai, 193–94
Yamada, Kho Tagae, 195
Yamada, Suzu, 195
Yamaguchi, Masaye, 189
Yamahiro, Kay, 189
Yamhill Public Market, 201
Yasui, Masuo, 186, 189
Yellowtail, Annie Walking Bear, 38
Young Men's Christian Association (YMCA), 167, 169, 174–75. *See also* Portland Vice Scandal
Young Women' Christian Association (YWCA), 64, 75, 145, 173, 175

Zeebuyth, Charles, 190, 192

EMIL AND KATHLEEN SICK SERIES
IN WESTERN HISTORY AND BIOGRAPHY

The Great Columbia Plain: A Historical Geography, 1805–1910,
by Donald W. Meinig

Mills and Markets: A History of the Pacific Coast Lumber Industry to 1900,
by Thomas R. Cox

*Radical Heritage: Labor, Socialism, and Reform in Washington and British
Columbia, 1885–1917,* by Carlos A. Schwantes

The Battle for Butte: Mining and Politics on the Northern Frontier, 1864–1906,
by Michael P. Malone

*The Forging of a Black Community: Seattle's Central District from 1870
through the Civil Rights Era,* by Quintard Taylor

Warren G. Magnuson and the Shaping of Twentieth-Century America,
by Shelby Scates

The Atomic West, edited by Bruce Hevly and John M. Findlay

Power and Place in the North American West, edited by Richard White
and John M. Findlay

Henry M. Jackson: A Life in Politics, by Robert G. Kaufman

Parallel Destinies: Canadian-American Relations West of the Rockies,
edited by John M. Findlay and Ken S. Coates

*Nikkei in the Pacific Northwest: Japanese Americans and Japanese Canadians
in the Twentieth Century,* edited by Louis Fiset and Gail M. Nomura

Bringing Indians to the Book, by Albert Furtwangler

Death of Celilo Falls, by Katrine Barber

The Power of Promises: Perspectives on Indian Treaties of the Pacific Northwest,
edited by Alexandra Harmon

Warship under Sail: The USS Decatur *in the Pacific West,*
by Lorraine McConaghy

Shadow Tribe: The Making of Columbia River Indian Identity,
by Andrew H. Fisher

*A Home for Every Child: Relinquishment, Adoption, and the Washington
Children's Home Society, 1896–1915,* by Patricia Susan Hart

Atomic Frontier Days: Hanford and the American West, by John M. Findlay
and Bruce Hevly

The Nature of Borders: Salmon, Boundaries, and Bandits on the Salish Sea,
by Lissa K. Wadewitz

*Encounters in Avalanche Country: A History of Survival in the Mountain West,
1820–1920,* by Diana L. Di Stefano

*The Rising Tide of Color: Race, State Violence, and Radical Movements across
the Pacific,* edited by Moon-Ho Jung

Trout Culture: How Fly Fishing Forever Changed the Rocky Mountain West,
   by Jen Corrinne Brown
Japanese Prostitutes in the North American West, 1887–1920,
   by Kazuhiro Oharazeki
In Defense of Wyam: Native-White Alliances and the Struggle for Celilo Village,
   by Katrine Barber
Gold Rush Manliness: Race and Gender on the Pacific Slope,
   by Christopher Herbert
*Reclaiming the Reservation: Histories of Indian Sovereignty Suppressed and
   Renewed,* by Alexandra Harmon
Pioneering Death: The Violence of Boyhood in Turn-of-the-Century Oregon,
   by Peter Boag
*The Forging of a Black Community: Seattle's Central District from 1870 through
   the Civil Rights Era,* second edition, by Quintard Taylor
*Seattle from the Margins: Exclusion, Erasure, and the Making of a Pacific Coast
   City,* by Megan Asaka
*Oregon's Others: Gender, Civil Liberties, and the Surveillance State in the Early
   Twentieth Century,* by Kimberly Jensen